"Terri Apple's book is a must-read for any the world of voiceovers. She covers everything there is to know and then some! Talk about a book that has it all—Terri has the market covered!"
—E.G. Daily (voice of Tommy Pickles in *Rug Rats*, Buttercup in *Powerpuff Girls*, Babe in *Babe: Pig in the City* and many more)

"If you're contemplating a career in voiceovers or already are in voiceovers, there's no better book to read than Terri Apple's *Voiceovers*. She's an expert and a great actress!"
—Debi Derryberry (voice of Jimmy Neutron, Alexa from the Diva Stars collection by Mattel, Shelby in the soon-to-be-released "The Legend of Secret Pass" and many more)

"I recommend Terri Apple's *Voiceovers* whenever I teach seminars or even when someone asks me how to get into the business—It's just easier to refer to Terri's book and expertise."
—Kat Cressida (voice of ESPN Draft 2010, Chevrolet, McDonald's, animation, video games, voice-matching, and hundreds of others)

"Terri is one of the top voiceover actresses, as well as fully informed on everything you need to know to make a go of it in the business."
—Dan Gilvezan (voice of Radio DJ on *3rd Rock from the Sun*, Spider Man, Dennis the Menace, and many more)

"You gotta read Terri Apple's *Voiceovers* if you want to get all the goods on making it in voiceovers."
—Danny Mann (voice of Duracel and hundreds of others)

"I recommend Terri's book when someone comes to me and wants to know, 'Is there anything else I can do to move my career forward?' Terri's tips and techniques are proven to work."
—Erik Seastrand (Head of Voiceover Department at William Morris Agency, Los Angeles)

"Some people aren't really that aware of just how big this business is—despite hearing the people who work in it every day. What made Terri Apple's *Voiceovers* really stand out to me, is that although there are more books hitting the market in recent years, there still relatively aren't *a lot* specifically about voiceovers. With the use of the Internet nowadays making it easier to be a voice actor from anywhere, those interested in the field will be glad to have such a comprehensive guide to get started."
—Erin Corrado, www.onemoviefiveviews.com

"I was working long hours as a bank teller, not really interested in moving up the corporate ladder when my mom bought me Terri's first book. I loved the idea of making money living in a small town outside of Austin, Texas but had no idea how to pursue this business.... I started slowly (little help from my parents, thanks guys!) and started workouts; doing research; and finding the local agents, casting directors, production houses and ad agencies, per Terri's book. After about 8 months, I landed a few local gigs and now am doing quite a bit of local and regional work and well on my way to changing businesses!! Thanks, Terri!"
—Jordan B., Austin, TX

"I first went to a seminar that Terri was having in San Diego about 5 years ago. I always wanted to break into voiceovers, but had no idea how to do it. After buying her book at the seminar... I decided to scrap my plans to pursue journalism and work toward becoming a full-time voice actor. Well, years later, I was so excited to be sitting in [the] Buchwald Agency (my agent in NYC) when Terri walked in. I immediately ran up to her to tell her that she changed my life and career choice! I'm now happily living in NYC and making lots of big bucks!"
—Angela T., New York City, NY

"I've been a local DJ (in San Diego) for quite a long time, but didn't know how to break into the "biz" of voiceovers. Terri helped me turn my DJ job into full-time affiliate work, and now I'm making an extra $50 grand a year."
—Dave P., San Diego, CA

TERRI APPLE

VOICEOVERS

Everything you need to know about how to
MAKE MONEY WITH YOUR VOICE

MICHAEL WIESE PRODUCTIONS

Published by Michael Wiese Productions
12400 Ventura Blvd. #1111
Studio City, CA 91604
(818) 379-8799, (818) 986-3408 (FAX)
mw@mwp.com
www.mwp.com

Cover design by Johnny Ink. www.johnnyink.com
Interior design by William Morosi
Printed by McNaughton & Gunn

Manufactured in the United States of America
Copyright © 2011 by Terri Apple
All rights reserved. No part of this book may be reproduced in any form or by any means without permission in writing from the author, except for the inclusion of brief quotations in a review.

Library of Congress Cataloging-in-Publication Data

Apple, Terri
  Voiceovers : everything you need to know about how to make money with your voice / Terri Apple.
     p. cm.
  Includes index.
  ISBN 978-1-932907-90-2
  1. Voice-overs. 2. Television announcing--Vocational guidance. 3. Radio announcing--Vocational guidance. 4. Television advertising--Vocational guidance. 5. Radio advertising--Vocational guidance. I. Title.
  PN1992.8.A6A68 2010
  791.4502'8023--dc22
                               2010031112

Mixed Sources
Product group from well-managed
forests and other controlled sources
www.fsc.org Cert no. SW-COC-002283
© 1996 Forest Stewardship Council

CONTENTS

ACKNOWLEDGMENTS vii

INTRODUCTION ix

CHAPTER 1: IS THIS A REALISTIC CHOICE FOR ME? 1

CHAPTER 2: WHAT'S NEW IN THE VOICEOVER WORLD 43

CHAPTER 3: THE ART OF THE VOICEOVER 62

CHAPTER 4: FINDING YOUR TECHNIQUE AND EIGHT STEREOTYPES .. 80

CHAPTER 5: OTHER GENRES OF VOICEOVER WORK 112

CHAPTER 6: AUDITIONS: INTERPRETING THE READ AND TAKING
            DIRECTION 135

CHAPTER 7: YOUR DEMO CD 179

CHAPTER 8: COACHING AND BEYOND 196

CHAPTER 9: YOUR AGENT AND AVENUES OF BOOKING JOBS 206

CHAPTER 10: THE RECORDING SESSION AND TECHNOLOGY 235

CHAPTER 11: ADVERTISING AGENCIES, PRODUCTION COMPANIES,
             AND EVERYONE ELSE 254

CHAPTER 12: THE SOUND ENGINEER AND THE SOUND BOOTH 262

CHAPTER 13: THE UNIONS 270

CHAPTER 14: STEREOTYPING AND TRENDS 280

CHAPTER 15: GENDER, ETHNICITY, AND ACCENTS 288

CHAPTER 16: BECOME A MARKETING GURU 294

CHAPTER 17: MAKING IT IN MAJOR AND MINOR MARKETS 314

CHAPTER 18: TOOLS, TIPS, AND TRICKS 321

SKIN THE CAT 340

AFTERWORD 343

APPENDIX A: SAMPLE COPY 347

MY SIX-MONTH GOALS/PLAN 353

APPENDIX B: RESOURCES 354

GLOSSARY 373

INDEX OF TERMS 378

ABOUT THE AUTHOR 380

ACKNOWLEDGMENTS

I've had so much fun over the last thirty years learning, twisting, and finding my way through a vast variety of work in such a fun and interesting field. I never in a million years thought I'd make a living doing something that, as a teenager, I enjoyed as a hobby. Now, looking back, I'm so thankful for a career that has allowed me to expand my horizons and have the time to pursue my other loves — writing and acting.

Thank you to Michael Wiese Productions for allowing the creative juices of this book to keep on flowing and for allowing me to share my mass knowledge of the voiceover world with everyone who wants to know how to break into this fabulous career!

Thank you to Jeff Black for continued support and encouragement, to my voiceover agent and dear friend Erik Seastrand at William Morris Endeavor, and to my family — Mom, Dad, and Craig — for your love and humor through all of life's ups and downs.

Enjoy the book and may it shine luck and wealth upon you, bringing you one step closer to your voiceover dreams.

INTRODUCTION

Welcome to *Voiceovers: Everything You Need to Know About How to Make Money with Your Voice*, a real look at the ins and outs of making it in the voiceover business. Using one's voice to make money is a viable option for creative people just starting their career paths, for those wanting to change their careers, and for those wanting to know the ins and outs or "maintaining" an existing career. The world of voiceovers is vast! There are many opportunities for making money in the world of voiceovers; you just have to know where and how to look. If you are serious about making voiceovers your career — or just want to dabble with a new hobby — reading this book is a must! It will give you everything you want and need to know to move forward in the right way. Understanding the challenges and rewards is key to making a living in voiceovers. Hearing from the pros (myself included) what it truly takes to start a career and stay in this business, is essential to ensure that you are making the right choices as you move through the wonderful, lucrative, challenging, and creative world of voiceovers.

You've probably listened to voiceover talent on TV or on the radio and thought to yourself, "I could do that." This is a great way to start! Understanding trends and voiceover styles in the marketplace you want to enter is very helpful in deciding to be a voiceover actor. Just listening to the different voiceover styles used in various advertising campaigns can help you begin to understand the nature of the business and its trends.

Voiceover work has become an extremely popular option for people considering what to do for a living. (Know many other jobs where you can make six figures and wear sweats doing so?) In fact, doing voiceovers has become such a popular career choice that many professionals in other fields have turned their part-time dabbling in voiceovers into full-time careers. (A doctor friend of mine gave up his medical practice because he made more money, and spent less time working, by doing voiceovers.) Yet as rewarding as this career can be, it's also very challenging — and it can be tough to break into. Trying to make a go of it in voiceovers isn't a decision you should make lightly. Don't give up your job — just find a way to be able to audition, once the auditions start coming your way. After all, doing voiceovers means doing a kind of acting. You can have a wonderful speaking voice, but succeeding in voiceovers requires you to know how to apply that God-given talent in professional situations. You certainly can make a living (a very good one) in this business and not be an actor. Being an actor is not a pre-requisite to getting voiceover work. Understanding how to read copy and knowing how to use your personality (with the voice you were born with) is another thing! This book can coach you in how to use the tools you have, to achieve the life and career that you want.

CHAPTER 1

IS THIS A REALISTIC CHOICE FOR ME?

PEOPLE ARE ALWAYS SAYING TO ME THAT THEY WANT TO BREAK INTO VOICEOVERS. If that's how you feel, this is your chance. Age is no barrier, nor is appearance. And with the arrival of the Internet, doing voiceovers has become possible for anyone living anywhere in the country. Of course, it's always true that having a certain vocal style may qualify you for specific voiceover jobs, depending on what market the client is trying to hit and which age group, ethnic group, or gender they are trying to reach.

A great place to begin is to pick up a magazine (any magazine) and begin to read an article in a certain mood. The mood that you are in at the time — as long as you define what that mood is so you can find it again — is terrific. Begin reading the copy in that mood. By simply reading the article in the mood you are in, you will see how the world of voiceovers and thus, selling a product, evolves. Don't worry about how you sound or how to say the words. By reading in that mood, you should be able to understand the flow of words and sentences. Breathe where natural while you're in that mood. When telling a story or speaking to someone in real life, you certainly don't worry about how to tell the story. The story comes out of the mood you are in, before you even begin the story. It's the same concept with voiceovers. Once you are in that mood, just go for the story. The pauses are then dictated by the pauses written in the script. Where to breathe, pause, and continue is dictated by how the words are written and placed in the script or article. In life, you breathe when it is natural to do so dictated by your mood. In scripts or voiceovers, your breathing is dictated by your mood and the writer's intent. The writer's intent simply means the way that a script is written. Record your read. Start to understand how you sound and the natural rhythms that come out of the read by paying attention to the periods, commas, and writing style of the article. Did your mood sound like what you chose going in? That is, if you chose a mood other than the one you were in.

The key factor in doing voiceovers is to be able to change your mood for that particular sell, so that you are able to nail all kinds of reads and be more than a "one-note" actor. Sure, it's great to book a voiceover job, but the key is to book lots of voiceover jobs. Unless you have a specific quality to your voice that prohibits reading for all types of voiceover work, you should be able to read and book in most genres of voiceovers, not just one. Having this versatility is categorized as staple voice talent. If you have a lisp, or a very strong accent, it may prohibit you from fitting into the staple category. Don't worry about it for now. Just learn how to nail the reads and understand the scripts or copy you are handed when auditioning, so you will know how to be up for many types of voiceover jobs. You may also have the type of voice that works for only one or two general areas of the business. That's okay too! Not everyone can be a staple client.

▶   TIP: Your mood = the sell

THE VOICEOVER DEMO

After you understand how to read scripts (from classes, coaching, private lessons, agents, seminars, audiobooks, books, etc.), you will need a voiceover demo to procure work. The voiceover demo is your calling card. (See Chapter 6 for explicit details.) Just like an actor has a photo to show what he or she looks like, the voiceover actor has a voice demo that showcases his or her voice and range.

Hiring a producer is your best option for putting together your voice demo. You don't want to send out something mediocre that you put together. This is one area of the business that you must invest in to get the quality of work that will in turn lead to procuring an agent and/or manager. Your voice demo is sent to everyone by you and/or your agent from casting directors to writers, producers, agents, casting houses, and advertising agencies. Having the right kind of demo for the specific market is essential. There are several types of voiceover demos. (See Chapter 6 for more details.) All demos are one minute in length now. They are called teaser demos.

DEMO TYPES

1. Commercial Demo: commercial copy of TV and radio commercials; local, regional, and national
2. Animation Demo: can include video games, TV and film animation characters
3. Video Game Demo: video game characters, using real video game clips
4. Promo Demo: TV and radio promos
5. Narration Demo: narration clips from TV
6. Trailer Demo: clips of movie trailers
7. Audiobook Demos: audiobook excerpts; usually three or four genres adding up to 2 minutes is fine
8. Affiliate Demos: two separate demos (TV and radio); each one minute in length
9. Automotive Tags (tags that voice actors record for local, national, and regional auto dealers): usually for smaller and local markets
10. Answering Machine: usually for industrial, in-house, smaller markets, or corporate

It's essential to understand what area of the voiceover business you wish to enter and to work with a knowledgeable producer that can help you set goals and head down the right road. Once you have a great demo, you're ready to send it out to get jobs!

HOW MY VOICEOVER CAREER BEGAN

The story of my own voiceover career began when I was in my early teens. Even then, I had the deep, raspy, unique voice that has become my trademark today. Sitting at home in Kansas City, I would watch TV commercials and wonder, "Who are those people I'm hearing — the ones talking about the products?" I was intrigued, and I did some research. I found out that the voices selling products on TV and in radio commercials were actually actors and actresses working in a field I'd never heard of before. Sometimes the voices belonged to famous celebrities, but more often than not they were the voices of men and women who weren't exactly household names. I loved acting and realized that this was just another way to act. I thought about it and decided that this might be an avenue for my own creativity....

In other words, I was hooked. Doing voiceovers sounded like the perfect way for a high school student to make some extra money. Who knew it would turn into a profitable career for me? I began doing the legwork of making phone calls, finding the agents who represented local voiceover artists (which was easy, since there were only two in my hometown), making a demo CD, meeting the casting houses, production companies, ad agencies — in short, everything I needed to do to get started.

I also kept on listening to the TV and radio, paying closer attention to how the voiceover actors sounded. I started to read magazine ads into a tape recorder, changing my voice in different ways and listening to the playback. I also tried reading copy that I took from TV and radio. Eventually, I put together a homemade demo. The first agent who listened to my demo asked me, "Have you thought about being a secretary?" This was my entry into voiceovers. The experience taught me to overcome rejection, smile, and keep on keeping on. I said, "Thank you," and was on my way — with one agent down and one to go.

At the end of the day, I have to say I'm very proud of creating this career and thankful that I get to make a living in something that allows me to use my creativity and still have the freedom to enjoy my life.

I wish you good luck on your own voiceover journey. Just remember that in this business you are selling your voice. (Or, as I like to call it, the icing on the cake!) So sit back and enjoy your read. You're sure to get an earful — and your money's worth.

WHAT IS A VOICEOVER?

Let's take a moment to define *voiceover*. I'm sure you already know what a voiceover is, more or less, but it won't hurt to define the term, since we'll be talking about voiceovers throughout the entire book.

As defined by *Merriam-Webster's Collegiate Dictionary*, a voiceover is "the voice of an unseen narrator speaking (as in a motion picture or television commercial."

The American Federation of Television & Radio Artists (AFTRA), one of the two main unions to which voiceover artists belong (the Screen Actors Guild, or SAG, is the other) defines a voiceover performer as "someone who reads copy and is not seen on camera."

Most actors define voiceovers as "a great way to make a lot of money." Although anything you lend your voice to is considered a voiceover, the industry distinguishes between *voiceover commercials* and *voiceover narrations*. The difference has to do with the voiceover's length, as well as the speaking style used. A voiceover commercial for TV or radio is anything that lasts up to one minute, although infomercials run much longer. Most TV and radio spots range between ten seconds (these brief spots are called *teasers*) and sixty seconds. If you are curious about how long a spot is, get a stopwatch and time it. Anything over three minutes is considered voiceover narration. Commercial spots on TV and radio are usually 15, 30, or 60 seconds in length. There are tags (tag lines) disclaimers, donuts (inserts into existing commercials to change a price, date, or product within the store) and legal lines. (Refer to my "Skin the Cat" guide at the back of this book for a list of terms.)

CAN I MAKE A LIVING?

You've decided that voiceovers may be an interesting and even, lucrative, career choice or hobby. You think, "What a great way to make a living." You watch TV, listen to the radio, imitate those funny voices from your favorite animated show or movie and think, "Wow, that could be for me!"

Then you stop, reconsider, and say, "How the heck can I make a living in that business? Is it really something that I could make money at?" The answer is Yes! Yet, just like most other careers, there are steps, goals, techniques, and tune-ups that you need to know. No voiceover actor or one person can give you all the answers. Yet, this book comes pretty close! Do you want to know the "secret" to booking jobs and getting in the door? If you start with one foot in front of the other and are willing to take the appropriate steps, then you may just land yourself a little extra cash or a big wad of it.

Like all businesses though, if you are simply in it to make the moola, walk away now! You may book a job somehow, but re-booking takes time, work, and talent. Certainly starting with a unique, distinctive, or even commonplace voice will help — depending on the market you want to make a living in. Of course a great voice doesn't hurt, but you must know what to do with that voice to make a living.

Let's assume you're intrigued and want to know more about the business. There are several questions to ask yourself to see if you've got what it really takes to go for this — just like anything else you would be interested in pursuing.

A STEP-BY-STEP GUIDELINE FOR SELF-QUESTIONING

1. How's my voice and how do I determine if I can book jobs?
2. How do I go after voiceover jobs?
3. Once I invest the money for classes, coaching, and a demo, will I get work?
4. Do I understand the goals and obstacles and how to be proactive?

HOW'S MY VOICE?

This question is important for many reasons. Just as a unique vocal sound (or even a lisp, for that matter) can be a moneymaker, the natural rhythm, energy, and flow in which you speak, also is important. It's that age-old comment, "Everyone tells me I have a great voice!" Or maybe, "Everyone always comments on my voice and tells me I should do voiceovers." Or even, "I've always wanted to do voiceovers."

What most people need to understand, besides the fact that all of that is great, is there is much more to a voiceover than simply having a great voice. When someone says one of the statements above or explains, "My friends always comment that I have a great voice," I ask them back, "What mood were you in?" This throws most people off. When we are speaking, the voice always has an undercurrent of feeling. That feeling, underneath the voice, is what the friends are responding to. It's the emotion (or lack of emotion) that you are speaking with that is captivating your audience. When someone responds to your fabulous voice, with its energy, rasp, crispness, assertiveness, or humor; it is coming from somewhere within you. You certainly don't decide how you are going to tell a story before or while you're telling it. But your mood will pre-determine the way in which the story is told! Thus, "You have a great voice." Now it's true, some people do have cool voices. Some people simply have to open their mouths and out comes some really amazing sounds. Yet, I will still stand behind the fact that the person was in a mood, or there is a quality to that person that brings out that "swagger," "charm," "vulnerability," "sarcasm," or "kindness."

There is a natural element in everyone's voice which brings out a particular quality that resonates with others. Everyone has a personality. Once that personality is put into use, moods are created. Moods are the very thing that bring out a particular vocal quality. That is what we call *the sell*, what the voiceover actor sells to the consumer or audience. I will discuss this more later, but just remember that there are many steps and this is the first and most important one. This is the reason I like to say, "The voice is simply the icing on the cake." Without mood (i.e., eggs, milk, sugar, flour, baking soda, and vanilla), there would not be any cake. Similarly, a voice without mood (i.e., emotions like playful, excited, seductive, no-nonsense, matter-of-fact, tutorial, warm, pensive, etc.), would be a robotic slate of bland. I will explore mood, emotion, and flow later in Chapter 5. I just want to wet your appetite for understanding the entire world of voiceovers. It is not simply having a great voice that is important, but how to put that great voice to work to make you money. You certainly can get lucky doing the same character or voice over and over again, but you should understand how to read many types of copy.

Now that we understand there's more to the world of voiceovers than simply having a great voice, you still may ask, "Do I have to be an actor? The answer is No. However, by the same token, you must be able to read scripts, find beats in the copy, see the transitions (to be discussed more in Chapter 6), and know how to read for different kinds of jobs. If you understand how to take that great voice of yours and sell a product, without sounding like you are simply reading copy, then you have just as much of a chance — and sometimes more — than the seasoned actor. There are many different kinds of voiceover jobs and many different types of voice actors. Finding out what kind you are and where you fit in the world of voiceovers, is what you should pinpoint by the time you have finished reading this book. In fact, you should have set a six-month to one-year goal plan for yourself (see Chapter 18) and follow it closely to make sure that you are doing everything you can to be proactive in moving your career forward.

THE SELL (WHAT ADVERTISERS ARE LOOKING FOR: MOOD AND VOCAL QUALITY)

You don't have to be told you've got a great voice to get into voiceovers, but you do need to have a knack for reading and enjoying the process of reading. The audition essentially "prebooks" you for the job. You certainly can listen to commercials to understand flow, beats, and mood. You can even copy a voice that you hear on TV or radio, but don't forget to try to find out what mood(s) the voiceover actor was coming from. Write down what you think they were asking for when listening to the spots. Once again, that is called *the sell*. In every script that comes through to you, there will be specs (specifications) that will tell you what the advertiser, consumer, and seller is looking for. You (the voice) are the one selling the product based on the specs they are looking for. You are one of several actors (in your town, region, state, or country) that will fit those specs or stereotype. Here's where your real job begins. It is up to you, and only you, to nail that read based on what the script calls for. You are going to be asked to read the copy and are expected — simply by looking at a piece of paper — to determine how it is to be read.

Watching TV or animated movies and listening to the radio, are great tools for understanding how an actor booked the job. You must realize that everything you see and hear was at one point on a piece of paper with some specifications attached at the top. What you are hearing on air is the result of 10, 50, or maybe even 100 actors all reading for the same script, all maybe fitting into that same vocal quality, all sending in auditions and some one (that person you are hearing on air) booking the job. Don't let this scare you. Let it be a challenge. Everyone wants to break into voiceovers because it's lucrative, and believe me, it is. In fact, I say if there wasn't so much money to be made in it, I wouldn't waste my time coaching! That being said, there are several avenues of the business where one can make a good living without even getting into the union national market. I'll discuss this deeper into the book, but I just want you to understand every nook and cranny. As they say, "Leave no stone unturned."

Why not know everything there is to know about a field so that you are prepared and ready to conquer? And while you're at it, you might as well understand what it takes and how to get there. It doesn't hurt to "sneak" into the business knowing what to do and what words and terms mean. This will equip you to better understand as you work as well as how to work while you're in it.

Listening to TV and understanding the kinds of voices that are out there (also called styles of reads, stereotyping, and trends) will help you understand where your voice fits in the market (see Chapter 15). It's important that you are realistic about where you see yourself in six months, a year, and five years. This doesn't mean that you shouldn't set goals and even challenge yourself. Just make sure that you aren't kidding yourself and taking compliments from your mother, cousin, brother, etc. (Although nice, they may not have the best perspective on what makes a good read.) You need to align yourself with someone who knows the business: a coach, a demo producer, a casting director, or other voiceover actors (see Chapter 7). Everyone has to start somewhere — and this book is the perfect first step. From here, you will learn how to align, what to do, the right choices to make, and how to do this for the least possible amount of money. However, know that it is still an investment, and like anything else, it needs to be done right. Cutting corners for demos, coaching, and sound equipment isn't always the right way to go when first starting out.

You don't have to know your niche right away. Some people are staple voice actors which means they can read for many different types of voiceover jobs and genres and still book jobs. Other voice actors are clearly better fit for promos or animation. You'll find where you fit or how many areas you fit in as you learn the process of reading, understanding sells and moods, and what type of voice you have. Where you live may also be a determining factor for what kinds of jobs may come your way. The Internet has opened up the possibilities so that it is attainable for you to live in Idaho and book a job from New York City. All of these factors count more on having a good demo, being in with the right agent or manager who sends you the scripts to audition in the first place and where your voice fits into the marketplace. The last five years have opened up terrific opportunities for voice actors living in smaller markets all over the country to still see six-figure years without working 9 to 5. Understanding both the creative side (your mood, voice) and the technical side (technical aspects of your voice to change for different reads) is the ideal marriage that keeps you auditioning and being called back for more. Once you book a job with a company, they could hire you for the life of the run of the spot. Companies, ad agencies, and production houses all work on more than one project at a time, so you might be able to work on more than one account within that agency. The producer may also work freelance and can hire you for other jobs with other agencies. If you aren't right for a job that you initially read on, it doesn't mean that they won't like you for something else.

HOW DO I GO AFTER VOICEOVER JOBS?

There are two categories of voiceover jobs: union and non-union. You will only be sent to union auditions if your agent or manager receives union auditions and feels you are right for the job. You do not have to be in the union to read on union jobs, unless it calls for "union only" talent.. There are unions such as Screen Actors Guild (SAG) and American Federation of Television and Radio Artists (AFTRA) all over the country that determine fees, rules, and regulations (see Chapter 13). You will only know if a project is union or non-union if your agent or manager tells you so. You can probably tell if it's a very high-end or national job, but it can be misleading nowadays. There are many companies that choose to go non-union for talent and choose to do a buyout — buying out the talent for one fee for the life run of the spot. It's cheaper for the company than paying scale residuals, but the talent makes far less. This is why aligning yourself with someone that knows the business and can help you negotiate is better than registering yourself on a website like Voice123 without earmarking your auditions. Earmarking involves not finishing the entire script, changing a word, or changing the product so that the audition cannot be aired without you knowing. Sometimes, however, a site like Voice123 can be a great starting point for getting auditions and having the opportunity to read. I'm sure it's a Catch-22. You want to be reading for the big jobs, but we all have to read the little, local radio spots. (We call those the meat and potatoes of the business.) Don't be fooled — a life of local radio spots can be a career, making you more money than a lot of 9-to-5 jobs. The problem is, if you start taking these voiceover jobs for $50 a pop, $100 a pop, you may learn in the beginning, but you aren't learning in the right way, over time and you may not be taken seriously down the road.

You need to understand and give yourself goals so that you eventually find a niche for yourself. That niche could be working for five local clients that rehire you over and over again and pay you close to scale (even if it's non-union) or finding a niche for yourself within your voiceover community, so that you are getting every opportunity to read for whatever jobs you can. Union jobs will come through advertising agencies, casting houses, and your agent or manager. You can book a union job and make the money that comes associated with that. This steps up your game so that you get in line for bigger opportunities. You can go down whichever path you'd like; you just need to understand that in the beginning, you may not have a choice. Read for what you can, get your feet wet, be smart about it, and work closely with experienced people who can give you honest feedback.

Voiceover jobs can be found through your local advertising agencies, post-production facilities, local industrial companies looking for a voice for in-house marketing, local voiceover agencies, casting houses, or online resources such as Voiceover Resource Guide, Voice-overs.com, Voicebank.net. There are managers, such as my company ASE Talent, that send actors auditions throughout the country to read for. Look for these at *www.Voicebank.net* or other online sources. Voicebank.net is the premier site that you want your demo listed on. You must have agency or management representation to be listed on Voicebank.net. You can also go to websites of SAG or AFTRA to find all union agents (or see Appendix B: Resources).

For Voice123, you don't have to have a demo (although they post it if you have one) and you are sent auditions. This is great if you are just starting, but I certainly wouldn't stay with a site like that if you want to move up in your career and make more money. You will not be taken seriously by an agent if you say you are on Voice123. Most, if not all, of the jobs will be non-union and pay very little. This is what I mean when I say there are two categories of voiceover jobs. You might call one avenue *amateur* and the other avenue *professional*. You can make money in both, but in order to do voiceovers right, you must head down a certain path, with the option to change, branch out, and widen your view on the industry. The best way to get auditions (until you've aligned with an agent or agents in one or many states) is to blanket your town, surrounding towns, nearest largest city, and state with your demo. Get to know the casting directors, radio stations, production houses, and agents. Do everything you can in that particular city so that you are receiving auditions. They must know you exist. Winging it by sending in a home-made demo that you recorded with a cheap microphone, making up scripts; and not understanding the art of the read, the sell, and mood, is only going to get you knocked out of the game. People in the business know immediately what a homemade demo sounds like. Demo producers, although an investment like your calling card, are imperative to you getting in the door. Even then, it's not a guarantee. If you're a "newbie," you are probably going to have to resend (and resend) your demo — maybe even with some cookies or a nice note. Just like any business, you have to do a bit of legwork to get noticed. But once in a door, you shouldn't ever worry about them closing that door on you — especially if your demo is good, your reads are good, and you are easy to work with!

ONCE I INVEST MONEY IN CLASSES, COACHING, AND A DEMO — WILL I GET WORK?

You won't get work without understanding how to read. You may book a job without a demo if you know a producer willing to hire you based on your great voice. You certainly don't need to spend one, two, or three years in a school environment for voiceovers (although there are great ones out there like Kalmenson and Kalmenson in Los Angeles) and there is a ton to learn in the world of voiceovers (much more than could fill one book). This is why you do need coaching and you do need to receive real scripts that have gone to air, so that you understand advertising copy, beats, mood, transition, and so forth. There are bad scripts and there are good scripts. There are small, local spots that run one day, one hour, one week, or one month. There are national spots that run ten years. All of these are valid voiceover jobs and all of them are ways of working within the voiceover business. What you do need to understand is this: Having the tools to attack your career successfully is imperative for making your mark in this business.

I like to say it's best to "sneak in" without anyone realizing you never worked in the business. When a new casting director calls you in for an audition, you want them to say, "Wow, where have you been?" You don't want them to immediately understand how green you are by the way in which you read the copy. And believe me, they can tell by the first word or sentence that comes out of your mouth; by you not understanding flow or story; and by you not romancing a word or throwing something away. Don't fret! All of this can be learned and it doesn't take long. For example, I coach in a very no-nonsense, tell-it-like-it-is manner. Get rid of the challenges and understand the beauty and fun of every read. Learn how to bring out the best in your voice by finding the mood and creating the read. You must understand that although you may have an amazing voice, you now need to learn what to do with it for the appropriate copy. It is not just nailing a read once, but several times over and over again. This is called consistency and you'll become very comfortable with that term once you learn the art of reading (and there is an art to it). So first and foremost, enjoy reading, enjoy using your personality and find a great coach. Start with a Learning Annex type class if you want to. Take a one-day seminar. I do phone coaching that is very reasonable where you would be in a class environment, getting real scripts, and learning from someone who knows what she is talking about. Skype and webinars are also inexpensive ways to learn. I do both as well as others across the country. Just make sure that you are learning. There is so much information in this business that it can take years.

I'm still constantly learning and always auditioning. Yes, I still audition! It's an audition business — even if they know your voice, the want to know how you sound for that particular spot. Even if they request you personally. Once you are known, you may book jobs based on what you've done in the past. For the most part, however, I still audition like everyone else — even if it has my name on it. And guess what? I sometimes don't book the job. Just like you, I have to nail the read, understand the writer's intent and know which "Terri Apple" they are looking for based on the specs.

Here are the three main steps to follow to make it in voice-overs:

1. You must know how to read to get called in to read.
2. You (at some point) will need a great demo that represents you and the areas you want to pursue.
3. You must stay current and know how to market yourself.

Once you invest — and you should make a budget goal for yourself, but spend wisely — you will go about sending that demo(s) out to your community and beyond. You've got to give yourself time to get in with the proper people. You've got to let them listen to your demo and start to bring you in for auditions or send you out to read. You may have to get onto a few of the online sites to get your feet wet and get the chance to audition, but keep this information separate from your agent-to-be. Agents don't need to know that you are doing all these small non-union jobs. They want you to be taken seriously for bigger jobs. Once you decide what area of the business you want to go into and know where the work is in your town, an agent will help you understand how to go after that work. For example, say you want to pursue affiliate work, understanding the steps to take to pursue this business is very important (see Chapter 3). You can go after local grocery stores, in-house advertising, industrials, and local radio stations to try to get steady, weekly voiceover work. You can be a donut insert voiceover actor for local shops, businesses, and chains. You could do these voiceovers often. You could find work being an on-hold voice for major companies, understanding that you need that type of demo. Your agent will then send that demo out to potential companies. Any major company in your city, region, and state with a marketing division hires voices for these types on on-hold promotions. You may make a nice living doing several different types of voices, not just waiting to read on commercials that your agent may or may not send you. Understand that you must decide (or not) which area of the business you want to be in. Maybe you want to learn the entire world of voiceovers, which is great. That being said, a good coach will immediately help you determine (by where you live, what you enjoy, and your vocal quality) what area you should pursue to make a living. Just spending your money to not specifically go down a road would be silly. Although you may want to start in commercials, also dabble in video games, go for the affiliate work, and try for trailers. Understand that there is a way to read on all of these, if you get the auditions and if you live in a place where these auditions come. If you live in a town with production facilities for video games (call and find out or go online) you certainly can send or walk in your video game demo. You do, however, need a specific demo for each area of the business and it can get costly. That's why I say work with someone who knows and can help you put your money in the right place for the least cost. You want to invest wisely in a demo so that you get your money's worth. Most producers will give you a deal on more than one genre of demo, depending on what area you want to pursue. Doing an animation demo when you live in a town where there is no opportunity to book a job is silly. The chance of you getting a union audition with Disney to read for the latest animated movie is very unlikely. Having a good commercial demo for that same town and receiving a regular voiceover audition for Kroger or Walgreens is much more likely. Think smart and know where you are and what's available. Any producer or coach should know what market you live in and what's realistic and available.

UNDERSTAND GOALS, OBSTACLES, AND BEING PROACTIVE

First and foremost, deciding that you want to go for it and try to pursue this career (or hobby) is the best attitude to have. Next, reading up on everything you need to know about breaking into the business — as well as taking an active participation in watching TV commercials, listening to the radio; understanding current trends, styles, and deliveries — is equally important. On that note, study whatever area you are interested in breaking into. For example, if it's animation that really gets your fancy, then watch animated cartoons. Pick the area which you want to work in and learn everything you can. Within animation there's nighttime adult animation which tends to use real voices instead of character voices and there are Saturday morning cartoons which generally use more character-driven voices. Do you want to know about a specific actor, show, or production company? Wait for the credits and google the name. You can look up anyone online these days. If you want to know about an actor and find out what other characters he or she does, so you can understand actors and their range, this is a great way to do it. You want to pinpoint a production studio to submit your demo to and see what other shows they produce? Look them up, do some research, and send your demo CD. Interested in looping? Same thing: Wait until the end of the show, find the loop group in the credits and contact them.

It pays to take notes, do your research, and even underline suggestions that stand out to you in this book and use them as a guide to help build your career. When you go to the end of the book to the blank page listed as "My Six-Month to One-Year Goals/Plan," write down page numbers from this book and any advice and steps that you may take to make your career move forward. Check off your progress as you go.

It's very important that you make proper steps for yourself in building your voiceover career (or any career for that matter). Understanding that you need to be in contact (either by email, phone, Facebook, LinkedIn, Twitter, blog, drop off, in person) with anyone and everyone who could possibly move your career forward within the town that you live in, is step number one. Of course, this is after you have done your homework with a coach, class, and school and have a properly produced voiceover demo in the area in which you want to work. Once you've done that, you will need to send out that demo to all of the appropriate parties. Staying on top of this for at least the first six months of your career is key in getting in to read and audition for all jobs that are obtainable in your marketplace. When you feel you want to branch out of your market and understand the tools of the web, again, to go to Voicebank.net and research other agents, managers, production companies, ad agencies, and casting directors to pursue other avenues, areas, genres, cities, and markets. Voiceover Resource Guide (*www.voiceoverresourceguide.com*) is also an excellent tool, and all of the blogs and online sites I've listed at the end of the book can be used as a guide to help your marketing and pursuing of voiceovers and creating a working voiceover world for yourself.

Once you've set your goals, you must not allow yourself to get frustrated. Maintain being proactive and on course. Remember that everything takes time. That being said, you could book a job tomorrow, provided you follow the steps that you have to do to be heard. If a casting director or ad agency hasn't heard your demo and seen what you are capable of doing (a producer's job is to provide the best copy and vocal coaching to make your demo work for you at any particular time in your career), how will they be able to bring you in to read and potentially book you on a job? So, it's up to you to be proactive and not cut corners in the beginning stages of coaching, demos, etc. You want to be any fish in any pond, and the best way is to get in without anyone noticing how green you are. There are terms, or catch lines (see Skin the Cat) that you will need to understand. Most voiceover actors learn "on the job" and don't get the luxury of learning these phrases until they are thrown to the wolves in the middle of a voice session. It can be quite scary to be told direction and words you've never heard before, and be expected to implement them into a read, but this is a large part of the business — understanding how to take notes, make adjustments, and do them when asked. This takes time and learning but the more you do, the easier it becomes! With "Skin the Cat" terms to help you, you will understand the importance of learning the lingo in the business, so you can feel better affiliated and understand the process of working in the world of voiceovers!

VOCAL QUALITY AND MOOD

In TV commercials, the voiceover *helps* sell the product. In radio commercials, the voiceover is the *sole* element selling the product. In either case, though, the voice reflects a mood, and this is where particular voices and vocal styles come into play. All our voices can produce many different vocal qualities. If you're happy, your voice sounds different from the way it sounds when you're pensive or anxious. There's a big difference between a voice with a smile in it and one with a sharp, hostile tone. Although many people's voices may fit into a similar vocal category, there are always subtle nuances that make each individual voice unique: every voice has its own personality. Each of us also has a natural rhythm to the way we speak. Some of us speak very fast; others are very relaxed. But voiceovers require that you use your natural vocal quality and rhythm to create the specific mood that the advertiser and copywriter are seeking for a particular job.

Here's a quick exercise to show you just what mood can do — how the words you say and what you mean can be two *very* different things.

- **EXERCISE: *That's a Great Shirt***

Take a look at the following line: "That's a great shirt."

Now, take a piece of paper and write down some adjectives that describe different moods in order, one below the other: *relaxed, anxious, flirty, aggravated, sad, tired, excited, hurried, empathetic, bored.* (Think of some others for yourself.) Read the statement half out loud, half to yourself (like you're speaking to yourself but out loud), trying to convey each of these moods in turn. As you do, try to create the mood genuinely — from the inside out — not by "pushing" your read by intentionally changing your voice. Do not worry about your breathing: that should come naturally as you learn to use your mood to create reads. Just relax (if it fits the mood!). For now, this is playtime. Then read out loud, picking a person to speak to and a place. Make these real choices and you'll see how much more realistic the read will become. Advertisers are looking for you, in that mood, with a great vocal quality = real sell.

Your goal is to create a *real moment* — also known in the trade as making an *active choice.* A real moment can only be created by experiencing that actual emotion prior to reading — not by trying to manipulate your voice. Even a simple statement like

"That's a great shirt," completely changes in intention and meaning depending on how it is spoken. The voice itself is the icing on the cake. What you put into that cake is what makes it memorable. The emotion and mood you bring to a read is what creates a wonderful vocal quality and dynamic.

Take the "That's a great shirt" exercise a step further. Record your reads so you can listen to yourself. You'll hear just how different your voice sounds with each one. Now try combining a few adjectives to create a layered mood or make new little changes but still associated with that "mood." For instance, try reading the statement as if you're both hurried *and* empathetic. Or how about bored *and* on the go? Excited and flirty? Warm and sincere? Warm and content? Notice how the energy changes. What you're doing is upping the stakes, creating different moods and different styles within your own vocal range.

The following is how you will learn to break down scripts/cold reading. I will explain this again in Chapter 6, Auditions: Interpreting the Read and Taking Direction, but get loose and go with it in this order to give you a guide.

Line (or script): "That's a great shirt."
Steps:

1. Read the script.
2. Apply the specs (specs for this are adjectives you've written down).
3. Read line (or script) half out loud and half to yourself. (Find the rhythm, mood, and feel of line in the mood you're supposed to be in.)
4. Read out loud, in that mood

> ▶ TIPS: Pick a person to speak to in that mood. Look to the left to find the mood, if you aren't already in that mood. Looking to the left will help you "retrieve" the emotion, so to speak (based on a lot of studies).

You're ready to audition now. Picking a person gives you a specific choice of someone to talk to. As a voice actor, you don't want to simply tell the microphone.

▶ TIP: The minute you tell everyone, you tell no one. (It is not realistic and it sounds like you are talking to anyone.)

You should only tell everyone if the script calls for you to tell everyone. For example, the specs read: Female or male coach standing in front of team, talking to them. A diplomat at the podium addressing his or her country. Then you are okay to play it real. Otherwise, pick one person and tell them. They don't have to like ice cream or BMWs (although, who doesn't?), but it doesn't matter. Picking a person to talk to in a certain mood allows you to be real and breathe naturally while telling an un-natural story — a story you wouldn't normally tell in a certain manner. That's the art of voiceovers: learning to read copy in a natural way, while hitting the sell they are asking for. Letting the natural nuances of your voice come out while in that mood: this is the icing on the cake that creates uniqueness and let's you stand out!

Here's another exercise:

● *EXERCISE: My Mood Vs. What I'm Saying*

We've all had days when we've been in a certain mood but tried to cover it up because we didn't want anyone to know how lousy we felt. We also sometimes manipulate conversations or try to act like we are in a different mood. The tone of the voice usually wins, however. Regardless of what you say, it's how you say it that comes across. The tone of your voice wins.

Say the following lines in two different ways:
"I'm having a great day." (Say this in a sad or bored mood.)
"I'm having a terrible day." (Say this in an excited or flirty mood.)

Record both. See how your tone comes across, regardless of what you are saying?

Congratulations! You've just completed your first step into the world of voiceovers.

▶ TIP: While you might be *vocally* right for a job, it's your *acting* ability that will determine whether you get it. By marrying your natural vocal ability with your ability to create the right mood, you'll create the *sell* for the product.

Being able to create a particular mood or a point of view (POV) and applying it to a script is the number one skill you'll need to analyze voiceovers and book jobs. If you listen to yourself carefully, you'll hear that it's the mood that creates the vocal quality, not the other way around. When you start with a mood, you always have somewhere to go.

▶ TIP: Your job as a voice actor is to "nail" the read at the audition. You may not book the job, but you still must be great in the audition to even be in the running. Right vocal quality = right sell = cool voice.

PERSONALITY, ATTITUDE, AND CHARACTER

Having a good voice isn't everything. This is why I refer to the voice as "the icing on the cake." This means that the cake itself (your personality) is the key that determines how you say words, moments, and the story. In life, you tell a story based on your point of view (POV) which is already determined by your mood. In scripts, the mood (specs, adjectives, POV, and sell) is written for you. You can have a kind of voice that is very cool or has a rasp, but the sell itself, is determined by the producer, writer, or director of the spot and, in a sense, tells you how they want you to behave. Thus, the mood will come from that. You nailing the mood (being in the right one, for the right spot) is what gets you closer to booking the job. You don't have to be an actor to do voiceovers, but it helps to learn tools that get you into moods quickly and easily so that the sell comes across. You certainly don't want to just push flirty, playful, matter-of-fact, warm, hip, or other moods because the read could sound forced and phony. The trick is to get in the appropriate mood before you begin reading, so that the mood will sell itself. This becomes the sell of the spot. It's not you selling something. It's you *in that mood*, and that is the sell.

▶ TIP: Being in the mood before you begin the script is key to reading in the correct tone and style. Find the mood based on the specs, not the mood you are personally in.

Your voice books you jobs, but in order to think outside the box and book more than one type of read, you must understand that as many emotions that you have are as many vocal ranges you can convey. You'll still fit into a category or stereotype, but it will open your range and booking ability greatly.

HOW IMPORTANT IS MY VOICE?

What are three adjectives that define you? (Sassy, assertive, fun?) These define the natural stereotype you fit vocally. This doesn't mean you are in that mood all the time, but it's a general way to determine where you fit in the voiceover world.

Although it's great to have a "cool" voice or a voice that stands out from the norm — and may even be the key to landing a great career in voiceovers — personality, attitude, and character can actually be more important. Getting in front of a mike, saying the copy with the right delivery (the one the client wants), making it all come in at the precise length required — and keeping this up for many takes — is not easy, but I'll be teaching you the tricks you'll need to pull it off.

Personality is the way you read the copy, putting your unique character or flair into the read. Personality is your trademark — it's what makes your voice stand out from the competition. It helps if you can act, since your acting ability will keep you fresh and different every time you read. When you are at an audition and there are several actors who have a vocal quality similar to yours, it is your acting that will set you apart. How you define yourself as a person correlates to how you read copy. Your normal rhythms and natural vocal quality will always come through. This is your starting point. It is important to define your "signature" voice — the one you feel most comfortable using. How do you sound when you meet someone? How about when you run into someone you're unhappy about meeting? How about excited about meeting? Does your voice go up when you become excited? How about when you're uncomfortable? Lonely? Sad? Does your voice change? When you're arguing with a waiter in a restaurant, is your voice the same as when you're arguing with a family member at home? Does it matter whom you're arguing with? Does it change the way you say certain words?

All these differences are part of your unique personality. Bring all of them with you to your read. You may be able to copy someone else's voice, but you cannot copy his or her personality. That's why the best thing that you can bring to a read is your own, unique take on the commercial. There are limits, of course. Your success also depends on what the advertiser is looking for. For example, they might be looking for a fun, upbeat dad. But that still leaves the door open for interpretation, doesn't it? There are so many different dads out there. Age, ethnicity, energy, education — any of these might or might not be defined in the copy. It's up to you to find the right read for the spot.

▶ **TIP: Learn to read in the mood, find the beats of the copy, and your reads will be more natural, allowing the sell to reflect that and all of the cool dynamics of your voice to come through.**

▶ **TIP: Have a point of view (POV) and focus on one person to speak to, creating an active, real read.**

You being in a particular mood already will allow the texture of your voice to come through stronger than you trying to force a mood and selling something to an audience. The key is to speak to a person in that mood, allowing the quality of your voice to shine through.

Once you get used to reading copy and relaxing into it, the reads will come a lot more naturally. The rhythms written into the copy will be enhanced by your own natural rhythms and inflections. You will learn to find these as you practice, go on auditions, and start booking jobs. The more comfortable you become with yourself and your ability to audition and interpret copy, the easier the audition process will become.

Attitude is every bit as important as personality. It's the emotion or feeling that the copy dictates or that you bring to the read. Attitude is the core of the read. Your attitude, or point of view, is your base for beginning the read. You will know which attitude to put into the read depending on the specs. Just look on the copy for what they are looking for and put that mood into the read. The mood will lend itself to the attitude of the read, based on your behavior. Every time you read a piece of copy — whether it's animation, narration, a promo, or an ad — it's always important to have a point of view. Who are you speaking to? Who are you telling about this product, and what's the appropriate mood? If I know that I'm going to read for 7UP and need to sound hip, cool, and off-the-cuff (according to the description/specs on the copy), then I know that I should use those qualities within my personality. I have to get myself in that particular mood for the read. This mood will then bring out that particular vocal quality, not the other way around. The voice has to come from the inside out. If I try to push my voice to sound a certain way, the read won't sound natural.

Character defines personality and attitude. It's the specific version of attitude and personality. Your character is the overall persona that you are projecting into the read. Sometimes your character is nothing more than being yourself and putting that into the read. The issue of character comes up a lot in animation, when you're really trying to come up with a specific voice to fit the character you're playing. But it's just as important to come up with character within yourself to fit the reads of ordinary commercials for TV and radio. The difference is that you don't change your voice as much. You change your personality and mood. For commercials, character might simply mean using your personality to change a read's attitude — a way of saying something differently.

READING ACTIVELY AND MAKING FRESH CHOICES

Besides understanding your point of view, who you're talking to, and what mood you're in, it's extremely important to read actively. When you are telling a story, really communicate with your listeners. If you're excited and eager, the natural rhythm of the story will come from your energy. Use your hands to express your mood. The more you actively feel the mood you're in, the better you'll convey that mood to the audience and sell the product as the advertiser wants you to sell it. Reading something "actively" means that you are reading as if what you are talking about is taking place in the here and now. This means that you will be in tune with what you are talking about. You don't just play an objective part — like lending your voice to a project — you are "you" in a "mood" telling a story to a particular person. For example: "The all new Toyota Camry." You can just read it and wing whatever comes out, but that certainly will not get the job. Not only will you not be able to remember how you read it, but you may be in a different mood on that particular day.

Me in a playful mood talking to Rhonda (my best friend) hanging out at a diner, will convey this read specifically and naturally. Me in a warm, seductive mood talking to my boyfriend and hanging on the couch, will convey the line much differently and will bring out a different texture and quality to my voice. This is called making specific, active choices. The difference between this and real life is that in real life I pick the mood depending on how I'm feeling and whom I'm talking to. The volume (vocal level) is determined by how far or close the person is sitting or standing to me. The volume may also be determined by actions or locations: walking, running, jogging, stretching, hanging out drinking tea, or having a glass a wine with ambiance around me. In scripts, I'm creating all of that based on what the writer wants the mood to be. He or she may say, "I'm looking for Terri Apple," but understanding which Terri Apple (from which product I've sold) is key to me understanding the quality of my voice they are looking for. There are certain reads that will bring out more rasp, or convey more warmth, or more playfulness, depending on which specs they throw at me, so I know which personality or mood to be in.

Fitting into a certain category is part of the business (this means where you fit in the voiceover world and the types of voiceovers you will read for most often), but that could be age related, just as much as vocal quality. You want to learn to do all sorts of sells because it not only helps you in the audition process, but understanding how to work in a voiceover session, as well.

READING ACTIVELY

Let's say the read calls for you to be tired — yawning and stretching. To play this part realistically, you should actually yawn and stretch during your voiceover. This will *actively* convey that you're in that mood, being that character. Or what if you're supposed to be a woman in labor having contractions? Being as realistic as you can will certainly help you book the job. If you have to convey that you're about to give birth, what better way to do it than to really act as if it were happening? The woman who does the read while sitting quietly in a chair isn't going to book the job. The actors who make their acting as real as it can be are the ones who stay in the running. The client may get fifteen or fifty really great, active reads. At that point, they'll decide who is right for the job — who comes closest, vocally, to what they are looking for as well as whose interpretation they liked the best. They may like Actor A's read but prefer the vocal quality of Actor B. In such a case, they may either do callbacks, or hire Actor A and provide closer direction.

> ▶ **TIP: It is advantageous to audition well consistently. Being both creative and consistent will keep you in the running for future jobs. Casting directors love knowing that if they bring you in, you will always nail the copy — even if they don't book you. They also know that, sooner or later, you will book a job.**

Once you get used to reading copy and relaxing into it, the reads will come a lot more smoothly and naturally. The rhythms written into the copy will be enhanced by your own natural rhythms and inflections. You will learn to find these as you practice, go on auditions, and start booking jobs. The more comfortable you become with yourself and your ability to audition and interpret copy, the easier the audition process will become.

MAKING FRESH CHOICES

Making fresh choices simply means that even though you've already decided the mood you are in before you read the copy and worked it out in the cold reading process (your time looking at the script and breaking it down to be ready to go into the booth and read for audition), you will still be open enough to create a new moment when you are in that booth. You don't want to sound like you've read the script so many times that the read goes on auto-pilot. You want to stay connected to what you are saying, how you are saying it, and to whom you are talking to (the friend you've chosen). When reading a script, you don't want to "tell the microphone." You want to speak beyond the mike to a real person, having a real conversation.

VOCAL CONTROL

Your next step is to learn what mood your voice ordinarily conveys. When you talk to people, are you usually energetic? Somber? Flirty? Serene? Authoritative? Everyone's voice has a "stereotypical" mood — one that suits you and that you use most frequently in day-to-day conversation.

- **EXERCISE: Determining Your Stereotypical Voice**

To determine your stereotype or where you fit into the voiceover business, perform the following steps:

1. Write down (or think about) three qualities that define you. Stick to adjectives and mood words. The voiceover world mostly deals with adjectives; so if you're a logical thinker, get back to getting your feet dirty in the sandbox. Voiceovers are about playing and having fun and understanding the technical aspects of the business. Below are examples of qualities:
   Fun, Hip, Playful
   Calm, Flirtatious, Enterprising
   Mellow, Business-Minded, No-Nonsense

Note: Understanding how you come across is important. Your key words that you choose (although our voices definitely change depending on the mood we are in — see Chapter 6), will determine the comfortable place you find yourself most of the time. To get a better answer for this, ask yourself, "What would my friends/colleagues/spouse/parent say?"

2. Grab a magazine article, and start reading. It's that simple. Just read in the mood you are in. If you find that you are trying to sell the words or emphasize certain phrases, you are reading incorrectly for voiceovers. If you are staying in your mood and letting the words, phrases, and lines flow naturally based on your mood, you are reading correctly.

3. Record your reads. Just record three or four lines to determine that you are reading correctly. The breathing and pauses come from the mood, periods, commas, and the way a script is written on the page — not how you think you should sound or where you think you should pause.

▶ TIP: In life you breathe where it's natural, based on your mood. It's the same thing for voiceovers.

Beyond your natural stereotype, however, everyone's voice is capable of expressing many different moods; your voice naturally takes on many different inflections and tones depending on how you feel. Are you feeling angry? If so, your voice will sound lower and less expressive than if you were excited. Calm? If so, your voice will reflect calmness. It will be smooth and even compared to being excited.

Your moods create your voice and your style. If you've ever listened to someone who's always depressed, you'll recognize the bland cadence and drone in that kind of voice (which can sometimes be interesting for character reads and animation). When we seek empathy from other people, we try to manipulate them into feeling for us, so we create a certain emotion within ourselves (unless we already feel that way), which makes other people react to us sympathetically. Well, that's exactly what you do in voiceovers. Advertisers are always looking for something specific

— a certain read, a certain type of voice, a certain quality and mood. A script might call for a "female in her twenties who is hip and confident." Of course, we don't really know the vocal sound of "hip and confident," but we certainly know how to project that quality and mood. We can learn to pay attention to what happens to our voice when we are in a certain mood. People project a vocal quality simply by being in a particular mood.

Voiceover acting is more about selling an emotion (along with the quality of your voice) than it is about pushing words, sentences, and your vocal chords. Pushing your voice out there — without really developing a point of view or mood — will make you come across as fake and "selly." Voices reflect attitudes, and selling a product is simply selling an attitude. Most of the copy that you'll read at auditions contains direction, usually written at the top or bottom of the page. This direction tells you what the advertiser is looking for: age, gender, and attitude. You can pick your own attitude based on the product, on how the copy is written, and on the images you are shown (if the voiceover is for TV), but the copywriter already has an idea of what he or she is looking for. High-pitched voices tend to come across — or "read" — as young, shy, unsure, naive, fun, or over the top. Deep voices read as strong, authoritative, and in control. An older, strong-yet-soft voice tends to read as warm, trusting, loving, comforting, and empathetic.

ACCENTS AND VOCAL QUIRKS

Not only does everyone's voice have a certain quality, but some people's speech is also accented — either slightly or strongly. Other people may not have a discernible accent, yet the way they say a word or draw out a sound still sets them apart and creates a unique quality. Accents come from the region of the country in which you grew up or from your native language if you didn't grow up speaking English. In the voiceover business, there is room for both common, everyday voices as well as those that are more unusual. Accents, dialects, and even speech impediments also have a way of making it into the voiceovers. It just depends on the product and the area of the field. Voices that do not stand out are still often used to sell certain products. In fact, voiceover artists are sometimes hired specifically because they don't cut through or stand out. In advertising, there is often a need for a "mom next door," a "nosy neighbor," a "regular guy," or an "everyday, middle-of-the-road businessman." These voices' unique quality lies in their very *lack* of uniqueness: they sound like everyday people whom we are likely to listen to and trust.

On the flip side, many voiceover actors have a cutting edge, a vocal quality that absolutely stands out from the moment they say hello. Behind every voice, regardless of tone, lies its personality — whether overpowering or nondescript — which is used to sell the product.

Accents can work for or against the voiceover actor, depending on the commercial and the sell the advertiser is looking for. Dialect coaches work specifically with accents and dialects. Depending on the work you are trying to get, such coaches are likely to be very helpful. If, for example, you have a British accent but want to compete for American voiceover jobs that do not specifically ask for British speakers, you can work with a dialect coach to learn an American accent. Or you may have a Southern drawl, or a very heavy New York accent. This could work fine if a script calls specifically for a "Southern farmer with a twang" or a "fast-talking New Yorker." But if the read just calls for someone "warm, businesslike, and authoritative," your accent would not likely get you the job (even though there are many warm, authoritative, businesslike people from New York and the South). Learning how to eliminate or diminish your accent could therefore make you more widely marketable.

On the other hand, you may want to learn to speak with an accent or dialect so that you can audition for a wider variety of parts. Some commercials call for a specific kind of accent — Southern, Minnesotan, New England, New York, any of the many British accents, or even English spoken with different foreign accents. Even within one general area, such as the East Coast, there are many different regional accents. A trained ear can easily tell the difference between people from Bangor, Boston, New

York, Philadelphia, and Baltimore. Being able to handle them fluently will widen your range and enable you to audition for more spots. Similarly, speech patterns and dialects in one part of the country don't necessarily work in others. If you are reading for a job in a locality with a specific accent or pronunciation, it may be to your benefit to be able to reproduce that particular speech pattern. On the other hand, there is also a common ground — diction and ways of saying words understood all across the United States and Canada.

As far as lisps and other vocal quirks go, whether they're beneficial or detrimental depends on whether they're technical problems, health issues, or simply quirks. Voices that have a nasal quality can work wonderfully for certain character reads (voice actress Patty Deutsch has made a great career playing this kind of character), whereas someone whose voice isn't naturally nasal but who tries to imitate that quality may come across as being phony or overacting. Also, lisps and other vocal quirks can come in handy when doing animation jobs. On the other hand, pronounced vocal quirks will limit your ability to book other kinds of jobs, so it's in your best interest as a voiceover actor to know how to turn these qualities on and off as needed.

As always, your ability to book a job will depend on the copy, the current trends, and the personality that you put into your read. Add perseverance, luck, and a good agent, and you've got the right mix for success.

USING YOUR PERSONALITY

A voiceover tells a story from beginning to end. A great personality can convey the information in a real, conversational manner that makes the listener feel like the voiceover actor is a friend. It's not necessarily the voice per se that the consumer is listening to; rather, it's the voiceover actor's personality — *how* he or she is selling the product to the consumer. The advertising agency is entrusting the voice talent with becoming a product's spokesperson. They believe that you will be a core reason (in addition to any visual campaign) for the consumer to purchase the product being sold. Ultimately, voiceover actors are hired because of their talent in conveying information the way that the client wants it conveyed.

Do you ever wonder why, all of a sudden, you feel you *need* to buy Crest White strips — even though you've lived your whole life without them? Or, you just have to try that mocha latte skinny? Maybe it has to do with the someone's voice luring you in — the way the voice actor has told you about the product. In TV and radio commercials, there is generally one mood (or sometimes a layered mood) that dominates the entire spot. Hip and fun. Cool and energetic. Seductive and informative. If you watch TV and listen to the radio with this in mind, you will quickly become educated in the different types of sells. The client might just say, "Have fun with it" — and, as a voiceover actor, you'll know exactly what that means. When the client asks for "sophisticated yet warm," you, the actor, have to *become* sophisticated and warm to convey that feeling and bring out the appropriate quality in your voice. The same goes for "playful and whimsical." In the voiceover world, everything begins with mood. That's where your personality comes in. Yet another read for the same script might have you toying with "warm yet conversational," without losing the sophistication. This read will come across a bit more informal. As you learn to layer reads, you will learn how to play around with moods. Simply switching the order of the words in the specs can create a different read altogether. For example, if the script calls for warm, playful, and energetic but you lead with playful instead of warm, the read will flow differently. What you need to learn to do is nail the read so that you are able to create a vocal sell that fits what they are looking for. Being in the wrong mood (leading to the wrong vocal style) certainly can keep you from booking the job. Once you are in the mood, it's your job to follow the rhythm of each particular spot and find the natural flow. This can be a bit tricky when the copy is bad, but even then, someone will come in, read it, and make it work. (That's usually the person who books the job.) At other times, a script is so well written, so funny, so cute, you get the rhythm right away.

STEPS TO BOOKING THE JOB:

1. Be in the right mood (thus creating the right vocal quality)
2. Nail the beats and transitions (the natural flow of the copy — per the writer's intent — how they intended it to be told).
3. Nail the read (be in the right mood, have the right vocal quality for the job, thus leading to "love the voice").

VOICEOVER CAREERS

There are a number of very good reasons you might want to pursue a voiceover career:

- You get to escape from the 9-to-5 routine.
- You can wear sweats every day.
- You get to have fun.
- You get to create voices that constantly challenge you and make you grow.
- You get to be part of a creative process in a multimillion-dollar industry.
- You get paid to do something you enjoy.
- You can expand your horizons, simply by learning other avenues that you might want to pursue — e.g. animation, audiobooks, promos, etc.

Voiceover careers are for people who enjoy playing with different moods as much as they enjoy speaking. You can certainly work in the voiceover field if you possess a unique sound or distinct quality, and voice actors have been known to re-create the same mood over and over again, but being quick-witted and having an active imagination are key. Actors can do very well in voiceovers because understanding mood and character is crucial to understanding how to read scripts, although theatrically trained actors may sometimes go a bit overboard and try to enunciate too much. Finding the line between *raw* (unprofessional) and *polished* (too clean) is critical.

▶ **TIP: The sell will determine how raw or polished you should be.**

It's natural for a new voiceover artist to sound raw or unpolished, simply because they haven't gotten really comfortable with the copy and flow of words. The raw quality will work if you are playing a real person, who would naturally have a more raw sound. Some people book jobs specifically because they have a raw quality to their voice, while other actors naturally sound more polished. What the script calls for determines how raw or polished one needs to be. Some stage actors can be a bit too polished, thus pushing a read too much, or overacting. I say stage actors simply because they tend to emote a bit more, whereas TV and film actors will generally keep things pretty subtle. There's a market for everything, so it's just knowing where and how to use your tools.

CHALLENGES IN THE VOICEOVER BIZ

A voiceover career can be difficult in several different respects. For one thing, the business is cyclical: certain months and seasons are better than others, which means it can be hard to earn money on a steady, predictable basis — especially before you've built up a regular clientele. Holidays (and right before and after) are usually good times in the marketplace when advertisers spend a bit more on their advertising. Summer can be a bit slow, and the beginning of the year can be slower. There are certain categories that advertisers buy at certain times of the year. For example, beer and cars during a sports season. Also, you may be the hot commodity for a year, but then have a slow year the next. It's important to have an updated, current demo (every three to four years) and keep up your connections with people in the market, besides sitting at your agency, and letting them do the work. It's up to you to make connections and stay connected. A flyer, gimmicks — anything you can do to stay in their minds — is good for business. A reminder card or MP3 file of your current demo is great, too. Advertisers and clients change their minds about having a certain voice selling a product or simply tire of a voice and may want to go a different way. They may even want to try a different gender. They may decide to change the sell or type of campaign they started with. They might like a voice for one cycle or for one campaign but have a different idea the next time around. They might want to make a change to appeal to a different kind of audience. You may flip on the TV, see a commercial that you had previously been voicing, and be shocked to hear a different actor doing the voiceover. It has happened to me and, I'm sure, to many other voice actors over the years. Your client may have decided to change gender or vocal quality or simply to take a fresh approach to selling the product. It's just the nature of the business. On the other hand, you can voice a campaign or spot that runs for years and years. My "Got Milk?" commercial — "I don't think so, baldy!" — has reappeared for over thirteen years. I never know when it's going to show up. Phil Buckman has been doing a Carl's Jr. campaign for ten years now. Danny Mann is the Duracell bunny and has been for over ten years. Jim Cummings has been doing Blockbuster for years now. Tazia Valenza has done Soapnet for several years, and Gina Tuttle has been the voice of the Oscars for about five years now.

As much as you can have the same job for many years, you certainly don't know when they will decide to go a different way with something. Just stay sharp, on your game, and be easy to work with. You can't control if you are replaced. Also, you may not always book the job when you audition. In fact, it could take several (or hundreds) of auditions until you do book a job.

Many times I've auditioned, not gotten the part, and then heard the produced spot on the air. At that point, I've said to myself, "I could have done that, if I'd known that's what they wanted." The only things you have to go by are the specs and tone of the copy. Unfortunately, you may never really know what the client and ad agencies were looking for until you hear the spot on the air. (Sometimes even *they* don't know until they hear all the auditions).

If you don't book the job even after what you think was your best audition ever, you may never know why. It's more than likely that the client just wanted a different style of voice, and, of course, you have no way of knowing what the other voiceover artists did in their reads. Every voice actor puts his or her own spin or style into the copy. Even if everyone sounds vocally similar, there is no way to second-guess creative and technical choices made by other actors. That's why it's best to not be competitive with other actors in the voiceover field. If you are competitive by nature, compete with yourself, so that each time you read, each new experience you have, leads you to bigger and better jobs. But don't spend too much time worrying about why you didn't get the job. You may never know why. Audition and move on.

If you do get the job, you may find out about the booking a day after you've read, two weeks later, or three months later — the schedule can be unpredictable. Or a client may like you but not book you for that particular spot, yet two years later have a perfect job for you and call your agent to book you. You may never even audition for that particular job. Still, auditioning is always part of voiceover work, no matter how successful you get, and unpredictability is built into the business.

START-UP COSTS

Start-up costs for voiceover careers vary. You have one goal: to get work. But how? By having the talent, taking classes or getting coaching, and making a demo CD. After that, you generate work by sending flyers, updated CDs, holiday cards, and mass mailings to ad agencies, production facilities, networks, writers, producers, animation houses, loop groups, and casting directors. After the initial investment for your CD and classes, the cost depends on how much you're willing to spend on your ongoing career.

A big chunk of your start-up costs will go toward workouts and classes. You'll learn basic voiceover skills and essential information about the voiceover world, from the creative to the technical aspects. Gaining knowledge of the market; reading actual, produced scripts as well as creating your own scripts; and getting the chance to work out at the microphone are all part of learning the business. Understanding how to break down a script and give it life while standing before the microphone are key to getting work. Having a great voice isn't enough. Learning what to *do* with that voice is the key to a long and lucrative career.

Voiceover classes can run anywhere from $49 for a one-day seminar at the Learning Annex to hundreds of dollars for ongoing classes that teach you everything from how to breathe to how to work the microphone, how to interpret copy, how to create different moods and voices, how to audition, and how to book a job. Costs vary depending on how often the classes meet and who is teaching them. There are classes for all levels of voice actors — classes in animation, commercials, promos, narration, and looping (you'll learn more about these categories in later chapters).

You can even get private coaching. Coaching can range from $95 to $225 per hour depending on the teacher and level. (Some do phone coaching too, so see Appendix B for a list). Demos can range from $1,000 with some sound engineers and producers (ask around to make sure they know what they are doing) to $2,500. Demos can be pricey, but worth the investment. You need a well-produced demo to get an agent and get in with casting directors.

FINDING THE RIGHT PLACE AND PERSON

How do you find the right class for you? Choosing among them depends on your personal preference as well as your learning style. Classes in a school-like atmosphere where there are courses at many levels being offered on an ongoing basis may work best for you. Or you may take a great commercial voiceover class, get information about your demo CD, and work with a private coach. Start by asking around. Ask fellow actors if they've taken any classes they'd recommend. Call your local SAG or AFTRA office. Pick up *Backstage* and look through it. Check with your local theater bookstore. Call a local voiceover agent and ask whom they recommend, or go to *www.everythingvo.com*. Voicebank.net is a great resource to find agents, casting houses, and advertising agencies in every city in the United States. Appendix B contains a list of classes and teachers in Los Angeles, New York, and Chicago. Refer to *www.voiceresourceguide.com* for a more complete set of listings. The *Ross Reports* contains information on classes and teachers as well. (Appendix B also has information on this and other publications.)

Decide which area of voiceovers you most want to work in. If, for example, you're looking to do animation, try to find a great animation class taught by a working animation actor, producer, or casting director. It's always best to learn from someone who's already successful in the business. Quite a few casting directors, producers, and even other voiceover actors offer classes; some even produce demo CDs, so you won't have to take classes at one place and produce your demo at another. Successful professionals also know the best guest speakers to bring in, giving you opportunities to meet and greet agents, casting directors, or ad-agency writers.

Making a professionally produced demo CD can be expensive, but once you do one, you shouldn't have to keep spending for new ones. Simply add or delete from your current one as you start booking voiceover jobs. If you don't book right away but want to change up your demo, a producer should do that for you at little cost, depending on what they offer. I coach (both in-person and phone coaching) and do demos (my email: terapp3@aol.com) and there are many places and people to turn to that will help you get your career off the ground! (See complete listing in Appendix B.) As you start to get more involved in voiceovers you may decide you want an animation CD as well, or a trailer CD, depending on the kind of auditions you are going on. A producer will usually give you a better price as you either create new demo CDs or add more areas to your existing demo.

A demo CD should showcase the full range of moods, feelings, specs, and characters you are able to comfortably re-create, so a casting director can hear your strengths and your versatility. Making a demo CD without sufficient training, or before you are comfortable working with a microphone, is a waste of time and money. Sending such a demo out to casting directors and agents will also work against you: once they've heard a bad CD, they probably won't want to hear from you again. So hold off on making that CD until you have taken a class (or two, or three). If you've already got a demo CD, bring it to class. Let the teacher listen to it before you continue sending it out. A good teacher will be able to give you advice if it needs fixing.

You must also be able to re-create the moods you've put onto your demo at an audition, so there's no point in making a demo until you've become comfortable enough in your reads to look at a script cold, run it a few times aloud, and lay down the audition the first or second time you read the copy. If it takes you fifteen reads to get the read you want, you are not ready to make a demo CD; multiple takes indicate you are not feeling comfortable in your reads. A teacher can help you find the mood, beats, rhythm, and feel of a spot and show you how to loosen up and nail your reads more quickly.

OKAY, THAT'S GREAT, BUT HOW MUCH CAN I MAKE?

Voiceovers can be extremely lucrative. Of course, there are the start-up costs. These can only be avoided if you get lucky and book a windfall of voiceover jobs in different moods and styles that a producer edits into a great 1-minute demo for you, otherwise you've got to invest. It certainly can pay off, however. Voiceover jobs range (non-union and union) from $440 for a radio spot per 13-week cycle (union) to anything negotiated non-union (probably a buyout one-time fee) to network commercials that can pay six figures, depending on run, cycle, and re-use, as well as market played in (see Chapter 13). Promo voiceover actors can make a few million a year if they get with a network. They go into the network one to several times a day to update what's coming up next on the air. This is a daily job, so hope of running off to Europe to enjoy that cash, may be dashed. But the money is great. Animation and video games are other areas where you can make a lot of money. Also, you don't just have to do one spot and call it a day. A lot of work leads to more work and one job can lead to several running at once. The only "conflict" (per union rules) is that you cannot have more than one commercial running on TV with the same product. For example, you cannot have Toyota and Buick spots running at the same time. That's called a *conflict*. Radio doesn't have any conflict, and you can do voiceover for as many car companies as you get. Unless the actual company hiring doesn't want you to be selling for the competition. They can ask to hold you exclusively, and this is something that your agent can negotiate. That being said, there are many people across the United States and Europe making quite a nice living in the world of voiceovers!

WARM-UP EXERCISES

Let's end this first chapter with some warm-up exercises meant to get your creative juices flowing.

- *EXERCISE #1*

Let's start with some print-ad copy. Look through some magazines, and choose an ad whose copy appeals to you. Choose three adjectives and follow the same cold reading technique given for the "That's a Great Shirt" exercise. We're now picking three adjectives instead of just one. This is where the tricky part comes in. You have to get into that mood, so you aren't pushing the sell, but simply allow your read to flow from that mood. An example of three adjectives is: warm, relaxed, and real. Or fun, knowledgeable, and matter-of-fact.

Learning adjectives and understanding how to color words and phrases (even the entire script) is the challenge that you will learn to do. It's fun and interesting to see how your voice changes depending on the mood you're in. It's also interesting to see how the read changes by adding a certain adjective, or changing up one adjective for another. You can stay with the same magazine copy and change your adjectives to see how the read changes. Try this and record for playback. Notice how a line or word is romanced (enhanced, played with) differently when you put a different mood into the read.

> ▶ TIP: You won't find the mood in the copy. The mood is what you are creating before you begin reading.

> ▶ TIP: The minute you leave your mood, you've left the spot. This means that if you do not maintain that same energy and feeling you had from the beginning, your "sell" will not have stayed for the duration of the copy. Learning to apply that mood and staying in that mood is pivotal for booking the job. It's also important in the voiceover session later on!

- **EXERCISE #2**

Choose a print ad that has no copy — one that uses only an image and a brand name. Pretend you are a copywriter, and try writing some copy for the ad; a sentence or two is fine. Write down what you're looking for as if you're the copywriter sending it off to voiceover talent. Read the copy in those specs that you've chosen. See the sell. If you want to go further, create a campaign or a slogan/tag line for the spot. See it on the air. How it will sound? What kind of voice are you looking for? What mood is right for that image? Record and playback. Change your specs, or switch the order of the specs. Don't forget to look to the left to feel the mood and get into it!

- **EXERCISE #3**

Now, let's go on to radio and TV. Record one or two radio or TV commercials off the air. (It doesn't matter what the commercials are for.) Play the recordings back, and listen carefully to the voiceovers. What are the specific moods and vocal qualities of these voiceovers?

Write down what you think the advertising agency's specs were for the commercial — the mood adjectives and the direction regarding age, gender, and point of view. Now, listen to each spot several times and write out the copy. Do a few practice runs. Find the flow. Don't try to copy the voiceover actor in the actual commercial or mimic his or her read. Pretend you were handed the copy at an audition and that you're reading *without* ever having heard the person who booked that job. Record your reads. Listen to the recordings. Notice how differently something can be sold, regardless of the product, by creating different moods, or vocal qualities, in your voice. (Doing this exercise will also help you later on, as you learn to break down a script.)

- **EXERCISE #4**

Now, choose a piece of copy from the samples in Appendix A, and follow the specs written on the page. Audition using the cold reading technique provided, just like you would be doing if you were auditioning. Record and play back.

CHAPTER 2

WHAT'S NEW IN THE VOICEOVER WORLD

IN THE LAST FEW YEARS, THERE HAVE BEEN SEVERAL CHANGES WITHIN THE VOICEOVER MARKETPLACE. The talent has changed: What used to be a relatively small market within the three major markets (New York, Chicago, Los Angeles) has opened up all across the country. Talent can live and work anywhere. They can now send in auditions to agents, managers, and even ad agencies. They can book jobs from their own home and either be sent to local recording studios or work from the comfort of their own home if they have the equipment and the client is okay with them running their own session. I know a few people who work directly with casting companies to book jobs.

It used to be common to have one agent only in the state where you lived, but now many actors have more than one agent in more than one state. I know actors who have ten agents across the country! They have non-union agents, managers, and several scripts coming in from several different sources. This is great, but be careful that you aren't receiving all the same auditions. Agents and managers in different states may or may not receive different auditions. You may receive more or less from one agent than others, it just depends on the hustle of the agent/manager and where they are receiving their auditions from. Auditions come directly from clients, casting houses, producers, writers, video game companies — everywhere.

The advertising agencies have changed too. Clients are going outside of the box and hiring not only local ad agencies, but no longer are feeling the need for huge campaigns and spending an exorbitant amount of money to get their product out there. With the Web and so many other areas to sell products (iPhone, Internet), there's been a willingness to look for talent in smaller markets and choose actors who don't sound like everyone else in the market. Agencies are more open than ever to hiring real people with regional accents to sell their products. Voice agencies (non-union, fi-core, union, all genres) are popping up across the country. Local companies no longer feel the need to go to high-end agents to hire talent when they can hire locally and get the work done within the budget. With the Internet, the recording facilities can turn around projects a lot faster, and with equipment available online, the clients no longer feel the necessity to hire the best recording studio to do post-production on their job. They are more comfortable going local, understanding that if the equipment is just as good and the sound engineer knows what he/she is doing, the work will still get done.

The market itself has changed to reflect all the diversity in the United States today. There are a lot more openings for ethnicities and accents, uniqueness and eccentricity. It's the same with on-camera, so of course voiceover has followed suit, which opens the doors for a lot of individuality that may have otherwise been closed off.

The major reasons for this new edition are to inform you of all those changes and to give you firsthand knowledge of the newest techniques and tools in the field, so that you can effectively get work in the voiceover business. There's the technical side of the business including the use of equipment, there's finding voiceover work and how to get the right work for you, and there's the market itself. Your understanding of these key elements and having inside access will give you the edge you need to turn your interest in voiceover into a successful career.

This latest edition has been revamped with 70% new insider information that you won't learn in other books. I will guide you through every area of the voiceover business. I will show you exactly how to be successful at every level of your career, from auditions to demos to the right coaching, from finding work to keeping the work coming, from how to work in a voiceover session to how to behave with clients. I will explain all of the terms and tools you need to make it in this business. I will show you how to use your voice to your best advantage and give you the skills to help you succeed in your career. I've been a successful coach, author, and speaker for the past 10 years. I have direct contact with the top voiceover agencies and advertising agencies, and firsthand knowledge of how the voiceover market works and the latest trends in the business.

The differences between a successful voiceover actor and one who never gets off the ground have to do with how you go after the work, who you hire to produce your demo and, most importantly, knowing how to get out of your own way. I've found that defensiveness, stemming from the inability to understand direction from directors and writers, is the number one obstacle in the voice actor's way. The reasons an actor becomes defensive are either the inability to take technical or creative direction, which is a learned process, or their stubborn belief that a more knowledgeable professional would know how to lead them in the right direction.

You must understand that the only interest a voice coach, booth director, casting director, writer, agent or producer has is for you to book the job. Remembering this is key to you moving forward in the voiceover process. You cannot book jobs without auditioning. You cannot pass the audition without learning how to nail the read and take direction. You cannot learn how to take direction until you understand what that means. Sure, you may get lucky and book a job off of your wonderful voice if you have direct contact with an ad agency or casting house, but you most likely will have to work with a writer and/or producer as well as a sound engineer to perfect the read. That means you will have to know how to take any and all direction given to you while you are in the voiceover session.

Learning to take direction with the right attitude can be taught and can be quite an easy process. If you are unable to understand directions, you may come off as high maintenance or argumentative without even meaning to. Fear of not knowing how to give them what they are asking for can get you fired from a job or never hired again. So, being prepared to enter the voiceover field ready to do the work is key. It's not rocket science and it doesn't take years, but a frequent comment I hear when coaching beginners is, "I thought it would be much easier." Although after a few workouts, the talent suddenly changes their tune to, "Oh, I get it, this is great!"

Voiceover work is truly a remarkable choice as either a hobby or a career. Getting any work can be quite lucrative and certainly not time consuming like a 9-to-5 job. Committing to a few hours a day (or week) to get your career started is all it takes. Having the right tools, getting auditions, and working your way up the ladder are all part of making a go of it in the voiceover field.

Many voice actors who've been in the business for years have to revamp their careers. They may have to redo their demo to make it more current, or maybe a character or voice they did for years isn't popular anymore and so it's no longer relevant to the marketplace. Or they might want to pursue another area in voiceovers, even take coaching or a class to get their chops up. Having an agent doesn't guarantee that you will be brought in to read for everything you think you're right for. You may want to have a conversation with your agent, find another agent who looks at you differently, or add a manager. You may want to go after more than one agent (in a different state) to add to the auditions you're receiving.

First and foremost, with the changing economy, a lot of the advertising agencies previously working only in a union market have gone non-union.

WHAT DOES THIS CHANGE MEAN FOR THE ADVERTISING AGENCIES?

Budgets have been slashed because there is no longer the kind of money that used to be poured into campaigns. (This is a general statement. Certainly there are companies that still pour hundreds of thousands of dollars into advertising, but the economy has slowed the length of runs and where spots are run overall.) The first people to lose out on that extra income are the voice actors. Union scale means that regardless of the type of voiceover job you do, ad agencies are required, by law, to pay the talent the minimum. If they no longer have the budget from the client to do the type of spot they want, they go the non-union route. This means that the ad agency no longer has to abide by the union contracts that protect the actors. The upside for the advertising agency is that they can provide a much lower budget for the client and not lose them to a competing agency. The downside is that they must find a talent as good as the union actor that they had previously been looking for.

With union talent, the first call that advertising agencies make is to the voiceover agents. They then release a copy of the script(s) and have the best actors who fit their requirements read for the job. With non-union talent, many agencies won't be involved. They either have to work with actors who have gone fi-core (are willing to work outside of the union contract) or search through non-union agencies, management companies and other avenues to find the kind of talent they are looking for. For the advertising agency, sending a script directly to the voice agent cuts down on a lot of time and hassle. They are relying on that agent or agencies to do the casting for them and find the best talent for the job. Although they are still picking from reads to determine whom they will use, the agent has whittled down the choices by sending in only those closest to what the client is looking for. When it comes to non-union projects, the advertising agency now has to rely on lesser-known sources to book their talent. With today's market, non-union management companies are springing up across the country that help cast the work for the non-union projects. These non-union management companies, which are sometimes fee based for the talent and sometimes not, act as union agents to provide the ad agencies with the best talent for the specs.

What's good about this change is that the advertising agencies are more open than ever before to non-union talent and voiceover actors new to the field. Advertising agencies and casting directors are on the lookout for fresh talent to add to their pool. Once you are in with a casting house or advertising agency, you should be brought in every time they feel you are right for a job, especially if you nail your reads and are easy to work with. As well, with the tougher economy and lower budget projects, the client may not even go through an agency at all. They may put a cold casting call through the casting director or may call talent directly. With all of these non-union management companies (plus clients not wanting to hassle with agents), they may simply post auditions via management websites or other websites, and have you audition via MP3 audio file. Today, voice actors can make a good living without having to join the union or get an agent.

WHEN NEGOTIATING FEES, HOW DOES THIS WORK FOR THE TALENT AND VOICE AGENT?

The voice talent wants any job they can get, within reason. That being said, talent shouldn't just take any job they can get. Sure, there are steps that can move you up the ladder and there are ongoing gigs worth taking (local grocery stores, donut work, affiliate, promo, video games, training videos), but you should know how to negotiate and get close to the same fees that you would normally earn working in the union market. Although there are budgets on every project, there is room for negotiation, and you must employ yourself as a businessperson to ensure that you make enough money. Ask for help in determining how much you should make (be sure to check local SAG and AFTRA scales). Also, with a regular voice job, make sure you determine how long something will run and if they intend to pull from it for other spots. You can be hired with the same company for many years to come, but if they know they can get you for cheap, they will. And that means you have no room to negotiate. Turning down a job may be exactly what you need to do to work your way up the ladder and land the jobs you want. This doesn't have to mean union or national work. This simply means working smart and working in any capacity you can.

With the market opening to more opportunities than ever before in the non-union world, the agent/manager and client must work together to make sure that the voice actor doesn't get ripped off. In some cases, the talent may chase this work themselves and even negotiate their own rates, but it may be a difficult process if the talent is clouded by the desperation to work. At least with a manager or agent to ensure the talent gets as close to scale (and in some cases buyout residuals), they will make the money along with getting their voice on the air. A few years ago, when budgets were much larger, the thought of going outside of the union was unheard of. But agents generally want to book voiceover jobs for anyone they represent, so if a non-union job comes their way, they will ask the talent beforehand if they are interested. The talent has the ability to turn the job down or go fi-core if they are union and want to take the job.

WHAT DOES THIS MARKET CHANGE MEAN FOR NON-UNION AND UNION VOICE TALENT?

For non-union talent (people newer to the business or actors who've never gone union) it opens up new opportunities for them to not only get in with previously hard-to-reach advertising agencies, but to book auditions that only union talent was considered for before. Starting in the non-union market and moving into union jobs can happen as well. Today, there are ad agencies that handle both union and non-union. Once they are familiar with your work, they may bring you in for union jobs as well. If you read for a union job, even though you're non-union, you may still book the job, which will lead to more union jobs. There really isn't much difference between union jobs and non-union jobs. Budget is really the only thing that determines how much a company wants to spend for the talent and the campaign in general. Sure, some union jobs hire better writers and come up with better slogans (as well as good old residuals), but plenty of non-union jobs are well written, some by those same union writers and ad people, and can pay quite well. Just because something is non-union does not mean you aren't entitled to some sort of fee.

Working in Voice123 or doing "on hold" messaging is a form of working in the voice market, but most people don't consider that to be professional work. While it's important to work in the business, it's more important to work smart and sometimes turn down jobs that pay only $25 or $50. What you want to do is work in the voiceover field. The areas of the voiceover market (although, technically that would mean anything you use your voice for) are TV, radio, affiliate, promos, narration, video games, audio books, in-house training videos, online training/corporate videos, trailers, dubbing, looping and animation.

The first step in advancing your career is to channel the kind of work represented on your demo tape. If you have a video game demo but want to pursue commercials, you must have a commercial demo to get those auditions. To pursue the video game industry, tap all of the proper online resources (Voicebank, everythingVO.com, E3 Convention) and funnel your energy into that market, so that you can get those auditions. You don't need to wait for an agent to do that for you. Most of the time, the video games come through outside resources (such as mentioned above), so you can pursue that on your own. No longer do you need an agent to call you in to read for auditions. You have the ability to zone in on areas you want to pursue and follow your dreams. You do not need your own equipment or an expensive laptop to send in auditions. And you don't need to live in a major market to make a living.

For union voice talent, the new market may mean that you choose to go fi-core and work outside of the union so that you can still make a living. It may mean adapting how you've been working and auditioning to ensure that you are reading in the right way — ask a booth director or a casting director for feedback. A lot of times, voice talent blame everyone else for why they've stopped getting work, when it's simply that the market has changed. Maybe their style of reading is no longer what the market is looking for or isn't up to par. Union talent needs to do just as much marketing as non-union. Although they may work on more than one campaign or product at a time, there are usually several contacts to be made within every ad agency. The ability to make new connections helps ensure that you are considered for future projects. The market is ever changing and so is the staff within advertising agencies. You may have been in the business for a long time, but you may have lost touch with the younger and newer writers and producers. How do you find them? Pick up the Advertising Resource Guide or any online resource, *Adweek* or any other advertising magazine, or Voicebank, which has a thorough guide not only of advertising agencies, but industry names as well.

WHAT'S NEW WITH REGARDS TO THE TECHNICAL ASPECTS OF THE VOICE BUSINESS?

Technically, the business has changed a great deal over the last 5 to 10 years. Several years ago, the thought of doing a phone patch (voiceover session directed over the phone from another state) was unheard of. Most producers didn't want to hire talent for a job without first seeing and directing them. They weren't sure they could trust the sound engineer and the quality of the voiceover. Once phone patching and ISDN (a direct long-distance link to not only direct, but record from both sides) became a popular way of working in the business. No longer were companies bound to hire local talent only. Once they perfected the technical aspects and got used to not being in the same room as the voice actors, it became a widely accepted practice to hire talent in a different state from the advertising agency. As well, voice agents were uncomfortable having voice talent send in a read. This meant they had to let go of the notion that actors could not direct themselves. It still holds true that there is no replacement for being directed by a booth director who knows what they're doing. Direction is very helpful in communicating what the producer and/or writer is looking for. Usually agents still would prefer that you go in to read if you are local, but they are open to you sending the work in, provided you do it right and you are good at self-directing. Even if you are a request (they know your voice) and/or they listened to your demo, you will still be asked to read to see how you sound for that particular job.

In the last couple of years, the "snowflake" (mini-microphone) has become extremely popular for sending in auditions. It's cheap ($59 or less on eBay or craigslist), and you don't need to go into a small or padded room to read copy. It isn't adequate for voiceover sessions, but gone are the days when voice actors need to spend thousands of dollars to build a studio in their house. Many voice actors have converted a closet into a mini recording studio. But this really isn't necessary anymore because when you are hired for a voiceover job, you will be sent to an outside recording studio to do it. When you are hired for a smaller job that may require you to have your own recording equipment, there are so many other options, such as small recording studios that offer very low ISDN costs, that it really shouldn't be a determining factor in hiring you for the job. Spending all of that money (unless you're a musician and use equipment for other reasons) is really going overboard. Instead, invest your money in the right coach and have a well-produced demo.

If you want to have equipment other than the microphone to send in auditions, then research the proper Zephyr so that you are using the most compatible ISDN that most voiceover companies use. The only reason to have your own equipment is to save the advertising agency the cost of renting a studio (but they won't pay you the difference instead). Usually, they are cutting corners, and will ask if you have your own setup, but will still direct you over the phone. Problems can arise when you are doing not only the voiceover but playing sound engineer as well. You cannot cut and edit your own takes while you are in the voice session. You will have to "star" the reads they like and afterwards cut, edit, paste per direction, and send everything back to the producer. This no longer means you are simply a voice actor. You have now taken on the role of sound engineer as well, without the pay. Offering to do this probably isn't going to get you anything except a "thanks." If you are hired to produce the spot (cut, edit, music bed, sound effects), you are essentially being hired in the role of producer and should be paid accordingly. Make sure you understand what you are agreeing to. You don't want to do favors or be taken advantage of, all in the hopes of more work in the future. It's great to have the ability to write, produce, edit and direct yourself, and, who knows, maybe you'll even get hired by the advertising agency to produce other spots. Just make sure that being a jack-of-all-trades doesn't keep you from getting hired as a voiceover actor!

Usually, voice actors do not cut, edit or add music to their voice sessions. If you are hired and working from home with a director, you will be asked to provide the takes they want dry (voice and voice alone) and then convert the takes to MP3 files after you are done with the voice session. When you go to an outside recording studio, all of this is done for you. A "snowflake" or other microphone that you can attach to your computer is not appropriate for voiceover sessions. There isn't yet the type of equipment that allows you to ISDN via computer sitting in your home. (I'm sure there will be a time in the future, when, with the push of a button, you can delete all outside noise and send in crisp, clean auditions, be directed via Skype and call it a day!) If need be, voiceover sessions can be directed at your voice agency. The equipment they have is usually up to par with what is needed for a recording.

Get your own microphone to practice with, as well as for playback and to hear how you sound when reading a particular spot in a particular mood. If you don't want to invest in one, you can go to a casting house that offers $1-a-minute auditions. This can get costly, but you are getting great direction from a reputable booth director as well as stellar equipment so that your read always sounds technically up to par. There are also audition clubs springing up across the country (Garden of Sound Los Angeles) that for a nominal fee allow you to use their recording studio and send in your own auditions. They show you how to work the equipment, give you the time to read, cut, edit your work, and convert to MP3. You may receive several auditions from different sources, so having your own microphone will be helpful. Work with a coach and have them assess your reads to make sure you sound good and are reading in the specs.

I provide an online (or phone) service and in one workout or assessment, I can usually fix any problem that you may be having, even if you think your reads are perfect. Another knowledgeable ear is extremely important in helping you get out of your own way — and move forward.

WHERE CAN I RECEIVE AUDITIONS IN THIS NEW MARKET?

Let's start by telling you that in the "old days" the only real way to get auditions was through your agent or a casting director. You made a demo, you sent it to an agency and hoped to get called in. When they took you on, you waited to go in to read or they would send you to an outside audition (casting house, adverting agency, production company). Although those days still exist and that process is considered essential to working within the voiceover business, you no longer have to wait around to get to that level. Here are a few options:

- Online casting sites: Make sure when you send in auditions that you watermark your work. Do not read the entire script, or you can purposely say a word wrong so they can't simply go to air with your work without re-recording and paying you.
- Voicebank: There are several non-union (and union) companies that hire voice talent. You can start where you live and branch out from there. If you aren't having luck getting an agent in your state, don't worry. With online resources and the ability to direct long distance, companies feel more comfortable looking outside of where they normally do to hire voice talent. This means that some of those great auditions that were previously not coming your way are sent to smaller markets. Booking work has never been easier. If you get the job, you are sent to a local recording studio to record. It doesn't even matter if the spot airs in your region. You will be paid according to the negotiation made.

- E3 Convention (or any convention, actor fest, Voice 2011 annual event): Conventions are great opportunities for you to meet producers, writers, actors, and other voice performers. You never know where your next job will come from so educate yourself on the latest tools, equipment, what's hot, where to look for jobs, anything you need to know to stay current. I travel to do seminars (as do other voice talent and authors), and you should take advantage of these when they come your way. Usually seminars are not too expensive (I speak at SAG and AFTRA for free and other events for small fees), but the information you learn as well as scripts you take home and the opportunities to work out are priceless.
- Advertising agencies, casting directors, production companies, radio stations, recording studios: Don't be intimidated to send out your demo to anyone and everyone who can potentially hire you for a job. Make sure your demo is good and start making the rounds until you've blanketed your town. Any of the above can pull you in at any time and hire you to do a voiceover job. All of the above can keep hiring you for a job before you've ever even stepped foot into a voiceover agency's door.
- Dubbing houses/looping: If you have a specialty (such as fluency in a foreign language), take advantage of it by contacting a postproduction house that does looping. Look online for a list of companies and call them up or send a demo to them online. Most loop groups offer a chance to sit in and observe the work. Several loopers I know got started this way and now make six figures just looping shows or films and don't even want to read for commercials because the process is so comfortable and they have a regular schedule.
- Audio books: Check online or go to the library or bookstore and copy down the names of the companies that produce audio books. Contact them via MP3 or mail. Taking an audio book seminar can be instrumental in sending you to the right contacts and learning how to read for audio auditions and work in sessions.

THE DIFFERENCE BETWEEN SUCCESS AND FAILURE

The difference between your success and failure in this business is you. That's right, the problem is not your voice that's either too high-pitched, too normal, or too unique, because all of those qualities work in the voiceover business at some capacity. Nope, the ability to succeed in this business has to do with how much effort you put into it to master it.

One of the wrong ways to start your career is getting a voiceover demo done before you know how to read. You may say, "I've got a great voice, I make money in other areas, I can afford a demo, so what am I waiting for? I might as well get out there and start booking!" Great attitude, but it's a bit premature.

Why? Well, let's say you get a great-sounding demo, because you hired the right producer, they provided the right copy, and they were able to pull some range out of you so that you can land different types of jobs. It's premature because although the casting director may have called you in based on your voiceover demo and likes you in person, your ability to read is key in booking that job. The casting director may say to you, "I brought you in because I loved your BMW read on your demo and it's the kind of read we're looking for." This means that you will have to re-create that same vocal sound for this audition. If you don't remember the mood you were in when you created that vocal sound and you try to wing it, the read will come out sounding forced. The casting director may get frustrated trying to explain to you how to get that mood back, and will just expect you to get there however you did the first time. Remember, the producer worked tirelessly with you on your demo session to pull from you the very best reads that represent you. Then, you have to be able to do it repeatedly, so that you can book the job. If the casting director cannot get the desired read (and you'll only be given one or two chances to nail it), you probably won't get called in again by that director. They will think you don't know how to take direction, couldn't back up your demo, or don't know how to read. Word travels fast, and your opportunities could vanish overnight. It's hard to get a second chance in the voiceover business. Jumping in before you are ready can be detrimental to the career you are trying to build.

Getting in to audition anywhere and everywhere you can is the most important step in getting voiceover work. The more you read, the better chance you have to get hired and the better your reads will become. Getting comfortable in your own skin and being able to apply the right mood to copy every time you read brings you one step closer to booking. You may not get that job (or several in a row, for that matter), but as long as the booth director or casting director likes what you've done, you will be on the right track.

Remember, casting directors bring in voice actors who fit the specs that the client is looking for. They also will bring in actors outside the box to show something a bit different to the client. Sometimes this tactic works, other times it doesn't. If a casting director brings you in to read and you don't feel you are right for the part, feel free to ask what they are looking for. Use every opportunity you can to showcase your talent and demonstrate that you know what you are doing, are easy to work with and are able to be spontaneous and creative in your choices. Casting directors and booth directors don't have all of the answers that a client is looking for and sometimes they may not have much more that what they have already told you, which may not be much. It's your job to do well in your cold reading every time, then walk away from it and move on to the next audition. Voiceovers are a numbers game, and the more you look at the business as simply that, the less likely you will worry about every audition that you did.

Working voice actors who audition a lot are getting the practice, the experience, and the expertise of others to guide them in the business. You have to work responsibly and read every script as if it is a job you have booked. The time you have to cold read (look through the script, read it, make notes, do cold reading steps) should not be wasted on frivolous talk so that you don't end up winging it in the booth. The more you put into understanding the writer's intent (how something is written and meant to be read), the closer you are to booking the read. I've rarely gone into a voiceover session without booking the job from the audition. This doesn't mean that the writer or producer doesn't have other notes for me, but I understood and conveyed the message of the spot in the way they wanted it delivered.

Not understanding how to read something can have a devastating impact. Not only do you lose the opportunity to book that job, but also you may miss the opportunity to read again for that casting house, director, and client. It's not a matter of ego or coasting on your amazing voice; in fact, my voice is the last thing I think about when reading. That's right, I'm not thinking about how I sound or how I should say a word or a line. I'm simply committed to my mood and telling a story to a particular person. I allow the words to flow from the way in which the story is told. Most voiceover actors stick to this policy because it allows them to connect with the copy and not oversell with their voice.

The voice is the icing on the cake and can make or break you. A voice actor's inability to be flexible and change within their range is also a negative factor and can cause them to lose work. If you are constantly saying, "I just do my thing and that's it," or, "They can book me for me because I can't do anything else, it's just my voice," then you are getting in your own way. You are telling the advertising world that they have to come to you and work your way or no way. Unfortunately, the business doesn't operate that way, and although your particular voice may be hot one minute, the next minute it may not be. You will need to learn to create other vocal qualities so that you can fit other categories of reads. Then you will need to fix your demo accordingly, talk to your agent and start to read on other projects. Waiting around for that one read that you can nail and only working in one area will take away a lot of other opportunities and money. Your goal in the voiceover field should be to broaden your range and be able to do as many sales comfortably as possible.

The opposite of this problem is the voice actor who considers himself or herself a staple client and is horrified that he or she isn't reading on everything that's out there. Number one, you have to trust your agent(s) or why be with them? You have to understand that they have your best interest at heart, although they might not be aware of everything you can do if your demo doesn't show off your range. Worrying about why you are only handed one or two scripts, while the guy next to you (who may sound similar to you) has five scripts, isn't going to help your mindset. If you want to know why you aren't getting more work, once every six months you can take your agent to lunch or set up a 15-minute meeting to discuss the direction in which you want your career to move forward. Be realistic, but certainly tell them if you have an interest in, say, trailers, or animation, or you want to know why you aren't receiving copy for a certain category. Let them know if you feel you are being typecast in one area; they may need to hear you read on a script or two to see what you can do with your range. When they signed you (or pocketed you), they may only have had one type of read in mind for you based on your demo, what you have playing on the air, or even how you read in the booth. Also, agents like to take on categories of actors. You have to speak up and say something so that you get considered for more auditions than just the obvious choices.

Having a unique sound that is obvious for animation and yet banking on a commercial career is not the smartest move either. Although, you may have a unique voice and there are lots of great radio and TV spots that you will able to read on, make sure that you pursue the area that has the possibility of generating the most work. If you've got all the time and money in the world and want to explore every avenue, that's fine. But then you should work with or take classes from great coaches who can move you forward quickly and in the correct way. You will need to have the best demos to showcase that work. Then you will need to learn how to audition and work in a voiceover session. Many voice actors learn on the job, but working with a coach who gives you pointers and teaches you the terminology can only help you be more effective and easier to work with in a session.

If you become defensive in an audition or voiceover session, the casting directors, booth directors, and clients won't want to work with you. A defensive actor is one who argues or tries to defend their read after the casting director, booth director, writer, and producer have given their notes, directions or changes they want you to make. Remember that they are not telling you off, but are trying to get the read they are looking for. They are giving you either creative notes (warm it up, pull it back, have more fun with it, lighten it up, more matter-of-fact) or technical notes (tighten it up, you have five seconds to play with, go up at the end of that word, romance that line a bit more, throw it away more). Your job as a voice actor is to write down those notes, and immediately be able to make the necessary adjustments to get as close to what they are asking for as possible. Getting angry or frustrated even with yourself, and allowing them to see that, is a sign of being green. They don't want to have to hold your hand or fear they've insulted you. Asking too many questions, reiterating what they've already said to buy you time, or overanalyzing will only frustrate the client and give them the impression that you don't know what you are doing. You need to sneak into this business with an air of professionalism, learn to take direction without personal emotion, and give them what they want without hassle. This is a learned process, and you must have some patience with the process. It isn't something you can learn overnight, and I always coach my students on how to work through their frustration. You have to learn to stay out of your own way.

You can certainly book a job without experience, go into the session with the same enthusiasm and re-create the same read that booked you the job, and open yourself up to learning. A good director, sound engineer, writer and/or producer will know how to walk you through the session. Listening, being open and prepared is the best thing you can do to ensure that you have a session that goes well. When the director gives you notes that you don't understand, you can ask them to explain in a simple, direct manner. They may even give you a line reading to show you exactly how they want something said. Staying positive and focused will help you to work your way through the session. You are taking direction from someone who is leading you to exactly the read that they want. It's up to you to follow what they are saying, make the appropriate changes, and to create that read. They may say at some point, "we're not getting what we're looking for," and at that point you may need to step outside of the booth and try to have a conversation or five-minute break to collect your thoughts. They may feel you are reading differently than how you did at the audition or that you are bringing in something new that you didn't do originally. They may feel the reads are starting to sound too polished or too bright. It may have nothing to do with you at all, and the client (after listening to the session) has decided that you're the wrong voice for the job, or they've decided they want to go another way. Or, they may love your voice but have a problem pleasing the writer. There are so many issues that can arise, you just have to go with the flow and work it out the best you can. Stay out of your own way, work professionally, and have fun!

CHAPTER 3

THE ART OF THE VOICEOVER

THE VOICE IS THE ICING ON THE CAKE. I say this often because how you read something is more important than what your voice sounds like. Of course, your voice is yours and yours alone. Many people start out in the voiceover business because they've been told they have a cool voice, a unique voice, or an interesting voice. Voices can be intimidating, strong, quirky, preachy, whiny — you name a kind of voice, and the voiceover world has it. But there are also a lot of people working in the business who have everyday, common voices.

Why do they get work, too? Because ad agencies and producers also need regular voices to sell their products. They don't necessarily want the voice taking over the message.

They want a nice, everywoman/everyman voice for their everyday product. The voice is your tool for the voiceover business, and every working voiceover talent knows how to use that tool for each particular job. Even if many of the voiceover jobs you do have the same mood, style, and vocal quality, each read has to be fresh and alive. You have to read *actively,* acting as realistically as you can so that you come across as natural — even though you are selling something.

LISTENING TO YOUR OWN VOICE

Most people think that they know what their voice is like — but then they're shocked when they hear a recording of it. They listen to their voice on an answering machine and can't believe how it sounds. Whether we know it or not, each of us "sells" different moods every day, depending on what we are feeling, what we want from someone, or what we are trying to convey. Understanding just how you come across when speaking is vitally important in the world of voiceovers.

BREAKING INTO THE BUSINESS

There are three major voiceover markets: New York, Los Angeles, and Chicago. This doesn't mean that you can't or won't book jobs in the South, or Southwest, or anywhere else in the country. There is plenty of work in the minor markets, too. I know several people making six-figure incomes doing voiceover work in Texas, Kansas, and elsewhere. There is plenty of money to be made in the nation's breadbasket, the thirteen states in the middle of the country. And the outskirts of cities have many, many local jobs for nonunion actors; you just have to know how to find them.

    The major markets employ more talent, and the agencies in these markets land most of the large-scale, national campaigns, but you can make money no matter where you live — through local production companies, ad agencies, and radio stations. In fact, there's far less competition in the smaller markets, and local ad agencies will certainly be pleasantly surprised — and encouraging — if you know how to work in a voiceover session. Ad agencies love finding new talent, and they love people who are easy to work with and who bring something creative to the voiceover process. Production companies may hire you because you are local and nonunion, then find that you are easy to work with, and rehire you again and again. You may continue to work with that same company for many years to come.

    And nowadays, with the Internet, there are also a lot of jobs to chase online. Checking out voiceover talent online is a perfect way for casting directors to hear who's out there. Voicebank (*www.voicebank.net*) and *www.voice123.com* are two places directors often look. Craig's List (*www.craigslist.com*), *www.actorsaccess.com*, *www.lacasting.com*, and *www.nycasting.com* are all great sites that you can join to look for voiceover jobs. (Check the resources in Appendix B for additional websites.)

When you're just starting out, it doesn't hurt to take a job here or there for free or for very low pay — a onetime buyout of $100, for example. You have to start somewhere. (I wouldn't make a habit of this — you want to get to the union level and reading for jobs that can make your career. Getting stuck in a non-union, buyout world, may not lead you in the direction you want to go in the long run!)

Get known in your local area first by auditioning for student films, local commercials, and work at affiliate TV stations. Build your resume, learn how to work on mike, and learn how to be professional in a voiceover session. All this experience will be very helpful when you move up in the marketplace into a more competitive environment.

To get your first voiceover job (and no matter how successful you get thereafter), you will most likely have to audition. (Sure, you might get lucky — someone might hand you a spot. Maybe you're a friend of someone at an ad agency who likes your voice, or the local radio station decides to take a chance and use you for a commercial. But this is very rare.) And you have to be invited to audition: It's not a great idea to try to crash a voiceover audition. To audition, you have to know the casting directors — or, rather, they have to know you and your work and call you in for reads. Pick up the *Ross Reports* and look at the listings. (I've also listed the major-market agents in Appendix B, at the back of the book.)

For smaller, local talent agencies, do some research online, or call a local commercial casting house or advertising agency. Even post-production houses in smaller markets hire voiceover talent for in-house infomercials — and they may hire you without a demo CD. This is a great way to start in the business. You can view the business cards of the members of the Casting Society of America, a professional organization of approximately 350 casting directors in film, television, and theater, at its website: *www.castingsociety.com*.

There are several ways to find out about voiceover jobs. Your agent, if you have one, will send you on auditions (although you will continue to work actively on your career as well). If you don't have an agent, you can go after jobs on your own through production companies, ad agencies, and casting directors. In a small city, voiceover work, if produced and cast locally, may even come through the one or two recording houses in town. *Backstage* magazine is another resource for (mostly non-union) voiceover work.

Have your demo CD professionally produced: It will save you time and the headache of not knowing what you are doing or what you should put on it. Send it to local advertising agencies, radio stations, production facilities, recording studios, schools and universities that have a theater and/or film department, as well as any local company headquartered nearby that produces industrial DVDs in-house. (You can find this out through the company's marketing or corporate communications division.)

Looping houses are production facilities that look for voiceover actors to do background sound effects, vocal sound, or actual speech to create ambient sound. These jobs can pay very well — up to $1,000 per day, depending on the project and whether it's union or not. Most of these jobs are handled by "loop groups": post-production facilities with a stable of local loopers they can call when a job comes through town. You may also find luck in dubbing houses (provided you speak and/or understand a foreign language). For audio books, check the Audio Publishers Association's website (*www.audiopub.org*) for a complete list of its members.

A list of local casting directors can be found through the local unions, the online Voice Over Resource Guide (*www.voiceover-resourceguide.com*), and also on *www.everythingvo.com*. You can also call local advertising agencies and ask whom they do their casting with. If they do it in-house, find out whom to send your demo to. (Your demo CD, like a business card, will never be returned. You will send out hundreds over the years.) Try to establish relationships and build a clientele for your future by keeping a list of everyone you come into contact with. And always write thank-you notes.

OTHER EMPLOYMENT OPPORTUNITIES

You might find making a go of a full-time voiceover career tough, especially in the beginning. You are competing in a market inundated with people who've worked in this arena for years. In that way, it's just like any other business. Of course, it's also a lot of fun, challenging, and financially rewarding, so a lot of people are *very* interested in breaking into voiceovers. Clients are always looking for new talent. They're often interested in "changing things up" and being the one responsible for bringing new voices into the mix. Agents are always looking for new people to add to their roster and will love a refreshing spin on a read. They often take on new talent, even to "pocket" (try you out without signing) to see if you book jobs. Casting directors love getting professionally produced demos from new talent, especially if they offer something different from the table of talent they already bring in for auditions. If you have talent as well as an interesting voice, if you stick to your goals, and if you spend time and effort learning your craft, you just may succeed and make money in this business.

One of the nice aspects of voiceovers is that many new voices do manage to break into the business every year. Ad agencies are always looking for new and interesting voices that haven't yet cracked the marketplace. As long as you fit the description they want — and nail the read — you'll have the same chance at booking the job as someone who's been in the business for twenty or thirty years.

While you are improving your skills by taking lessons and auditioning whenever you can, you might want to call production companies that specialize in documentaries and in-house training videos. You can find these local companies by doing a bit of research. Call your local radio station and ask who the local in-house training companies are. Use the online resources mentioned in Appendix B. You can even go to your local grocery and department stores, or the stores in your local mall, to inquire about doing intercom announcements. Widen your horizons.

If you don't have a demo CD, follow another avenue until you can get one produced. Student filmmakers at local colleges might be looking for voiceover actors for their films. Check online under "voiceovers"; many non-union houses are looking for voice actors because they don't have the funds or resources to pay union talent. Many local advertising agencies and radio stations book non-union talent as well. This can be a great opportunity to learn your craft and make connections. Few people break into the business by reading for big national campaigns. Booking a local radio spot, doing an in-house training video, providing the voiceover for an infomercial — any of these can be a great training ground for the future.

PRACTICE! PRACTICE! PRACTICE!

Look at and listen to what's out there in the marketplace: Pick up a magazine. Read a book aloud. Watch TV and record the commercials. Watch animated shows. People often confuse doing voiceovers with doing voice imitations. It's all well and good to be able to copy, or "do," a voice you hear, but it's better to try to understand — by listening carefully — what the writer, producer, or ad agency was looking for when they hired that voice.

Don't do caricatures, yet be creative and "charactery" with your choices. What does this mean? Pick a character: A harried New York cab driver. A lisping, gum-chewing Southern hairdresser. A tough mafia guy. A lonely, nasal-sounding car mechanic. If you dig deep enough, I'll bet you can come up with vocal qualities based on these descriptions. If I add more adjectives — a *flirtatious*, tough mafia guy; a *bored*, lisping, gum-chewing Southern hairdresser — this will change the read. Or add a technical direction — deep rasp, smoky voice, flat voice. Now there's yet another layer to the read. First and foremost is finding the voice that fits the character, then you layer the read with mood within that character. (See Chapter 5.)

Remember what we said about character, attitude, and personality? You've got to play with your voice to develop different attitudes and moods. To play with your voice, try reading the TV commercials you recorded in a different manner each time. Do everything you can with the words, and be as silly as you want.

Now pick a few different characters for yourself and see what you can come up with. Be a smoldering sexpot, a mysterious detective, a yuppie tennis player at a country club, or a gas station attendant with a bad haircut. Create these characters, figure out how they would sound based on these descriptions, as well as how you think they feel. Each character and mood will bring out a different inflection and speech pattern in your own voice. Try applying some of the mood adjectives to yourself and listen to how your voice sounds.

Don't forget to practice different voices around your house and in your car. Start with one descriptive adjective, and then keep adding. See how many vocal changes happen because of the mood changes. If you're at home, record yourself and listen to the recordings. Sometimes you won't think you sounded different until you play something back.

WATCH, LISTEN, READ — AND RECORD YOURSELF

Watch television commercials. People are always telling me, "I heard such and such a commercial, did the voice, and knew that I could have booked that commercial." When I hear this kind of thing, I always ask, "What do you think the mood of that person was? If you had the script in front of you, what do you think the direction would ask for?" It's more important to get the quality of the voice and the mood than to merely copy someone else's vocal pattern. Copying another voiceover artist's vocal pattern may get you one job, but without a mood or point of view, it will be difficult for you to stay in the voiceover game.

Learn how to determine what kinds of spots you might be right for. When you hear a commercial with a voice that's similar in tone to yours, write down the mood adjectives that you think the script called for. Remember, everything you watch and listen to started out as a script. Before that, it was a concept/idea, so this should help you understand the process and where you fit in as a voice actor. Write out the script and try to come up with some reads of your own. Keep trying different ways to say the copy — appropriate to the product the commercial is selling, of course. Remember that whoever did book that voiceover job read that spot at least ten times — and maybe as many as forty times — during the voiceover session, until the producer, writer, ad agency, and client all got what they wanted. That's a lot of people who have to agree on which read goes on the air.

The visual design of a television ad can tell you a lot about what the ad agency and clients are trying to convey. What do they want us consumers to feel, to see, to understand? Was it designed for teenagers? Senior citizens? Harley-Davidson riders?

Listen to the radio. The voiceover is even more important here than on television — without visuals, it's the only selling tool. Pay attention to what kinds of voices are used most often. Who are the voice actors talking to? What kind of story are they telling? What makes you listen to a spot — or change the station? Do you think you will remember the commercial? Buy the product? Remember, the client is counting on that voice and personality to lure people into buying the product advertised. Even if the radio commercial is really bad, someone decided to air it, and someone got the job.

Write down the ad copy. Whether you're listening to radio or watching TV, write the commercials down and practice reading the copy. Don't imitate — just follow the attitudes and moods you hear. What is the person's point of view? Who are they addressing? Then create your own specs, including mood adjectives, and read the copy again. Read to yourself first, understanding the technical setup of the spot. Then, when you've gotten into the right mood, read the copy aloud. Then read it again. Before you record yourself, you should already be in an active state of creating a mood and ready to read. The recorder (or microphone) is simply a tool for conveying the mood to a particular audience. The energy and quality comes from inside of you — not from the mike or recorder.

Now record yourself. After you've recorded a spot in a number of different ways, play them back and listen to your tone, your breathing, your timing, and your pacing. Time the commercial so you know how long the actual spot is, but don't worry about getting the commercial "in time" right away. It's more important to find the mood first. Once you've hit upon the right mood, the pacing (or rhythm) of the spot will become more natural.

There are several steps to reading a voiceover commercial. The first (and most important) is to find the mood. The right mood *is* being in the right vocal quality. Understanding the specs and finding the right vocal quality while in the mood is very important in booking the job. The second is finding the beats or transitions (the way a script is supposed to be read, based on how it is written). You should find this in the script, as you learn to read and get comfortable in seeing scripts and being able to understand how to break them down. (See Chapter 6.) Every script has a rhythm and flow to it, and it's up to you, the voice actor, to find that in the script. You can book a job based on your vocal quality, but it's important to understand the way a script is written and make it sound natural based on what the writer/producer/ad agency wants. Commercials come in many different time lengths: Five-second tags, fifteen seconds, thirty seconds, and sixty seconds. Infomercials can be much longer. The only way to determine the length of a particular spot is to record the actual commercial and then time it from copy start to copy finish. Once you find the right mood, you can try to record it "in time." We'll discuss timing in more detail later on.

When I was just starting out, I diligently went through real ads in magazines and read them aloud. I bought a recorder and recorded myself. I tried to create as many moods as I could come up with by looking at the image in the ad and reading what the ad said. I invented cartoon characters, drew them, and gave them names. Then I gave them distinct walks and mannerisms. This helped me find their voices. I would record everything and time it. If I was basing my reads on a regular commercial, I would time the commercial so I'd know just how long the spot was supposed to be. While I watched TV, I would write down and time the ads. Then I would read a spot and see if I could fit it in that time. Knowing commercials helped me understand what the clients and ad agencies were looking for. It also helped me decide whether I was pursuing the right career. Could my voice be cast in that commercial?

The secret to doing voiceovers is to make the copy sound real for yourself. If you believe the copy you're reading aloud, then you will get an audience to believe it and buy the product. That's what the ad agencies want: a unique voice that will help sell their product. Do that, and you'll have some happy customers!

LEARNING TO RELAX

Your auditions and jobs will go a lot better if you learn to relax. Relaxation techniques like meditation, hypnotherapy, and yoga are all great ways to relax your body and to open up your lungs so you can speak for a longer time without taking so many breaths. When you're recording, your breathing should also come as naturally as the sentences you speak in everyday life, and when you're feeling relaxed, you breathe less frequently. Work out. Cardiovascular fitness makes it easier to breathe and gives you better lung capacity.

Think about times when you've been very eager to tell someone something. Notice how you can get a lot more words in a sentence? When you're agitated, you may breathe more frequently and heavily. How about when you're bored or tired? Your breathing becomes a lot slower, your rhythm calmer. Breathing changes with energy, and energy changes with breathing. Your breathing should be second nature — a natural part of your energy. The way you convey sentences when in a certain mood in ordinary life is the same way that you will convey the meaning of a voiceover commercial or animated character. In other words, breathing grows out of your mood. We do not lead with our breathing — we lead with the mood, and the breathing follows.

WARM-UPS AND COLD WATER

Personally, I don't perform any warm-up exercises before auditioning, although many other voiceover professionals do. There are a number of things you can do to warm up vocally. You can do deep breathing, visualize restful places, or use other relaxation techniques. I simply look at the audition copy, apply the appropriate adjectives, and go ahead with the audition. I like to keep it simple so my creativity can come through. This also keeps the reads fresh every time.

As for quenching your thirst and getting your voice ready, plain cold water is the best thing you can drink. Soda constricts the muscles in your throat, makes you burp, and creates phlegm. You really want to avoid bubbles, especially during a voiceover session in which you'll be reading the copy over and over until the producers get the read they want. You want your voice to be as consistent as it can be, especially if they need to cut a line from one take together with a line from another take. Tea is good for sore throats — and so is honey — but hot drinks can also constrict throat muscles and make your voice deeper and raspier — which is a good thing only if that's what the read calls for. If you have a cold and a raspy voice on a day that you audition and you happen to book the job, you'd better keep that cold all the way through that voiceover session! You'll be hired for what you did at the audition, and the job itself might start the next day — or three weeks later, depending on deadlines. That's why it's important to keep your vocal register consistent, remember what you did, and be able to re-create it.

▶ TIP: Eat an apple a day. No, I'm not just saying this because my last name is Apple. (I don't make any money when you eat an apple!) Believe it or not, apples are great for keeping your throat open and the juices flowing. There's something about the texture and consistency of an apple that cleanses your palate. So it's true what they say — an apple a day, or at least on the days you're doing voiceover sessions.

CHANGING YOUR OWN MOOD

There are many, many different kinds of reads — different styles, different moods. There is the hip, cool read. The matter-of-fact, off-the-cuff read. The fun, energetic read. The warm, sophisticated read. The wry, ironic read. There are so many, in fact, that it would be impossible to name them all. What's important is for you to learn to create the mood given on the audition copy.

You may have a naturally sophisticated, laid-back vocal quality. When you're handed copy that says the voice should be sophisticated and laid-back, you're already there — unless, of course, you've just come from a fight with your boyfriend or girlfriend and you're very agitated. In that case, you'll have to create a laid-back mood on the spot. If the read calls for light, fun, and energetic but you're feeling tired and lethargic, you have to create the mood of you feeling fun, light, and energetic.

Remember, anything that is pushed will not come across as natural. Voiceover actors learn to become "schizophrenic" in their behavior. Once you're done with the read, you are more than welcome to go back to your lousy mood! Things work similarly with the technical qualities of your voice: rasp, pitch, tone, throatiness, and the like. If your voice has a natural rasp and the copy calls for a rasp, don't overemphasize this quality in your voice — just read naturally.

USING YOUR BODY

During the read, you'll either be standing or sitting. To some extent, this may depend on the sound booth you are using: Some have a very small space and don't provide a chair or stool. It's up to you, usually (depending on space), whether you sit or stand. I suggest standing to keep the diaphragm open, which makes it easier to breathe, unless the read is very casual or there's a ton of copy, narration, or audio book, then sitting may do. Whichever position you're in, limber yourself up. Keep your body movements free. Keep it real. Use your hands as you normally do when you are talking. (I often use my hands to make a point, for example.) Use your body and go with the flow. When I did a campaign for Home Base (a chain of housewares stores), I stood with my feet apart, hunched over (in front of the mike, of course), and held a pencil while I read. It was the only way I could get into character.

Look at your body language when you're talking to someone. Use it the same way for voiceovers. A buddy of mine,

Jim Cummings, a well-known voice actor who is the voice of Blockbuster (among hundreds of other advertisers), stands with his hands crossed over his head while he reads. It looks odd, but it works for him. That particular stance keeps his voice flowing, and he books many, many jobs.

As you work more and begin to understand your craft, you'll develop your own physical style. Whatever is comfortable for you is okay: crossing your arms to emphasize a point, standing with your feet spread apart, clenching your jaw. As you practice, play around with your stance as well as your voice and speech patterns. The way you stand and the way you hold your hands, your head, and your body will directly affect your read.

When I was doing the Home Base campaign, the character was flat and monotone. At first I didn't realize how my body was acting. Once I became aware of it, I couldn't do the commercials without holding a pencil in my hand and standing in that position. I tried reading the copy while sitting — to no avail. It just wasn't the same. I had conditioned my body, voice, and mind to believe that this stance was best suited for the character.

Certain reads lend themselves to standing in certain ways. If you are yelling off microphone (to give the impression that you're in another room or across the street), you'll need to stand farther from the mike than you normally would. Do the opposite for an intimate read: Stand very close to the microphone and speak softly.

REAL LIFE VERSUS "REEL" LIFE

Physical positions and movements can affect all aspects of your read. By changing your stance at the microphone, you can change your state of mind. Try the following exercise. First, look at these lists of emotions and physical attributes:

Emotions and Physical Attributes
Frustration: stuffy nose
Excitement: sitting with your feet far apart
Boredom: sitting with your legs crossed
Seductiveness: crossing your arms in front of you

Agitation: putting your hands behind your back
Fatigue: laughing
Sincerity: yelling
Sadness: crying

Now try combining some emotions with some physical attributes. Choose one item from each list and combine them. Try reading a piece of copy (maybe one of the samples from Appendix A) using that emotion and that attribute. Then try using two attributes from one list and one from the other — mix it up and see what voices you can find. This is the way you build a repertoire of characters.

When you are speaking in your everyday life, you make these kinds of movements and changes very naturally, without noticing. Your voice may rise or fall by as much as an octave depending on your mood. You use different voices to stress a point, to relax, to talk on the phone. Understanding these different "characters" in your own voice will help you immensely when you are trying to understand and read copy. The big difference is that you don't pre-plan your voices in real life; unless you've studied yourself carefully, you probably don't consciously remember which inflection you use when, for example, you excitedly jump up and down and say, "Oh, my gosh!"

Our moods and emotions have a great impact on how we "deliver our lines" in real life. Other people know what we are feeling only because we're expressing our moods and emotions, whether we're aware of it or not. Ever notice how, when you ask someone, "How are you?" and they come back with a terse, "Fine," that you instinctively know that they are not fine? You can read that they are upset. Becoming aware of these sometimes subtle signals is essential to interpreting voiceover copy and doing great reads.

When you are auditioning or doing an actual voiceover session, you're usually working in a very small space. There is a microphone; a stand, which is provided to hold the script(s); a chair to sit on (if you want to) — and you. You won't be able to move around very much, so you'll have to take those large movements you've worked on and condense them — make them work for you in a small space. The tricky part is to do it in a physically smaller way while still "selling your read" — making what you are saying sound real.

DOING NARRATION, PROMOS, AND ANIMATION

There's lots of other work in the voiceover world besides commercials. To begin preparing yourself for narration jobs, practice by reading print advertising copy, as well as magazine and newspaper articles. Pick up a book and read from it. Rent documentary DVDs and play back television shows that you've recorded, writing down the voiceover copy so you can practice reading it. Talk to the people in charge of hiring at local production or post-production facilities, and ask them about the possibility of your doing documentary or narration work. Always leave a demo CD behind. (Leave appropriate demo for area you want to pursue.) Doing the narration or voiceover for industrial films is another great way to get started in the narration and promo field. To practice doing promos, record and then write down some of the short phrases and sentences promoting upcoming shows that you're always hearing on television and radio — things like "Fire on the freeway!" and "News at eleven." Practice these as you would any other reads. You can listen to promo/narration/audio books/all areas at *www.voicebank.net*, go under agents and listen to demos.

For animation, the advice is similar. Create some animation characters — even try your hand at drawing them. Think about what they would say and how they would say it. Make an animation CD using the characters you've created and trying all sorts of different voices. Weave a story by having the characters talk to each other. Watch animated films and TV shows to see what kind of voices are out there and what your competition will be like. Animation voiceover classes will teach you how to imagine voices and then how to take them from your mind to the microphone. (See Chapter 5 for a fun exercise to help create voiceover characters.)

VOICE TO VOICE

AN INTERVIEW WITH BECKY BONNER

Becky Bonner is a successful voiceover actress and producer who also works as a booth director with the William Morris Talent Agency in Los Angeles. Like a casting director, the booth director directs talent during an audition. I began by asking Becky how she got her start in the business, and she took it from there:

"I answered a blind ad in the *Hollywood Reporter,* and my day job became manning the receptionist's desk for [famed radio commercial producers] Dick and Bert, whose company later became the Famous Radio Ranch. Thus began my long and fabulous association with Dick Orkin and Christine Coyle, who taught me how to write and produce comedy radio spots and made me fall in love with the medium. Since 1985, when I first started producing and writing, I have worked, and still work, with the Radio Ranch as a writer/producer, been a freelance radio writer and producer, had my own production company, worked with a partner to write cartoons and theme-park attractions, produced radio promos for network TV shows, taught voiceover classes, directed some special projects for AFTRA and the Museum of Television & Radio, and, through it all, managed to keep my own acting career going. Mostly, of course, in voiceovers.

"The voiceover business definitely has changed over the last five years. For the better, in that there is definitely more copy coming into the agencies. Just look at the increase in the number of cable TV networks needing promos and running spots that need voices, albeit for a reduced pay rate. The end result, I think, is anyone looking to get into this business really needs to have his or her chops honed. The competition is fierce and not for the faint of heart.

"The biggest challenge of being on both sides of the glass, so to speak, is to park my producer's hat at the booth door. Once I step in front of the microphone, someone else is in charge. No making suggestions to my fellow actors; no deciding for myself what direction the spot should take. I don't like to put myself in spots that I have written or am directing; I like to wear one hat at a time. Also, I hate having to edit and mix my own voice. By the end of the session I'm always asking, 'Whose idea was it to cast her?'

"The most common mistake most voiceover actors make is overthinking the copy, and thus overreaching on their reads. Usually, the first response is the best. When I'm auditioning actors and they ask for one more read, I very seldom use that last read. It often comes out sounding too studied, too fake. Now, sometimes, an alternate approach emerges that floors me. But that is pretty rare.

"As a voiceover actor, you are going to have literally hundreds of auditions. You are the best you can be at any given moment, on any given day. Do your read, and then let it go.

"A voiceover performance is definitely an acting performance. It takes craft, skill, and talent. Unfortunately, unless you have an interesting 'voice print,' you aren't going to make it. (Could be interesting, compelling, pretty, strange, whatever — something that makes people want to listen to your voice.) It's pretty much equal parts, I think. Just because someone has said to you all your life, 'Gee, you have a great voice, you should be on the radio,' doesn't mean you should. You belong there if you are also an actor, can read copy, have acquired the necessary microphone skills, and, oh yeah, get a lucky break or two.

"When I am auditioning actors, I certainly welcome questions, love to hear interesting approaches, and, like I said, if there is time, I will allow for an alternate read, although I might not use it. I don't usually give playbacks during auditions because of lack of time. And because actors never listen to the big picture — they get hung up on a single word, the way they did one particular line, sold a joke — whereas I'm listening for many, many other things in the audition.

"The most important aspect of auditioning for a V.O. job is to relax. No single audition will make or break you. If you've done your homework; if you've honed your skills; if you've taken your time with the copy so you know who you are, who you're talking to, and what the story is that you are telling; if you walk in confident and competent, then you'll be fine.

"Since I now am a booth director for a major L.A. talent agency, and I direct the same actors on a daily basis, I have come to know who wants input and who doesn't. I will always offer something if I feel an actor has missed a moment or not told the story well. And if an actor asks for input, I will always give it, even if it's just to say, 'You did great, let's keep it.' But I also want to respect the choices that the actor has made. That is part of the process, and I'm there to direct that actor in that performance, not to turn out a series of auditions that all sound exactly alike. My job is to make sure that every actor leaves the booth feeling like they have given it their best shot. I know for sure that I have helped some actors find some moments that led to their getting the job. I hope to God I have never given an actor such a bum steer that they didn't get the job.

"I mentioned the big picture before. The director/casting director is listening for everything. Sometimes we just know something about how the job should be approached; it can be something as specific as input from the client or as intangible as a gut feeling that comes from twenty-plus years in the business. I always give that information to the actor up front. I'm not saying actors have to do everything we tell them. But they should always know that we do have their best interests at heart. After all, when they do well, we do well. Their job is acting; ours is casting and directing. We all want to impress. We all want to get the job.

"I do think that I do know when someone has absolutely nailed an audition. I have, however, given up trying to second-guess clients and ad agencies. Who knows what they have in their black little hearts? (Just kidding.) No, really. I am sometimes surprised when someone doesn't get a job. Since I think I work with a terrific set of actors, I am never surprised when someone books a job.

"I think it helped me to be on all sides of this business. I don't think I could've lasted this long if I were just sitting home, waiting for the phone to ring. Does this mean everyone should go out and try to be a triple-threat multi-hyphenate? Not really. I say be open to the opportunities that present themselves. I didn't set out to be a radio writer and spot director. But when the chance came up, I didn't say no. That's the first rule of improvisation, actually. Never say no. Say yes, and build from there. This is a town where everything changes in a heartbeat. Be ready."

CHAPTER 4

FINDING YOUR TECHNIQUE AND EIGHT STEREOTYPES

EVERYONE ALWAYS ASKS ME IF I HAVE A TECHNIQUE. I really don't. I don't breathe in a certain way, try to push a certain rhythm, or make sure I read the copy the exact same way every time. What I do is act. I make sure every piece of copy is real for me, and that every piece of dialogue comes across as if I'm truly speaking to someone — that it doesn't sound forced or rehearsed. When you overanalyze a script or work too hard on particular aspects of the dialogue instead of on the emotional story behind what is being said, you'll find you get lost in the words instead of conveying the story.

To use your voice appropriately, you have to use your personality appropriately. How? Read the copy or script through. Is it funny? Is it serious? Is there room for your own personality to come through? Is the copy written so that when you read it, it comes across naturally? A lot of times copy is not written well — a sad fact. You may find it difficult to say lines that don't feel like something you'd really say. That's where your acting ability comes in. You must be able to make the copy sound real, even when you're acting a part you know nothing about.

Notice that, once again, we are not starting with the voice. Instead, we're working from the inside out. (Remember my theory that the voice is the icing on the cake?) So what if you've got a great voice? (Not that I'm taking anything away from a wonderful, delicious, meltingly sensual voice or a fun, quirky, weird, high-pitched tone.) Do you know how to use it? Do you know how to sell the product by using aspects of your voice? Being able to sell that product to an audience without sounding like you're reading copy is where your own special technique comes into play.

Read the copy the way the writer intended it. Every script has a natural rhythm and is trying to tell a story, even if it doesn't make sense to you. Every script is written with a purpose, no matter how silly or serious the text may be. You will find the natural flow and beats as you read a script and learn to analyze copy and cold read. Bring your personality and the appropriate attitude to your read, as per the specs.

It is your job as the voiceover actor to bring life to the script. The writer hears it a certain way in his or her head. Your job is to read it and make it real. This doesn't mean that you'll read the copy in the exact same way that the writer mentally hears it. In fact, when auditioning, you won't always be able to figure out just how the writer intended the copy to be read. You may not get the job simply because another actor reads the copy the way the writer envisions. This is just part of the business.

THREE BASIC RULES

Here are three rules that will help you no matter what you're reading — and no matter what your own personal vocal style may be.

Rule No. 1: Imagine you are speaking to a real person.
Pick a particular person. Sue from accounting. Your best friend, Jim. Your crazy Aunt Dolly with all the cats. Do not speak to everyone all at once, or someone you randomly ran into on the street. Be specific. This will help in giving you a POV (point of view), which is what you start with in life every time you have a conversation with someone. A point of view allows your personality to shine through, making the read real no matter how brilliant or boring the copy is. It relaxes you and gives you a greater sense of control over your read. It also allows a real story to develop,

ensuring that you don't sound like you're reading from a piece of paper, full of fake emotion.

Rule No. 2: Breathe.
You want to breathe naturally in the mood you are in. When you're speaking in life, having a conversation, you don't think about your breathing — it comes as you tell your story, where it's natural to do so.

After reading through the copy a few times (silently first to get a feel for the copy, then half out loud/half to yourself to find the rhythm of the spot, and finally, aloud, the way you intend to read it in the audition), find comfortable points within the natural rhythm of the sentences to exhale and inhale. Add the specs or mood adjectives and begin to read the copy in the right mood. Notice how your voice sounds. Breathe naturally. You can tell a story and breathe naturally whether you are taking a brisk walk or taking a sauna.

Don't forget to breathe. Breathing is very important in a read. Some copy is written so that you don't have much time to breathe. A lot of scripts are written with run-on sentences. You may read something and wonder, "How am I going to get through that sentence?" If you're unintentionally short of breath, or if you're not breathing in the right places, you will have trouble conveying the message of the script. (The only time being short of breath works is when you are reading a script that calls for the character to be short of breath.) This is why it's important to create a mood — so that the breathing will come at natural pauses and places within the copy: periods, commas, and other pauses. Look for the rhythm in the copy. The closer you are in mood, the closer you will be in time.

The more you practice, the more breathing seems second nature rather than an obstacle to overcome. If I'm in the mood of the read, I don't have time to ask myself when I need to breathe. It happens naturally at the appropriate times and per the punctuation in the script. Think about how you breathe in everyday life. You certainly don't pay attention and say to yourself, "Oh, yeah, I'd better breathe now." It's the same in voiceovers; knowing when to breathe just feels more complicated because you are putting all your energy into trying to concentrate on the script, and standing in front of a microphone with headphones on. As long as you are in the moment, talking to a person and relating your story (the copy or script) to them, you can't lose. An ad executive may not hire you, but he or she may say, "I love the way that person interpreted the copy. No one else did it like that."

Rule No. 3: Find a technique or way to read the copy that works for you.
I learned how to develop different moods and different types of reads so that I could land as many different types of voiceover jobs as possible. Develop your own style and technique — whatever works for you. Never copy another voiceover actor. Instead, create and develop your own inner voice and strength.

Don't worry if your vocal style seems similar to that of other voiceover actors: When you bring your own "inner voice" to the read, the unique qualities of your personality will come out when you read. You will often hear the same voices over and over again pushing the same product: again, no need for concern. Although advertisers like to rehire actors, they are always looking for new voices: people who will bring a fresh perspective to the world of advertising. Sounding like other actors is bound to happen. There are only so many "reads" and styles out there. It's up to the casting director, ad agency or agent to put you on a particular script and audition.

Understanding what you're right for and expanding your reading/acting skills will be important in the process of auditioning. You want to be considered a "staple," able to read for a variety of jobs/genres. Being a "one-note Nancy" isn't the way to go. If you can nail a certain type of read but no other, you need to work on your range as an actor. Learning this skill is as simple as using your personality, where appropriate, to add range (vocal and emotional) to what you are brought in to read for. A great producer will know what and how to bring these reads out of you during the voiceover session. Your variety of moods (vocal qualities) will help lead to future voiceover jobs. It's important to understand adjectives and moods so that your read can reflect that. You also want to be able to remember easily what mood you were in when you booked the job. Nothing is worse than not being able to re-create that great read that booked you the job in the first place!

METHOD ACTING

When I started taking acting classes, there were so many different acting techniques to choose from. Some acting teachers believed in the Method (where you re-create a past emotion, mood, or event and bring it into a current situation). Others did "objectives," working strictly from the written word. (Laugh here. Cry there. Yell on this line. Be annoyed on that line.) Some classes were mechanical, others technical, others natural — some were even surreal.

Of course, you have to decide what works for you. I cannot tell you to study or learn a certain way. But if you've never picked up a script or done a voiceover before, I can tell you which way is easiest and works best for me and hundreds of other voice actors working today. My own background is Method training. Do I use it in my voiceover work? Absolutely. Sure, when you're doing voiceovers you're heard but not seen. And sure, reading commercial copy is sometimes a little less dramatic than doing a scene from Ibsen or Chekhov. But the main idea is the same. Your acting and interpretation have to be grounded in reality, whether the copy is about fire safety, Coors beer, Ford trucks, Toys for Tots, McDonald's, AIDS research, or Barbie's summer corvette. Your ability to incorporate your individual style into each read is extremely important.

Once a voice or style of voice becomes popular, many clients will want to use a similar voice, feeling that this will help their products sell. But even when voices sound similar, each has specific nuances that make it different from other voices. When I started out, I did not intentionally try to follow a certain trend or to have a certain style of a voice. And I still don't view my work as others sometimes do. ("Oh, she does that flat read.") I can absolutely do that "flat read" — but I can do several other types of reads, too, all depending on the copy. I can be high-energy, funny, sardonic, witty, warm, supportive, energetic, and several thousand other things. Get my drift? You have to be able to evoke those emotions in yourself and bring them to the read. Remember, your vocal style is only one layer of what you can do as a voice actor, especially if you plan on staying in the business more than a season or two. It's important to be a good reader and actor, too.

HUMOR

Humor is always a bonus, especially for radio copy. If there's humor in the dialogue, you need to find it and use it if it's fitting for the spot. Part of understanding how far to go as a voiceover actor is understanding how much fun to have with the copy. As a general rule, actors can improvise with radio copy. This means that they can add or play with a word or two. You certainly don't want to change the entire dialogue (don't disrespect the writer of the spot even if you think it's terrible). Adding what we call a "button" — a funny word or two at the end of the spot after the last person speaks — is also okay. (Ask a professional how to do a button, so you don't walk over someone's lines.) A casting director or booth director can help you through a button — a touch of humor, a smile, or a bit of irreverence into the read can be helpful in booking the spot.

You always want to work the humor or find it in a spot. Ignoring or not making something funny that's written to be funny can be an error of judgment on your part. The best thing you can do is be coached on how to see reads for what they are, interpret that and read the script accordingly. Practice, practice, practice, until you get really good at reading scripts and understanding beats. Humor, of course, is a pretty broad category, and there are still choices to make: Should you be ironic? Subtle? Abrasive? Childish? These are only a few of the options, and each will affect your read and the way you sell the product differently. You choose these adjectives based on the adjectives they are asking for. It's kind of your guide to follow, like instructions. You are still being you, the actor, you're just being you in that mood (the adjectives, specs, mood, sell) they are asking for, on any given script.

Stand-up comedians do especially well in radio because the medium accommodates their brand of improvisation and spontaneity. A facility with quick banter and the spoken word is very attractive to casting agents. By the same token, many theatrically trained actors tend to overact with voiceover copy, indulging and embellishing a bit too much. Voiceover acting is all about keeping reads real, natural, and conversational. Some advertisers even hire nonprofessionals for voice jobs because they tend to sound real — if a bit raw and unpolished. As a voice actor, you will have to find a happy medium between these two extremes.

FIRST PERSON

This quote comes from voiceover actor John Thoms:

> "In this business, I think there is a misconception that bigger jobs are somehow different than the smaller ones — whether people think that bigger jobs are harder to attain, or that bigger jobs are the only jobs worth changing one's schedule to facilitate. I recently had the experience of challenging the 'big job versus small job' misconceptions. I was in Vegas for a wedding, and my agent called to tell me I booked a small radio job for a regional bank. I hesitated to take the job for reasons of convenience but pulled it together and left the festivities of Vegas behind to make time for the job. It was only when I showed up to this so-called small radio job that I looked at the copy and saw that there had been a slight misunderstanding. The 'small' job I had regarded as somewhat unglamorous was in fact for the voice of a national car campaign. In my experience, your small jobs could in fact be a big job in disguise! Either way, ya can't beat the free coffee."

UNDERSTANDING LANGUAGE

Understanding language and being able to interpret and speak it properly are very important in the world of voiceovers. You are representing a product through speech and mood. Correct pronunciation of words is a must. Depending on what part of the country you are from (or from out of the country), you may pronounce words differently. Understand the importance of language and accents where it's appropriate. Understand that where you live in the country has a direct reflection on how you read and how the words come across. If you have a quirky speech pattern or a lisp, you're going to need to correct this problem unless you can use it to your benefit in humorous reads or animation. If need be, see a speech pathologist or take a diction class to work on your enunciation and speech patterns. I often direct students who have problems with swallowing words, speaking too quickly, or mumbling. Your goal should be clear diction and a smooth word flow, without over-enunciating any one word. Practice by reading from books. If you're not sure how to pronounce a certain word, look it up in the dictionary or ask someone.

All languages have a natural rhythm and fluidity. French people seem to come across as passionate. Americans seem a little more casual, while the English have a more proper, formal sound. If you were to do voiceovers in another country, you would have to learn how the people of that country inflect certain words, the kind of humor they use, and the way they say certain phrases.

Of course, accents and tones vary from region to region even within the same country. Many Midwesterners have an obvious twang, and I (a Midwesterner) am often told that my voice has a regional sound. I say certain words in a certain way, and my voice has a natural rhythm that has to do with where I was raised and the way I learned to speak. People from different regions even use different words for the same object or product. Do you call it a sack or a bag? Soda or pop? A pocketbook or a purse? Do you stand in line or on line?

In most advertising, you won't hear the language used incorrectly. You also won't hear any fumbling of words or phrases — unless it's deliberate. On a national level, advertisers want all of us to be able to relate to what they're selling, no matter where we live or how different we may be. The language we use differs from one region to another, one town to another — even from one group of friends to another. But the language of advertising usually takes the middle of the road, so that everyone will understand the message: "Buy this product."

INTERPRETING CHARACTER

When you're given copy to read, it will include a basic direction telling you about the kind of character the client is looking for. For example, a radio commercial script might say, "Girl next door, friendly, upbeat, late twenties." The way you read this copy will depend, however, on how you interpret it — how you see the script. Twenty different people will interpret this young woman twenty different ways — and give twenty different reads. No writer, director, or casting person can tell you exactly how to do a read.

The one thing you will have in common with the other voiceover actors (besides maybe sounding similar in vocal quality) is that you all have, or should have, broken down the read with the proper beats and way to tell the story. Most of the actors who end up in the running will have hit the beats and told the story in the way that the writer/advertiser/client wanted it read. It takes practice and time to understand the way that scripts are written. The more chances you have to audition, the better you'll get. This is why people take classes, to learn to improve their reads. Most voice actors who audition a lot get the opportunity to read all the time. Before you get an agent (or, even if you have an agent but aren't called in a lot), you won't get the chance to read lots of scripts. See as many scripts as you can (the way the advertiser wrote them) to understand the full dynamic of how to read copy. There are times when all talent reading for something will sound alike.

When you enter an audition waiting room, you may find several other women there who all sound very similar to you and to one another. This is because the client is looking for a specific vocal quality. It is the actresses' job to use their vocal quality in a friendly, upbeat way. This may come more naturally for some women than for others.

Now, here's an example of some copy for this "girl next door, friendly, upbeat, late twenties" character:

> I was having coffee with Beth, when the phone rang. It was Sue. She's yelling into the phone, "JCPenney is having a half-off sale. Want to go?" So, I'm thinking, Are you out of your mind? See you in five.

It's your job as the voiceover artist to bring life to this character. If you get the job, you're going to become the character. Any pauses, squeaky noises of excitement, or sarcastic tones are up to you, based on choices you've made. Initially, as the voice actor, it's up to you to "apply the specs" to the read. This means that even though you may mostly fit the category you're reading for, you still may have some work to do. You need to understand if it's TV or radio. Understanding the specs/adjectives and being in that proper mood before you read will ensure that you stay in that mood all the way through. For example, if you enter an audition for JCPenney in a bad mood, how will you nail the read if it's asking for upbeat, friendly? You have to work the exercise I devised (see Chapter 3) to learn to "get in the right mood." If you're already in that mood, you're halfway there. Remember: mood first, beats second.

Nailing a read every time you audition is a must to be considered for booking. The better you become at auditioning, the better chance you will have of booking jobs and understand how to work in voiceover sessions. Like everything in life, practice and understanding key words are key.

When you get into the session itself, the writer or director may ask you to emphasize something differently or change the way you're reading a certain word or phrase. You may re-read the same script thirty or forty times in a voice session until they get the read they want. But during the audition, you'll get much less input. The casting director or booth director may tell you to "warm that up," "have more fun with it," "pull it back," or "keep it more conversational." They may tell you to "add a smile" or "be more playful." Some direction may be technical while other direction may be creative. But that's about it.

As the voiceover actor, you're the one who decides how to say the lines. Usually, once you have a grasp of the language for that particular spot, the dialogue will become natural. It's important that you don't change the idea of the copy. It's important that you don't put a pause where it's not written. By that same token, it's important to pause where it's written, while making a natural acting choice within that mood. Making the copy your own and changing the interpretation or way something is said are two totally different things. Learning to improvise within what's written (loose, fun feel) so that it sounds like it came from your mouth and not a voice actor on a mike, is pivotal for many reads. Once you're connected to the copy, in the right mood, you shouldn't be worrying about how to say each word or whether to make your voice go up or down. As long as you're "in the read" (that is, sounding like a real person), there are thousands of different interpretations you might have. Once you get the mood and specs of the spot, let the lines flow naturally instead of dissecting each and every line.

> TIP: Once you're in an upbeat mood, you'll notice how the ends of words stay up, because you're excited or upbeat. By being somber, content, or matter of fact, notice how you say the same lines — the words will naturally go down or stay even. This doesn't mean that once you're in the voiceover session they won't direct you to say a line or phrase a certain way, or "make sure you go up/down on that word." It's impossible to know every way someone wants a line read. We only have the notes and direction from the writer, the script and whatever someone tells us they are looking for. We still have to follow the mood, so that the words come naturally from that mood. Reading more playfully will naturally color and romance words more, where as reading more flat or matter of fact will give the words less emphasis. These are just technical notes that become obvious when you read and the more you read. Part of your job is knowing what to color or romance within a script — they don't tell you every line and how to read it. (That can come later in the session.)

Character descriptions can change the entire mood of a read. Let's look at one more: "A woman in her fifties, working three jobs, tired, bored, witty." Now go back and read the copy about the JCPenney sale as this character. I'm sure you can come up with at least three different reads (or more) for this character — and that each read will be different, because you are working in the moment, telling the story, relating real emotion. If you're a man, change the character to a male character and try the same thing. You might have some trouble with the character description — you might think, for example, that there's nothing in this copy that could allow the character to be witty. Or you might not know how to act as if you're working three jobs.

Descriptions can be tricky, but you must look beyond this to try to understand what they are looking for. The point is that the ad agency created the description — and it conveys the style of read they're looking for. Do you see how little your vocal quality matters to the read? Yes, there might be a word about voice quality in the description; it might say "warm," or "older," or "raspy," or "quirky." But the rest of the description will have absolutely nothing to do with your voice — and everything to do with your attitude and personality. This is why your interpretation of the character is so important. As well, don't worry about the age category — if you are handed a script, just play the adjectives. Simply get into that mood, find the rhythm, beats and transitions. You can't worry if you sound too young or too old. Understanding the right kinds of adjectives to put into the read, based on what they're asking for, is the most important part of nailing reads. You can sound older/younger depending on adjectives you've added to the read (listen to how your vocal range changes, per mood/adjective choice). Look at it this way, overall you won't be handed something that the casting director, booth director, writer/producer, or agent doesn't think you can read for. It's your job to read it. It's their job to have you read for it. If you're confused by direction, you can certainly ask for more of an explanation. Be prepared to get lots more or nothing. Sometimes all the direction they give is what you already have in your script. Sometimes it's very little or one word. It's part of your job as the voice actor to work that out on your own and do well in the audition.

ACHIEVING EMOTIONAL DEPTH

Your emotions affect the read as much as your personality and vocal characteristics do. The writer or director will tell you what they want in the read. Here are a few of the (many) emotional descriptions that you might see in the script for a commercial:

sad, happy, enticing, empathetic, nurturing, caring, content, sincere, serene, honest, wise, strong, assertive, aggressive, nonchalant, playful, provocative, flirty, warm, real, gal to gal/guy to guy, witty, charming, detached, rude, tired, bored, warm, hostile, aggressive, assertive, irreverent, reverent, sexy, snobby, slow, energized, hyper, and maudlin.

Get the idea? There are so many different ways of feeling. The depth of the feeling is another matter, however. How far should you go with your emotion? Well, it depends on what the writer or director wants. You don't want to overact or overemote — to be too snobby, too bitchy, too sad, too excited, too passive, too anything. Keep it real. Try putting a few emotions together and see what you get. How about trying a few different emotions — and combinations of emotions — with this line: "Isn't the moon beautiful?" Try it warm and friendly. Try it upbeat and excited. Or, how about sardonic and flat? Matter of fact and off the cuff? Seductive and empathetic? I want you to understand that there are different depths and levels of emotion. Something can be read in a way that's both businesslike and witty. They don't necessarily cancel each other out. If you're given the direction "businesslike but witty," it means that you should read the copy intelligently and informatively, but you should give it some wit, too. Make it fun. Just because a read conveys information doesn't mean it can't be funny. A read can be both raspy and sarcastic. The "rasp" is just your natural sound; the "sarcastic" is how you sell the copy. There's no end to what a client might ask for: "raspy sexy," "smooth sexy," "high-pitched sexy." Each of these three reads will come out sounding different. Three different emotions. Three different depths. Each one can be pushed or pulled back — made stronger or weaker in tone, character, and level. If the direction says "smooth sexy," take away the rasp. If the writer or director says, "smooth it out," that means they want you to even out the words as they form in your mouth. You might have been making the read too "choppy" — breaking up the words too much and interrupting the story's flow.

There are the emotional components and the technical components. Then there is your voice. Together, these form the voiceover.

PHRASING

There are several ways to approach the issue of phrasing. Part of your job, as a voiceover actor, is to look at how the writer wrote the copy on the actual page of dialogue you are reading. The writer will have phrased the dialogue in a certain way. Certain words or lines might be boldfaced, italicized, or typed in a different font. A line might be punctuated in a strange or surprising way. A phrase might be followed by three dots, indicating a pause. Or a sentence might be broken apart into two or more lines on the page. Take, for example, the sentence from above: "Isn't the moon beautiful tonight?" Now, let's change the way the line appears on the page and see what happens:

> Isn't the moon beautiful ... tonight? Or how about: Isn't the ... moon beautiful tonight?
>
> Or: Isn't the ... moon, beautiful. Tonight?

Don't these changes alter the read? Indeed they do. Ad copywriters do these kinds of things on purpose. They want you to read the dialogue a certain way.

Always make sure you clearly enunciate the name of any product. Don't make it so obvious that it sounds like you're trying to push the product down the listener's throat — that's called "billboarding." Just make sure that you don't rush right through the product name.

Your job is to read the copy and see whether it makes sense the way it's written. Often, after you've studied the copy and read it aloud a few times, you'll discover the natural phrasing of the words. But sometimes there is too much copy for the allotted spot and the way the direction calls for it to be read. If you have a problem with the script, the casting director or booth director can be a big help. In an actual recording session (as opposed to an audition), the director, working with the writer, may even rewrite the script or change the copy.

THE COPY'S APPEARANCE

The way the copy looks on the page — the typefaces used, boldface, italics, color, and so on — will affect the way you react to it. The choice of font can actually tell you a great deal about how the client wants you to feel when reading the copy. Certain fonts are used to project a certain sell. Boldface type is used to stress certain words. Words in italics may convey a feeling of delicacy or secrecy. Small type may give you the feeling of a more intimate, conversational read, while all caps will make you feel you should be louder or more aggressive with the copy.

There's an analogy to visual advertising. Think, for example, of billboards, restaurant and retail-store logos, and other kinds of signage. The writers and designers who create such signs put a lot of thought into how the buying public will react to them. Not just the words, but also the fonts and colors used will influence whether you buy an advertised product or even walk into a store or restaurant. A very casual font will seem more inviting than a staunch, sharp letter. As you go through your day, take a closer look at all the signs you see, and ask yourself about the moods they're conveying. Does a store's sign match the feeling you get when you enter the store? And what about "official" signs — traffic signs, directional signs, and the various other kinds of signs created and posted by the government? You might notice that, in general, such signs use workaday fonts like Times Roman or Helvetica. What kind of feeling do these signs convey?

How does this correlate with the job facing the voiceover artist? It may help you to understand the writer's intention. It's just another level to explore as you interpret your read when auditioning. Think, for example, of how the writer's use of capitalized-versus-lowercased words might affect your read of this copy:

> "SAVE $1.00 off your next purchase of TASTY CHICKEN TACO Supreme, The next time you come into TACO TACO. SAVOR the munchies!"

Of course, copy doesn't always look like this. Often, it's written in plain typewriter style. When writers add these nuances, they're doing so for a reason, and you should read accordingly. There isn't a secret code that tells you how to treat a boldfaced word, but the general feeling is that you should emphasize it.

▶ TIP: You need to create relaxation in your work, not nervous energy. So before a read, breathe. There are a number of deep-breathing exercises that you can use to relax. Here's one: Take a deep breath, inhaling through your nose; hold the breath for a few seconds and then exhale through your mouth, expelling all the air from your lungs. As you breathe, concentrate on thinking calming thoughts. Do this ten or more times, and you will calm your mind and be able to concentrate on the work.

TIMING

The timing of a spot is very important. Is the commercial a thirty-second radio spot? A sixty-second TV spot? The issue of how much information can be fit into a certain amount of time — the amount of radio or TV time the client wants to buy — is always a pressing one. By the time the voiceover artist gets the copy, it's been through a number of rewrites, often because of time constraints.

If the client says, "We want a thirty-second spot for radio, we want to fit in this much information, and we want to make it fun and upbeat," the ad agency writer has to create copy that's brief, entertaining, and informative. He or she has to write the dialogue around the information. That information is the last thing to be edited out of the copy, because it's what the client wants to convey.

While timing is the first thing the writer and director work on, be sure you already know the copy and the mood with which you're going to work; don't time the copy first. The closer you are in mood, the closer you will be in time.

Timing tells you two things about a read: First, it tells you how fast you should go. What is the pace of the script? If the copy is wall-to-wall dialogue — meaning that the dialogue fills up the entire read without any pauses or time for music or sound effects — you will need to read accordingly.

Second, if you know the time of the spot and the length of the script, you can figure out what the writer intended. If there's comparatively little copy, the writer probably wants the read to be slow and casual. If there's lots of copy, the writer probably wants you to be fast-paced and energetic. Sometimes the spot is thirty seconds, but even after you've done the read several times, you find you just can't do it in thirty. At that point, the writer will have to shorten the script, taking out unimportant words or words that aren't "selling points" (information about the product). The point is to give you more time — and for the writer to get the kind of read he or she wants.

PACE

The pace or speed at which you read the copy depends on how the writer wrote the spot and how the director wants it read. Each script will have a timing at the top. If it doesn't, your trained eye will let you know how long a spot is. You can always ask the booth director if you want to know the length. It's important that you remember to nail the mood first. The closer you are in mood, the closer you will be in time. Your pace of the read depends on the setup of the copy, how the writer wrote the spot(s) and how they want it read (pauses, beats, commas, dead air). Your job is to find a comfortable pace that fits with what they are looking for. The pace also has to suit the rhythm and sell of the spot. It's also part of your job to find the natural rhythm and flow of the copy. Once you find that rhythm, you should be able to read the copy in the time allotted. Writers are well aware if a spot times out long (goes over the allotted time). It's not your job to change the copy or try to go faster to make the read work. It is part of your job to nail the read closest to fitting to time, based on the mood that they are looking for. All of this takes practice and knowledge. (After you do voiceovers for a while, you'll see that three seconds, long or short, can seem like quite a lot of time.) Find the mood and then find the pacing and timing. If the mood isn't there, it won't matter that you got the read in time. The read will come across as technical.

There are many different ways that a spot can be read. Advertisers want a real, conversational read. So breathe naturally and read like you're talking to someone. The pacing will come naturally.

TAKING THE DIRECTOR'S ADVICE

The director of a voiceover session will usually offer advice. You may read the copy one way, with a particular inflection or emphasis, but the director may have a completely different take on the read — perhaps something you never even thought of. The director may stop you in the middle of a take and have you do the read in a completely different way, or tell you to make your voice go up or down, to slow down, to speed up or to "romance" — emphasize or play with — certain words or phrases. You may not even see the point of the direction, but the director is the boss and knows what the client is looking for. The director may have you do many reads, with several directional changes, to get just what he or she wants. In the audition process, you are going to have to figure out all of these nuances on your own, based on the information you are given within the copy. Once you are in the voiceover session, working with the writer and director, they more than likely will give you more specific notes.

ACCENTS AND DICTION

When you are doing voiceovers, you have to work at eliminating any noticeable regional accent unless it fits with the copy description or you're doing a "charactery" read. At an audition, you may find yourself thinking, "Hey, this character would be funnier with a Southern accent." So ask the casting director if you can do a Southern accent during an alternate read — a different take on the script that incorporates the original specs, but adds to them or deviates from them somewhat. (Alternate reads provide ad agencies with new perspectives on their own scripts; however, not all casting directors permit them.)

Although you must be capable of clear diction, whether you use good diction on a particular job depends on what the director asks you to do. I once created a character who had sloppy speech patterns, and it worked for that job. Usually, though, good diction is essential. If you can make your dialogue sound crisp as well as conversational, you have a winning combination. By saying most reads should be crisp and conversational, don't take this to mean that you must over-enunciate the words in order to make your point. Don't take this to mean that all reads should be read in the same tone, pace and rhythm. Part of being a good voiceover actor is to understand direction and what exactly the potential client is looking for. Also, understanding and hearing the commercial in your head is imperative in making it work on paper and on the air.

TONE

Certainly you can remember your mother saying, "Don't you take that tone with me!" It wasn't what you were saying, but the bratty tone with which you said it. Well, every voiceover, whether for a commercial, animation, promo, or narration, also has a tone — the general feeling the client wants to convey: serious, businesslike, comedic, conversational, dry, thoughtful, or bratty. Once you read the copy through and decide on your mood, the feelings you convey will help set the read's tone.

The tone of your read can be affected by where you stand in front of the microphone and how loud you are being. If you are very close, with your mouth almost touching the mike, your tone will be more intimate. If you are standing farther away, yelling from the sidelines, your voice will be louder and your tone more energetic. (Generally, your mouth should be about two inches from the microphone. Keep the same distance from the mike during your entire read, unless the direction tells you to do something different.)

Don't confuse tone with either attitude or pitch. Tone is your vocal quality and the general vocal feeling of the spot, whereas attitude is the emotion you are feeling as you read. The attitude affects the tone, but it's not the same thing. Pitch and tone are also different. Pitch is a measure of how high or low your voice is — like notes on a musical scale. Just as people have natural moods and come across a certain way, voices have a certain natural pitch.

Pitch can be affected by mood and tone, however. Tone can cause your pitch to go higher or lower than normal. (Conversely, a director may ask you to change your tone while maintaining your voice's natural high pitch: to play with a mood within your vocal range.) Or you may be asked to go outside of your vocal range — to "sound deeper." The pitch of your voice can also help set the tone. Because pitch relates to emotional state, excited voices tend to go up in pitch, and introspective, intimate, or depressed voices tend to drop lower in pitch. You can learn to play with pitch to convey different feelings, attitudes, and tones.

Learning to do this will make you more employable. A student of mine has a naturally high-pitched voice. I've since taught her to speak more warmly, intimately, and seductively, and her reads have become much lower in pitch. Her natural speaking voice has remained the same, but she has broadened her vocal range and can now audition for types of reads that casting directors had previously not considered her for.

> ▶ **TIP:** A "level" measures the volume of your voice. When the sound engineer asks for a level, speak a few words from the copy using the same tone of voice that you will use when you read. Once you establish a level, keep it consistent — don't suddenly get louder or softer during the read. "Getting a level" isn't only required for determining the volume, it's also useful for determining how you'll read the script during the take. Go ahead and take advantage of the sound level time to play with the read, get used to the copy and be present. You will continue to read the copy until the sound engineer says, "Great, we got it." At that point, you will be ready to lay down the read (read the copy in its entirety).

DEALING WITH THE HAZARDS

Lots of things can go wrong during a voiceover: You can pop your P's, spit, lose your breath, mush or swallow your words, cough, choke — or even realize, suddenly, that your arm or foot has fallen asleep. Any hazard you can think of can — and will — happen to you at one time or another, even if you're a seasoned professional. The hazard can come from the sound booth or writer/director side. Anything can happen, from not getting the proper approval on a script to a microphone malfunction, to booking overtime for studio usage if a voiceover session goes over the allotted time. As for you personally, you cannot expect to read perfectly every time. Something will get caught in your throat, you'll feel a sneeze coming on, or you'll be in the middle of a read and lose your place in the script. Relax. There is nothing you can do. Popping P's is normal. If you have a tendency to pop your P's or to slur certain words, the sound engineer, after hearing you read, will put a filter on the microphone. This will protect your read so that every little squeak and pop won't shoot out and be so easy to hear. To avoid popping, make sure you're aware of which letters you tend to pop, and don't over-enunciate words containing those letters.

What about detectable breathing? You cannot read a spot without breathing. Your breathing should come as naturally as it does when you're speaking in that particular mood. When you're excited, you'll squeeze more words into a sentence; when you're relaxed and taking your time in telling a story, you'll breathe less often and more deeply. Your breathing will also depend on where the writer wants you to take natural breaths based on how they have written the copy. This is learned in coaching, training, and sometimes even on the job. You can't control every single line reading and breath, but the more obvious choice within the script is most likely the best one. You'll have to learn to read over and over again, while keeping the breaths in check and natural. The more voiceovers you do, the more control you'll have over your breathing. Cardiovascular exercise helps — and swimming is a particularly good way of improving your breath control. So is quitting smoking, since smoking leaves you short of breath.

(Some breath sounds can be covered up in editing, and breaths between words are sometimes edited out digitally by the sound engineer to shorten the length of a spot.) It's not your job to read an entire script, or even a long line for that matter, within one breath, unless there's a time factor. When you're reading disclaimers at the end of scripts, you will be asked to read quickly and in time. There is a certain trick to reading fast, while maintaining your rhythm and flow. Practice with the following script.

- **EXERCISE: Read the Disclaimer Copy**

Try reading the following disclaimer copy to see if you can read it in one breath. The second read should be with one breath and within ten seconds.

> Call now and receive two cellular phones for the low price of $19.95 plus shipping and handling. No money down; no hidden fees. Call now for details. 1-800-BUY-2-CELL, that's 1-800-BUY-2-CELL. Terms and conditions apply; see store for details. Offer ends October 31, 2007. Some restrictions apply. Offer is not available in Kansas or Florida. Call for local rates.

Have fun trying! This isn't just a timing exercise, but also to practice maintaining breath control and sounding like you know what you're talking about. Your mood for a disclaimer should be sincere, straightforward and spoken with a quick flow. Tripping over words, losing the pace, and/or losing mood takes you out of the spot (and out of the running for the job).

WHAT'S NEXT?

You've learned the basics about your "icing" (your voice), so relax, take a deep breath, and put the information in the back of your mind. Next, it's time to let your creativity come forward. This is the most important part of your read. Now that you have the technical knowledge, you can rely on your natural talent to read the spot.

At every audition, I go in, study the copy, incorporate my ideas, find the character, and give the best read I can. Then I leave. I don't worry about how my voice sounded. If I book the job, then I book the job. I can't worry about what I did right or wrong. If

I go in with the attitude that this job isn't a requirement for my happiness, then I am able to do good work. It doesn't matter if they want me or not. I'm free to experiment. Technique is whatever you make it. My technique is to get out of my own way so that I am there for the copy. I read for jobs that I'm well known for — the flat, sarcastic type of read — but whatever attitude they call for is what you should be available to do. I've booked just as many jobs outside of my range, or normal flat character, as I have within it. I want to book as many jobs in as many areas as possible. So, to do that, I must understand how to read and how to interpret whatever comes my way. Just make sure that your read is coming from somewhere: a story, an idea, a person you're thinking about, a character, a feeling, a mood, a topic, a vocal range, or an emotion.

And then remember: just breathe.

STEREOTYPES

WHERE DO I FIT INTO THE VOICEOVER WHEEL?

There are several different types of "sells" in the voiceover business. Sells are tools (actors' voices) that are used to promote products. The following stereotypes are general terms that may be associated in the voiceover business with certain styles of reads. You, the voice actor, fit into one or several categories, and your agent/manager/casting director/advertising agency will bring you in for auditions accordingly. Although you may be typecast in one particular area as far as voice quality is concerned, your acting ability as well as your ability to change your mood will have a direct result on what you are brought in to read for. Your ethnicity, race, gender and age certainly play a role in the type of voiceovers you will book. Some actors have a repertoire that allows them the flexibility to do numerous voices and characters, whereas other actors feel limited by their own vocal quality and range. Understanding but not being limited by your range certainly will open up your wheel and where you fit into the voiceover world. Many companies like to use certain types of sells (voices) to lure the customer in. Luring a customer in can be done in hundreds of ways, but to make your life a bit easier, I've picked several of the top sells that are seen quite a bit in specs when hiring for jobs.

THE P AND G READ

The P and G read, affectionately known as the Proctor-Gamble read because of its smooth, smiley feel, is a very popular one. The term is used for many national commercials or brighter reads that require a smooth, warm, natural sound when selling household products, hygiene, and any daytime product geared to women. Usually the P and G read is referred to women, often in the age range of 17 to 30, but they can be a bit older depending on the product. You know the type, they all have that smooth, easy, smile that sells you anything during the day. When they ask for a P and G read, a voice actor knows to kick it up a notch. This is a certain sell the client is looking for. P and G ads also usually run nationally, and the residuals are amazing. New York City, Chicago and Los Angeles are the majors for P and G reads, but nowadays with your agent online, you could book a P and G read anywhere. If, for example, an ad agency (such as Bernstein-Rein in Kansas City) has a client and is looking for women for a spot or campaign, they won't necessarily send the scripts to the three major markets. They may have a great relationship with one of their local gals or have someone new in mind and audition them locally. It doesn't matter where you book. If the spot runs nationally and it's union, you make the same residuals as everyone. Now, you may be asked to read for something that isn't national, but the specs still say P and G read. Want to know what a P and G read sounds like? Turn on daytime TV for a few hours and listen away. You'll know what I'm talking about. Yes, it's a vocal quality as well, but it's also in the mood: young mom, gal-to-gal, warm girlfriend, secret keeper, strong head on her shoulders, sound advisor, trusting friend.

THE SEDUCER OR SEDUCTRESS

You've heard him or her. They lure you in with their breathy, deep, strong, romantic ways. They tell you that you must buy this product. They get you with their smoky, raspy vocal quality that seems to have a life of its own, even if they're throwing away the words. They sound like the Marlboro man, or anyone who possesses some unique quality that makes them stand out simply for having a cool voice. Understand that this is still a sell. Yes, certain actors have vocal qualities that make them right for certain jobs and other actors with different vocal qualities won't even read for the same parts, but once you fit into a category, you will probably read for things that fit your specs. You hear the Seducer or Seductress quite a bit on promos, late-night TV, nighttime commercials, car and beer commercials, generally anything that calls for a harder, sexier sell and a lower-range voice to sell the product.

The Seducer or Seductress is definitely in charge. They know how to stimulate the audience's senses and charm them into wanting whatever product they are selling. This doesn't mean that they are forcing you into buying something. A strong voice can simply inform you in a quiet, docile manner and still reel you in. They can be dry, playful, smart, seductive, alluring, manipulative, or contrived. It doesn't matter. However they do it, you want, you need to buy that product or your life won't be the same. At least that's what that advertiser is hoping.

THE CHEERLEADER AND THE ENERGIZER BUNNY

This voiceover actor has more energy than he or she knows what to do with. Actually, if they're a working voice actor, they do know what to do with all that energy — put it into the read. An experienced voice actor understands how to play with a read but still stick to the copy as written. There are moments of improvisation, but we're not referring to that here. What I'm referring to is the bright, fun, crazy, zany read that you hear on the air. Whether on radio or television, that actor just pulls you in with a fun, energetic voice. A read may sound pushed if the producer or writer has asked for it that way in the session, but remember usually the voice actor has nailed the read during the audition.

A script that calls for the actor to "have fun with it," "play with it," or is "open to interpretation" is where the Energizer Bunny or Cheerleader soars. Not to be confused with the P and G read which can be bright and warm, the Energizer Bunny and Cheerleader have oomph that you don't hear in any other commercial. They stand out because of strength, smile and ability to sell with a convincing energy all the way through the spot, without being over the top. The over-the-top quality that you hear may be a casting choice and not an actor choice. Because some actors will take an over-the-top read way over the top and may not book a job because of it, it's important to know what is an over-the-top read and how far is too far. The Cheerleader or the Energizer Bunny knows how to invite you into the spot without you even knowing why or how, you just know you want to listen. The advertiser counts on this to sell the product. They use this voice as a marketing tool.

Several actors and vocal qualities may fit this spec, but it's the voice actor's ability to use acting skills that book the job. Understanding volume, energy, and what the term brightness means are equally important. Possessing a natural rhythm and comic timing are also critical for this kind of read. While the script may not read funny or actually be funny in any way, it still may require a sense of timing in your read. When spots have to be read in a certain time to fit the ad buy, you, the actor, have to be able to understand how to nail the read for mood within that time frame. Running long or short, losing energy half way through, or picking up speed simply won't work. Your job as a voice actor is to provide the mood they are looking for within that particular read. The ad agency (or whomever is hiring you for the job) will listen to several voice actors that fit the category before making a decision.

THE GUY/GAL NEXT DOOR

They sound like everyone and no one. Nobody special, nothing dark, ominous or grand about his or her voice. Just what the advertiser ordered. They sound like everyone you speak with ten times a day. The guy at the grocery store, the gal walking her dog, the person you ask for directions. There's nothing special about their voice, because the advertiser is looking for a regular Guy/Gal-Next-Door read. Terms that may be applied to this read are "guy next door," "girl next door," "keep it real," "off the cuff," "nice neighbor," "friendly patron," or anything else that keeps you sounding like a real person. A real person versus a voice actor who puts all the correct pauses, spaces and nuances in the read to sell the product. While the polished voice actor brings life to the read that an actual guy next door won't, some advertisers are looking for the real feel of a real person. Don't be fooled. Keeping something real is just as much of a learned skill as "faking it" to sound a certain way. It's simply a delivery. Now, if a voice actor has a really unique voice or something that makes them sound too exotic, they probably won't read for this type of spot, anyway. Having nothing special about your voice may be the exact thing that books you the job.

PUSHY PAULA/PETE

The in-your-face read can also be called a hard sell. Any commercial with the message "you have to buy this product" is a hard sell. A loud voice, an assertive voice, an aggressive voice, a bright voice, an extra smile — these are the vocal types that do these ads. Advertisers are not looking for the old lady or the sweet kind neighbor voice for these ads. Although you may be able to play this type of read, having a lower vocal register definitely gives you the upper hand in booking this kind of job.

  Even before bringing on an advertising agency to create ads or campaigns, the company may already have the type of voice (if not the exact voice actor) in mind. Depending on what they are selling, they will look for a voice that hits their target audience.

During football or any sporting season, you will hear a lot of in-your-face reads. A strong, assertive, bright voice is needed to sell tools, equipment, cars, beer, or anything that targets a male audience.

Depending on what a company is selling will determine the voice they choose to sell the product. Voice is a major component in selling a product, and advertising agencies go to great lengths, ensuring that the company hiring them will have several different voices within the range of in-your-face to choose from for the job.

THE QUIRKY NEIGHBOR

Contrary to the regular, non-imposing voice that sounds like an everyday person is the annoying neighbor, the high-pitched kid, the overbearing mother-in-law. While a lot of these types of voices can be created within acting, and experienced actors know that getting into that mood will create a voice to fit these specs, having a voice that stands out in an interesting way will help in booking these jobs. I'm talking about the commercial world and animation as well as video games. Having a unique vocal quality, whether really high or really low, definitely has a place in the voiceover market. The skills to just be yourself and show your acting chops both come in handy. You may need to offer a few choices when auditioning (alternate read), and your ability to sound like two different overbearing mother-in-laws may be imperative in booking you the job.

The ability to be the character without pushing it is equally as important. If you go over the top and have a very forced read which doesn't sound real, there's a good chance you won't book the job at all. Being real while delivering lines, even while playing an over-the-top character, is a learned technique. Understanding how far to go with a character, staying within the boundaries of making the character work, is also very important. As the actor, you must understand where your voice fits into the marketplace, know your range, and use that tool (your voice) to fit the specs as best as you can in a number of different reads, sells and scripts.

NO NONSENSE NED

This is the casual, off-the-cuff opposite of the in-your-face read. It isn't defined by being bossy, rude, arrogant, playful, or offensive. It isn't trying to be a sell, sincere, over the top, kind, informative, or evasive. It's simply being real. Use the term "raw" if you like. No Nonsense Ned isn't concerned with you liking him. He isn't trying to talk you into buying anything. In fact, he/she makes you feel like you can if you want, but there's no pressure. This approach is great for giving you information in a non-informative manner. Unlike the dry, sarcastic sell, this simply lays it on the line. Like it or not! Some voices may play into this better by not trying as hard. There are certainly voices that do different sells better. But you must learn how to un-sell as well as sell. In fact, the better your ability to just be real and in the moment while delivering copy for this type of read, the more likely you'll get the job. Anything too funny, smart, pretentious, witty or trying too hard definitely is not the read of No Nonsense Ned. Although, similar to the next door neighbor in keeping the reads real, the neighbor may have a bit more smile or earnest delivery. And, unlike the next stereotype, Dry Dana, No Nonsense Ned isn't trying one way or the other to sell you anything. No Nonsense Ned's non-sell is what will make you want to buy the product. He/she will seduce you with their authenticity and direct manner of speaking.

DRY DANA

Dry Dana fits many different worlds. Certainly one thinks of sarcastic when defining this read. Other words commonly associated with Dry Dana include witty, off-the-cuff, wry, matter-of-fact, no-nonsense, telling it like it is. Dry is simply a specific point of view to start with. Vocally, it means you are at a lower register in your voice, speaking at a slower pace, but not all the time! When other adjectives are added to the list, the read changes. For example, adding wit to the read will probably speed it up. Off-the-cuff lends itself to a "gotta go" mood. Dry reads definitely have an element of humor (or lack thereof) and more character than your everyday read. This is a particular sell and understanding how to do a sell is key in moving your career forward. Don't simply copy a voice; learn how to create it from inside.

THE KNOW-IT-ALL

Although many of the sells could easily be mixed and matched, the Know-It-All is the voice that instructs or informs you. They certainly seem to know what they are talking about, simply from the weight of their voice. Unlike Pushy Paula, The P and G, and the Cheerleader, the Know-It-All doesn't get big, bright, or too smiley. They simply inform you in their authoritative kind of way. We listen because the voice carries weight. We believe they have the authority to know of what they speak. Specs that fit into the Know-It-All category include smart, educated, sincere, knowledgeable, tutorial, effective, professorial or any other adjective you can come up with to define intelligent. Many times, advertisers will use more than two or three adjectives (and even the name of a smart actor or two) to help you understand exactly what they are looking for. Learning how to apply the specs to the read will make it that much easier for you to book the job.

VOICE TO VOICE

AN INTERVIEW WITH CHRIS ZIMMERMAN

Chris Zimmerman is a successful casting director and the director of many animated programs. Her extensive resume includes *Star Trek Voyager, Giant Bomb, Bionic Commando, Questfan, Mortal Kombat, Jonny Quest, G. I. Joe, Captain Planet, Dumb and Dumber,* and *Swat Kats.* She has also cast and directed animated television episodes, CD-ROMs including *The Blues Brothers* and *Fish Police,* and live-action movies, movies of the week, and public service announcements (PSAs).

What do you look for in a voice?
Everything from a rasp, speech pattern, attitude — all that can help identify a character. A lot of times it's the delivery rather than the actual voice qualities. When you audition, you'll get to

read a paragraph or two, or a scene, with another actor. What nails the job is when the actor finds something to bring the character to life.

Work the script. Use your odd speech patterns. The person who gets the job is the one who sometimes breaks the rules, who doesn't read the script the same way. The person who hones in on the life of the character will get the job.

What about improvising?

Be aware of who you are auditioning for. Improvising can be helpful to you; it makes you seem funnier. Don't overdo it or you will kill your audition. Use it for the character. Don't show off. I don't mind improvising if it is appropriate to the scene and to the character.

What will help a voice actor get rehired after the voice session with you?

Show me your creative spark as an actor. Listen to the director. Hear what I ask for and respond. Attitude is a big requirement. I want actors to act, play, and bring life to the room. You also need to be pleasant and easy to work with. The people who are willing to give 100 percent while they are there will definitely be back.

How do you feel about getting unsolicited animation CDs?

If a CD looks professional or is from a union member I will accept it. I try to listen to as many as I can. You need a CD to get in the door. I've never hired directly from a demo CD, but I have called people in from the demo CD. The voiceover CD is the calling card.

What makes a voiceover actor good in your book?

They become the character.

What advice would you give to new talent or to someone who hasn't booked a lot of animation?

Get as much experience as you can in front of the microphone — actual jobs, auditions, or workshops. Be comfortable in front of the microphone. You can't watch yourself; you can't be afraid to make a fool out of yourself.

Do you hire a lot of celebrities for voiceover jobs?
Yes, but I prefer to hire the person who is right for the part.

How closely do you work with the animators?
Some animators will come to the session to watch the actors so they can match the facial expression with the animation.

Any final word of advice?
Just free yourselves up to live the character. Free yourselves up as actors and *be fun!*

● *EXERCISE: Animation*

This exercise is a great way to find characters and voices.

1. Draw a picture (elaborate or stick figure, have fun with it, be creative).
2. Name your character and give it three adjectives to describe it.
3. Write two or three lines of copy to go with your character.
4. Create a voice and stance — read the copy.
5. Add a mood to go with each line/paragraph of copy. See how your vocal range changes as you change mood.

CHAPTER 5

OTHER GENRES OF VOICEOVER WORK

THERE ARE MANY WAYS OF MAKING MONEY IN VOICEOVERS. We've talked a lot about commercials, which are the most viable kind of voiceover work. But many people make a healthy living in the other areas discussed in this chapter. But just because you work a lot in one area doesn't mean that you will find work in all of them. Follow your gut, find out which area of the business you enjoy the most, and concentrate on pursuing that area. Some voiceover artists who work in looping (background voices and noises for film and television) find it hard to break into animation or promos. By the same token, many commercial and animation actors have a difficult time breaking into the tight-knit world of looping (which is also known as audio dialogue replacement, or ADR). Each one takes a particular talent and focus.

Keep auditioning in as many different areas as you want to break into. Do note, though, that each requires its own demo CD. Interested in audiobooks? You'll need an audiobook CD to send to the audiobook publishers, so they can hear how you read in this genre. You may start with one demo CD and gradually build to several demos or one CD encompassing many areas of the business.

I started by doing regular commercials but wanted to break into promos. Interestingly enough, just as I wanted to start doing them, my agent started getting calls for me to go to some studio auditions for promos. I started booking. My voiceover world now consists of commercials, animation, promos, and narration. Although I'm open to other areas of the business, this is where I've found the most success. A friend who does a lot of animation work also works part-time in a loop group. Using your talents in multiple areas will give you more chances to make money. As you'll read in the interview at the end of this chapter, voice actor Hillary Huber does quite well filling in her downtime by reading audiobooks.

LOOPING (A.K.A. ADR OR WALLA)

Working in looping, or ADR, doesn't require any particular type of voice, but it does require plenty of acting skills. Loopers create background noise (a baby crying), ambience (people talking at a party), or sound effects (hiccups) for a scene while following the film as it is projected on a screen. Looping (which, besides ADR, is also called *walla* — the terms are interchangeable) is done during post-production. Breaking into looping is not easy. You will need to join a loop group. Loop groups usually hire the same actors over and over again, and the same set of actors usually work together for particular television shows or films. There are several loop groups, mostly in California — some union, others nonunion. Getting a recommendation from someone in a loop group is the best way to break in. But don't forget to send your CD, too. (One loop group is listed in Appendix B.)

Audit or take a looping class to learn what the craft requires. Watch TV and look for the loop group information in the credits. Contact the post-production facilities in your town and ask if they have loop groups. Becoming one of a post-production house's loopers is also a great way to get on their radar for future voiceover jobs. Contact the production offices of small production companies that come to your town through your local film commission and ask if they are doing post-production locally. Even if they're not, you can find out if they need any looping on the set: they may want to get some background ambiance or dialogue done right after a scene is shot. Walla lines are written before shooting, usually by the director of the project, but they can also be improvised by actors, depending on the director of the walla group. Acting experience is necessary; the ability to do accents and speak foreign languages often comes in handy. Previous experience in voiceovers also helps.

There are two ways to do looping. One involves scripted background dialogue; the other, improvised dialogue. For example, you may be hired to walla an entire hospital emergency-room scene that has twenty or more actors walking through it. The loop group will record the voice dialogue for the whole scene. It's an interesting illusion: although the camera is pulled back far enough that you cannot see who is saying what, you still get the feeling that the characters and background actors walking through the scene — everyone from the ER nurse speaking over the intercom to the patient lying on the gurney — are saying the words you hear. Or you may be asked to do a weather report, something you will have to write down and then act out. That's when improvisational skills come into play. You'll be asked to come up with phrases and dialogue to match what is going on in the scene. This is called improvising copy for dialogue.

If the director of the film or TV show doesn't like the voice of an actor on-camera, a looper may even be hired to dub that voice. While watching the scene, you will read the dialogue and match the picture — making the scripted words match the movements of the on-screen actor's mouth. Obviously, this requires acting, because you must also re-create the on-camera actor's emotional tone with your voice. Looping is sometimes referred to as being part of a vocal orchestra. You need to work well within a group. You need to know when to be loud, soft, angry, nice, sad, or happy as you duplicate the exact mood of what's on the screen. When looping, it's important that you always face the microphone — even though you may be several feet away — to allow room for the other loopers to move around. Sometimes, several loopers may stand together in a crowd, in front of many microphones, looping the same scene at the same time. For certain scenes, you have to know how to change and improvise dialogue rapidly as you see the scene unfold in front of you. You can join as many loop groups

OTHER GENRES OF VOICEOVER WORK

as will take you. Most loopers know each other, because it's such a small market.

One problem with looping is that it precludes having a full-time job and takes away from the time you have to go on auditions. When you are hired for a project, you usually have to commit to the entire shoot. A looping day can exceed eight hours, and the looping project can go for several weeks at a time. With a TV or radio spot, you may only be in a session for an hour. (By union rules, if you are kept longer than one and a half hours per spot at a commercial voiceover session, you must be paid extra. Many voice actors actually do several voice jobs a day.) Agents, therefore, usually prefer to book you on commercial or animation jobs because their own remuneration is better (agents don't make commission on loop groups), and there is a chance for you to do more work.

On the other hand, once an actor gets in with a looping director or group and becomes a regular, it is possible to make six figures a year, especially at a loop group that does a lot of projects. Some loopers even get residuals for their work on feature films and animation, depending on their contract.

Here are some looping dos and don'ts, which come to us courtesy of Sandy Holt's Loop Ease, a successful loop group in Los Angeles:

- *Do* come to the session prepared. Know the material you are looping. Know which genre the material belongs to (drama, comedy, science fiction).
- *Do* know your jargon: military, scientific, period piece, medical, police, fire, action.
- *Do* be a team player. Accommodate other actors and your sound engineer or whoever is running the session.
- *Do* take direction well.
- *Do* follow what is going on in the story.
- *Do* pay attention to each scene on the screen even if you're not looping that particular scene. You need to know what's going on from one scene to the next.
- *Do* empty keys and change from your pockets and remove jewelry and anything else that might make noise.

- *Don't* talk during the playback of what you've just recorded.
- *Don't* talk during a take unless you're supposed to.
- *Don't* purposely drown out other actors unless you're doing a scene in which you're supposed to be louder than they are.
- *Don't* ever use proper names of products (such as Sony, Coke, Nike, Reebok, or Tide). Use generic terms.
- *Don't* overpower the other actors. Keep your voice quality and dialogue appropriate for the scene — to match the other actors in the scene.
- *Don't* use negative tones or dialogue during walla (unless the scene calls for a negative mood).

VOICE TO VOICE

AN INTERVIEW WITH JOE CAPPELLETTI

Joe Cappelletti is a professional looper. A few of his recent credits include *Entourage, The Hurt Locker, Crazy Heart, The Good Wife, Gilmore Girls, Dear John, Californication,* and *The Fourth Kind.* You can find his full resume posted on his website, *www.thefinalword.org*.

Tell us how you got into the business.
I got started in the voiceover business shortly after I graduated from acting school — the American Academy of Dramatic Arts in New York. I had done a commercial (on camera) for a company — Road Hawk Car Batteries. They seemed to like the character I created — a New York gear head who really loves his car: "It's got a 440 high-performance engine. It's got a chrome blower and two fours!" So they decided to do a couple of radio spots with this character. I'm sure it would be scary to see that commercial today. (I remember that hairdo well.) But, what the heck, that's what got it all rolling. Things in motion tend to stay in motion, right? Isn't that a law of physics or an ancient Chinese proverb?

I became interested in the group ADR area of the business when I discovered that this work provided the opportunity to make a meaningful contribution to all kinds of projects — from films and television to web launches, commercials, video games, anime ... you name it!

And every job is different. Sometimes we are required only to create large group sounds. On other projects, we may be asked to voice-replace an entire character to picture. This means you (the audience) are seeing a character on screen interacting with another; however, you are not hearing that actor's voice. You're hearing the voice of a skillful voice actor who has learned how to dub — to seamlessly say the words in sync and with the appropriate feeling, so as to convince you that you are hearing the actor you're seeing. It's challenging but great fun! When we dub Japanese anime the challenge is even greater. We have to match the lip movements that were originally drawn for a character speaking a different language.

Thankfully, we share this responsibility with the adaptor and director. In other areas of ADR, we provide all the background voices you hear discussing technical jargon in police situations, in hospitals, auto body shops, the play-by-play of sporting events, radio programming, and commercials — to name a few.

How do you go after jobs?

Wouldn't you like to know! You realize you're asking me to reveal my trade secrets! This is our Barbara Walters moment. This is the one everyone else is afraid to ask — but they want to know the answer. Good for you for asking the tough questions for your readers! I have been hired by people who work in just about every rank in the chain of command that you can imagine — from directors, producers, and studio executives to my immediate supervisors. So you can see that the marketing aspect for this job is very labor-intensive and time-consuming.

The truth is, as with any business, you have to be extremely diligent to generate opportunities, and this area of the entertainment business is no different. What makes it perhaps even more difficult is the fact that the person doing the hiring can be different for every job. And often is. And you never really know who has the final say until you find yourself on the stage with your group … or not. I've been on both sides of this. I've had a date in the books and a cast set for a project that never happened. I've also worked with directors, studios, and productions "that only work with " (add the name here). The fact is, this is a town of plenty. And I genuinely believe that there is enough to go around for everyone with the requisite capabilities who loves the work enough to commit to always putting forth their best effort. By that I mean training, continuing to work out, and always looking for opportunities to improve their game.

What skills must a looper have?
First and foremost, I look for an *actor*. By that I mean one who has the ability, based on experience, to make the leap of embodying other people believably, moment to moment, in an imaginary circumstance. In doing group ADR effectively, the work we do on a soundstage must translate to whatever scene it is that we are covering on screen. We must be so convincing in our characterizations — at once completely engaging, yet subtle — that our work should appear as though we are the characters in the given environment. Our overriding goal and *responsibility* is to bring life to the scenes around the principal actors — without drawing any attention to ourselves. I know this seems counterintuitive for an actor, but it's a necessary and vital adjustment. The work by its very nature is intended to be dynamic yet unobtrusive. People make the mistake of thinking that group ADR is just a bunch of unintelligible voices in a crowd. The uninitiated wrongly assume that if one possesses the ability to carry on a conversation in English, that's all that's required. Seamless ADR demands an acute sense of awareness of all the conversations going on around you, as well as the ability to fully invest in your particular interaction. Improvisation acumen is a must. So is the ability to see and match lip-sync with improvised dialogue.

Other important qualities include, but are not limited to, a positive, enthusiastic team attitude; a facility with dialects; a well-rounded education; a willingness and ability to do research; the ability to take direction; and also, I believe, a sense of gratitude for the privilege we enjoy to work on projects that have taken years to get off the ground.

Can group ADR be a full-time voiceover career?
Sure. I know there's a small — very small — group of voice actors that make the vast majority of their income from this work alone. They tend to be the most experienced — some with twenty-plus years in the biz — and work with the biggest ADR companies several times per week. Some of these actors work exclusively with one group; others freelance.

For most voice actors, group ADR is just one outlet for their talents. I actively espouse the importance of diversification — *all* of the actors I hire work in other areas. There are opportunities in video games, promo, narration, websites, commercials, foreign dubbing, and voice matching.

How do you break in?
There's no simple answer here. My recommendation is to take an acting class. Take an improv class. Practice reading out loud every day. Watch TV shows and movies and listen for the group ADR. Does it work? What would you have done differently? Obviously, you're interested enough in this aspect of the business to have bought this book. That's a great step. Keep reading. And don't be afraid to ask questions of actors that are more experienced than you. This is a wonderful community of professionals, and information opens doors. Just make sure that when that door opens, you're ready. There are a lot of extremely talented people that are currently working all the jobs in town. I think good questions to ask are: Is there something about my work ethic or particular skill set that can enrich this work in a new, exciting way? What's singular about you?

I've yet to discover shortcuts. I think it's possible to land some jobs — again, opportunity is plentiful. But to have a sustainable, meaningful career, I think one must always try to best your previous outing — to figure out a way to raise the bar and challenge those around you to do the same.

JINGLES

Jingles are the little songs — tunes and lyrics — that sometimes accompany commercials. Jingles are usually sung by in-house singers at production companies, by actors who are known in the field, or by other singers known for their jingle work. Some post-production facilities even specialize in jingles. (Famous singers and songwriters will also sometimes sell the rights to a song for a flat rate for use in a commercial.) Many singers are eager to break into the jingle business because the residuals are on the same scale as those for voiceovers or doing on-camera work. Animation actors must sometimes sing as part of voicing their animated characters, and they may then be hired to do jingles because they get known as voice actors who also sing. But in general, the jingle business is a very tight-knit community.

Local companies often write their own jingles and hire local talent to sing them. National campaigns that don't use celebrities will usually rehire the same jingle actors again and again. Because jingle singers are required to sing the same thing over and over, and change tempo, mood, and rhythm to please the producer and client, singers with voiceover experience are often favored. For those voiceover actors who are also singers, jingles are yet another type of work they can pursue.

INFOMERCIALS AND IN-HOUSE TRAINING VIDEOS

The voice talent in an infomercial explains a product and sells it to the audience. In a training video, the talent explains a set of procedures or conveys important information to viewers — usually the employees of the company producing the video. (Companies producing training videos can range in size from small, local firms to huge multinational corporations.)

You can audition for infomercials through your agent or through production companies. Trailer houses may also cast infomercials. There are several local production companies across the United States whose bread and butter is in the infomercial and in-house training world. You can pursue in-house work by contacting large companies and speaking with the department in charge of in-house training. Ask them if they are seeking voice actors for their training videos or DVDs.

Infomercials and training videos are a great way to break into and learn about the voiceover business and to get used to working with a voice director. Many of these jobs work the same way as commercial sessions: success involves balancing energy, vocal creativity, active choices, and the technical aspects of the script.

DUBBING

Dubbing requires you to use your voice to jibe with someone else's. As a dubber, your job is to read a script while trying to match the on-screen actor's tone, vocal quality, and timing. Dubbing work can be found through post-production companies or through your union.

Most dubbing is for films and television programs being translated from one language into another — for example, a French or Spanish film being dubbed in English. You may need to know the original language so that you will know just when to say the lines of dialogue. The particular sound and vocal texture you try to achieve depends on whose voice you are dubbing.

From time to time, voiceover actors may be called in to dub a line of dialogue in an English-language film. Let's say an actor who has only a single line in a film is shown on camera, but in such a way that you never see his or her face; the director may hire a voiceover actor to dub the line instead of calling back the original actor for one of several reasons: (1) The director might have not liked the placement of the actual line and wants it to be spoken earlier or later. (2) The director may have not liked the actor's voice. (3) The actor wasn't available to do the dub. The voiceover actor will try to match his or her voice quality to the other person's — or at least try to match what they think that person would sound like. Timing is very important in dubbing, because you need to match the voice to the picture.

ANIMATION

Voiceover actors who do animation create voices for characters in the enormous and ever-growing animation market. It used to be that animation consisted of little more than Saturday morning cartoons and the occasional animated film. Now, you'll find animated video games, multimedia infomercial presentations, prime-time TV shows, and many more animated films — and, of course, those Saturday morning cartoons are still on the air.

Success in animation requires that you have an acting background, as well as an interesting voice. Animation uses many different kinds of voices; the important thing is that you be able to do unique things with your voice. Some voice actors are naturals for animation. Ever talk to someone whose voice is noticeably quirky? Chances are they'd be suited for animation. Remember all those weird voices that you've done for years at home? Start putting them to work for you. Try to see how many different voices you can come up with.

Although the animation market is large and can be extremely lucrative, it is relatively hard to break into. The best way to enter the animation field is to take a class — or marry an animation director. (Well, it worked for a friend of mine.)

Here's a quick animation exercise to get you going. Take a piece of paper and draw a character. It doesn't have to look professional — it can be a stick figure with a hat and poncho. Or it can be a very elaborate drawing. It doesn't matter. Now, give your character a name, and describe it with a few adjectives. Write them down. Say you draw the stick figure with the poncho and hat, and you name him Mr. Taco. Now, Mr. Taco is suave, debonair, and cocky. Got it? Next, write down some dialogue for your character. Don't go into overdrive and write a two-page script. Keep it simple. Write three lines. Create a scene.

Here's mine for Mr. Taco:

> "Well, aren't you a pretty little gal? Mosey on up here and let me buy you a gin fizz."

> "You see that? He's snoring in the middle of the bar. Knock his chair over."

> "What's that? Heck no, I haven't played poker since ... Tuesday."

It doesn't matter what the character says; what matters is that it's *your* creation. Now, attach those adjectives (just like we did in the commercial voice exercises) and find your mood and voice for your character. Then say the lines. Record yourself. Play the recording back.

You've just created a voice for an animated character that can be used for your animation demo and for many animation auditions in the future. You can even use that particular voice for other characters. (The casting director doesn't need to know that you're really using the voice of the drawing of your teddy bear for the alien on his new animated series!)

Try this exercise several times. How many voices can you come up with? Remember, do what's comfortable for your voice; you don't want to strain so much that you won't be able to re-create that character week after week, year after year, if you book a job.

There are also live-action films that use voiceovers in the same way that animated films do. For example, the *Babe* films — *Babe* and *Babe: Pig in the City* — were live action films in which real animals were given human voices and personalities (courtesy of voiceover actors, of course). The *Babe* movies did so well that the market for live-action features really opened up. Movies such as Disney's *Whispers: An Elephant's Tale* followed, and today there are hundreds of live-action projects.

Here are some questions that people looking to break into animation frequently ask — as well as my answers:

Don't celebrities get most of the animation work?
Yes, celebrities do book a lot of the lead roles in animated features. Their names are used to market the big-budget animated films. But some of the most talented and versatile actors working in animation are non-celebrities who specialize in the art of voice acting.

Is there work on foreign animated films?
Yes, there is. In fact, I do a lot of English-language looping and dubbing for Japanese and French animated films. Film actors tend to do very well in dubbing and looping because they do a lot of looping for their own movies. They learn to lip-sync and loop really well.

What are "classic" characters?
Classic characters are the characters everyone comes to know from popular animated movies and TV shows — ranging from Winnie the Pooh (voiced by Jim Cummings) to current classics like Tommy Pickles from *Rug Rats* (voiced by E. G. Dailey in the feature film as well as in the hit TV series). When a show becomes as popular as *Rug Rats,* it can turn into a lucrative franchise for the voiceover actor, leading to work on feature films, theme park voiceovers, video games, talking toys, and commercials. The classic character will always be voiced by the same actor, and that actor will continue to make money as long as there are products — from movies to dolls — featuring that character on the market. If you do the voice for a classic character, you may have work for years!

Is the animation market changing? Is there a market for "real" character voices as well as cartoony voices?
Yes, there's a market for both. In fact, the market for actors who can create human-type character voices is growing — although there's always room, of course, for those far-out cartoony reads.

By the way, there's a great book on the market called *Word of Mouth,* by Susan Blu, which talks about creating voices for animated characters and gives a lot of information about the wonderful world of animation.

VOICE TO VOICE
AN INTERVIEW WITH DEBBY DERRYBERRY

Debby Derryberry is a well-known animation voiceover actor, whose voice has starred in dozens of animated films and TV programs.

First, let's get your resume out of the way. What have you been doing recently?
I'm Jimmy Neutron. I'm Judy on *Jumanji.* I'm Zatchbell on Cartoon Network. In the Diva Starz collection from Mattel, I'm Alexa. And I'm Shelby in the upcoming movie, *The Legend of Secret Pass.* I also did *Tasmanian Devil* and was Tinkerbelle in *Peter Pan and the Pirates.*

Wow, quite a list! How did you get started?

I was living in Nashville doing jingles and I sent my demo CD to Los Angeles. Ginny McSwain, an animation casting director, responded because she liked the CD. She told me that I would have to move to Los Angeles to get work. When I moved out here, I resubmitted all of my CDs again. Ginny set me up a meeting with an agent, and he signed me. That was nine years ago.

How do you create the voices that you do?

By the picture. I try to look at the picture — if they have one — or the character description. If the character is nerdy, I try to stand the way that I think the character would — do the physical aspect of the character. I try to emulate the character. It helps to create the attitude of the character. The attitude is much more important in getting the job than "tweaking" it a certain way.

What's your signature voice?

I'm the little girl. Either the bratty girl, or the upper-crust snobby girl, or the sweet angel girl. It depends on who is casting. Each casting director may see you in a different way.

What was your first job and how long did it take you to book it?

I booked my first job after my third audition. It was a special on TV called *Dixie's Diner.* I was a Southern-belle pig. Then I booked *Tiny Tunes.* My next job was *Peter Pan and the Pirates,* with Tim Curry. They signed us to sixty-five episodes. I was Tinkerbelle's first voice.

Sixty-five episodes is what we all want to get. Are most of your animated series for sixty-five episodes?

Usually they don't sign you for that many. That is rare. A show may go for that many episodes, but most likely, unless you're a celebrity, you will be paid per episode, no matter how many you do. They will pay you for the pilot, then thirteen, then if you're lucky the show goes to sixty-five! Disney pays residuals for ten reruns, right up front. Most shows pay you for residuals each time it plays. We all work for scale, day-player rates.

Any other characters that you specialize in?
Interestingly enough, I get a lot of work doing "infant cries." There is a big call for them, and I'm their girl. I looped an animation feature with infant cries.

Do you do a lot of looping?
Yes, I do animation, looping, and regular voiceover commercials.

Which do you prefer — looping or animation?
I enjoy both. An animation day is shorter for better money. You will work on a TV show for four hours and a looping session for eight.

What about residuals on animation features?
You get the residuals when it goes to video. The big money is in video sales. I giggled in *Toy Story,* and the money has been great. Animated Disney makes you a lot of money. On TV, you get the residuals when they rerun the show.

Do you still have to audition for a part on an animated show?
For principal roles, I do. For special guests spots, they usually just call me in. I started out doing a special guest for *Casper* and they liked what I did, so it turned into a regular role.

How do you stand out in animation? Is their room for improvisation?
Absolutely! It's what makes your character stand out! If you can get away with improvising, then go for it! Incorporate it into the character. You still have a certain time frame that you have to stick to, but there is room to play within the read. Improvising is what can make you stand out, and take you from being a special guest to a regular role. There is always room for padding.

Can you give me an example of an improvised moment?
Sure. On *Bobby's World,* there was a line that said, "Ouch, I hurt my knee." I changed it to, "Bobby, I have an abrasion."

What did the director do?
They loved it. In fact, they sometimes have the animators come to the voiceover session to meet you and watch what you do while

you're recording. They want to see how you are reading the copy — what your physical body is doing. How you're holding your arms or squishing your face to get that certain sound or attitude. I've watched the cartoon at a later date and seen that my character is doing the same physical act that I did in the session. I've seen Tinkerbelle cross her eyes in a scene where I had crossed my eyes saying the line in the session. The animators saw it and loved it, so they incorporated it into the character!

That's great! Do you have any ritual that you go through for your voice?
I read the script. Highlight my lines. I do all my improvisation the night before the audition. Be ready! I read the verbal cues in the script. Running, jumping, out of breath, throwing a ball. You have to know when to incorporate a "humph" or heavy breathing within the sentence. If your character is falling, know when to get louder, to yell, to get softer. To make it seem like you are really doing these things. The description of the character helps tell you what to do and what the character is like.

How many characters do you think you have inside you?
Off the top, I would say about twelve. Within those twelve, I have about ten different dialects for each character.

Which dialects?
Oh, I can do Texas, Georgia, New York, England, Ireland ... and Valley Girl, Russian, Norwegian, and a bunch more.

How do you create new characters?
You find them within the pictures, the auditions, the copy. What the character says, how they act, how they look. Sometimes if it seems that they would have a lisp, or braces, or glasses. All in the style of the character.

Do you have any advice to new talent trying to break into animation?
Remain humble. Be persistent. Get your CD out. Resubmit every six months. Keep taking classes with casting directors. It is very important to know every casting director in town. I still bring my

CD to auditions. I just dropped it off for a certain audition and they happened to like something on there, so they hired me for another role as a special guest, not the audition that I originally read for. So, it's always good to have your CD to show your range.

How tough is it to break in?
Extremely tough. It's very competitive. The casting directors have their favorites. I would spend all of my money on meeting the casting directors. Go to classes!

What's a normal weekday like for you?
Well, if I'm on a series, we work once a week. A normal schedule for a show would be Tuesday two to six. Otherwise, I may loop nine to six and during lunch run across town for an audition. Or I may do a voiceover session from ten to two, grab some lunch, and run around to several auditions all over town.

NARRATION

You'll find voiceover narration on television, radio, industrial films (noncommercial films for particular industries), infomercials, documentaries, and theatrical films. The narrator is the person telling the story — conveying the story in a certain mood, just as on TV commercials and radio. The narrator's mood and flow allows the story to unfold with rhythm. Narrators may have a certain style or flair to their voice, depending on what the show is or what kind of story they are telling. Producers and directors look for a certain vocal quality to match the type of story they are telling to that particular audience.

Small industrial films and in-house video work may be the easiest work to get in smaller markets, or if you're nonunion. Local TV and radio shows, fashion shows, in-house store promotions, projects with ad agencies — all need narrators. Postproduction houses may also hire a narrator for a project once it is in the final stages.

In-house and industrial films are "non-broadcast," meaning that they are used as training films for employees and will not be shown on TV or in theaters. This work can be either union or nonunion.

CDs AND DVDs

Voiceovers are also used on various kinds of educational and entertainment-oriented CDs and DVDs. The voiceover artist might tell a story as an image appears on screen or be a character in an animated story.

The multimedia field presents great opportunities for voiceover actors, as all types of talent are needed. The unions are just beginning to gain control of this work and set the pay scales for it. Meanwhile, companies producing CDs are hiring on a daily basis, so you or your agent needs to come up with a fee. The hours can be long and the work is tedious, but there will be a great mass of work in the near future. If you are nonunion, this is a good area to try to go into.

PROMOS

Promos, or promotional spots, are the essence of an entire commercial whittled down to a single phrase. TV promos are teasers for upcoming shows: "Next on *Grey's Anatomy*." "Tonight on CNN."

You can get a feel for what promo voices sound like just by watching TV. The vocal quality tends to match the tone of the show being pitched: light and casual for lighter, fun shows and more serious for *Dateline* or other serious programs. The Lifetime network uses very smooth, deep, warm women's voices; whereas ESPN, the sports network, goes for a manlier, throaty quality. How about news programs? They tend to use conservative, authoritative voices. Think Dan Rather.

The promo world is exciting. You can go from doing the promos for a local TV or radio station to doing national promos in Los Angeles or New York. The work is steady and it pays well. Dominated by men in the past, the promo market has begun to open up to women. Many networks now use female voice talent to sell certain shows. Although male voiceover actors still get most of the promo work that runs on nighttime network television, I anticipate a time in the near future when more women will be invited into this time slot, as well.

The promo market requires a strong voice as well as the knowledge of how to read this kind of copy. Some teachers specifically teach promo and narration reads.

Different networks and shows use different kinds of voices and vocal styles. If you want to pursue promos, you'll need to include a promo segment on your demo CD. To listen to some sample promos, go to *www.voicebank.net*. You do not have to be a member to use this site. Click on House Reels, go to a particular agency, and pull up its talent base, which contains one-minute teasers — samples of each member actor's work. From there, you can listen to any number of voice demos in many areas of the voice business, including promos. (Actors cannot post their own demos — they must be invited onto Voicebank after obtaining an agent or manager.)

TRAILERS/TEASERS

Trailers (also called teasers) are mini-commercials for TV shows or films. A typical movie trailer will tell you everything you need to know about a full-length feature in less than a minute. If done well, the trailer will sell you the story — pulling you into the product so that you will want to see the whole thing. Most voiceovers for trailers are done by men, but a few women are starting to do them, as well.

Do some research and find out which postproduction companies produce trailers. Mix Magic, in Hollywood, is a well-known trailer house. Once again, you will need a produced demo CD specifically for trailers to send out.

There are several popular trailer actors, and many trailers use the same voice actors over and over. The most famous is Don LaFontaine (*www.donlafontaine.com*), whose rumbling bass-baritone often seems inescapable at movie theaters. Film studios like a certain vocal quality when selling their films, and they know that certain actors can provide it without sounding phony. John Geary and Jim Cummings work all the time in the trailer market (check out *www.voicebank.net* or their websites to listen to some of their work); in fact, about ten guys do most of the work. Nonetheless, there is work in the growing market of trailers for movies that go straight to video.

AUDIOBOOKS

The audiobook market is huge, including best-selling fiction and nonfiction, how-to books, classic literature, medical books, and more. If you are good at reading aloud, then you should have success in this market, as that is what you will be doing — reading from the actual printed book. Audiobooks can use all sorts of voices, depending on the subject matter. There are two types of audiobooks: unabridged (the full text of the book) and abridged (a shorter version).

A number of companies across the United States specialize in producing audiobooks. You can find them on the Audio Publishers Association website (*www.audiopub.org*), which contains a complete listing of its members. Send out your demo CD to those you are interested in working for. The hours can be long, but the pay can be good. Although some audiobook jobs are handled by AFTRA and go to celebrities, others remain nonunion, and this market still hires unknown talent. Because of the amount of text involved, recording audiobooks requires a lot of patience, as well as a nice, smooth tone.

Can you make money in any or all of these fields? Well, the truth is that any voiceover talent can make money in several different areas of the business. Some actors work in one area more than others and get known for certain kinds of jobs and characters. Others seem to have a knack for several different voiceover areas and manage to find work in all of them.

VOICE TO VOICE

AN INTERVIEW WITH HILLARY HUBER

Hillary Huber has been a successful voiceover talent in Los Angeles for sixteen years, voicing thousands of commercials — including ads for Toyota, Birds Eye, Boeing, Ford, and McDonald's. She is also a critically acclaimed audiobook reader. Her audiobooks include *The Light in the Piazza,* by Elizabeth Spencer, *A Field of Darkness* by Cornelia Read, and *A Map of Glass* by Jane Urquhart. Along with veteran voice actor Pat Fraley, Hillary teaches audiobook workshops that cover everything from how to enter the market to performance skills to self-directing. Here's what she said to me:

> "Fifteen years ago, after bouncing around many different careers, I decided to try my hand in the voiceover arena. I took some classes, made a demo, got an agent, and started working. Right. Wish it had been that easy. Doing voiceovers is the greatest job in the world. When I entered the market, the rest of the world didn't yet know this; but now they do. It has gotten even more competitive and even harder to break into. The Internet has revolutionized the way we work, opening up jobs to people worldwide. While I have had the great fortune to make my living solely as a commercial voiceover actor, I realized that as I got older and the market got more competitive I would need to broaden my areas of expertise. Enter the wonderful world of audiobooks.
>
> "You need to realize that this is probably one of the easiest voiceover markets to break into. There are no agents. There are seldom auditions. You simply forge a relationship with an audiobooks company. Pat Fraley and I researched some books and decided that *Pentimento,* by Lillian Hellman, would be perfect for me. We recorded a short demo of me reading several selections from the book and sent it up to Blackstone Audio. Alas, they could not secure the rights, but when we then suggested *A Very Easy Death,* by Simone de Beauvoir, they took the bait and said I'd be perfect for it. I had my first audiobook deal. What's interesting about this story is that we approached them with an idea — essentially saying, 'This is how we can make you money,' not, 'Please hire me to read your books so I can make money.' We are currently on our twelfth project with Blackstone.
>
> "I produce my audiobooks — meaning the publisher sends me the book, I prepare the script, do all of the research, record in my home studio, and deliver the raw tracks to the publisher, who then edits them. I'll often hire a composer to write a few short pieces of music for the intro and closing credits. Being my own producer affords me the freedom to work around my commercial voiceover career. I never miss an audition or a job.

"Another route is to become a 'gun for hire.' You make a demo, generally consisting of three short excerpts from books demonstrating your particular skills. The demo is no more than three minutes total. You send your demo to small and medium-sized audio publishers with the hope that they need your talents and hire you. You then show up at a prearranged studio, read for six to eight hours a day, and go on your merry way. Scripts are prepared for you, research is done for you. It's a lot easier, but you don't have the control to work around your schedule, and I find this vital.

"Reading audiobooks is grueling work. It's a marathon. Primarily, you must be a good reader. You must be able to wind a story and interpret themes. You must be a good actor and really pull the words off the page. Unless you choose the nonfiction route — medical, scientific, history, etc. — you should be facile at character work. Some audiobook narrators make no effort to change their voice in order to differentiate between characters. Frankly, I find doing so essential. Your job isn't to trick the listener into thinking different people are speaking, but a little vocal characterization can really help illuminate the characters and the story.

"How long does it take to read a book? Well, that depends on the length of the book! I'm a pretty good reader, and I don't make too many mistakes. A 300-page book generally times out to ten to twelve finished hours. I can read that book in about fifteen hours. I'm only good for about four-hour sessions. My brain starts to shut down after that.

"Something you need to understand about the audiobook market is that 90 percent of the readers are people you've never heard of. 'But wait!' you're saying, 'I've seen celebrity names on the spin racks at Barnes & Noble.' Yes, you have, but they read the abridged versions. *We* read the unabridged.

"What does it pay? Let me say straight out: reading audiobooks is not nearly as lucrative as the other voiceover areas. You are usually compensated based on the finished hour-length of the book. For beginners, this could be as low as $50 per finished hour. For seasoned pros, that number could reach as high as $800 — even more for the real big shots. But keep in mind that this is for the *finished* hour. If it takes you twenty hours to read a ten-hour book, you only get paid for ten hours.

"That being said, reading audiobooks has been the highlight of my career. It is the most creative and the most fulfilling. At the end of the day, I get to look at my shelf of books and feel as though I am leaving some beauty in my wake.

"I suggest you check out *www.audiopub.org*, the Audio Publishers Association website. This is a clearinghouse for all things audiobook. There is info on how to become a reader; there are links to all of the publishers, as well as narrator profiles. Also, *www.audiofilemagazine.com* lists reviews, interviews, etc. If you are interested in classes, go to *www.patfraley.com*, and look for upcoming workshops. During our Audiobook Event you will learn about entering the market, performance skills, and how to bid a job. Listen to audiobooks. Check them out of the library or join *www.audible.com* and download them. Listen to samples and familiarize yourself with what is out there and who is reading what. This market is growing rapidly. I suggest you get in on the ground floor!"

CHAPTER 6

AUDITIONS: INTERPRETING THE READ AND TAKING DIRECTION

AT FIRST, I WAS KNOWN FOR "BUSINESS/ STRAIGHT" READS, and then I was known for high-energy reads — until the Home Base campaign came along. All of the sudden, I became the stereotype for the "flat" read. I didn't set out to do that. It just happened. I created different types of reads for each type of product according to what the advertiser was looking for. Sometimes, that's the best way to find different types of reads to add to your imaginary "Rolodex of voices."

It's very common to get known for a certain type of read, either based on your voice or an energy that you project. But no matter what you're reading, you've got to *start with the script.* Here are some pointers:
- Read the script to yourself to get a feel for it. This will help you understand the writer's intention as well as how the ad agency is trying to sell the product to the public. (Sometimes, simply by reading the copy and understanding the rhythm — as well as knowing what kind of voiceover work you usually book — you can get an indication of where to go with the script.)
- Look for adjectives describing the mood. If there are none, ask the casting director what the client is looking for.

- After you've found the mood description, apply that mood to the script.
- For TV, pay attention to the fonts used for the copy and how the copy is set up on the page. If it's a radio script, what's the music bed like? Sound effects?
- Read the copy aloud a few times in the proper mood.
- Imagine the person you'll be "talking to." (This is called *personalizing* the script.) It will make your read more specific and real.
- If you are reading for a campaign, once you've found the mood, apply that mood to all the scripts. To find an alternate read (another way of reading the script), add more adjectives, changing your mood. Remember, you still want to stay in the same basic emotional area that the spot's specs call for.

And here are some dos and don'ts that I hope will also be helpful:
- *Do* know what the product is and market it's geared to.
- *Don't* get ahead of what you know! Try to keep your reads simple and flowing. Find the rhythm.
- *Don't* assume you know how to sell the product better than the advertiser! The copy tells you most of what you need to know.

As I say, it's important to know as much as you can about what you are selling. If it's radio copy you're reading and there is no image, you've still got to know what the client is selling and what they're trying to say. You may not always be given the luxury of direction. You can tell a lot from the copy, from what it says, from what the product is, and from all the other clues we've already discussed. (For some samples of copy for TV and radio spots, see Appendix A.) If you do have a picture to go by (for TV or animation), this can help in determining character.

DIRECTION

Direction is usually written on the script. The direction does not, however, give you a complete or perfect answer to the puzzle of how to read the spot. Use the direction as a guide. If you do not have any direction to follow (this does happen sometimes), then you need to follow your instinct — and the casting director. If the direction that appears on the script confuses you, just realize that some of the ins and outs of this business will take time to learn. Your understanding of scripts, copy, specs, and direction will grow as you audition, practice, and take classes. The more jobs you book, the easier it will become to understand copy.

When you're auditioning, you may not always be told how the script will ultimately be used. Your agent may only know the time and place you must show up for the audition, and perhaps the name of the product. As you get more experience in the world of voiceovers, you will be able to recognize whether a script is for TV or radio by the way it is set up. Radio copy is pretty easy to spot — usually it will just have the length of the spot at the top, along with the name of the ad agency and the specs. The script for a TV commercial can be as simple as an image of a dog being petted by its owner, with a tagline underneath. Because the medium for which you're auditioning will affect your read, ask the casting director before you start if you're not sure which medium the spot is for.

Let's run through this copy for a made-up cat food commercial and analyze it:

> Violet Variety Cat Food. Make your cat purr for life!

First, decide what *type* of spot this is: What's the style of the spot? What type of read does it call for? The more copy you read, the easier these questions will be to answer.

Here are some adjectives that could be applied to this spot: soft, sexy, intimate, and playful. These adjectives will allow you to come up with a selling style and create a read. See how many reads we can come up with just from the name of the product and a tiny bit of copy? This is the same process you will go through with every commercial you read for. Now, try reading the Violet Variety Cat Food copy with one adjective, then another.

After you've done that, try another two or three reads, putting two or more of the sells together for each read. Try a sexy read and add another adjective. Record yourself, then listen to how your read sounds. Do you hear how each time you read the copy, a different vocal change and energy comes out of your voice?

Now, take a few minutes, grab your recorder, and look through the sample copy in Appendix A. Pick one or two spots. Spend some time looking at the direction and deciding what kind of sell would be most effective.

Let's try another bit of copy:

> There were 134,000 smoking-related deaths last year. Should I reserve a plot for you? This message has been brought to you by the California Anti-Smoking Alliance.

This is what's called a public service announcement, or PSA: an ad for a not-for-profit organization. Dealing with a serious subject, it tries to reach us with assertiveness, information, and a touch of sarcasm. The way you read the copy should reflect that. So give it a try: attempt this read with authority, knowledge, sarcasm, empathy, and warmth. Try giving it a straight, matter-of-fact read, then a sexy read, then a read with an edge.

PUSH/PULL BACK

Pushing and *pulling back* are terms applied to certain words or phrases within a script — or even to the entire script. How do you know which words or phrases to push? Which ones to pull back on?

Understanding the mood of the copy is the first step. Do not attempt to work your script *technically* before you find the mood. Work from the inside out. As I like to say, doing voiceovers is like baking a cake. You can't put the icing (i.e., the voice) on before you've mixed together the eggs and flour.

To *push* means to *stress* certain words. Other, similar terms used in voiceovers are *billboard, romance,* and *emphasize.*

Pull back means to go easy on the read, to underplay it, to be more casual, or loosen up the read. The terms *throw away* and *be off-the-cuff* have a similar meaning. By pulling back, throwing away, or being off-the-cuff, you give the read a more informal delivery.

Sometimes the copywriter will underline certain words or phrases so you will know which words they want you to emphasize or romance. Directors use both terms when asking actors to enunciate or play with a certain word or phrase in the script. This might be the product name, or simply words that the ad agency deems important. The copywriter might also include this information in the direction that appears in the script — or indicate it by using a bolder font or underlining those words.

Although the copy is written with certain beats and line readings in mind, it is up to you to make it natural and fresh. Don't overanalyze the copy. Read through the script, and apply your point of view, adjectives, and specs. If you find places to romance, underline them. Don't obsess over decisions about where or when to push the copy: anything that's too planned will sound fake. The most natural read that fits the attitude is the best choice. This is what is called *making it your own*! Overanalyzing only leads to losing the meaning of what you're saying.

ATTITUDE

Attitude is the point of view that you take with the script. When you hear a commercial, one of the first things you notice in the voiceover is the attitude. Attitude is just another term for point of view. Copy is generally written with a certain attitude in mind. The client has approved the writer's copy, and they want it read a certain way. This sometimes means that they will give you line readings and show you exactly how they want you to read the copy — including tone, timing, energy level, and feeling. (Line readings are generally given in the voiceover session itself.)

If you are auditioning or just interpreting the copy by yourself, you need to remember that you cannot read the client's and writer's minds. You don't know *exactly* what they want. Sometimes you'll book the job and hit the nail right on the head, and sometimes not. Your job is to *try* to give them what they want in the attitude they want. Copywriters hear things in a certain way, and it's up to them to decide if the read works for the product.

Hiring you for the job is only part of the process. They also have to please the client.

Sometimes the client and writer or producer will have different ideas on how to sell a spot. It is up to the producer and writer to get the right read from you, while making the client happy and giving them what they want without losing their original vision for the spot or campaign. If they book you on the job, they will tell you to emphasize certain words or to go up on a word or down on a phrase. You must make choices within the direction you are given. Once you're in the voiceover session, you may even be asked to do several different types of reads — even though they hired you on the basis of the read you gave in the audition! But be open to having a good time and playing with the script. Staying out of your own way and giving the client what they want is the most important thing you can do in a session.

DIFFERENT WAYS OF SELLING

Below are some different types of sells and what they mean. Experiment, making active choices about the moods you use and feel. If you feel sexy, you'll convey the message flirtatiously. If you feel bored, you'll convey that sense of boredom in the sell. If you feel invigorated — you've got it! — you'll convey excitement. Every read begins with a mood or point of view.

SOFT SELL

Soft sell is a term for a type of sell that is quieter or more intimate — usually for an actress selling products women tend to buy, or selling to an audience of women. The read should be gentle, romantic, warm, caring, loving, and feminine. A soft sell can be done in many different ways; these adjectives are just meant to give you a starting point from which you can experiment. Although a man can do a soft sell, the term *soft sell* rarely appears on a script intended for a male actor. The terms *light, off-the-cuff, real, warm,* or *easygoing* are used instead.

Here are a few kinds of products that generally call for a soft-sell type of read: lingerie, cat food, feminine hygiene products, makeup, hair care, and products relating to "sensitive" issues, such as health, medical, or dental problems. But don't let this list confuse you, because many of these products could just as easily be sold using a ...

HARD SELL

A hard sell is right at you and in your face. No playing around! This is a tough, strong, assertive read. In the 1970s, advertisers went for the hard sell in a big way. BUY! BUY! BUY! Then, in the '80s, they made a lot of fun of the hard sell — but you still were being pushed to BUY! BUY! BUY! In the '90s they just threw things in your face but acted like they didn't care. They got you on the subconscious level — the gut — but it was still BUY! BUY! BUY! It was still a hard sell. Just like the soft sell, the hard sell can be approached many different ways: loud, soft, strong, relaxed, angry, or happy, happy, happy! The wording and the direction are what make it a hard sell. Let the product and the copywriter's direction be the guide to your approach to this sell.

FLAT READ

In a flat read, you read the copy without energy or care. Although the read is laidback, it's meant to grab the listener's attention. This read is done in a calm, low monotone and at a relatively slow pace. A flat read is considered a "character" read. In a flat read, nothing affects you. Nothing is pushed. But you can still do a flat read many different ways. You can add any number of adjectives — flat but with some energy, flat but informative, flat with a smile (also called a wry read). The flat read, the dry read, and the wry read are all very similar, although there are subtle differences among them.

Within the flat read is dry, wry, off-the-cuff, thrown away, matter-of-fact, guy-to- guy, boredom, and sarcasm. (Any of these fit into the world of dry. You should always refer to specs and the script to fully understand the type of read they are looking for.)

STRAIGHT READ/CONVERSATIONAL READ

A straight read is matter-of-fact, off-the-cuff, and real. A straight read is usually businesslike, but it can also be conversational. As with the flat read, the straight read opens itself to many different interpretations. You can read something "straight yet informative."

You can read it "straight with a smile." Straight reads are often used when the advertiser just wants to sell you information. Period. But it's still a read — and a deliberate one. A straight read may be directed toward a more sophisticated audience. Rather than trying to hit consumers over the head or push them into buying, advertisers are trying to talk them into purchasing something by appealing to their wisdom and knowledge. Usually, scripts have many adjectives to describe what they are looking for. The read may call for more than just a straight read. It may say straight with a smile. Straight, upbeat. Business, warm. The businesslike read doesn't try to elicit laughs; it uses the product itself to impress the consumer.

You will hear the term *conversational* a lot. Advertisers love a conversational read. Why? Because it sounds natural. A conversational read is exactly like an everyday conversation. Nothing is phony. Conversational reads are very natural and not planned or forced. They're guy-to-guy, gal-to-gal. A lot of radio copy will include the direction "conversational." Conversational reads also often call for other adjectives: conversational and wry, conversational and informative, conversational and straight, or conversational and warm.

SEXY READ

A sexy read, obviously, tries to seduce the consumer. It may be relaxing, inviting, invigorating, nurturing, playful, teasing, cunning, or flirtatious. Many adjectives can help further define "sexy" — and may work for a particular product. Within your sexy read, use some of the adjectives just given to deepen your read and give it more pull. This is how you add life to your dialogue — by making choices within a general characterization.

HIGH ENERGY/ENERGETIC READ

This read is fun, playful, and excited. It summons your enthusiasm. You can certainly get any number of different reads out of the direction "energetic," depending on your vocal quality and your level of excitement. You can be energetic and fun. Energetic and relaxed. Energetic and conversational. Energetic and gregarious. Energetic and nervous. Certain products are typically sold in certain stereotypical ways. Certain types of sells just seem to go with certain products. For example, advertisers usually use a soft sell to pitch cat food and laundry detergent to a female audience, but a harder sell for SUVs and beer, which are typically pitched to men. As you learn to listen more closely to the commercials you hear, you may begin recognizing voices — and noticing that these voices (and a certain kind of sell) are often used for a specific kind of product. Pay attention to the voices, the sells, and the different attitudes they convey.

There are many kinds of reads and sells. I've only given you a few that you should know because they commonly come up in direction.

THE COMMERCIAL AUDITION

I got called for an audition in the Valley, forty-five minutes from where I was working as an assistant at a Los Angeles talent agency, and I had to lie to my boss to get there. It was for a campaign for a company called Home Base. They had seen everyone in town, including big names like Julie Kavner (Marge on *The Simpsons*). The audition specs called for a female with a flat, wry delivery.

Afterward, I thought it was the worst audition I had ever done. I went in and basically threw the read away — read it in a very flat, dry way). I called my agent and told him how badly I thought it had gone. Cut to: I booked the campaign for the next three years, and that job led to many others — and created an entirely new genre for women voiceover actors. The moral: Trust your gut, do the best job you can do, and then *let it go!*

If you've been called to audition, congratulations! You got one. (And it may have taken a while, too.) But now you need to know what to do. Chances are, your first audition won't come through an agent but rather through the work you've done up until this point: those classes, those nonunion projects you've worked on, and those contacts you've made. But whatever it was that got you in the door, you got it! Treat this voice audition like the first of many: you will be doing a lot of cold reading over the course of your voiceover career. Your job as a voiceover actor is to audition. And audition, and audition. You need to learn how to read great, often, and correctly — in that order — to book those jobs and make some money. A little luck and timing doesn't hurt either. Oh yeah, and that great voice!

BUT DON'T COUNT YOUR CHICKENS ...

When auditioning, it's important to keep in mind that you may not be right for that particular job. Being right for a job means being in the right vocal category and mood. You may be the wrong vocal quality or wrong mood simply because of your natural voice or by a choice you've made. You can't help age, gender, ethnicity, and vocal range, but you can learn tools and tricks to help you become "right" for as many jobs as possible. Being wrong for a job can simply mean in the wrong category. Even so, it's not wasted time: They've heard your voice, and maybe you'll be right for something down the road. You may read for a role and not book the job, even though you felt you did a great job. Every once in awhile, if you aren't booking, feel free to ask the booth director, casting director, or agent to give you an assessment of your reads. Your vocal quality is your natural sound when you speak. Your rhythm is the pace at which you speak. It and your tone determine whether you can match the writer's intent. What is the advertiser trying to say and how are they trying to say it? It's your job to try to convey the writer's intent during your audition. The rhythm with which you speak can convey the message correctly or incorrectly (to the ad agency's ears, that is). You can have a great read and a great audition but still not book the job. That's because you didn't hit the nail on the head from the writer's or ad agency's point of view. Having the wrong rhythm, emphasizing words in a way that they feel is inappropriate, pushing a read — these are all things that will keep you from booking the job.

If you have the vocal quality that the ad agency is looking for, you have a leg up. If they're looking for a man in his mid-thirties with a slight English accent — whose voice is upper-crusty, well-read, and authoritative — and if you fit that bill vocally, then you are one step closer to the job. But you still must compete against several other men who also fit this breakdown, or spec.

WHEN I AUDITION

When auditioning, the first and wisest thing to do is to read the copy, apply the specs, and use your personality (appropriately) to set you apart. Follow the cold reading steps every time you read. When I prepare for an audition, I read all the parts (if there is more than one character). I try to see what the writer's intent for the spot is: Is it humorous? Warm? Informative? Playful? This tells me how to read the copy — which mood or point of view I have to adopt. As the talent, I have to know *how* to tell the story before I can tell it.

YOUR MOOD = POV

Have you ever been in *no* mood at all? I didn't think so. You're always in some sort of mood. "Tired" is a mood. Even "numb" is a mood. Anxious, angry, bored, impulsive, nervous, excited — these are all moods that we've all been in at some time or another. And when you are auditioning, it's best to make *active* choices about your mood. This means that if the specs say I'm pregnant, about to give birth, and madly in love with my husband, I have to *act* that way. Never mind trying to fake it. I need to get into that emotion and act. My voice is a reflection of my mood. You can tell how someone feels by the tone of his or her voice.

This leads us to rhythm. The rhythm in which you speak is also dominated by your mood. Excited? Can't wait to tell someone the story of what just happened to you? What happens to the rhythm of your voice? Speeds up, right? Get a lot of words in quickly, don't you? Why? Because you can't wait to tell your friend that story! How do you breathe? Probably not as slowly as when you are in a calm, relaxed mood, sipping hot tea, and watching a sunset. If you go from being excited to being calm and relaxed, doesn't your voice reflect that change? Your voice is determined by your mood, and voiceovers are really just a reflection of your mood. As voiceover actors, we sell the public our mood and personality. Yes, the listeners are hearing a voice, but there is always some sort of mood behind that voice, selling in some particular way.

When I have an audition and I know I'm one of thirty, fifty, or even a hundred women trying out for the same role, the only unique thing I can bring to the table is my own perspective, my own point of view on the read. If I choose to ignore the specs that the ad agency has provided, that's my choice — but those specs are a blueprint for what the agency is looking for. If I don't have specs to go by, how will I know where I should be coming from? Just by reading some scripts, you know you're supposed to have fun with them or do them warmly, but these are pretty general instructions. That's why the specs usually try to lock you into something and get you going on the right road for that particular commercial.

It's also important to have an *alternate* read ready to add to your audition, in case the casting director lets you do another read. Have an idea of exactly what you think is right for the commercial, based on the specs and script, so that you can add a slight twist if you are asked for a different interpretation. This is where rhythm can come in handy. You've already got the initial mood. Then, let's say, you feel (or the casting director suggests) that you should slow down on the second read. You keep the same mood while slowing down your pacing and rhythm. Keep in mind that you're still reading within the time allotment, as well as the same general setup of the commercial. You're still paying attention to the script's exclamation points, question marks, font changes, or words that have been underlined for emphasis. Doing an alternate read doesn't mean changing the specs to something completely different from what the ad agency is looking for. But if you feel you could have warmed up the read, been more conversational, had more fun with it, added a bit of sophistication, then go for it in your alternate read. As long as it fits with the original specs and is different from your first take, it's fine.

In radio, it's fine to add a word or improvise a bit. Your audition is the time to explore some improv or add a "button" — a funny comment at the end of the spot. But be careful: learn the basics *before* you begin to improvise. And make sure you know when and how improvisation is appropriate. (Taking a class is a great way to find out.) A comedian friend of mine always complains that he never books a job in voiceovers. It turns out that he improvises during auditions quite a bit — in fact, every time he auditions. Casting directors were actually using him as a wild card — to change up the auditions and provide contrast for the other actors doing straighter reads. But his improv never worked for him; it actually got in the way of his booking a job.

COLD READING STEPS

1. Read the script to yourself, without acting, to get the writer's intent. See the moments, pauses, and beats. Find the humor, see the script.

2. Apply the specs. Learning to mix those adjectives into one great read is key!

3. Read half out loud, half to yourself — you're finding everything now. Getting a feel for the script. Add a person to talk to (close friend, hubby, mother, boss) in that mood.

4. Read the script aloud to get the flow of the copy and pacing.

▶ TIP: The minute you read to "everyone" you're reading to "no one." Picking a person is key in making specific choices. We don't talk at someone; we share information and stories with someone in a particular mood. Reading copy is a lot like speaking in life. The difference is, we don't pre-plan our moods and stories beforehand. With voiceover, we have to create the moment "now" even if we're not in that mood!

STEREOTYPING AND BRANDING

Listen to commercials on TV and the radio. What are the moods you hear in the voiceovers? Authoritative? Hip? Antagonistic? Pompous? Listening for these differences will help you understand vocal mood and range. Yes, it's true that once you book a certain job, you may find yourself doing that same voice or mood over and over again. This is the world of stereotyping, and there's nothing wrong with it. If this voice or mood lends itself to certain products, and if you're making a lot of money, who cares? If your "warm, young mom" voice is working for you, apply it to any and all reads that fit that spec. At least you know that advertisers like your voice and that you are bookable. As long as you are making active choices while you read copy and do jobs, you are still coming at the work from a new perspective. Even if every job sounds like "warm, young mom," each product is different, and so each spot will have a different quality from that of the other spots you do.

You may be asked to re-create a vocal quality that you used for a particular spot, which in turn may lead to a campaign. In a campaign, your voice will appear on several commercials for the same brand or product. You may be reading different copy, but your mood remains the same. In fact, your voice becomes part of the brand, and people start to associate your voice with that product. Other ad agencies may also begin to associate you with that particular vocal quality, that particular selling style. They may like the way your voice sounds, the quality it brings out, and the way the public responds to your voice, and they may want to hire you for their spots or campaigns.

While you're becoming bookable for a certain type of read, continue auditioning for work requiring other moods and styles. It's important that your agent doesn't keep you from these other auditions, even though they may seem a little outside the box. Just because you are booking lots of "warm, young mom" reads doesn't mean that you shouldn't be handed other copy that is right for you and your age group. It is your responsibility to remind your agent of your full ability and range as an actor (and to make sure these other moods and styles are represented on your demo).

STAPLE CLIENTS

Yes, certain qualities in your voice lend your voice to certain roles. Yet many actors are able to become staple clients with their voiceover agencies, meaning they are right for several different types of reads. They are more versatile and can represent everywoman or everyman. Being a staple client means you'll be auditioning several times a week, which, of course, opens the door to many more opportunities. And the more opportunities you get (and the better you get at your reads), the better chance you have of booking jobs!

As I've said before, it's very important to nail your reads every time you audition, regardless of whether you book the job or not. Each time you do a read well, you get closer to booking jobs. A spot will eventually come around that you *will* book; it may just take some time. I always say, "Treat this hobby as a career, but know it's just a hobby." That is, put your energy and time into it, but know that you can't take it too personally.

It's a competitive business, and it stays competitive no matter how long you've been in it. It's important to follow the trends. There are always new voices and character styles out there, dominating the marketplace for a period of time. Your voice and style may have been hot years earlier, but it's no longer the new, hot voice. The world of advertising is ever-changing. Your voice may not fit the style that advertisers are currently looking for. The only thing you have power over in the voiceover business is to give a good read and go on with your day.

DEALING WITH YOUR FEAR

Don't let the audition scare you. Don't drive yourself or the casting director crazy by overanalyzing. After all, this is only one audition; there will always be another around the corner. Still, you should treat each audition as an opportunity. Be prepared, and do your best. There are a lot of voice actors but only so many auditions; all you can do, really, is the best job you can, and cross your fingers. One day, a job will come along that you will book.

The casting director will tell you if the commercial is for radio or TV, and whether it's national, local, regional, or cable. But, actually, it's usually easy to tell if it's radio or TV copy by the way it's written. TV scripts usually have the audio/voice copy on the right side of the paper and a description of the corresponding video/visual on the left. Radio copy will be set up in paragraph form so that it can be read easily. (Sometimes, scripts for TV spots do not contain a description of the visual. If you're unsure, simply ask the casting director whether the spot is for TV or radio.) The copy will most likely have the name of the advertising agency on it (unless it's a top secret project).

Put the same amount of professionalism into every audition you do. If it's your first audition ever, you might mention it to the casting director — but don't make a big deal out of it. Make sure that you get to the audition early enough that you have time to read over the copy and know the way you'd like to read before you get into that voiceover booth. It always helps to act like you know what you're doing, even if you don't.

DRESSING FOR THE AUDITION

Considering that I go through most of my days in sweats (I work out in the morning when I don't have a session), it's safe to say that the dress code is casual. It's a running joke with voiceover people that whenever we see someone dressed up and wearing makeup, we casually ask, "on camera?" One of the treats of the voiceover world is that you are being heard, not seen.

That said, it's always a plus to look professional. Sometimes you might meet with the client; although you are being considered strictly for your voice, these same clients probably do the casting/producing for the on-camera part of the spot you are auditioning for (if it's for TV, that is). I've had the experience of booking the on-camera part after the client saw what I looked like, simply because they liked my look. I had already booked the voiceover session; they were going to begin casting for the on-camera role, but they chose me. When I know that I'm going to a session or a studio, I'll try to get a little dressed up. As always, the way you dress makes an impression.

THE AUDITION PROCESS

You will get the call for an audition from your agent or, in some cases, the client. If you don't have an agent but dropped off your demo CD with a casting house, the casting director will call you directly. Having liked what he or she heard on the CD, the casting director will bring you in because the house has something you're right for. Many people still get auditions this way.

The agent or casting house will give you a very precise time for the audition: for example, 10:35 AM or 4:50 PM. Auditions are scheduled at regular intervals — every ten or fifteen minutes. You may be paired with someone, which means you really need to be on time. If it is absolutely impossible to make it at a certain time, let the person who called know when you respond to the call. If possible, they will try to reschedule you. But realize that auditions happen very quickly, and they may not be able to accommodate your schedule.

NO ADVANCE COPY

The cold read is the essence of the voiceover audition. Unlike auditions for other acting jobs, voiceover auditions do not fax, mail, or deliver the copy to you ahead of time. (The exceptions are animation and some narration auditions.) You can't pick up the copy beforehand or take it home to study. The voiceover audition process just does not work this way; the copy is available only at the audition session. You therefore have to learn how to be spontaneous and to prepare yourself quickly. If you feel shaky and insecure, get to the audition early, find the copy you are reading (don't sign in if you're early and want to study it), and go into another room, a hallway, or outside to study it. Do whatever you can to be ready.

SIGNING IN AND WAITING

Get to the audition early — by twenty minutes or so — so you've got time to read over the copy and specs. You can ask your agent if you can pick up an animation script the day before an audition, but it will only be possible if the production office has a copy and you are reading for a large role. For the most part, you will just be called and given a time to show up to read.

The waiting room will most likely have a sign-in sheet, which is mandatory for all SAG and AFTRA auditions. The copy will be in the waiting room. Because the individual auditions follow one another very closely, there may be several other voiceover actors there (from several different agencies) whom you will be reading against.

There may be actors who will read with you in a group read, or you may be reading "wild" by yourself, even though there are other actors roles. You also may have been brought in for a one-character script, known as "a single." You may know these actors or you may not. If it is a group read, you will not know with whom you are partnered until the casting director comes out and tells you, unless it's written somewhere near the sign-in sheet.

EXAMPLE:

Mom	**Dad**	**Announcer**
Beth Smith	Dan Applebee	Danny Mann
Diane Willis	Steve Mackell	Terri Apple

This is a sheet that shows you the roles being auditioned and the person(s) you are reading with. It may be listed by time, so you know who your partner is. If you are reading "wild," it means that although there are several roles in the script, the casting director (or ad agency) may choose to have read you separately. This means that you will need to read all the characters, but only read *for* your role. You will read each line, with a slight beat between each line, staying connected (in mood and pace) with the script as it's written. Casting directors do not read the other parts. Neither do the booth directors. It's up to you to understand the feel of the script and read it as if you understand what's going on. You may do the voiceover session the same way. It's up to the individual hiring you for the job.

If you know who you're reading with and they are there, you can ask them if they want to "run it," or practice. If they don't, don't get discouraged. Some people have been in the business for a long time and don't feel the need to study their copy with someone. Whether you're reading alone or with a group, you must wait until you're called to audition.

But there is a mandatory one-hour time limit on waiting periods per union rules. (It's up to you to say something in nonunion situations. If you feel you're being taken advantage of, say something — in a nice way.) If you have to wait longer than an hour, the union fines the casting house and they have to pay you a fee. Try to be patient and easy to work with. This doesn't mean you don't want to say something if the hour is coming up, you just want to make sure you aren't stepping on any toes that may hire you in the future.

PREPARING YOURSELF

The waiting room for a voiceover audition can be one big party. Remember, you are dealing with actors — and usually funny ones, at that. They all have a story to tell. (The atmosphere in the waiting room can, however, vary depending on the time of day and the amount of copy.) If you want to ensure peace and quiet for yourself, you'll usually have to go into another room or move outside.

Some people just look over the copy once or twice before going in to read. Others spend ten or more minutes underlining the words they want to emphasize and marking the copy up with arrows indicating how they want to inflect certain words. Use any method that helps you give the best read you can. I think the easiest way of breaking down a script is to follow these steps:

1. Read the script objectively to yourself. Determine if it's for TV, radio, or animation. Find the natural flow within the writing. Identify the sound effects (SFX) and the music bed, which will be indicated on the script.

2. Look for the specs. Now it's time to attach your mood to the copy, per the specs.

3. Read the script half out loud/half to yourself (not a loud whisper, but not full volume). Attach a person. Decide then who to talk to. They do not have to love BMWs, ice cream, or that particular shampoo. It doesn't matter if they like the product, you're simply telling one person in that particular mood. The other aspect of telling one person is where you are telling them — this is a real situation and place. This real situation allows you to be at that "vocal level" without pushing your voice, worrying about how loud (or soft) you should be. Breathing should be natural as well because you've chosen a mood. Just breathe where it's natural for that mood and per the beats in the script (pauses, periods, etc).

4. Read aloud at the exact vocal level and in the mood and tone you will be using to read the script when you get on the microphone. Read the copy a few times.

At the audition itself, do not let the microphone intimidate you. The microphone is merely a tool. The read on the microphone is an extension of what you've already worked out outside of the booth. Do not become more intimate (quieter) or forget your point of view or whom you're talking to just because you're in front of the mike. This is why it's so important to workout and practice with a great coach. You have to learn how to work off of the microphone (finding your read) just as much as on the mike (after you've found the read). You are still making "fresh" choices (actively reading in the there and now) while you're on the mike. There are moments to play, have fun, and take beats or pauses, which are important in understanding the script and telling the story correctly. Understanding how to take notes and direction is just as important as getting the audition itself. You must understand what key terms mean and how to apply them. Your ability to prepare yourself quickly will improve the more you audition.

SOME KEY TERMS

(SEE SKIN THE CAT ON PAGE 340 FOR A FULL LIST.)

Warm it up: add a bit more smile, friendliness, but not louder.

Pull it back: a bit less of whatever you are doing, but not different.

Have more fun with it: a general term used when someone seems stiff or too polished; reading with a bit more "looseness" or "playfulness."

Romance it more: adding "flavor" and pushing (not prodding) words; landing within words a bit longer, to create more passion and color in your read. You have to learn the difference between being in the mood and allowing those colors to come out vs. pushing the words simply to make them stand out.

Throw it away: this means you may be sounding too prepared or "ready." You can also sound too "selly," strong, bright, friendly, upbeat, etc. Throwing a read away means to just say it and be done with it. It's both a technical term and a creative term. You must know when and where to apply it, based on knowing the script and specs.

Any of the above terms (and all listed in Skin the Cat) can be used in auditions and voiceover sessions.

IN THE BOOTH

When it's your time to read, the casting director or an assistant will come to get you. There is also a chance that the commercial's director or copywriter may be there to direct you — especially if you are auditioning at the advertising agency itself. (This is very common in New York City and Chicago.)

If there are headphones available, they will either be on the floor or on a mike stand. If you want to use them while recording your audition, wait for the sound engineer to tell you it's okay, then put them on and adjust them until they're comfortable. (The headphones will be marked *L* for "left" and *R* for "right," and you will be able to adjust the volume.) Some casting facilities do not provide headphones. Using headphones is a personal preference: You do not have to put them on. If you do not wear them, you won't be able to hear your own voice the same way those listening to you can hear it.

When I teach I encourage my students to use headphones so they get comfortable hearing themselves and learning how to manipulate certain moods, reads, and styles. I think it's important to be able to hear yourself inside the "cans" while reading and acting. I also think it's important to be able to hear yourself in your headphones during playback and understand the direction someone has given you. This enables you to better understand how to warm up your voice or to pull back if necessary.

The casting director will speak to you through the talkback microphone, which allows the people outside the recording booth to communicate with you. The casting director will ask for a level — at which point you should read a portion of the copy at the same sound level at which you will record.

Now is the time to ask any questions you may have. If you don't understand a word or phrase, are confused by what the ad agency is looking for in terms of voice quality or character, or if you are concerned about the pace, ask! Keep your questions brief, however. You're just one of many actors who are reading, and the casting people really don't want to deal with anyone who is insecure. But if you truly have a concern, voice it.

If the copy does not say what the timing is and you need to know, ask about that, too. Doing the read in the proper period of time may help you book the job. If the ad agency hears fifteen reads for a thirty-second spot but you were the only one actually to read it in thirty seconds, they may go with you just because they know that you can get the read done in time. Most casting directors will not let you go much over the time allotted for the commercial, but they are more concerned with getting a good read from you to put on the audition CD.

The closer you are in mood, the closer you'll be to the time (although some radio copy is overwritten.) But, in general, the closer you are in mood and rhythm to what the advertiser is looking for, the closer you'll get to the timing of the spot. Don't worry if you're a second or two over or under; once you hit the mood, you'll be able to adjust that aspect in the voiceover session itself.

The better you get at reading and understanding scripts, the better you'll get at nailing the mood and reading to time.

THE READ

Should you sit or stand while reading? This is up to you. Personally, I feel that you get a fuller vocal read by standing. Your diaphragm can get cut off when you sit, and a lot of casting houses already have the microphone set up for you at the standing level. (They just adjust it for height when each new person comes in to read.) Standing also allows you to move your body more freely, which is especially important if you're creating characters. The casting director will ask you to slate your name and begin. (*Slating* is just stating your name and the name of your agent or agency, if you have one.) You will then begin take number 1.

If you mess up, they will stop recording and begin again. You might only read one to three times, depending on whether the casting director is getting what he or she wants. Read the copy as many times as they ask you to. If you're asked to read again, the casting person will tell you what they didn't get with the last read, and what they want this time. In fact, if they don't like the way you're reading something, they may even stop you in the middle and have you start over.

If *you* ask to do another take or an alternate read and they let you do it, it had *better be* a different read. Don't waste their time. Follow your instinct. If you want to get a little crazy or off-base with the alternate read or you feel the copy should be read a certain way, ask if you can do a take that way. Don't go overboard, though. Remember, the casting director has a lot of people's voices to record.

The casting director will move you smoothly through the audition. He or she may ask for a few different types of reads (and may send more than one take to the agency). He or she may play back the audition for you, letting you listen to what you have just done and asking you to make changes in the next take. Take this opportunity to analyze your work. The casting director may have you do another take because he or she wants you to do it differently — maybe more laid-back, or warmer, or whatever. Or he or she may let you choose how you want to do it the second time around. But most of the time, casting directors will want the first take to reflect what they and the ad agency are looking for. (By the way, one of the best compliments you can receive is having the casting director be happy with your read.)

IMPROVISING

Improvising is sometimes encouraged and sometimes not. It's a touchy area. If you feel that improvising will help, take the risk — but I'm a big believer in improvising *within* the lines that are written. This means following the script but romancing certain words more, playing with the copy a little bit, and adding sounds that are natural to the character. It doesn't mean changing the word *house* to *mansion.* The writer has written the spot in a specific way for a specific reason, and the voiceover actor is there to get the words across to the audience the way the copywriter wants them said.

Many voiceover actors will improvise with radio spots. There is more room for improvisation in radio. If you are reading for a "wild and crazy guy" and you are supposed to "have fun with it," then feel free to improvise a little. Just be prepared to pull back for your next take. The casting director will tell you if it's too much.

In radio you can use much more of your personality to tell the story. There is a beginning, middle, and end to a radio spot, even if there's a "slice of life" feel to the script. Actors doing radio spots together will tend to "out-button" one another. A *button* is a word or short phrase — usually humorous — that's added at the end of a spot. Sometimes, one actor will add a button and then another actor will add *another* button — this can go on for quite a while! It's best, though, to tell the other actors that you will be putting a button on at the end of your character's line, so they're prepared.

For TV, though, you should read the copy as written. Don't improvise or (for example) laugh for a TV spot, unless the script calls for it.

WHEN THE AUDITION IS OVER

When you're done reading, thank the casting director and walk out of the room. If the script in the booth was placed there for all the actors to use, then don't take it with you. If you were using your own marked-up copy of the script, and the casting house allows it, you can take that one home if you like.

You can never go into the audition room to hear what someone else is doing, nor can you ask to hear your read after the fact. If you don't like the way you read, a casting director will sometimes let you re-read, if you ask. But if you were not given any notes or directional changes while you were in the audition, they were probably happy with what you did. Feeling like you could have read better or differently is inevitable, especially when you're first starting out, but the more you read and the better you get, the more you will learn to trust your instinct and judgment, and simply move on.

A FEW DOS AND DON'TS

Here are a few things to keep in mind while auditioning:
- *Do* make sure that you felt natural and confident and that you did the kind of read you set out to do and that they asked for — in other words, that you did the best job you could.
- *Do* pat yourself on the back.
- *Do* let the read go after you've left the audition. Don't second-guess yourself after you've read.
- *Do* take the copy with you, if they allow you to. It's always good to practice with later.
- *Do* thank the casting people for having you come in to read. They spend a lot of time organizing their lists and deciding whom to bring in. They narrow it down from quite a few people, so the fact that they thought of you means they like you and think you have a chance of booking the job.
- *Do* leave them a current demo CD. You can hand it to them, drop it off if you see an office around, or mail it to them.
- *Do* leave quietly and quickly. Standing around and gabbing may give them the impression that you have no other

auditions (let them think you're busy and working) and may distract people who are getting ready to audition.
- *Do* forget about it and head to your next audition with a positive attitude.
- *Don't* ask them to critique you. You can ask your agent to call them later if you feel the need for feedback. (Your agent may or may not do this, depending on the casting house and its policies.)
- *Don't* ask for advice. The casting people are busy, and the audition is not the time or the place. If you want advice, ask the casting director if you could drop by for five minutes some afternoon or during a slow period.
- *Don't* call your agent to see if you got a callback. Your agent will call you if you book the job or if they express interest in hearing you again.

GETTING THE CASTING DIRECTOR TO REMEMBER YOU

The best thing you can do, of course, is to nail your read. Be polite, nice, and professional. Bring something unique to your read. Give it your signature, or demonstrate a certain flair with the copy. The casting director (or ad agency exec) knows that all the people they're auditioning have the potential to do the spot. They know that each of the ten actors they've called has the voice it takes to book the job. They expect you to know how to break down a script and read it within the specs that the copy calls for.

Always be as quick in the booth as possible. Don't waste their time with silly, irrelevant questions. If you have a current demo CD that they don't have, leave it. Many casting directors audition for several commercials a year and deal with a lot of the same advertising agencies over and over again, so you may go back to the same casting house many times throughout the year.

SPECIAL KINDS OF AUDITIONS

The audition process doesn't always work exactly the same way. You may be asked to audition with a scratch track. You may be called back to audition again. Or you might have to do what's called a demo. Here's some more information about each of these special cases.

SCRATCH-TRACK AUDITIONS

A scratch track is a non-air, demo version of the commercial for which you will be doing the voiceover. At an audition, you may be able to watch a scratch track and read "to picture" while watching it. Seeing the picture will give you an idea of the mood and style of the spot. Sometimes, someone in the creative department at the ad agency may even have recorded the copy for the voiceover on the scratch track — as a placeholder of sorts — to begin to give the client (and you) an idea of the mood and attitude of the final spot. Recording to picture is usually done if the talent is hired by request or if it is very important for the spot to be recorded in an exact amount of time.

A scratch-track audition can also be done for radio. Obviously, radio copy doesn't contain notes on visuals. (See the sample copy for TV and radio ads in Appendix A.) A radio scratch track will be an unfinished audio version of the commercial for you to follow along with once you go into the booth. On the scratch track, you will hear a voice (usually the writer or producer of the spot) reading the copy. Do not get confused by this voice. You will not record your voice while the scratch track is playing. It is merely an aid to help you better prepare for your read, to guide your timing, or to demonstrate a vocal tone and style.

The casting director will play the commercial a few times so that you can get a feel for it. Take mental notes, or write some notes on the copy — places to take beats, places to go faster, which words are spoken with which visual (if it's a TV commercial). The ad agency wants your voice to match the spot's timing and visuals. Of course, if you book the job, you will redo your read when you go in for the actual recording session. When a commercial is partially completed, a scratch-track audition is used to get a feel for how it will sound with your voice.

CALLBACKS

Callbacks are not as common in voiceovers as in on-camera work. Usually, the client will listen to the audition CD once and decide which voiceover actor to hire for the job. If, however, you are called back, you will be asked to come in and read again, sometimes as soon as the next day. But you might also be called back a week later — or a month later. It all depends on when the commercial is being recorded.

If the agency can't make a final decision or hasn't yet heard what it wants, you may be called back, either to the ad agency or the casting house, to read again. They might be unsure whether to use a man or a woman, or they might be having trouble deciding between several different types of voices. Treat this audition just as if it were the first. Be on time, and study the copy. They may give you different direction. Follow what they say, and read the copy again.

A callback means that you are in the running for the job. If you've gotten a callback and want to know if they've cast the job, ask your agent. Most likely, he or she will know — or can call the ad agency to find out. Sometimes, however, commercials are scrapped altogether. Perhaps nothing worked: the copy, the concept, or the voices. Or the client simply might not like the commercial that the ad agency wrote. They might drop the campaign or hire a different ad agency. There's a lot more involved than just your voice.

DEMOS

A demo is a non-air version of a spot. An ad agency may be using it to bid on an account that it's trying to win away from a competing firm. Or an agency may recruit a group of "civilians" (people not in the business) to listen to or watch the demo spot and voice their reactions. If the demo is eventually broadcast using your voice, you will then be paid the higher scale rate (also called an "upgrade") as well as a residual for each time the spot airs. The unions keep track of what is aired, and if your commercial does air, you will then be paid accordingly.

If the demo is a nonunion job, the terms will be negotiated by you (or your agent), the producer, the writer, and the director. If you want the experience, work for less money. A nonunion, non-air demo is still worth doing if you need it for your CD. You can request the CD from a nonunion demo job, and if the commercial airs, you can negotiate a further fee based on the fact that it aired. Nonunion commercials usually only pay a single fee. Budgets are small, and there are no residuals.

Demo jobs are fairly common. The more people at an ad agency involved in a spot, the more creative minds there are. This means more discussion and less agreement on the spot. They may not even know if they want to go male or female. The demo allows all parties involved to pull you into a recording studio and work with you for up to an hour and a half. This is the maximum time, per union rules, that one session can run. If they use you for longer than that, they will have to pay you the demo fee again.

Usually, they will bring you in and have you read the copy a number of ways. They will not let you know right then if you've booked the spot, because they'll still be seeing other people and discussing the final outcome with the client. If, months later, you happen to see the spot on the air, but with another actor doing the voiceover, it just means that they decided to go a different way with the spot. The voice that airs may have nuances that are similar to yours — but with differences that made the agency choose the other actor over you. Sometimes you won't know the reason for their choice.

I once did a demo for a campaign for Nestlé Sensations. I auditioned, then got called back. After the callback, the ad agency called my agent and hired me for a demo. I went back to the ad agency's recording facility and did four spots, each several different ways. I heard nothing. Several months later, I had my agent call the ad agency to see if the spot would be airing. The ad agency said that they were still studying the spots and weren't really sure if they would ever play. I still have not heard them on the air and I'm not sure if they will ever come out. I got a one-time demo fee, and that was it. But if they ever do air, I will be paid an upgrade and will begin seeing residuals every time they air.

BEFORE YOU READ

QUESTIONS TO ASK YOURSELF

Here, just to help refresh your memory, are some questions to ask yourself before you audition.

Who am I talking to?

Finding out the targeted demographic and age group for the commercial helps you discover whom you are talking to — and therefore your point of view and mood.

What am I saying?

First, read the commercial to yourself. Then read it again, this time aloud. Look at the specs. Understand what the copy says. How is the product being sold? Is the commercial funny? Sad? Does it push you into buying the product subtly or boldly? Get what kind of story or message the commercial is pushing. Every piece of copy tells a story, even if it's badly written.

What kind of a message am I trying to convey?

Am I trying to scare teenagers into being aware? Am I trying to teach responsibility to drivers? Do I want the audience to subscribe to a certain newspaper, buy a certain brand of toilet paper? Am I trying to open your eyes to the beauty of a particular brand of contact lenses? The words, my voice, and the image (if it's for TV) will sell the product.

What is the mood or attitude of the spot?

The mood and attitude are the feelings you get when you read the spot. Is it sophisticated? Alluring? Funny? Is the copy trying to make the audience laugh? Is it serious? Hearing the voiceover on TV or the radio after it has come out may give you a good idea of what the client was going for on that particular spot. Sometimes it's hard to understand all the pieces until you hear a commercial on the air. But even then it may not make much sense to you. You must resign yourself to that. That's the way the client and ad agency wanted to convey their message. It's what worked for them.

What are the specs telling me in terms of how to read the spot?
The description on the copy or the casting director's instructions will tell you what the copywriter is looking for, what the attitude is. Most likely, the script will include some adjectives that try to convey what the copywriter is looking for in terms of character, vocal quality, and mood/style/sell. Audition accordingly.

How do I find the rhythm in a spot?
Usually, just reading the copy will reveal its natural rhythm. But the way the copy is set up on the page, the font that's used, and the style of the spot, as well as the music bed, sound effects, and anything else that's happening in the spot (including the visuals in a TV spot) will help you break the copy down to find its natural rhythm. Part of your job as voiceover talent is finding the rhythm in each spot you read.

WHAT'S NEXT?

Okay, so now you've done it — you've completed the audition. Now what? Now forget about it and move on. Don't start calling everybody to see whether you booked. But *do* do the following things:

- Write down the name of the ad agency and send them a current CD.
- Keep the copy to practice with.
- Keep a record of all the contact people at all the ad agencies you audition for (and the agencies' addresses), so that you can send them holiday cards, mass mailings, and so on.

These are all smart business tips and will help you get future jobs. As for this audition? Let me say it again: Forget about it! Once you've read, it's over with. Move on to the next one. If you book the job, you might find out later that same day, or the next day, or two weeks later, or six months later. You never know when a job will come around.

Auditioning can turn into a numbers game even if all your reads are good. You might book the job with your first audition, or you might not book anything until the hundredth audition. Each audition leads to the next. You will get better each time. Keep at it, and have fun. Somewhere along the way, you'll book a job. By then, you'll be scheduled for five auditions and three callbacks — and you'll have to check your date book.

VOICE TO VOICE
AN INTERVIEW WITH CARROLL DAY KIMBLE

Carroll Day Kimble is the head of Carroll Voiceover Casting, one of the top voiceover casting houses in Los Angeles. The agency has cast several national commercial campaigns and is always open to new talent.

How do you go about the casting process?
First, the client calls me; then they fax over the script. I spend a lot of time imagining a voice for the spot. I listen to CDs. I remember the voices of people I've called in. My clients rely on me to bring in the ten or so best voices for the job. I usually don't put a lot of voices on the CD — just ones I think could book the job. Then I call the agencies, and the talent comes in. If a casting director calls you in, you have a much better chance of booking the job.

How do you find the talent to bring in?

Usually through the talent agencies. I also have developed relationships with talent and will continue to bring them in if I feel they have read well.

Will you listen to a CD that someone has dropped off?
Sure. I prefer to go through an agent, but only because if they book the job I know exactly where to find them. Depending on the spot, sometimes I have to cast very quickly.

If you hear a CD you like, would you recommend the person to an agent?
Sure. If I hear something really unique, I may call an agent I know well and say, "Hey, you've got to hear this guy!" It's really helpful to be in the unions, though.

Do you have a stable of talent that you call in?
Yes. Every casting director has some talent they can rely on to deliver 100 percent every time.

How does one get in the stable?
Relationships develop over time. I like someone with range, someone who takes direction really well. Someone who brings life to the script! An actor who is passionate about what they do, how they read, will blow me away.

What do you like from an actor once they come in and read?
It's a casting director's dream to know that a talent can walk in and nail it on the first or second take.

Do you have any influence once the CD goes out? Influence as to whom they hire for the job?
Sometimes the client will call for my recommendation. Other times, I might call them and say, "Hey, Terri Apple nailed that read." They may listen or they may not. Usually it's up to several writers and producers. Other times, they will call me just to book the spot. I'll read it and begin my casting process and think of who to call in or book for the spot.

Does a client hire more than one casting house at a time?
Rarely. Usually, that only happens if the first casting house couldn't find anyone suitable. Sometimes the casting specs will change as well.

What would you say to an actor who goes from being busy to slow and back again?
The business changes. Sometimes there are specific casting specs. They want a really raspy smoker's voice in a male or a smooth, raspless voice in a woman. It depends on the client, the job, and the season. Everything changes. Women with texture were in. Then they're not. Then it's back again. Just depends on what sells at the time to the client.

So what's the philosophy for actors to follow?
Just keep working and practicing. The ultimate goal is to get out to the casting houses and read!

OTHER KINDS OF AUDITIONS

Previously we dealt with one type of audition — the typical audition for a radio or TV commercial. Now, let's take a closer look at some of the other kinds of auditions you might be called for.

ANIMATION

The animation audition follows the same process as that for commercials, although you will probably go to Disney, Warner Bros., or the production facility producing that particular animated series or film rather than to an independent recording studio. Or you may go to a casting house that's doing the casting for an animated series, video game, or TV show.

Once again, you will enter a waiting room and sign in. You will most likely know which character you are reading for because your agent will have told you when he or she called you with news of the audition. Then again, there may be several parts for you to try out for, each requiring a different vocal quality — or the casting director may love your voice and think you might be right for several different parts. There is also the chance that the casting director or production house will call you in without being sure just what they want you to read for.

In any case, you will show up and look over the copy they ask you to look at. For an animation audition, you may be given a sketch of the character and a verbal description as well as the copy itself. A picture is a great tool for deciding what kind of voice to try. You may see a drawing of an elephant wearing boxer shorts and have to come up with your own version of how that elephant should sound. The verbal description may contain several elements. For example, it might say, "Flippo is slow but not dumb, pensive yet determined. He's a tough, rebellious teenager with a heart of gold." This kind of description is very common. Your job is to interpret how you think Flippo should sound.

In animation, you really have to bring the written words to life. There won't be a television monitor at the audition showing your character in action. The only visual you will have is the sketch. Sometimes the animator will be at the audition, but at other times, the animated show won't be anywhere near completion. Maybe all that the animators will have at this point are character sketches and a story line. They may be waiting for the voiceover actors to flesh out the characters they've drawn before they come up with an entire show. They may be waiting to hear voices that they feel fit with the characters they've imagined to complete the process.

If you are called in to read for more than one character (which happens quite often), just find the right changes in your voice and perform the different characters in the ways that fit what you think they should sound. Unlike commercial copy, audition copy for animation — also called "sides" — is often available to be picked up or copied beforehand so that you can study it. Ask your agent for the sides, or drop by the studio to pick them up. Take them home to work on them a day or two before if you are able to.

Sometimes there will be a completed script for you to read for an animated movie or TV series. This will give you a full sense of the story line and of how your character develops throughout the show. In an animation audition, you'll want to make sure to give the character you're reading for lots of color and depth. If Flippo is falling over the side of a cliff only to land safely on a cloud, incorporate that idea into your read. Make sure you sound like Flippo falling off the cliff (exasperated noises and all) only to be comforted by the cushioning of a feather-filled cloud (ahh!). The character must feel lifelike. As an actor, you have to make *active choices.*

If you don't book the job, you'll be able to see who booked the part when the show comes out. Sometimes the writers, producers, and director are looking for something very specific. At other times, they may have *thought* they were going one way with the casting but then decided their original specs just weren't right for the character — even though you read perfectly for the specs they gave you. Or another actor may fit the vocal job perfectly and blow them away. Taking that animation class and having an up-to-date animation CD is the key to staying ahead of the game.

LOOPING

To get into looping, you will need to find the loop groups in your area and give them a call. Find out if they will accept your CD. They may offer classes or allow you to come and sit in to watch and see what it's like to loop. (You may have to pay a fee for the privilege.) This is a very good way to break into the business, since there aren't that many loop groups, and it's a pretty small niche. (Looping also pays well, which adds to its exclusivity.)

Once you've hooked up with one or two loop groups, it will be easier to network with other loopers, find out about other projects, and get additional work. Looping on a film or TV show can mean *big* residuals. You can also contact post-production facilities and production companies or networks to find out how you can become part of their stable of loopers. Most loop groups are in the larger cities where many TV shows are shot and films are produced, so if you want to loop, it pays to live in Los Angeles, New York, or Chicago.

DUBBING

Don't confuse looping with dubbing. Dubbing means matching your voice to that of an actor on screen — in other words, recording *over* what's already there. Many dubbing jobs are translations from one language into another, so if you're fluent in a foreign language, this may be a perfect career for you.

At a dubbing session, you go into a studio in which a chair and monitor have been set up. The copy in front of you is in the language you'll be speaking. The scene will come on the screen in the language it in which it was originally recorded. You will then match the tonality of the voice you are hearing (sounding as much like the person on screen as possible) and say the words to match the actor's mouth movement. Dubbing requires lots of patience and talent.

Call dubbing houses to find out about dropping off your CD and auditioning. (It's especially good to find out which dubbing house in your area specializes in the language you know.) Foreign voiceover actors work all the time, dubbing TV shows like *Desperate Housewives* and *Grey's Anatomy* for foreign markets, as well as miniseries, made-for-TV movies, and feature films.

PROMOS

TV and radio promos encourage viewers and listeners to stay tuned for upcoming shows. Promos are done for network shows, their affiliates, cable TV stations, and shows in syndication. The major TV networks are ABC, NBC, CBS, and FOX. Affiliates are the local stations in cities around the country that broadcast shows for the networks as well as their own local programming. Cable TV stations (like CNN) are not available via public airwaves but only by subscribing through a local cable service provider (although many cable TV stations are available nationally). A show in syndication has been sold to run in whatever market will pay money to run it. Shows that have either been in production for a long time (like *The Simpsons*) or that are no longer in production but have run for many years (like *Seinfeld*) are now in syndication on both network and affiliate stations across the country.

Voice actors are hired to do promos for networks, affiliates, cable stations, and shows in syndication. Network promos and affiliate promos are similar types of jobs. The same voice actor may be hired for both, or the local market may decide to hire a different talent to voice its station's promos for a particular show to differentiate it from its mother network. Promo copy is usually very short: "Tonight at nine on Fox 11, *Desperate Housewives*."

The purpose of a promo is to either prevent people from changing stations or to get them to tune in to a program at a specific time later on. Bumpers are a special kind of promo that run *during* a TV show, rather than beforehand. During a bumper, a voiceover actor is used to remind the viewers what show and station they are watching. Because promos help create a show's image, they are treated with the utmost importance.

To audition for promos, you may read at your voiceover agency or go to a network or a production studio. These studios and production facilities have their own casting directors. You may also work directly with the booth director and sound engineer (depending on the size of the studio, this may be the same person). You sign in, get your copy, and wait to be called in. The setup is the same as for a commercial audition: You'll go into a booth. There will be a microphone and headphones. There may be a TV monitor in front of you showing the promo. The casting director is in an adjoining recording room that may or may not be visible through a glass partition. (In many studios, the booth is quite a few feet from the main recording room.) You will speak with them through your headphones and microphone.

You will begin reading to the actual promo after hearing a series of three beeps. (This cue, which is also used in looping and dubbing, lets you know when to start talking along with the visual.) You will read some or all of the copy, depending on what they want. They may ask for a second read, telling you to read slower, deeper, faster, or more energetically. The casting director will record your takes, and then you will leave.

The voices used in promos differ, according to what's being promoted. A lot of promo voiceover work goes to men, but from time to time you do hear women. I'm known in the promo world for a fun, energetic read, and, depending on the TV show, I'm often called in to audition for that type of read. As you watch and listen to TV, notice how the promos aired on a given night have a voice quality that matches the programming, depending on whether it's serious or funny. Steve Mackell, who is the voice of the NBC lineup on Thursday nights, is energetic and zany. But the voice that promotes the show *Dateline* is very deep and authoritative, which suits the seriousness of the show and the age group at which it's aimed. It wouldn't be appropriate to have a spacey teenage girl saying, "Tonight on *Dateline*: The War in Iraq." You wouldn't take it seriously, would you?

Promos are a very big deal. With just a few words, you are representing an entire demographic. Learning to audition well for promos takes practice. It also takes knowledge of the special jargon that's used in the promo world. For example, if you're doing the voiceover for a TV promo, you might hear the term *SOT,* or *sound bite.* This refers to the sound that's already in the scene included in the promo — usually from the program being promoted itself. The voiceover will go around and in between words of the actors in the scene.

Here are some terms commonly used in the promo world:

SOT: Originally "sound on tape," it now stands for "sound on CD".
Cans: Headphones
GFX: Graphics
Graphic lower third: The bottom third of the TV-screen image, where the station will put the tune-in time and the station's logo. (This third is reserved for the station ID.)
Graphic upper third: The top third of the TV-screen image, where the station puts the name of the show.
SFX: Sound effects
Tagout: The wrap-up in the promo — the line at the end that's always used for that particular show. For example, "Judge Judy. She's ready to rule."
Timing: Reading "to picture" and fitting the timing of the voice-over read to the SOT.
To picture: Reading the voiceover copy to the image on the monitor — the visual of the spot that will air.
Tune-in time: The time when the program being promoted will air. In addition, the director of the promo may use industry jargon when directing you.

Here are some phrases that might get thrown your way:
Give me a level: Read some of the copy at the same tone and sound level at which you'll be recording. (This technical direction enables the sound engineer to adjust the microphone and headphones.)
Open it up: Take more time for the read; stretch it out. You can do this by changing your pacing, getting more relaxed and intimate with the read, as well as by romancing and playing with certain words in the copy.
Tighten it up: Make the read quicker; take less time to get it all in.
Split the difference: Try to get your read "in the middle" of the last two takes you did — somewhere in-between. This can refer to timing, tonality, or even attitude.
We're speeding: We're rolling CD. We're getting ready to record.

NARRATION

For a narration audition, you will generally have longer copy than for a promo or commercial. Since you will most likely be narrating an entire show (or an industrial video), the producers will want to hear a smooth, consistent read that jibes with the subject matter.

The narration copy will include direction, with specs describing the kind of voice and attitude the producers are looking for. You probably have been called in to audition because they have a copy of your demo CD that your agent has sent, so they will have a pretty good idea of the quality of your voice. They certainly won't be looking for a zany character read, but, depending on the job, they may want a sweet, high-pitched voice or a low, deep-throated one. Often, men with deep voices get the narration jobs, but not always. Women do a good number of narration jobs.

DEMOS FOR ANIMATION, LOOPING, NARRATION, AND AUDIOBOOKS

Just as for commercials, there are demo auditions for animation, looping, narration, and audiobooks, and the audition process for these categories is basically the same as for commercials. A demo gives producers a chance to hear you in their studio together with actual visuals.

For an animation demo, you might be pulled in to read your character(s) with other actors who are also being considered for parts. You might be doing the demo because the animated film or TV show has not yet been sold. The director may want to lay down an entire episode and then see if he or she can sell it. You might also be called in to do a slightly different version of what you did at your callback if they still feel that you didn't quite get the read. The directors, writers, and producers will work with you until they get what they want. You may be recorded alone, while another person's read is played back for you to react to. At other times, you will have to use your imagination and pretend to be reacting to another voice that hasn't been recorded yet.

The same goes for narration, looping, and audiobook demos. You will meet with the writers, directors, producers, and sound engineers and record whatever copy they give you. If they like your voice, and if the product (whatever it is) gets sold, then you will be called back in to do the real session. The demo will only be a small portion of the job. A narration can sometimes be several pages long. Looping an entire movie can take days. And recording audiobooks is a very long process, so they will only record part of the book for the demo.

VOICE TO VOICE

AN INTERVIEW WITH MASASA

Actress and voiceover talent Masasa was the voice of Sarah, the psychic, in *Team America: World Police,* the exuberant locker-room correspondent Tally Wong in the 2006 incarnation of MTV's *Celebrity Deathmatch,* and Condoleezza Rice (and others) in *Friday: The Animated Series.* Her many other credits include the stylish narrator of the yearly special *InStyle Celebrity Weddings* as well as various fun and exciting animation, video game, and commercial projects (*X-Men Legends, Shark Tale, Dead or Alive Paradise* to name a few). A Canadian by birth, Masasa is the child of a Zimbabwean father and German-Irish mother, and our interview partly focused on the impact of race and ethnicity on a voiceover career.

How did you get started in voiceover work?

I got into voiceover work literally with a little help from my friends! When I first moved out here [Los Angeles] to pursue acting, my first day job was as a receptionist at a major animation company, where I would speak with Jess Harnell (*Drawn Together, Pet Alien, House of Mouse, Animaniacs*) on the phone rather frequently. He always used to say, "Masasa, you have *got* to get into voiceover!" At the time, I barely even knew what voiceover was, but after much encouragement (and prodding), I finally took his advice and asked him how to go about it. He referred me to a demo producer — Chuck Duran — and I got one made. As luck would have it (once again), my friend Larry Hummel (formerly of ICM) had just gotten a job as an assistant. He brought me in to read on a project and I booked it. I also happened to book the next two projects, so they signed me, and the rest, as they say, is history.

Do you find that you have to fight for certain scripts to read for, or that you are stereotyped by your ethnicity?
One of the great things about voiceover acting is found in the name itself: *voiceover*. Ideally, in most cases one's voice should trump one's ethnicity. That is, of course, if the actor, regardless of race, has mastered the nonregional accent most voiceover actors strive for. Since I was raised in Canada and Upstate New York, and I am the product of a biracial marriage, I think that came naturally to me. Having said that, there have been times when I auditioned because they were looking for an African American for the spot, but at the same time got overlooked for the broader, standard or announcer reads. If this occurred within my own agency, I would simply request that I read for the latter. (I do *not* recommend this for everyone, though, as it does drive agents *nuts*!) However, when it comes to outside casting agencies, I tend to sit back and let them do their jobs. After all, most of them are good at what they do, and I have found that over time they pick up on how diverse your range can be. In my experience, most casting directors who used to bring me in for primarily African American spots have broadened the range in which they see me, and, as a result, I now have more diverse opportunities.

What do you feel the industry generalizes on when casting a script, as far as ethnicity, background, and social status go? Or do you feel it's strictly based on vocal quality?
Customarily, the advertising industry does tend to try and reach particular specific demographics, and therefore they personalize their approach to that audience. This is certainly true of gender and age. So, understandably, race is also sometimes taken into consideration. In general, there is a difference in speaking patterns amongst the various races and cultures in this country, and that does usually need to come across in the voice, particularly if the spot is targeting a particular demographic. For any reads that specifically say the character is African American — commercial

or otherwise — I use a dialect that is recognizably so. (I have come to affectionately refer to this as a "blaccent.") Sometimes casting specs have referred to the character as being "street" or "urban" — terms I have never cared for because they are often used as a kind of shorthand for the entire black experience. Additionally, I have seen some cases where the copy is written in slang or "Ebonics" even though the vocal qualities of the actor's performance should create whatever nuances need to be heard in order to portray the character's ethnicity. I once even encountered some audition copy in which a black employee referred to her supervisor as "the boss man." Yikes!

What is the kind of read or sell that you are known for, or that you usually bring to a script?
I would have to say that I am generally good at doing a straightforward, wry, cute, British, edgy, smooth, Australian, jazzy, robotic, New York, everyday, elegant, African, comedic, authoritative, childlike sort of style. In other words, I have no idea!

Tell me that cute story about your friend who booked the job over the others.
I have been fortunate enough, as have some other black actors I know, to be cast in several roles where the ethnicity was not specified as being African American. And I am grateful that so many advertising, video game, and animation producers and directors are aware that it's all about the performance and not the race of the actor. Here are a couple of interesting examples of the flipside of African American casting:

The first involves a friend of mine — fellow voiceover actor Vanessa Marshall. She plays the role of the eight-year-old African American character, Irwin, on *The Grim Adventures of Billy & Mandy*. How did she, as a Caucasian actress, get this role, you ask? Well, apparently she was the only actor who, when auditioning for the character, did *not* assume the typical "blaccent."

As for myself, one of the tools I use to determine the tone of the casting of a particular spot is to simply scan the room. What are the other actors like? Are they younger, older, professional, casual, black, white, Asian, or any other ethnicity? On one audition, I noticed a casual, youngish, Caucasian vibe in the room. Other than that, there were no specs on paper describing the female characters in the spot. I went into the booth with another actress, read the spot a few times, and then exited out to the waiting room, only to notice there were now a few black actresses in the room. "Uh-oh," I said to myself, realizing that I had mistakenly failed to portray the African American ethnicity in my read. I mentioned this to the casting director, who confirmed that my character was indeed supposed to be black. I was then told not to worry because "sometimes the client just needs to know that you are" — not necessarily to hear it. That turned out to be the case here, as I did in fact book it. So, it just goes to show you that you can never quite anticipate the outcome of *any* casting, even when it comes to race.

CHAPTER 7

YOUR DEMO CD

DEMO CDS ARE TYPICALLY 1 MINUTE IN LENGTH. The demo CD is your calling card. It is a compilation of either real or made-up voiceover jobs (depending on if you've booked jobs and what genre they are in). Most commercial demo CDs include parts or pieces of five to eight spots. The spots are very brief to showcase the product and mood, about 5 to 20 seconds each. The CD usually fades or cuts from one voiceover spot into the next once the mood and product name are heard. When creating your CD demo, keep in mind what's current and trendy, as well as what makes your vocal style different. A mix between local, regional, and national is a good combination for your demo. You'll also want a blend of radio and TV spots on your demo.

A good voiceover producer is key in putting together a great demo for you. This is one area you definitely don't want to skimp on. Having a friend that runs or owns a recording studio for music, isn't a voiceover demo producer. A voiceover demo producer knows exactly how to get the best out of your voice, the type of sell that will work for you and the range needed on your demo. He or she will know to use real copy from real scripts and not make things up. Writing your own scripts is not a good idea. Ad agencies can tell if a script or copy is not professionally written.

Having a demo CD is a requirement in the voiceover business. A good demo can be a very effective way to showcase your voice and your range of moods, styles, attitudes, and characters. You will need a demo CD to secure an agent and to get auditions, and you will regularly use it in mass mailings to casting directors, production companies, and ad agencies. There are several different types of demo CDs. The kind of CD you do will depend on which area of voiceovers you want to work in, and remember, an entire demo CD is only 1 minute in length.

Before you make your own CD, listen to other people's demos and ask around to find a producer. You don't want an entire CD of fun, high-energy reads. One fun, high-energy read is enough. Then move on to a different sound and mood. Your CD compilation should be a varied. Trust your producer to put together a great demo. This demo doesn't guarantee you an agent. It can help in getting one, as well as getting into casting directors and ad agencies. You will use this in every place you try to get work. Understanding that the demo is a representation of what you do, will allow you to understand the voiceover process better. The demo can be filled with you doing "fake" spots. This means that you didn't actually book the voiceover job. As you book jobs, you will begin to remove the "fakes" and put the real spots onto your demo. The goal is to have all real spots. But, again, you will still want to have a variety of vocal qualities/moods on your demo to show range and what you can do as a voice actor. Demos will be in categories, so as you book work (or want to obtain work) in other areas, you'll need a voice demo for that area of the business.

DEMO CD BASICS

A demo CD shows prospective agents and clients just what you can do with your voice (but not all that you can do). As a collection of various commercials and/or voice variations compiled from both radio and TV spots, it showcases the different moods and tones you're capable of and demonstrates your range and your vocal and reading ability. There are commercial demos, as well as demos for animation, promos, trailers, audiobooks, and narration — almost any area of voiceover work. In this chapter, we'll discuss each type of voiceover demo CD.

CDs sent out without agent representation are called *unsolicited* CDs. Unsolicited CDs can be sent to anyone who could potentially hire you for a job: radio stations, film and trade schools, advertising agencies, theaters, production companies, postproduction facilities, trailer companies, loop groups, audiobook publishers, casting houses, and animation companies. They can even be posted on the Internet, on websites such as *www.actorsaccess.com*, Craig's List, and *www.voice123.com*. If you're sending out CDs, call first to find out who is in charge of an organization's voiceover division and send your CD directly to that person. A demo CD may just get thrown away, but then again, the person who receives it may pop it into the CD player and give it a listen.

Many of the CDs you send out may simply be discarded. Today, you have to make a lot of copies as well as MP3 files to send to various ad agencies, agents, and casting directors. Your best bet with casting directors is to walk in with your demo and make a face-to-face connection, if you can. I recommend making twenty-five CDs to start. And make sure that your name, telephone number, and email address appear on the face of every CD you send out. If you have an agent, ask before you send to all of the casting directors and ad agencies. You will follow the lead of the agent to know who you should send out to. Make sure you understand your boundaries. They may encourage you to make connections, or they may want to make these for you. It depends on the size of agency and leverage they have within the voiceover community.

"FAKE" CDS

People who are just starting out in the business commonly use "fake" CDs — CDs that don't demonstrate your real experience (because you haven't got any!). If you have your fake CD professionally produced, the producer will usually find scripts for you to read and direct you. Most people start voiceovers because people have told them they have a great voice. Then they take a class and realize that voiceovers involve a lot of acting work and that their voice is secondary to their ability to read copy. When you do your CD, make sure you vary your reads/sells. Once you've got a hip, cool read, don't repeat it. You do not need two examples of the same type of read. Each read on the CD represents a job you could potentially book. Play with your voice, making adjustments to find different attitudes. Let the reads flow naturally instead of working your voice. This will open up your reads and prevent you from pushing. Think of your voice simply as a tool for relaying a message.

Using acting as a tool will change the way you sell each commercial. You will be amazed at how many different tones and textures come out of your voice when you begin to tell a story. Instead of worrying about the words on the paper, think about how to deliver them. Imagine yourself as strong, businesslike, and authoritative. And then as soft, sexy, and flirty. And then as bored, matter-of-fact, and wry. And then as excited and energetic. Every voiceover demo should be unique for that the voice actor (and producer). You don't want to copy voice demos, but you can certainly listen to them to fully understand how they are put together and what makes them flow.

I strongly advise against making a homemade demo CD. The production quality will never match that of one that is professionally produced, nor will a music producer understand voiceover copy, where to cut, what to put in what order or how much, and music beds/sound effects. In addition, if it's just you doing all the recording, listening, and producing, you cannot be as objective as you need to be. A professional producer, by contrast, will understand what makes for a good read — and will know whether the reads on the CD are different enough from each other. You may find it hard to hear those differences in energy and mood.

You may find a producer who wants you to write the copy for your CD yourself. This is tricky, and again I would advise against it. Copy you write yourself will probably sound like you wrote it yourself. It might be cute and sweet, but it won't sound like a real spot, and ad copywriters will know the difference. (Of course, some real scripts are badly written — but remember, they were actually produced, which means that they were approved to go to air.) Use real copy instead.

You can find lots of copy to use in magazine ads and radio and TV commercials. It's much better to "borrow" that copy than to write your own. Of course, as you audition and book jobs, you will build up a collection of real spots that you can use on your CD.

You have a bit more freedom with animation CDs because you can make up both the characters *and* what they say. Although, it is better to use real copy and real jobs. An animation CD should feature five or six different character voices. If each character has just one line, you may want to add a few more characters — but keep the total time to 1 minute. The same applies to promo and narration CDs: keep them under 1 minute. And all CDs — of whatever type — should have a nice flow and rhythm. If you want to do video games, you will need a 1-minute demo for that, as well. A mix between animation and video is fine to start out, but when you work in both areas, you'll eventually want to have different demos for each.

Music and sound effects help make the read sound professional. Make sure that the music beds or sound effects fit nicely with the copy you're reading and the products you're selling. The producer you select should be able to include music or sound effects on your fake CD.

Your CD *must* be a compilation of different types of spots. By all means, use your first few real jobs on your demo, but include some "fake" reads to fill it out with enough material to send to casting directors and agents. Never send just a single spot; they'll ask, "Where is your demo?" or say, "Send me your demo, when you do it."

So, how do you go about deciding what to put on your fake CD? The first step is to get a good demo producer to tell you. But let me give you a few hints. Let's say you're a deep-voiced man and you think you do a great "John Goodman/good ol' boy" type read. That's where you begin. Find copy that's appropriate for that style of read, and read it. Then, for the second read, use the strength in your voice for a hard sell for GMC trucks. Push this read out; have fun with it. Then look for a straight read — something like a coffee commercial or a jeans ad. Be the regular guy, conversational and relaxed. Then find a "good husband" piece of copy — perhaps dialogue with your "wife." You can have another person's voice on your demo — just make sure that the other person's read doesn't overpower your own and that this spot isn't the first one on the CD if the other person has the first line. Your demo showcases you and your voice/moods, not the wife. The only good in putting on a double (more than one character) is if it showcases your voice and ability to act. If you do include one of those mushy, lovey-dovey husband/wife spots on the CD, then the next read should be dry and off-the-cuff — maybe a beer commercial. Get the picture? So many choices! This is part of the reason you need a good producer that understands what goes on the demo CD.

INCLUDING NON-AIR/NON-BROADCAST SPOTS

The terms *to air (on air)* and *broadcast* mean that a spot will air on TV or radio. *Non-air* and *non-broadcast* are the opposite: spots designated by either of these terms will not appear on TV or radio. You may get paid for some non-air/non broadcast work; for example, you might do an in-house job for an ad agency demo for which you'll be paid. (In such a case, the agency won't yet have sold its campaign or spot, but because they like your voice, they'll want to hear how it sounds with a TV spot's image or a radio spot's music bed in a preliminary version of the commercial.) There are many different reasons you might be paid for a non-air or non-broadcast voiceover spot.

Even if you've been paid for them, non-air/non-broadcast voiceover spots are considered fake spots in terms of your demo CD, even though they are produced to sound like they've aired or could air. Nonetheless, there is nothing wrong with using a non-air demo on your demo CD.

By the way, nonunion jobs are often for broadcast, either in smaller markets or even national. With today's economy, quite a few advertising agencies that were union are now looking to hire nonunion talent. (They pay less and they don't have to pay residuals, per union rules). As a beginner, you'll want to take all the jobs you are offered. Each time you get one of these jobs, whether paying or not, ask for a copy so that you can use it on your demo.

EDITING THE CD

The spots on your demo CD should flow seamlessly — they should be woven together so there's no separation between them. If you can afford to hire a producer and sound engineer to put your CD together, they will edit it for you. If you must do a homemade CD, don't "label" each spot before it comes on. Announcing each spot will make your CD sound choppy. Just put the commercials on the CD, back to back, and let them run.

A demo CD is like a story. You're taking the listener on a little journey. Some people will only listen to the first couple of spots, so keep the CD moving along at a nice pace. Once you've shown the mood and product, move on to the next spot. Diversify the reads: if you have a high-energy read, follow it with a matter-of-fact or authoritative read, then follow that with quirky character read. And remember what's on your CD. When you book a job, the producer might say, "We loved that 7-11 spot you did on your demo." At this point, you say to yourself, "Okay, in that read I was cool — hip yet playful." Then use your memory of that read to reproduce that vocal quality. Every spot has a point of view, and this 7-11 spot represented you in your hip, playful, cool attitude — which in turn booked you the job with that particular producer. You may have been hired to do a Toyota spot, but when the producer says that he or she liked what you did for 7-11, you should apply the mood from that spot to the Toyota commercial.

THE COST

A professionally produced demo can run anywhere from $1,000 up to $2,500, depending on the producer. Demo CDs aren't inexpensive, but you should be able to write off the cost as a business expense. The CD is your calling card, so make it the best you can.

One way to save money is to rent studio time and work with the in-house sound engineer to record, but still hire a producer to direct and produce the demo. Depending on the studio, hourly rates can run from $75 to $300. The sound engineer will do the technical work (per the producer) and edit the CD to the producer's specifications. A producer/director will usually charge a flat fee for studio time, recording, and editing. You will record the spots together. The director will then edit the CD and get it to you when it's produced. If you're not sure whom to hire, ask around: word-of-mouth is a great way to find someone. If you hear a demo you like, ask who produced it. But always listen to other demos someone has produced before hiring him or her to produce yours.

THE MASTER CD

A master demo CD is the CD from which you make copies. This is what you pay all that money for, so protect the master by keeping it in a very safe place. Some actors also keep all the jobs they do on a master CD, so they can cull from the work they've done over the years for a demo CD.

A demo CD should be good for two to five years, depending on how much work you get in the meantime. Once you have a master copy of your demo CD, you can add new work to it as you get jobs — and edit old work out. This work is also done by a sound engineer at a recording studio.

You can burn copies of your CD on your home computer — if you have the time. But since this can be a slow process — and since you'll want to have a lot of CDs on hand — I recommend having your CD professionally duplicated. The studio where you record your CD can copy them, although this is an expensive way to go. There are also production houses that specialize in CD duplication that are much less expensive. The more CDs you order at one time, the less each one will cost. The cost can vary from $1 to $3 per CD.

AFTER YOU'VE SENT THE CDs

After you've sent your CDs, wait two to three weeks before following up with prospective agents to give recipients time to listen to them. Voiceover agents usually listen to all the submissions they receive on a specific day during the month. (You may want to ask the front desk, or the agent's assistant, when this day is.)

If an agent is interested, he or she will usually contact you, although it doesn't hurt to call: sometimes they'll have heard your CD and really liked you but not had time to call and ask you to come in. You may be called in to meet with the agent or to audition for a specific job so they can hear how you read copy and find out how you handle an audition situation. Don't call creative directors, producers, or casting directors. If they like you, they will keep you in mind and may call you directly to read for a spot. Email is another great way to get your voice demo out there and get listened to.

That doesn't mean you shouldn't follow up at all. Every three to six months, send the casting people a new CD, an email, or a postcard listing the latest jobs that you've booked, especially if they are currently playing on air. You need to remind them that you're still out there, and that they can call you in when they have something that's right for you. Do the same with smaller production facilities, which are always looking for nonunion or last-minute talent for radio spots, industrial videos, or local TV commercials. Don't get discouraged. Success in this business takes time.

YOUR CD AND YOUR AGENCY

Once you have an agent, make sure that your agency always has plenty of copies of the latest version of your CD. The agency will be sending it out to all the ad agencies and casting directors in town. (Even with so much work being done online today, many agents and agencies still work with discs rather than electronic files.) Having your CD professionally duplicated takes a few days, so don't let yourself run out. Always keep a small supply for yourself for your own mailings.

Your agent will also add the content of your demo CD to Voicebank, an online casting service used by ad agencies to search for voice talent. Voice agents upload their voice talent onto the site so that creative directors can hear the voice talent pool within each agency. The agency can then download the sound file and email it to its client. You may also want to have a website of your own (or at least a page on MySpace, Facebook, Smallworld, or any networking site), where you can upload your demo so people can access it immediately.

This is a wonderful tool for your business and for getting jobs all across the country. And, of course, you can always email your CD demo anywhere in the world. Your agency will also have a *house CD* — a master CD that includes samples of *all* the voices the agency represents. The agency will usually make a new house CD about once a year, submitting to ad agencies, producers, writers, TV stations, video-game producers, animation houses — any place that hires voice actors. The tracks on the house CD are usually categorized into Men and Women, Announcers/Promos (Men and Women), and Animation (Men and Women). There might also be categories for celebrity talent and for Spanish-language voiceover actors. When the agency asks you for work to include on its house CD, they will want a copy of the 1-minute demo for the house CD. This is called the *house minute*.

MASS MAILINGS

Mass mailings consist of sending or dropping off your demo to all of the local casting directors, production companies, and advertising agencies. I do mass mailings of my demo CDs — and so should you. I look online to find ad agencies in my general area that I've never worked with. I also check out advertising agencies in neighboring towns and send them copies, as well. I live in Los Angeles, but I contact companies that might hire me in Orange County, San Francisco, and elsewhere. In fact, now that the MP3 file format makes it so easy to transmit high quality electronic sound files quickly, I can get hired all across the country. Prospective clients can hear my voice and know that they can hire me to work in my home studio or a professional sound studio nearby and still get the same quality as at a recording facility. It's a good idea to do mass mailings a few times a year, especially during slow periods (the summer and the late fall, right before the big holidays). You can also email your demo to producers, ad agencies, and production houses as MP3s. Update everyone on your latest voiceover job, campaign, tag, animated show, or anything you've done. Send new demos, cute notes, and any other marketing tool you come up with. And don't forget anyone during the holidays.

ADDING TO YOUR DEMO CD

Each time you do a spot, get a copy of that spot(s) from the ad agency. If the spot is finished, you may get a copy while you are at the session. If not, it will be sent to your agent — or you can give them your home address and ask them to send it directly to you when it's completed. Sometimes, ad agencies will charge you $20 to $35 to mail you the CD, but sometimes they'll do it for free. (They might also email you the copy.)

Add new spots to your demo CD as you go. If you get a couple of jobs, wait until you've got all the copies, then add them to your demo. Every time you go into a studio to work with a sound engineer, you'll be paying the studio's minimum hourly charge, so make sure that you're not going in there to add something every two weeks. As you start booking more work, you'll also want to remove old spots — or spots you don't like as much — from your CD. Either way, keeping a copy of everything you've done is smart business. You may want to pull from it later to do further demos. You may want to change up your demo or just listen to old reads that you booked through the years. I have several boxes mixed with cassettes (yes, back in the day), videos, and CDs all with my old spots and campaigns. It's fun to look back and see the way the market and advertising has changed over the years.

RE-DOING YOUR CD

You should redo your CD every two to three years. It's a good thing to do even if you're just adding a new spot or two, mixing it up a bit, trying a new style of read, or adding a mood, since you're bringing something new to the table and giving the ad agencies something fresh to hear. Unless they are spots that you are well-known for, you don't want spots more than five or six years old on your CD. Don't worry if you don't have a lot of spots for your demo; if a read sounds good and it's getting you auditions and work, keep it on the demo. If you've got nothing new to add, you can get by with your current demo for a few years. Just make sure you watch TV and listen to the radio, stay aware of the trends and styles that are out there in the marketplace, and try to keep current. You can always rent studio time, hire a producer, go back into the voiceover booth, and record a new, more current spot to add to your demo. Some producers will even add new reads, up to a certain amount of time, for free. When I produce demos, I offer the talent up to six months to change a script, if they want.

DIFFERENT DEMOS FOR DIFFERENT AGENTS/AREAS

Depending on the size of your agency and the number of different voiceover areas you want to pursue, you may wind up with an animation agent, a promo agent, and a commercial voiceover agent. Each will require a demo CD for his or her particular area. A smaller agency might have only one or two agents. They might cover all voiceover areas or limit themselves just to commercials. But if you're pursuing work in a few different areas, you'll still need a demo CD for each one. If you're just starting out, this might be too costly, so pick one voiceover area and focus on that one first. After you begin to get work, you can spend the money and time to branch out. Or you may find that you are highly successful in one area and work a lot less in another. Put your energy into the area that makes money for you. You may even find that you begin to book voiceover work in another area *without* having that particular CD. Great! Just take the work that you do generate and use that to build that CD. It will be much less expensive for you to use materials that have already been produced rather than starting from scratch.

ANIMATION CDS

When putting together an animation CD, follow the same guidelines as for a commercial demo. It's best to hire a producer to help you put together the best possible demo. While you can try to find some good cartoon copy, it's also okay to write your own. (In this one way the process differs from commercial demos.) Watch kids' shows to get a good idea of what is already on the air, so you can make sure that the pieces on your CD sound like what you might hear in an animated TV show or movie.

An animation CD will feature different vocal styles and ranges to showcase your vocal quality and the different kinds of voices you can do. As with a commercial demo, the CD should be no longer than about 2 minutes. Again, you should listen to some samples on Voicebank to get an idea of what your CD should sound like. You don't want to put ten or more reads on the demo — that's way too many. Five to eight characters is plenty. As with a commercial CD, you should replace old work with new pieces as you begin to book jobs. Over time, you should also edit your CD to make room for other, different reads. Voiceover actors who are well-known in the field may have more on their CDs, simply because they *have* more work to use. But they still follow the basic guideline and keep the demo at the appropriate length. And even if someone becomes well-known in animation, he or she will still try to keep the demo current, to show off all the different voices he or she is capable of doing.

PROMO CDS

Promo CDs should be 1 minute in length. Promos are brief spots that promote upcoming shows, and a promo CD might contain reads taken from prime time network television ("Next on *24*"), or local-affiliate voiceovers ("The Evening News at six on Channel 13 with Ron Smith"), or cable TV ("Tonight on CNN — German shepherds: the truth among the pack"). Just as you vary the content of your commercial CD, including spots for both TV and radio, you should do the same for promos, especially if you've never done this kind of work and you're making up the content.

Don't just do national network–type promo work: include promos for the local affiliate market as well. The affiliate market can be very specific. Radio affiliate audiences are often divided by genre, such as country, pop, rock, easy listening, sports, and the like. Listen to samples on Voicebank before putting together your CD, and vary your reads to showcase the full range of your abilities.

TRAILER CDS

A trailer CD should have five or six different trailer voiceovers. These can be a mix of TV, radio, and movie trailers. Most trailer voiceovers are done by men. (We all seem to have been trained to believe that men's voices are more businesslike and authoritative than women's, and the public seems to respond better to male voices on movie trailers, although women are beginning to get hired in this field — depending on the film, of course.)

Trailer work is a tough niche to break into. Most work is done on a buyout basis (meaning you get a flat, one-time fee), although some trailer jobs' contracts include distribution deals and residuals. There are companies called *trailer houses,* which deal specifically with trailers, and it's to these companies that you should send your trailer CD. A company called Mix Magic in Hollywood is one such house. Howard Schwartz Recording Inc., a recording studio in New York City, works with quite a few trailer houses in New York and likes keeping trailer demos on hand in case a producer asks about voice talent for a future job.

DUBBING CDS

Those new to this area are going to need a separate dubbing demo CD. But if you speak a foreign language and have worked in the voiceover field for a while, you'll be able to use your commercial demo CD to audition for dubbing jobs: your previous work will stand on its own, and you will be hired because you speak the right language and your voice is similar in tone to that of the person you will be dubbing. For dubbing jobs into English, understanding the language of the films and programs you dub will enable you to follow the cadences of the actors' voices. Your fluency in the other language will be a big part of why you are hired. The ability to follow another actor's timing and rhythm will also be important.

AUDIOBOOK CDS

An audiobook CD should contain clips of three to four pieces in different genres. As with any demo, it's best to have it professionally produced and edited. If you've done audiobook work previously, make sure you get copies and use pieces from them on your CD. Just like a commercial CD, an audiobook CD should showcase different styles of reads. Each piece should be from fifteen to forty-five seconds in length, and each should fade or cut into the next. A total of one and a half to two minutes is plenty. But do demonstrate your range and abilities with different styles of books and different moods.

NARRATION CDS

Narration copy is long — it comes from shows like documentaries — and, as with audiobooks, brief pieces from each of the narrations you're using are edited down to make a 1-minute CD. To create a fake narration CD, read the first 30 seconds or so from two or three scripts with different subject matters. That will be enough to demonstrate your range.

LOOPING CDS — NOT NEEDED

Here's some good news: you don't need a separate looping CD. Your regular commercial CD is fine, although if you want looping work it's a good idea to show off your range by including some of your quirkier accents, some background noises, a baby crying, or anything else you can do. The bad news, at least for those who live in smaller towns and cities, is that most loop groups are in Los Angeles, New York, and Chicago. Since most of the work that loop groups do is for movies and TV shows, they're in the places where most of the shows and films are produced. A good way to break into a loop group is to sit in — if they allow you to. Also, offer to work for free in the beginning, and work your way into the group!

BRINGING YOUR CD TO AUDITIONS

It's good to bring to an audition that new CD the casting house hasn't yet heard. If you've just made a CD in a new area — animation, promos, or whatever — and you know that the casting house casts in that area, then by all means bring it to them. If you audition at an ad agency, leave a CD at the front desk or bring a few to distribute to other copywriters at that agency. Even if you've done work for an ad agency before, there might be a creative executive working on another campaign who's never heard your voice, so bring along a CD just in case! If you are reading for a director, you can certainly hand him or her a copy of your CD.

J-CARDS FOR JEWEL CASES

A J-card is a cover that slides over the demo CD's jewel case. Check with your local duplication house to find out where in your area you can get them printed. Putting a J-card cover on your CD isn't a necessity, but it does help your CD to stand out. The cost of printing J-cards ranges from $1.25 to $3.00 a copy, depending on how many colors you're using, the paper stock, and whether you use a graphic designer. Well designed J-card covers are expected in California; in New York, a good demo, a quality CD, and a clean, simple cover are at a premium.

Something catchy that emphasizes your name or the type of voiceover you do is always good for name recognition and business. I used to use the slogan, "An Apple a Day." My colleague Kat Cressida uses a very cute marketing concept involving a Kit Kat bar. Anything unique can be good. It doesn't have to be high-end graphics to get your CD heard. If you're good at graphic design, feel free to get creative and design your own J-card.

Always include information about your agent and your union affiliation on your CD — either on the J-card or on the face of the CD. If you do have an agent, the agent's logo and contact information is enough. The duplication house should have your voiceover agency's information on hand. If not, ask your agent for a label with his or her agency's logo and have it duped onto the face of each CD. If you do not have an agent, specify that when submitting CDs to casting houses.

Also list your union affiliations on your J-card or the CD itself. If you are nonunion, however, provide that information through a note, or email it along with the demo. An agent or casting director may like your voice and bring you in for a union job. If you book the job, you will have to follow union rules. Whether you are union or not, always be honest about your union status.

CHAPTER 8

COACHING AND BEYOND

TAKING CLASSES AND SEMINARS, DOING ONLINE WORKOUTS — anything you can do to move your career forward and learn how to read copy — is imperative to working in the voiceover business. As a voice actor, you have to understand that it's rare to go straight into an audition, nail the read and get hired for the job with absolutely no training or history of working in the voice field. What you can do is lure an agent or casting director and even ad agencies in with your amazing voice. From there, what you need to do is learn the correct tools to work with in the industry. Mastering both the creative and technical aspects is important in advancing in this business. Maybe in the old days when the market was much smaller, it was easier to sneak in and learn on the job. Today, because the market is much bigger and the competition is stiff, it's very important to learn how to market yourself effectively as well as to work easily with the director, producer, sound engineer and/or writer in the voiceover session. This book is a great resource to help you along your journey, but it doesn't take the place of a class or a good coach. (When I have time, I coach via phone, online, and in person. There is a full list of coaches in back of the book or go to *everythingVO.com*.)

Find a coach or teacher who knows the voiceover business. Where you live will help you determine which classes to take. If you live in a small town where voiceover work is harder to get, you may need to compromise and take an acting or diction class instead of a voiceover class. Such classes are often offered by continuing education programs at community colleges, universities and local drama clubs; there may even be an acting school in your area.

Also check the local papers and the Learning Annex (*www.learningannex.com*), which offers a variety of classes in sixteen cities in the United States and Canada. You might also call SAG (the Screen Actors Guild) or AFTRA (the American Federation of Television & Radio Artists). Either of these unions should be able to help you find classes near where you live. Search the Internet for voiceover schools, acting schools, voiceover training, production facilities, and the like. Finding a great teacher who knows the business is the best way to get started in the voiceover field. You will have lots of questions, and he or she will have the answers.

BEGINNING-LEVEL CLASSES

There are several types of voiceover seminars and school courses for different areas of the business. For example, the Learning Annex offers one-night intensive seminars taught by well-known local voiceover actors. These classes, which cost about $40, teach basic information about the voiceover business. Depending on the class, you may even get to play around with real copy and a microphone. The Learning Annex also offers longer workshops (lasting from four to six weeks) that emphasize diction, breathing, interpreting copy, and reading for radio and TV. Call your local Learning Annex or look on the Web for details.

Most of the teachers and trainers listed in Appendix B offer both ongoing classes and private lessons focusing on certain fields within the voiceover industry. Classes generally run from four to eight weeks. In a beginning class, you'll learn how and where to stand or sit, how to interpret copy, how to vocalize copy, and how to give different kinds of reads. You'll work with moods to create different vocal qualities and find your style or stereotype. You'll have time to read alone and to work with other people. Some classes will give you a CD of your completed work to take home with you, which you can use for practice and review. Schools such as Kalmenson and Kalmenson in Los Angeles (listed in the back of the book) are dedicated to every aspect and level of the business. Private coaches can instruct you at every level. A beginning-level coach should give you copy in the area you want to pursue to take home for practice outside the studio, and tools to help you learn how to read copy correctly. After the first workout, the student should leave with a course of action as well as the tools to begin understanding how to look at scripts and begin to nail reads. Spending time in a voiceover booth is important, but developing skills such as how to do a cold read before you go into the booth is even more important.

INTERMEDIATE-LEVEL CLASSES

In intermediate-level classes, you'll be working with other students who may have some professional experience, and the work will be more advanced. The copy will be a little more difficult (perhaps longer and more intense, with meatier dialogue, thicker accents, and different textures than you might be used to). The class may concentrate on a particular sell or area. The teacher may concentrate on transitions and beats to help you understand the way a script is written. Or they may bring in "reading to time" while incorporating the mood. Intermediate-level classes are really great for honing your skills, learning how to interpret copy, and mastering your reads. These classes may include appearances by guest speakers from advertising and voiceover agencies, as well as working voiceover actors, all of whom can give you the inside scoop on the business.

ADVANCED-PRO CLASSES

It's a good idea to take an ongoing workout class. You want to work on scripts that are written by ad agencies. Or even if you are working alone from home, you can easily get scripts from TV or radio by copying down the dialogue, adding your own specs and recording your reads. Play them back to see how close you got to the read that is playing on the air. Try not to copy the voice as much as find the mood that the specs were asking for. Understand that every spot that goes to air started out as someone's idea, then went to paper, then through an entire audition process, writing changes, and finally got approved for air. In the advanced-pro class, you should learn how to nail your reads every time and walk away confident. You also must learn how re-create what you did in the audition for the job. You are given direction in all workouts, classes and coaching, but usually in the audition the direction is very specific and short, whereas in a voiceover session direction can be long and notes very detailed.

CLASSES IN SPECIFIC VOICEOVER AREAS

There are classes available for every type of voiceover out there in the marketplace. You can get coaching in person, online, or over the phone. You don't have to be in the same room as the coach, although at some point you will want to work out on a microphone. First and foremost is understanding your reads before even getting onto the microphone. There are private and group classes in everything from audio books, dubbing, looping, jingles, affiliate work, promos, trailers, narration, animation, video games, industrials, and commercials.

In animation classes, you'll learn how to invent voices and how to manipulate your voice for new reads. You'll read and record actual copy used for television and film animation. You'll compare your work with that of your classmates and find out what makes one read so much better than another. There are also narration classes, audio book classes, promo classes, and classes that offer "to picture" experience — to teach you to read copy as you watch an image, just like what happens in an actual voiceover session for a TV commercial. All these classes teach you the ins and outs of the voiceover session and prepare you for job situations. If you've done a few voiceovers and want to learn more, study a different area of the business and to work out take a more challenging class. Class sizes vary (anywhere from seven to twenty students) and usually try to simulate the atmosphere of a real recording studio. As working voiceover actors, we get the opportunity to practice every day while auditioning for potential jobs. We may read for months and not book a job, or book a job three to five times a week. It depends on the client, the current trend in the business, and your agent getting you in to read.

Before you sign up for a class, make sure that the instructor will provide the students with experience working at the microphone and reading copy as well as giving you the tools to break down scripts. If you are daunted by the microphone, there is an option: in some classes — including a very well-known class in Los Angeles — you read copy aloud without a mike. This can be a good way of learning to interpret copy and to get comfortable reading without an intimidating microphone two inches away. Remember, your vocal ability comes from your acting and your mood, not the microphone. Once you get comfortable reading aloud, then when you are at the microphone you'll see it simply as a tool to sell your read and help you tell your story. Learning to read on the microphone, with and without headphones, is also important. I usually like my students to learn with headphones on first, so they aren't intimidated. It depends on the environment and class. Trust your coach to get you from A to Z in a timely, professional manner. And assess your progress. Are your reads getting better? Are you able to get through reads faster? Are you able to break down scripts quicker than before? When listening back to reads and taking direction, does it sound like you're improving? Understand that it's not all about "good" and "bad" reads, but getting the mood, time, flow and beats right.

WORKOUTS

All classes should provide a workout atmosphere, in which you are given copy and go into the booth to read aloud, either alone or with others. You will listen to copy and analyze it. You'll probably read it a number of ways and with different partners. The teacher will play the read back for you, give you pointers, and send you into the booth again to try a different read. There are also ongoing, professional workout classes, which are great for working voiceover actors. Even if you work a lot, there is always more to learn, and you'll want to get on that mike and practice as much as possible. These classes are usually taught by working voiceover actors, producers, or casting directors. In such classes, you work alongside other voiceover professionals who know how to book jobs. They are in the loop, and you will learn the ropes from them. In most voiceover workout classes, you'll be given real scripts that are actually used in auditions. This will allow you to see what's out there in the world of voiceovers today, so that when you're ready to audition, you'll already have a sense of what voiceover copy looks like, as well as the different specs and styles of reads. In smaller towns, classes may only offer local or regional copy, but this is great to learn from as well. All voiceover actors, no matter where they are in their careers, still do local and regional jobs. It's not all about nationally broadcast commercials. Small, local radio spots can fill many a slow month for the voiceover professional. That's why we call them the bread and butter of the voiceover world. Many times, those spots pay the bills! For information on specific classes in the Los Angeles, New York City, and Chicago areas, see Appendix B at the end of the book.

VOICE TO VOICE

AN INTERVIEW WITH MARLA KIRBAN

Based in New York City, Marla Kirban trains, directs, and provides guidance for many aspiring voiceover amateurs and professionals alike. You can find out much more about her career, past and present, by visiting her Web site: *www.marlakirbanvoiceover.com.*

Can you tell us a bit about your history in the voiceover business?
I guess you can say that I started on the path to the world of voiceover after I graduated from Emerson College, in Boston, with a theater education degree and a minor in speech. I taught public speaking and oral interpretation at Stratford High School in Connecticut. Years later, Charles Rosen, from Charles Rosen Casting in New York, asked me to direct a voiceover commercial audition for Mercedes Benz. I realized that I had a natural ability to direct talent and had an ear and a love for voiceover. I

then went on to Los Angeles and worked with Jeff Danis at ICM. I helped cast and direct fabulous talent in its voiceover department. I have, since then, moved back to New York and have been teaching, inspiring, and motivating voiceover students.

What do you think is the biggest difference between the L.A. and New York markets?
Honestly, with the Internet, MP3s, and more talent owning home studios, everyone in New York has the same opportunities as talent in L.A. The only thing that I can think of is the fact that animation is predominately in L.A. So if I have a student talented in animation, I recommend L.A., as I did with Dana Snyder, who is the milkshake in *Aqua Teen Hunger Force.* Animation directors use the same voiceover actors most of the time for a number of different roles on an animated series. So if your idea of an animated cat's voice is "meow," think again about animation — you really have to be exceptionally gifted.

Is there a greater need for voiceovers these days?
I would say that in different venues there is. I think there will be more use for voiceover talent on the Internet, as that medium is continuously growing. The development of new cable networks will lead to the use of more promo voiceover talent. With TiVo, customers are now given the opportunity to skip over TV commercials, and I sometimes worry about that. But there will *always* be radio — and products to sell!

Do you think voiceover is an option for actors these days?
I think every actor should have a voiceover demo. It's another opportunity and a way to make some money. I'm surprised when students of mine graduate from college with a theater degree and no tools to market themselves in the real world. They have no acting reel or voiceover demo CD. They have no tools to enable them to make a living commercially.

Tell me about your classes and your Web site.
I have some of my students' demos on my Web site, and having them on there gets my students agents! Bryant, my engineer, and I write all the copy ourselves for the demos. We individualize

everyone's demo, so each is unique. We also try and make each demo funny and entertaining. In addition, I coach one on one, whether it's for commercials (radio/TV), promos, narration, animation, or even trailers. I remember working with Howard Parker, one of the top trailer voices. Having done so many trailers, every time he opened his mouth to voice any commercial, he sounded like he wanted to kill someone: his voice is deep, dark, and edgy. I was able to help him lighten it up.

I have seminars during the year where I bring in L.A. and Chicago voiceover professionals, such as Ginny McSwain (animation director), Jeff Danis (agent extraordinaire), and Harlan Hogan (Chicago talent), to talk to my students about marketing. I offer something called "pro jams," where actors who already have demos continue to work on their craft in a group setting. I select copy for each individual, and everyone in the class contributes comments and direction to one another. It's not only a blast, but it's an excellent forum to learn from others' mistakes. I also send some of my students out on auditions for non-union casting. Casting directors and various companies call me for my talent, so I do a lot of casting as well. Sometimes I may even send a student out before they are actually done with their demo, so if they book the gig, they've paid for it already!

What do you feel are the top qualities a voiceover actor can bring to the table?

A voiceover actor needs to be able to tap into his or her emotions and turn on a dime within the copy, as well as visualize who they are and who they are talking to, and be free enough with themselves to let go and become vulnerable. I always feel an improv class is a good thing to take while learning this craft. I want students to be open and free when they learn and realize it is a craft and, like any other craft, it needs to be honed. The other thing: an actor *cannot* think of him- or herself, his voice, or what he is doing as he is doing it. "Be of service to the copywriter" is what I always say. It's about way more than your voice!

How important is the demo?
It's everything. It's like your 8 x 10 glossy. But don't do a demo until you are ready. I could bring anyone in and give line readings, and my fabulous engineer, Bryant, could make it sound amazing. The demo will get an agent's attention. But you have to be as great as that demo. If you can't analyze copy or figure out the points you need to make, you will never book a job and your agent will realize that you don't know what you're doing pretty fast.

How hard is it to get an agent in New York — and do you need one?
I have a lot of students who have gotten agents. It depends on what an agent is looking for. I had a fabulous young British guy who I knew, once he learned the craft, would be a hot commodity. And he turned out to be because, of all the years I've been teaching, he was my first young British talent, and there is commercial copy out there for his type. Agents don't want versatility: They want to typecast you. If an agent needs your type on their roster, then you get a call. However, because a lot of non-union jobs are popping up on the Internet, on *www.voiceover123.com* for example, there are students who get a lot of work even without representation.

Can you have more than one agent in New York?
You can freelance with some smaller agencies, and I recommend that at the beginning. The more opportunities you have, the better.

How would you say it's best to go about meeting agents, casting directors, and people at ad agencies?
There are places like Actors' Connection and Edge Studio, which sponsor evenings with voiceover agents at which you can meet in a group and then audition for them.

What do you look for when teaching?
I look for people who are open, smart, have a good sense of humor, are willing to have fun, and who can leave their "shame" at the door. Being self-conscious does not work. I tell students to think of class as clown school. If they can't do it, then I don't work

with them. I only take on people who I believe have a chance to be successful.

Any words of wisdom, advice about marketing, being proactive, and turning voiceovers into a lifetime career?
You need to be able to sell yourself. Carry that demo wherever you go, because you never know who you may run into! Voiceover careers just don't happen overnight. Make sure you have a great demo and that you are able to back it up with a great audition.

CHAPTER 9

YOUR AGENT AND JOB AVENUES

Getting an agent or manager is important in booking jobs. Depending on the state and the union rules (SAG and AFTRA), having more than one agent may not be allowed. Check with your agent who's signing you. Some will want exclusive representation, while others may not mind you being with several different agencies. You may see some of the same auditions, but it's up to the agency if they will allow you to read on both. At some point, you will want to find an agent to further your career.

The voiceover business is extremely competitive, and it can be difficult to get representation. If an agency wants to take you on a trial basis, let them. (This trial basis is called "pocketing," and I discuss it in more detail later in the chapter.) This not only enables the agent to see whether he or she wants to sign you, but it also lets you see what the agent can do for you. It affords you the time to make sure that you and the agent are a good match, and that he or she can get you the kinds of auditions you think you're right for.

No agent can possibly get a hold of every piece of copy that's out there. There are far too many agencies and far too much talent competing for work. On the other hand, Voicebank, together with your agent's connection to ad agencies, should certainly yield most of the scripts appropriate for you to audition for, regardless of where you live.

So how do you know if an agent will do a good job for you? That's a tricky question. Is the agent well known and well respected within the industry? Start by asking other voiceover actors the agent represents, and find out how often they are sent out to read. Ask them what kind of copy they generally read for: Radio? Television? National campaigns? Animation? Remember, different voice actors will read for different types of jobs, so don't expect exactly the same kind of attention or results.

SAG and AFTRA will provide a list of union agents by fax or mail; the lists can also be found on their Web sites. You can also check *www.everythingVO.com* or *www.voicebank.net*. These Web sites have complete lists of union and non-union agents across the country. (Membership is not required to search these sites for agencies and managers.) They even have demo recordings that you can listen to if you want to hear the competition at a given agency or to find out how many actors with vocal qualities similar to yours a particular agency represents. (Appendix B at the back of this book also has some agent listings.)

If you live in a smaller market, look through the listings under "Talent Agencies" in your local yellow pages. Call local production companies and the casting directors in town; call the on-camera commercial agencies to find out whether they have voiceover divisions. Check with your local film commission. Call the creative directors at local ad agencies; they may know the agents in town. Take classes. And ask everyone you know in the voiceover field whether they can recommend an agent to you. See if a colleague can set up a meeting or pass along your demo.

Also, in a smaller market, there may only be one or two agencies in town. Check *www.voicebank.net* or *everythingVO.com* for local listing of agents. You will want an agent or manager who's on Voicebank — a vast amount of scripts come through there and ad agencies use Voicebank as a trusted tool for auditions. You cannot get onto Voicebank as a talent unless you have representation. Drop off, mail, or email your demo CD to the local agencies, or call them and ask to set up a meeting to discuss representation and how they select their clients. Usually, you will be asked to mail in or drop off a hard copy of your demo. (Your demo should contain samples of all areas of the business you want to work in — list commercial reads first, unless you are simply pursuing animation, promo, affiliate, etc.) Give the agency time to listen to your demo. Remember that they get thousands of submissions and have to listen to each one. A sure way to not get called in is to make a demo that doesn't follow protocol for what to put on and how to read. While waiting for a response from the agent(s), don't hesitate to drop off, mail, or email copies to local ad agencies, production companies and casting directors. Casting directors are known for bringing actors in even without an agent. If they like your demo, they may call you in to read. Do not drop off head shots with your voice demo unless they've requested it or they cast on-camera, as well. Drop off a basket of cookies instead or simply be professional, pleasant, and nail your reads when you are asked to audition.

If you find some agencies you think you might like to work with, check out their reputations. Talk with people who have worked with the agents and the talent they represent. Talk to your union to make sure the agencies are reputable. You want to be with a hard-working agency that is making the phone calls, getting the copy, and sending its clients out on auditions. Who else does the agency represent? You can listen to their client list on *www.voicebank.net*, where full demos are listed. If the agency has a reputation for sending out actors who read badly at auditions, ad agencies and casting directors may decide not to include that agency when they send out scripts in the future. Some questions you shouldn't bother the agent with. Voicebank has a list of clients that agents represent, so if you want to know your competition, listen to their demos. Asking how many other actors sound similar to you is okay, but don't get overwhelmed. Learn to ask the right questions, and not ask the wrong ones!

WHAT TO ASK WHEN MEETING WITH AN AGENT

- Will you bring me in to read for other areas, such as animation, if you think I'm right for something?

- If I want to pursue other areas of the business (promos, narration, trailers, etc.), are you willing to consider me in those areas before or after I've done the demo?
- How many other actors with voices similar to mine do you represent?
- Where do you see my career heading? What kind of jobs do you think I'm best suited for based on my demo?
- How many times a week on average will I be coming in? Going to casting houses? Ad agencies?
- Do you have an animation, promo, or narration department? (The amount of promo and animation work in many cities is limited.)
- If I sign with you, are you open to me having representation in other states? Is a manager okay?
- Is it okay if I send out my demo(s) to the casting houses, or would you prefer to do it?
- How many agents does your agency have that solely represent voiceover? Each department? (There may be one or several agents for each department depending on the size and state.)

If there's only one agency in your town that has a voiceover department, you won't have much choice about where to go. But if they are signatory with the union, they have to follow the rules just like every other agency. If they are non-union, they still might get a lot of scripts and be a good place to start. Non-union copy can lead to union copy. Ad agencies work in both union and non-union, so once you're in with an agency, they may bring you in to read for anything (union or non) that they think you're right for. Making and keeping relationships besides your agent is key to being brought in to read for jobs and being considered for future work.

Have reasonable expectations about what an agent can accomplish for you. Remember that an agent may have many other clients that he or she is trying to get work for. Even if you have an agent, there is no guarantee that you will get jobs. The agent will get you in the door, but you have to do the rest. He or she can push you for a job or get people to hear you read, but the agent can't make them hire you. That is up to the client — and the quality of your read. Everything is about auditioning, no matter what level you're at. I still read for every future job. Even people I know making seven figures audition for jobs. Once in a great while, you'll get a call and cast, but usually I read for the audition and get cast from that.

Your agent can set up appointments for you to meet casting directors, but a casting director will only see you if he or she has something for you to read. You may be sent with your demo CD when you have an audition. Your agent may also send your demo CD to the casting director, who will listen to it and bring you in to read when he or she is casting something appropriate. That way, the casting director can get familiar with your voice in advance.

SECURING AND KEEPING AN AGENT

Keep in mind that most voiceover agents rarely do "generals" — meetings with talent whom they are not interested in representing. Even if someone refers you to an agency, you will most likely be asked to send your demo CD before you are permitted to set up a meeting to discuss representation. (Dropping off a gift basket with your CD is always a good call.)

This business is a bit of a Catch-22. You must have a demo tape to secure an agent, regardless of whether it is a fake CD or contains real to-air commercials. Once you've done your demo, it's time to get out there and try to get an agent. Of course, when first starting out, depending on the number of choices in your city, you'll want to find someone who is truly excited by your talent, your voice, and your demo — regardless of your history in the business.

If you are newer to the voiceover game, you're likelier to get a friendly reception at one of the smaller, boutique agencies, which have fewer clients, less internal competition, and newer voiceover talent. Getting into a large voiceover agency when you've just started in the business isn't always a smart idea, anyway. It's very easy to get lost in the shuffle, and you might find yourself not getting called for auditions once you've read a few times and haven't booked. They may put you on the back burner or take you out of rotation for the simple reason that they have several other clients who do book auditions, and they need to send out those working actors first. For an agency, it's very important to send good voiceover talent to every audition they supply for an advertising agency or casting house. A good voiceover actor makes an agent look good.

You may get an agent with your first submission. If not, you'll have to keep submitting your demo to other agencies. Send to two or three, then wait about two to three weeks to see if they call you. If not, call to find out if they've listened to your demo, or when they listen to new demos (some agents listen to all incoming CDs at a certain time of the month). It may take you six months to a year to find an agent, so don't become discouraged!

In the meantime, you can go after a lot of work for yourself by developing relationships with casting directors directly. They will bring you in if they feel that you're right for a job, regardless of whether you have representation. Casting directors can also help you get an agent, so get to know all the casting houses, ad agencies, and production facilities in your town. (Sometimes, this is easier in smaller markets, since there's not much competition.) Keep plugging away. Keep sending out those demo CDs. When an agency is interested in meeting with you, they will set up an appointment for you to come in, go into the booth, and read. They might hand you new copy; if they like your audition, they might even submit your audition to the ad agency that sent them the copy. (If you book the job off the bat, they'll take you on.) Or they might have you read some older copy for a commercial that has already been cast, just to see how you read and what you can do. It's also important for them to hear you read several different types of copy, so they might hand you a character radio spot as well as a national TV spot. Your job is to break down the copy, analyze it, and give it a cold read.

You may get fifteen minutes to look at the copy, or they may allow you to take the copy home to get more familiar with it. If you take it home, it's not a bad idea to call a voiceover teacher and set up a private session. Bring the copy to the session, and show the teacher what you intend to do with each spot. Let him or her help you break down the beats and get the right mood so you can nail those reads. You don't want to do a lousy audition. You've got to impress the agency — not just with your demo CD but also with the way you read in the booth.

Once you've read, the agents who've come to listen to you may discuss your reads with you, or they might ask you to meet with other agents at the agency. They may decide to take you on right then and there, or they might have to discuss the decision and call you back. Once they've decided to take you on, get the agency logo label from them so you can add that to your CD. (You'll want to put the logo on your CD and then resubmit it to all the casting houses, with a brief note letting them know that you now have representation.) Casting houses prefer to deal with agents. Once you've secured an agent, let the agent work for you. Let the agent call you in for auditions and get your name out there to the right people. This may take a bit of time, but trust your agency and understand that by taking you on they've shown that they believe in you. That they believe in your talent — especially if you've never booked a job before — is huge! It may take some time, but you'll be on the way to auditioning for and booking jobs and moving up in the ranks!

FINDING AN AGENT IN A SMALLER MARKET

When I first started out in Kansas City, it would have been easier for me if I had had an agent, but the one I went to see told me to become a secretary, so I was a little turned off. I had to show him I could get the jobs on my own. I took my demo cassette — which was homemade! — around and dropped it off at all the advertising agencies and independent producers in town and even at the sound studios. I started getting calls from the demo. Then I started to get work.

A few years later, I did get an agent — the only other one in town at the time. By then, I had done several voiceover jobs, and he had copies of my demo to send out. At that time, there wasn't a recording facility at his office (which was just one room), so I always got sent out to audition. I was one of about five people doing voiceovers in Kansas City. Most of the others were DJs for the local radio stations. There weren't many voice actors pursuing that market. But I kept myself competitive and got to be well known. I didn't join SAG until I booked my first national spot, so all the work I did was non-union. Eventually, I did enough work to finally make a real demo, but my homemade demo had been enough to get me my first ten jobs. These days, things are more competitive, and self-made demos just won't cut it, but I think that as long as you hustle, you can still get work in a small town. Having an agent definitely helps, though, because you may not know any of the casting people in town. An agent will be able to hook you up with everyone, and it's much easier to book jobs through an agent.

Start by calling your local union office for a list of local agents. Call (and always ask the name of the person you are talking to) or drop by the agents' offices — in a smaller town, why not show them your face? The agent may not be able to meet with you just then, but you can drop off your demo CD with the receptionist (and make sure that you also get the name of the person you are dropping off the CD with). Don't forget to include an inquiry letter with your CD (see the sample letter on the next page). If you've done any voiceover work, make sure you mention it in your letter: "I am the voice of Mr. Potato Chip Diner, Rex's Hamburger Haven, and Topsy Tipsy Ice Cream in Shawnee." (If your CD is all fakes, you obviously won't supply that information when writing such letters or sending e-mails.)

If the prospective agent likes you but not your CD, he or she may ask you to get a new demo done before agreeing to take you on — and may refer you to a good sound engineer and/or producer. But the agent might take you on with the CD as is. When you go into a meeting with a prospective agent, be upbeat and positive. Talk about any jobs you've done, any casting directors or ad agencies that already know you, and any classes you've taken. If you have no experience at all, that's okay.

Let the agent listen to the CD and be the judge. The agent may send you to a class — or give you your walking papers. If he or she feels you aren't ready for an agent just yet, don't worry.

Thank the agent and ask if he or she can give you any suggestions. Call the local colleges and try to get some nonpaying voiceover or narration work. Do take a class. Keep practicing reads. Call local production houses and see if you can get hired for some non-union work. Maybe someone will hire you for a job, like your work, and hire you again.

Don't get discouraged. Everything happens in steps. Just because one particular agent doesn't take you on doesn't mean that you aren't good. You may just need more practice and someone to give you a chance. Or the agent may not be looking for talent in your vocal range or age category: to avoid conflicts of interest, an agent may not take on any new talent in a given area once he or she has several similar clients. If you can't find a voiceover agent in your town, call the on-camera commercial agents and ask if they would consider having a voiceover department — featuring you.

Sample Inquiry Letter

> Date
>
> Address
>
> City, State, ZIP
>
> Telephone Number
>
> E-mail Address
>
> Web site address [if you have a Web site]
>
> Agent's Name
>
> Address
>
> City, State, ZIP
>
> Dear Mr./Ms. Wonderful [put the person's last name here],
>
> Per my conversation with Becky Wilson, I have enclosed my commercial demo CD. I am currently seeking representation and would love to set up a meeting with you at your earliest convenience. I look forward to speaking with you.
>
> Happy listening!
>
> Sincerely,
>
> [Your name here]

THE AGENT'S ROLE

An agent represents you and your talent. He or she is there to send you out on auditions, help land you jobs, and keep you working in the voiceover industry. The agent works closely with ad agencies, casting directors, and the voiceover talent to keep up on what's being cast and getting the best scripts for his or her clients. In return, the agent gets 10 percent of the fee for every job that you do. Here are some typical ways in which your agent might help you get jobs:

SPECIFIC REQUESTS

Specific requests are handled either at your agency's office or at the facility that requests you. In most instances, your agent will receive a request for you to read for a spot from a client, ad agency, or casting director, and you will then either be sent the copy/script or go to the ad agency, production office, or casting facility for the audition. But in other instances, based on your demo CD or your previous work, your agent will get a request for you to audition along with other talent who sound similar to you. These auditions may even be handled at your agency and the reads sent to the ad agency on CD. The ad agency or casting director will listen to all auditions submitted, decide whom they like, and then play those for the client, who will decide whether they want to hire you for the job.

    The client may give the agent or casting director guidance on how they want you to read the copy, or they may simply say, "Have her do her thing." Every voiceover actor has his or her own style. An experienced voiceover professional knows that "doing your thing" means that you should give your "trademark" read. Even a trademark read can be tricky. When I see a request for a "Terri Apple" read, I still need to look at the specs to understand which Terri Apple they want. Is it my dry read, my flat read, my fun read, or my energetic read? I have developed so many different moods and vocal qualities over the years that it's very important that I understand what they're looking for in terms of mood and energy.

It's only when I have this information that I can give them the read they're after.

▶ TIP: Depending on how your agency operates, you may want to use a cell phone so that you can always be contacted whenever you are needed. A last-minute job may come in, and you may be the one who gets hired — or you may miss out if they can't reach you. Unless you formally "book out" (tell your agency you are unavailable for any auditions or jobs on a given day), the agency will assume that it can book you for a job — including a last-minute job. (You should always book out if you know you're going to be unavailable.)

Even if you are out of town, however, you can still arrange to do a voiceover job remotely via phone patch. Nowadays, many voiceover sessions are done without the actor and the producer or the casting director ever meeting face-to-face. The audition and the session are all done by audio only — which makes perfect sense in the voiceover world!

GROUP REQUESTS

An ad agency might call your agent and say, "We're going to send over this copy for M&M's, and we want to hear six of your best men in their late forties who sound like the guy next door." Or they might say, "Please have Tim Martin, Joe Dunn, Terry Smith, Stacy Allen, Jeff Forrester, and Joe Blake read on this." But if they just request six people in a certain category, it's the agent's job to choose six people for the read. Now, the agent might have twenty-five clients who could do this particular read. But the agent will base the choice on his or her best six clients in that particular category. If the agent can throw in a few more, he or she will.

The ad agency may have called three or four other talent agencies as well. When they get the audition CDs, they will listen and decide whom to book for the job. If the ad agency doesn't get anything they like on the first go-round, they may opt to farm the audition out to a voiceover casting house.

SPECIFIC AND GROUP REQUESTS

An ad agency or client might call your agent and say, "I'm sending you some copy that I would like to hear Terri Apple on, but could you also put another three or four women on who are similar?" This happens when they know they like your voice but they may not have sold the client on hiring you. They want to hear how you sound on that particular spot, but they also want to give the client some other options.

When you go into your agency to read, the agent will tell you that although the ad agency has requested you, other people are reading for the spot as well. You do your best read within what they are looking for. If you're worried about typecasting, ask to do an alternate read — although the casting director may have asked your agency not to send one. (We will discuss alternate reads in later chapters.) And although it would be fun and helpful to hear how other people at your agency interpret the same copy, you will not be allowed to hear the reads of the other actors — so don't ask. (That is what classes and workouts are for.)

Conversely, a specific name may come to mind when the ad agency describes what they are looking for, or the agent may suggest someone he or she thinks would be right. If the ad agency trusts the agent's opinion and gives him or her the option of choosing someone, you may book just because the agent threw the job your way without your ever auditioning. (That's what the phrase "throw you a job" means.)

URGENT REQUESTS

An ad agency or client might call your agent and say, "I have a radio spot that I need a raspy female for. Who can you get me by three o'clock today?" At that point, the agent will see who's available. At my agency, if you are not available on any given day or week, you call in as soon as you know and they book you out on a board. Then, if a casting house or ad agency requests you for an audition or job, the agent immediately knows to say that you're unavailable. Once you've booked out, the audition is gone. Casting houses do not wait around to let you audition when you get back to town the following week. Auditions go quickly, and so do jobs. Most working voiceover artists rarely leave town. They know that a big job may be just around the corner and that one day out of town might mean missing the big audition. If you do go out of town, it's very important to check out recording studios wherever you are headed, so that you can e-mail an audition back to your agency, if necessary. You don't want to miss out on a national voiceover job worth thousands of dollars just because you decided to go to Mexico for a few days! It's also good to know about recording studios at which you can record jobs out of town just in case a regular client calls wanting you for a spot — or if you've booked a voiceover job that you auditioned for sometime during the previous weeks. If they can provide a phone patch, you can do the job from wherever you are on vacation — as long as there's a recording studio in the vicinity.

An urgent request can come at any time. I was once out to dinner in New York City when I got an urgent call from my agent in Los Angeles. They had a studio booked in New York, and I had to leave in the middle of dinner to do some TV spots for Toyota. Even though I had traveled to New York, I hadn't booked out — on purpose. The ad agency wanted me and had a deadline, and I happily went to work.

GENERAL AUDITIONS

Casting directors call agents when they have audition copy/scripts. If you don't have an agent, but they feel you are right for something based on your demo they will call you directly. As soon as your agent gets the call, he or she will call you, and that call might come in at any time of day, which is why it's best to make yourself available 24/7. Sometimes, there's a very quick turnaround (due date) for the read, or the time that it goes to air may be very tight!

Being constantly available is tough, but a necessity. When I was starting out, I waited tables at night and worked part time at a talent agency — and had to sneak away to get to auditions. I didn't want to miss a potential job. Nowadays, with the ability to send auditions back via email (MP3), you may have a bit more time to send and receive auditions. You certainly don't want to miss any opportunity to make money. Casting directors will call you in to read — that's a must. I've never been sent an audition from a casting director to read from home. Only auditions that come through your agency are available to send in if your agent okays it.

Remember, a job may be booked for 7 a.m. in Los Angeles to meet deadlines at an ad agency in New York City, where it is three hours later. It's generally okay to travel on weekends, which are usually free, although animation jobs do occasionally happen on Saturdays and Sundays. And the deadlines on non-union work tend to be a bit more flexible. (Although, with non-union they may want to use you on a Saturday or whenever they can get free time in a studio where they're recording.)

The casting director is the intermediary between you and the client. When the casting director has the auditions in hand, he or she sends them to the ad agency. The client then picks the person they want to hire for the job. Casting directors have files of voice talent they've either used over the years or found recently, and many demo voiceover CDs too. Your agent will send your CD as well as the agency's house CD to the casting directors, so that they have your agency's full talent roster. If an agent feels that certain voiceover actors aren't been called in, he or she will mention it to a casting director.

AGENT PUSH

The agent may call casting directors and ad agency creative directors to let them know about the new talent he or she has signed. The agent may push to have a particular client read for a particular product. Also, the agent will send out your demo CD in response to any request that comes in and will often submit your CD to all the ad agencies, casting houses, promo houses, producers, and production companies. It's the agent's job to keep on top of which ad agency has which clients and which casting house is casting for which projects — and to keep up good relationships with the casting directors and advertising agency staff.

ONE-STOP SHOPPING

Some ad agencies will send copy/scripts directly to the agent. They do this for several reasons. They may know that the talent they want is at one particular agency. Why send the copy out to casting directors when they can shorten the audition process? If an ad agency can hire all the talent for the spot(s) from one agency, it saves them a lot of time and they don't have to pay a casting director to do it for them. They just call the agency and hire directly. You will be called into your agency to read for any and all copy that your agent thinks is right for you. Your agent will schedule a time for you to come in and read. You may have to negotiate the time if you have other auditions. Let your agent know about all your other appointments as soon as you make them, so he or she can work around your schedule. Again, agents will assume you are available if you have not booked out.

VOICE TO VOICE

AN INTERVIEW WITH ERIK SEASTRAND

Erik Seastrand is vice president of the voiceover department of the William Morris Endeavor Talent Agency in Los Angeles. Also an attorney, Erik has worked as an agent since the early 1990s.

What do you look for in a voiceover client?

I look for an interesting, unique quality that separates that particular voice talent from the rest. There are two sides that I look for — the talent side and the business-savvy, responsible side. I need to have talent that not only knows how to read, how to act professionally in a voice session, but also has a great business sense. This is a profession that requires you to pay attention to current trends as well as always update your CD.

Are you open to bringing in new talent?

William Morris is an established agency with established talent. However, with a great referral, we will listen to new talent. If an ad agency producer called me up and told me to listen to so-and-so and sent the demo, I would definitely do that. We are interested in categories in the sense that we sign people and take them to the next level. This can be a voice actor who is not getting the attention from their current agent and has an interest in more opportunities that we can possibly provide, or an actor who happens to be at a top agency but doesn't feel they are getting the proper attention. As an agency, we are interested in partnerships, where we are providing opportunities (scripts, auditions, introductions) and you are bringing your talent. We need talent to show up on time for auditions and sessions, know how to read, and be professional. At the end of the day, we are working together as a team.

If you're new talent, you've got to be able to sound like working talent. In other words, you'd better be able to fool us when we listen to your demo CD. You don't want to send in a demo that sounds like fake reads, badly done. Your demo must sound professionally produced, as well as show your acting ability. When you are called in to read at your agency, you must know how to lay down a script and understand how to apply the mood to create the right read. You need to know how to nail the read. Booth directors are there to give notes, but you need to bring your "A game" to the read and be able to take the notes they give you.

Your agency is not meant to be a training group for voice talent. We are here to help actors achieve goals and to present opportunities.

How do you feel about voice actors having home studios?
I understand the changing advances within the industry, and we'd be crazy to not adapt with it, but, that being said, when we get last-minute projects (which we do quite a bit), those that are in the office and available will get the first shot, if they fit the specs. The turnaround time can be very small, and to fax the scripts to someone who may or may not be at their house to record the project, and trust that they will self-direct and get it back to us — as well as us having to then listen back, do cuts, edits, and upload the project separately — is difficult. Still, we understand people have trouble getting to sessions and/or being unable to get to the office to read. And we represent quite a few people who do have

agents in other states, so we understand the need for the MP3. But there has to be a lot of trust between the talent and agent to assume they will give the copy the best spin, know how to lay everything down, and get it back to us in a timely manner.

That said, what is your feeling about actors being represented by more than one agent across the country?
It becomes difficult if, for example, the actor is represented by an agent in the Midwest and has a local or regional car account running. That means we cannot include the actor for any car accounts that could possibly run nationally (making the actor and the agent a lot of money). A car account that runs nationally is obviously going to be more lucrative for all involved, so we have to be careful and not create conflict between the agent, ad agency, and talent. I do feel that talent should be business-savvy, create relationships, and be professional at every voice audition and session they do. Keep records, keep your demo CD current, be aware of trends. Also, knowing your limitations as a voice actor is important. This doesn't mean that you shouldn't pursue other areas within the voiceover field, but you must understand how to achieve in that area, the proper training to take, and the right areas to pursue within which you can achieve success.

THE COPY AND YOUR AGENT

Scripts come into your agent's office from ad agencies, producers, Voicebank, and other sources. Your agent will distribute the scripts to the appropriate talent along with any information/specs the ad agency or other client has provided. The actors read the scripts, and the recordings are submitted to the script's sources. This process may keep you in and out of your agent's office — and outside casting houses — every day of the week, depending on the number of scripts that come through.

Most A-list talent agencies receive the same scripts, but some voiceover agents will receive different copy depending on the relationships they have formed with outside sources. As long as your agency is affiliated with Voicebank and the unions, however, it should get most of the same major scripts as the other agencies, although your agent will still have to do the work to secure and maintain relationships so you get invited to auditions. (Being on Voicebank doesn't by itself ensure that your agency will get all the scripts.)

YOUR AGENCY CONTRACT

Usually, you sign with an agency for one year. After that, they may want you to sign a longer two- to three-year contract. Before signing such a contract, however, you should make sure that you are happy where you are — and that the company is constantly working for you. If you think you aren't being sent out as often as you should be — that you're being "shelved" — have a conversation with your agent. You may find out that they don't feel all that secure about you, in which case you may want to leave that agency and go with another. If you haven't booked a job in the past three months, the agency is legally required to release you from your contract and let you pursue other agents. (If, however, you've been called for a job but have turned it down, the agency does not have to let you out of your contract.)

YOUR AGENT AND YOUR MONEY

Union rules state that your agent gets 10 percent of all the money you make from all the jobs you do. This includes residuals. (Your contract will say the same.) Simply put, every time you do a job or it reruns, the agent gets 10 percent of whatever you receive. Depending on the job contract, this fee is sometimes included in your payment — essentially, your employer pays your agent's fee; at other times, this fee comes out of what you are paid. The payment process usually works like this: The ad agency or other client generates a check and sends it to a payment service, which sends it to the accounting department of your agency, which then deducts its 10 percent commission and sends you a check for the balance. Sometimes, however, the client's check is sent directly to you. If you receive such a check, make sure that you call your agency's accounting department and let them know you've received the payment directly. Then write the agency a check for 10 percent of the amount and send it to them. If you forget, the agency's accounting department will deduct that amount from your next check. Even if you get a job on your own or through other sources (contacts, friends, business associates, boyfriends, girlfriends, your mother, someone else's agent, lawyers, or the president of the United States), you are still required to pay your agent his or her 10 percent fee, because you are under contract.

Your agent is your protector. When you're hired for a job, he or she will negotiate all aspects of the deal, getting you the best pay for the work you do. The union establishes a base fee (called scale) that the ad agency must pay you. Depending on your union status, your years in the business, the amount of work you've done, and whether or not you've got a lot of things running, however, your agent might be able to negotiate a higher fee. (Talent who work more often get paid a little more.) Negotiating your fee is the agent's job. If you feel you've been working for scale for too long and want to be paid more, speak with your agent. Work together to get you the most money for particular jobs. A lot of very well-known voiceover actors still work for scale, because the competition is tough and the ad agencies know they can get any number of qualified voiceover artists for a job. Your agent will also negotiate holding fees — the fees an ad agency pays you when they are not sure whether they will broadcast a commercial you've done. These fees prevent you from recording commercials for competing products.

BEING POCKETED

Sometimes, an agent might want to take you on as a "pocket" (or "hip pocket") client. This means that the agent will postpone signing you to a formal contract until he or she sends your CD (and you) around to see what kind of response you get. It's a kind of trial run. Even if you are very talented and work a lot, an agency may not want to bring you in immediately if it already has a lot of people with voices similar to yours on its roster.

When an agent pockets you, he or she will treat you just as if you were a client until deciding whether to sign you or let you go. If an agent pockets you, wait for six months or so, and then talk to the agent about what the next step should be. If the agent doesn't want to sign you — and if you're not getting a lot of auditions — you may want to start submitting your CD to other agencies to see if there's a better place for you to be. You may be pocketed by more than one agency. Agencies usually dislike this arrangement — preferring to represent an actor exclusively — and it is a bit more common in New York City than in Los Angeles.

CHANGING AGENCIES

If your contract has expired and you are not happy, you can leave your agency with no further obligations. If, however, your contract has not expired and you are unhappy, then you should still think seriously about changing agents. Before you make that decision, however, make sure that you aren't frustrated with yourself over your lack of bookings. Ask yourself if it's really your agent who is at fault. Agents do sometimes pull auditions, or ask casting directors not to send them on to a client because they didn't like your read — sometimes even without telling you.

If the agent really isn't getting you out there, if you haven't been booking jobs lately (whereas you used to all the time), or the agent seems lazy to you, have a talk with him or her. But maybe you'll find that it's your attitude that's to blame, or that there's some sort of miscommunication between you. It's your job to make sure you get what you want from the agency. Here's a little advice, so you can give your agent a push before you heave-ho the relationship completely:

- Set up a meeting to talk about marketing strategies.
- Ask the agent why you're not getting out as much as you used to or coming into the agency to read as much.
- Make a list of clients you've worked for in the past that the agent can call.
- Listen to your CD together. Analyze it. Make changes if necessary.

- Have your agent listen to your auditions and give you feedback.
- Gently push the agent to broaden his or her thinking about the kinds of voice jobs you can do.
- Get an animation, promo, or narration demo made, so that the agent will bring you in for other kinds of auditions.
- Do a mass mailing of your demo CDs yourself. Set yourself the goal of meeting five new creative directors by sending CDs to people you've never met before.
- Impress your agent by taking a class — even if you feel it's unnecessary.
- Tell your agent how serious you are about making this a full-time career commitment.
- Ask your agent what else you can do to help your career along.

Try making all of these changes, and see what kind of response you get. Give the agent three to six months. Taking these steps may establish a new relationship. Your agent may suggest a new workout class or another area for you to pursue within the voiceover field. You may find you were simply taken out of rotation — that your agency stopped sending you to audition because you hadn't been booking very much — and that speaking with your agent has turned things around. But if nothing changes and you are still not satisfied, leave that agency. If your relationship has indeed soured, they may even be happy to let you out of an existing contract even if they've sent you on one or two auditions in the previous three months.

Once you decide to leave your agency, call around and set up meetings with other agents (or ask some casting directors who know your work to help you set up meetings). Meet as many agents as you can. You want to make sure that your agent wants the same thing for you that you want. (But be realistic about this — every voiceover actor wants to make a million dollars a year.) You want to make sure the agent believes in you and will push you. Maybe you weren't happy with your last agent because you found out that copy for a few national commercials came into the agency and you never got called in to read for them. Or maybe you weren't getting sent out to other places often enough. This might also be the fault of the casting companies. Unfortunately, no agent holds all the cards, and sometimes it's a crap shoot. Be open and honest with prospective new agents. Let them know the kind of money you've made over the past few years. Make sure they represent people in your financial range. Coming in as an agency's top breadwinner is not necessarily a good idea; you want an agency with other powerful, working voice actors — an agency that attracts ad agencies and production companies looking for talent, not one where the rest of the talent is mediocre or doesn't work very much. Make sure the agency is the kind of place where you can grow.

A new agent needs to know how to market you and get you out there, so make sure that the two of you are on the same page in terms of your goals. If, for example, you want to start auditioning for promos but have never done any, make sure the agent is willing to help you pursue this. Make sure that your promo demo CD isn't going to be sitting on a shelf somewhere, waiting to be dusted off. When you change agencies, make sure your demo CD has the updated information on it, and send out CDs with a short note to the casting directors to let them know you've changed agents. (The new voiceover agency will inform them, as well.)

WHAT YOU CAN EXPECT OF YOUR AGENT

The agent's job is to market your voice, make sure that the powers that be know you, and help you get jobs. The agent will make calls, submitting your name for jobs, and will send your CD around to casting directors to encourage them to keep bringing you in for auditions. When you book a job, the agent will negotiate the rate and talk with you if it sounds shady and he or she thinks that you shouldn't take it.

Your agent may have lots of clients. If you become well known in the business, your agent may get requests for you directly, and you may be a top booker (getting a lot of jobs). Or the agent may have to work extra hard to get the casting directors to see you. An agent's job can be difficult because he or she has to push you and get you the work. But an agent does a lot more than just making cold calls. Your agent will also be speaking to the producers, writers, directors, and casting houses he or she knows, pushing you for jobs. A good agent also does his or her best to make sure that your reads are up to par and suggests changes that you might make to enhance your performance and get more jobs.

WORKING WITH YOUR AGENT

If you have an occasional question, call your agent. Don't call every day just to gripe or to ask if you got a particular job. If you get the job, your agent will call you. Sometimes the toughest thing about working in voiceovers is worrying about whether you got a job. But you may be reading for twenty commercials a week, so just keep on moving. If you book, your agent will call. You may also have weeks when you have no auditions. This is normal. Every week is different, and whether you're auditioning or not depends on what's happening in the advertising world, not on your agent. Your agent has nothing to do with how the advertising world runs. As long as your agent is connected and usually gets good copy, there's nothing more you can do. The ad world goes through slow periods (especially at the end of summer, right before the rush of fall). Don't worry, it always picks up.

Build your relationship with your agent(s) very carefully. Make sure that your personalities are working together smoothly. You don't want to annoy your agent by calling every day. You don't want to besiege him or her with questions like, "How's it going?" "How's my career?" "Why didn't I get those last ten jobs?" "Why didn't you get me in for that bleach commercial I heard on TV, with that voice that sounds just like mine?" First of all, your agent may not have gotten the copy for the bleach commercial. You can't know whether the bleach commercial was cast in your town or somewhere else. And your agent has no control over changes in the ad world. Advertisers may like one sound for a while, then move on to another, and then come back to the original. Sometimes you just have to hang in there and keep reading. You shouldn't pester your agent — but you should keep in touch.

You should make a call to your agency once every couple of weeks to check in. Ask for your agent, but if the agent can't take your call, just have a quick chat with the assistant. A quick, "Hi, it's Steve Jones, just checking in," will do fine. Making friends with the assistant is a great way to ensure you get called in. Assistants see all the copy; they're in the meetings at which the agents cast their talent pool, and it doesn't hurt to have them think of you and say, "Hey, how about Steve Jones for that Mazda script?"

Give your agent reasons to stay enthusiastic about you. Finding a new way to read, a new avenue to submit your demos — anything to create a good buzz around your career and to keep the agent interested — is always a good plan. And giving the agent a nice gift for the holidays is a great gesture.

Remember that your agent cannot possibly know of every audition in town. The agent can only do so much. He or she has to be making the calls, of course, but the casting companies and ad agencies also have to do their part — letting the agent know about upcoming auditions. Still, there may be times when you hear about an audition that you think you're right for but that you haven't been called for. What you should do depends on how you hear about it. If it's at a casting studio, call your agent and ask if he or she can possibly get you in. The agent may call the casting house and ask. But that doesn't mean the request will be successful. The casting house may already have filled its roster for that audition and won't be able to squeeze anybody else in.

If you are at a reading at a casting house audition and happen to see other copy that you feel you'd be right for, ask the casting associate or casting director if you can read for the other project. More often than not, they'll be very nice about it and be willing to include you in the audition. If, however, you hear of copy/script that came in to your agency that you didn't get to read for, you're in a tricky situation. Think twice before calling and complaining. If you work a lot, it may have been an oversight. But just because you think you're right for something doesn't mean that another actor isn't, too — or doesn't read better than you, more consistently. You don't want to undermine your agent's judgment, and you don't want to do something that may make you feel worse than you already do. If you call, be prepared to hear something like, "Yes, we know you exist, but we only could bring in ten people and, unfortunately, we didn't feel that you were as strong for this as some of the other people we represent." Don't make your agent look stupid; you really need to trust that the agent will bring you in every time he or she thinks you are right for a read.

If you feel you are constantly missing out on reads that you'd be right for, do talk with your agent. But remember, too, that it's usually only the big bookers who always get to read all the copy that comes in, and that if you're a newcomer to the business you simply may not be first and foremost on the list. Agencies rotate their client list, which means that they try to put as many people at different times on reads. These can seem unfair and strange. You certainly deserve every opportunity to read on every script that comes through your agency's doors that you are right for, but sometimes it just can't happen — there may be too many actors in one particular category. There may be a special request or something about the project, only your agent knows. There may be a specific note from the ad agency that asks for only a certain number of talent on that job. The agent has the authority to pick who reads for which jobs. Try to be great at every read and be easy to work with, so that you will get in for as many as possible!

AUDITIONING/RECORDING AT YOUR AGENCY

Most agencies have a recording booth (or several) that they use to have you come in to read. Some have more booths and microphones than others — it depends on the size of the agency and its budget. Recording studios generally have two rooms — one to hold the recording equipment and the other for the voiceover actors to do their work. The two rooms are separated by a glass wall so that the talent can see the casting person. (I've been to some talent agencies where the studio had just one room, in which the casting associate perched in a corner, working with the equipment, as the voiceover actor worked at the microphone.) You may also walk into a room shared with a casting or booth director and they may record you onto a computer through a microphone.

(Be prepared to read wherever they place you!) That being said, there are several types of recording studios (Walla Walla, dubbing, v/o, music) that are many different styles and sizes.

The process of reading at your agency is basically the same as what you go through when you audition at a casting facility. The agency has set up an on-premises recording booth to make it easier for the ad agency to submit scripts and get recorded auditions back, eliminating the need for a casting house. You may find yourself going in to your agency to read every day of the business week, or you may only be called once every few weeks. It all depends on how much copy is coming into the agency and how much of that copy your agent thinks you are right for. You may be considered a staple client (someone who books a lot of jobs and who is considered right for many different types of reads), or you may be stereotyped and brought in only for specific types of reads.

When your agency has a script that's right for you, you'll usually be called the day before the audition or based on when it's due and how your agent is casting. But some scripts come in at the last minute, which means you may get a call to come in immediately. Sometimes, the agency will want everybody who's reading to be there when they open at 9 a.m. so they can be done with the casting process by 1 p.m. Sometimes, they'll bring people in all day long. When the agency calls you to come in, confirm the time that they give you. If you can't make it at that particular time, let them know. They may or may not be able to be flexible. They might have you scheduled for a group read (with more than one person in the same spot), in which case the specific time is important. Or they might just ask you to pick a time that's convenient for you. But they're usually working within a pretty small window. For example, if a script comes in and the auditions are due back to the ad agency in two days, then your agent has to bring in all appropriate talent, audition everybody, and e-mail the auditions to the ad agency within that time frame. Great agents try to turn around the auditions as quickly as possible so they're the first to be heard in the decision process.

VOICE TO VOICE
AN INTERVIEW WITH JEFF DANIS

Jeff Danis is currently a partner/owner of the DPN (Danis, Pinero, Nist) Agency. Formerly, he was a voiceover agent and the head of the Commercials/Voiceovers Department at ICM (International Creative Management).

You started in the advertising business?
Yes. I was with an ad agency in New York City for ten years. I did everything from head of casting, to talent, to payments. Then I worked at J. Michael Bloom as an agent, took a year off to be a casting director, and then came to Los Angeles to start the voiceover department at ICM.

Why did you want to go into voiceovers?
I knew they were the thing of the future. I knew that the money potential for talent and agents was big. As a voiceover agent, you have more control of someone's career. There is more longevity in a voiceover actor's career than on-camera commercials.

What do you look for in a voiceover client?
Earning potential, unique voice quality, good acting ability. Also, I think a comfortable persona and the ability to read a script are very important. Many actors have trouble with the commercial rhythm. Some stage actors tend to be too broad with the copy, while some film actors tend to be too intimate. There is a definite rhythm to the read. Actors should watch TV commercials and listen to the radio. Ninety-nine percent of the time, the obvious commercial read books the job. All TV commercial reads should fit these ideals: Give it warmth! Give it a commercial read. Most of the time that will get you the spot or get you close. Voices may sound different, but there is still a definite rhythm to the read. The way a sentence ends. The tone of the voice. Also, timings are very important. Timing has to be there.

How do you differentiate the clients on your list from one another?

Everyone has something different. It is very important to know your clients. I keep a roster in my head. If a producer calls, I know in that minute that I can go through my list and be able to tell them who can do what kind of read. It's very important to know my clients, to know exactly what they are capable of. A lot of producers count on me to help in the casting process. They can call me up and say, "I need a couple for this spot. The woman should be sardonic, the man should be nerdy." I can cast that spot in a matter of minutes and know that my clients will be at that job.

What suggestions do you have for someone who comes in to read?

Technically, your voice should be present on the mike. Make sure that the headphones are up; make sure that you are centered to the mike. I, as your agent, need to be able to showcase you the best way I can. When you go in to read, the very first and very last question that you should ask is, "What am I saying?" If you cannot answer that question, then your read is not the best that it can be. The interpretation of the read is very important. A lot of people may read for a job, but the interpretation, the acting, is what gets you the job. Convention is out. They want unique personalities now. They want the copy to come alive, your unique personality to come through.

How many clients do you put on an audition CD?

It depends on the copy. I will stick as many people on a CD as I think are realistically capable of booking that job. It may be anywhere from five to fifteen people. You have to remember that we may or may not be the only ones in town getting the copy. Sometimes, with large campaigns, it may go to us and a few more agencies that each put ten or so people on — and it may also go to Chicago and New York. Sometimes more than one hundred people can be up for the same job!

What do you expect from the voice talent?

I expect them to make the voiceovers a priority. I have one client who has a great voice but just doesn't book the reads. I have faith in him because I know that he will work. I continue to work with them. Practicing reading is important.

I think it's a great workout just coming into the booth, even if you're not booking. It gives you a chance to read copy, hear what's in out there in TV land, and get the rhythm down.
Absolutely. The truth is, a great TV commercial read can be learned. It is more important to know how to act than to have specific voice quality.

What does it take to make it as a voiceover talent?
Opportunity and ability. Rhythm is everything. Unique personality. I've heard some great voices, but they didn't have any character in their voice. The best reads are the actors who understand what they are saying. Commercials have a simple message: "Buy this product!"

What is the difference between a voice agent and an on-camera commercial agent?
An on-camera agent will have many more clients. Clients can easily become overexposed. Ad agencies like to see different faces. An actor can be on two or three commercials and they burn out. A voiceover talent can do a lot more work. The agent and talent can make a lot more money over a longer period of time. The voice can work for many years — there's much more longevity and potential. I also have more control with my clients than if I were an on-camera agent. I can cast the spot and send work my clients' way a lot easier than on-camera agents can. I have a lot more opportunity for work for my clients: radio, TV, looping, animation, nonbroadcast, industrials, promos, and CD-ROMs.

Let's end this with a bottom line. Do you have one?
The talent has to be A-list. All the good intentions that an agent has are only as powerful as the talent is. On that same note, as talented as the talent is, they are powerless without a great agent behind them!

CHAPTER 10

THE RECORDING SESSION AND TECHNOLOGY

CONGRATULATIONS, YOU'VE BOOKED A JOB! Hopefully, it's the beginning of many to come. Now it's time to record the spot — and get paid. Your agent will call you to give you the time and date of the recording session. Or, if you got the job on your own, the casting director or person in charge will call you directly.

Recording sessions vary according to where they take place, how the recording is done and the kind of job (commercial, promo, narration, animation, etc.). Some voiceover professionals record all jobs in their own home studios. But when you start in the business, you'll be going to professional recording studios for the session.

The ad agency will call your agent to book you, based on the expiration date of the project, the availability of studio time, and the schedules of the writer and producer. Once the session has been booked by your agent, the time is confirmed and cannot be changed unless there is an emergency. The ad agency will have gone to great lengths to find an available studio and to make sure you're available at a given time. Studios are rented by the hour, and the client has booked you for a specific amount of time. If you have to cancel or change at the last minute, inform your agent immediately so you can reschedule the session. You don't want to be replaced by another voice actor and lose the job — as well as the potential for working with that client again on future projects.

Per union rules, producers are allowed to keep you for an hour and a half per spot. For commercial sessions, you will usually be booked for one or two hours. If you're recording several spots, the client may book you for several hours. The only thing you need to bring to the session is your voice. Once you arrive at the studio, check in with the front desk. Tell the receptionist that you are the talent. The receptionist, who has a list of everything that's going on in the studio that day, will ask which job you are there for, hand you the copy (if it's available), and tell you which studio you're recording in.

RECORDING THE SESSION

There are four basic ways to record a session: in person, in town; patch (phone or land); in person, out of town; and MP3.

IN PERSON, IN TOWN

If you, the ad agency, and the client are all in the same city, you will work with the ad agency personnel (and perhaps with a representative of the client, as well) directly, in person. You will go to a local studio and into the booth. The sound engineer will direct you through levels and the mike setup. You will be introduced to the person who will give you direction. (Direction covers everything they want from the read.) The client's representative may or may not be at the session. If the client's representative isn't there, the ad agency copywriter or creative director in charge of the account will direct you.

On the other hand, the client may provide quite a lot of input — together with the ad agency's creative director. You may sometimes feel that you are being pushed in many different directions while trying to give the "creatives" what they want — which may be very different than what you did at the original audition. Remember, you are there to make the client(s) happy. They may not even know exactly what they are looking for until they hear it. Work with them and give them options.

Once the ad agency people get the basic read they want in terms of mood, point of view, and vocal quality, they then work on getting the read *in time.* They've chosen you because you are the voice they want, but they will still want to manipulate and play with your voice until they get the precise read they're looking for. You may read the copy once or you may read it thirty times during the session. Getting the right read is a mix between creativity and technique.

After the session, they may call the client (if the client isn't at the session) and play the takes they like for them. They may ask you to stay to make sure the client gets the read they want. Or, if they release you before they've gotten the approval, you may be brought back in, paid another session fee, and asked to do some more takes of the same commercial — known in the industry as a "re-record."

Recording studio setups vary. You'll usually be in a booth whose acoustics are specially designed for sound recording. If this booth is next to the room in which the sound engineer and the client and ad agency people are working, you'll be able to see them through a window. If the voiceover booth is separate, you will only be able to see each other through a closed-circuit TV monitor, and you will have to communicate through the headphones and microphones. At some network promo rooms, the setup is even simpler: You will sit in the same room as the recording engineer, with a small TV setup so you can record to picture, or a small monitor on which you can watch the spot and then record "wild" — without timing yourself to the picture. By the way, some studios have valet parking — but some don't. In any case, if you drive to a session, you should allow yourself enough time to park and make it to your session with plenty of time to spare. They may only have fifteen minutes scheduled for you, depending on their deadline. Time is tight in this business!

▶ TIP: This extremely useful tip comes from voiceover actor Dan Gilvizian: "Avoid spitting on the glass while recording. It grosses people out and makes that sound engineer's job a lot harder."

PATCH (PHONE OR LAND)

For a phone patch, you are in the studio recording the spot, while the producer, client, director, and writer are patched in — from another studio or from several other locations. For a land patch, the producer, director, and writer are in the studio recording the spot, while you are patched in from another studio. Patches are used because the various people involved — you, the producer, the client, the director, the writer, and whoever else is participating — are in different parts of the country. For instance, you might be in Los Angeles, but the client is in New York, and the writer and ad agency are in Denver. The entire patch session will be conducted through the headphones and microphone. The sound engineer will be the only person physically there with you during the session.

The sound engineer will handle everything technical — the headphones and microphone — and will then call the client. As the session begins, the engineer will put you through to the writer or producer (sometimes the same person), who will direct you throughout the session. The client may be on the line as well, just listening to the session. Do not touch the microphone. Adjusting the mike is the sound engineer's job — and the engineer doesn't want anything to get broken. If you are having a problem with the height of the mike (or any other technical problem), let the sound engineer know, and he or she will adjust it. Pick up your headphones, but wait to put them on until the sound engineer tells you it's okay to do so, because they may be doing some technical things that result in a loud, headache-inducing tone if you have the headphones on. Once everything is set up, you are clear to put the headphones on and get ready to record.

During the patch, you'll hear the direction from the copywriter or producer through your headset. It's usually the sound engineer in the studio where you are recording who will give you the take numbers and any technical information. The sound engineer will also give you your timings, slate each take, and cue you to begin your read. But it may be that the sound studio calling in will also have a sound engineer on the line handling takes and timings. Sometimes, both engineers will be slating and recording.

It is up to them what they want to do. Just follow the instructions from whoever is slating you and telling you what to do. When you are done with each take, the writer/director will give you a new piece of direction to guide you through the following take. It's a good idea to make notes on your script, writing down each change as they give it to you, so you remember what to do for your next take.

IN PERSON, OUT OF TOWN

An out-of-town ad agency may choose to fly you in rather than work with a patch system. Some agencies and clients feel they can't hear you read as clearly over a phone line as they can if they are right there with you. (The ad agency would spend just as much on a digital phone patch as on your airline ticket, so it really doesn't matter to them in this regard.) If they fly you in, they will cover the airfare and give you a per diem, which should cover the cost of a meal and local transportation. The union sets a minimum amount for the per diem, but depending on the city you're going to, you may be able a negotiate a higher amount. If the per diem doesn't cover your expenses, tell your agent. You should be given enough. On most of these jobs you fly in and fly out the same day. If the job requires more than one session or it isn't completed in one day, your overnight expenses and per diems are usually covered for the duration of your stay.

MP3

"MP3ing" is the term used for transferring voiceover data via the Internet. Many voiceover actors who record from their home studios use MP3 technology to send out the audition, demo, or session recordings they do at home. If you are hired for a voiceover job but no people from the ad agency or client will be sitting in with you, this is the perfect way to record the job and send it out. The client can then download it from the Internet.

SOME TERMS YOU NEED TO KNOW

You're bound to hear some industry jargon while you're at the session. Here are a few important terms you need to know:

Hot: When you hear a buzzing or screeching noise in your headphones, the headphones are turned up too high. The sound engineer will say, "Your headphones are hot," or, possibly, "You are feeding back," which means that your voice is pushing back into the studio and you will not be able to record.

Level check (also called a **sound check**): The sound engineer will check the loudness of your voice as you speak into the microphone. For the level check, start reading the copy or script, beginning at the top, and continue reading until the sound engineer has adjusted the levels so that the spot comes out crisp and clear. If you plan to yell at a certain point in the script, yell during the sound check so the sound engineer can anticipate that level of sound. During a phone patch, the sound check will be done over headphones by both the client's sound engineer and the sound engineer working beside you.

Slate: "To slate" means to say your name and the take number. In an audition, you may say the take number, but in a session the recording engineer will do it. Before each take, the engineer will recite the name of the product and call off the take number. Then the ad agency will pick the take or takes they like when they edit the spot. They may combine pieces from two or more takes when creating the final spot.

Timing: The timing is the time allowed for you to read within the take. Just because a commercial is a thirty-second spot doesn't mean you will read for the entire thirty seconds. The spot may include four seconds of music. There may be an announcer, or another actor playing another part. You may only have ten seconds to read your part.

RECORDING REGULAR BROADCAST SPOTS

A regular broadcast spot is one that will be going on the air — either television or radio. You will go in and do the session, but the ad agency may want to piece together portions from many different takes to get the voiceover they want. It's the final, edited version that will go on the air. You may ask for a copy of the spot. If they finish editing it during the session, the sound engineer will simply make you a copy and give it to you. If they don't finish it, the ad agency will take your home address or the address of your agent and mail or e-mail you the completed spot.

▶ TIP: Make sure that your headphones are set properly. Both you and the sound engineer can adjust your headphones. Your controls are attached to the headphones next to your microphone. You should be able to hear yourself and the sound engineer talking. But the headphones are there to enhance your read, not confuse you or force you to push more than you want to. And you don't want to hear your voice through the cans louder than your actual voice. Hearing yourself louder in the cans will tend to make you speak more softly and intimately, which won't work unless that's what the read calls for.

RADIO SPOTS

A radio spot might be a "single" (just you, alone), a "double," or even a group read. (For more on doubles and groups, see below.) The spot may or may not include music and sound effects. If it does, the person directing you may already have set up the music bed and sound effects and may want to play them for you so that you get the rhythm, mood, style, and flow of the spot. They may even feed the music and sound effects into your headphones so that you can read along with them. Or they may choose to have you read wild and then add the music and sound effects in post-production. Obviously, a radio spot will air only on the radio. If you do a TV version of the spot (or a TV spot that's part of the same campaign), you'll be reading different copy. (Refer to Appendix A for some examples of radio spots.)

Just as in other kinds of recording sessions, the session for a radio spot will begin with the engineer asking for a level. Then you'll begin your takes. The engineer and ad agency people may play back the takes they like until they get the read they are looking for. They may ask you for several different moods or for technical changes. Learn to listen to what the director or copywriter wants from you. Stay out of your own way. Offer an opinion if they ask for it, or if you truly do understand what they are looking for and think that this time you can nail the read. Sometimes they don't know exactly what they are looking for, so they may want several different options. Be accommodating and willing to play around. Once you've got the mood of the spot, they'll want to focus on the timing and on laying your read down to the music bed or to the other voiceovers in the spot.

TELEVISION SPOTS

For television spots, there may or may not be a storyboard or moving image (scratch track) for you to coordinate your voiceover with. If there is a scratch track, you might be asked to follow along to picture while you read. Or they may show you the spot first, then have you go into the booth and read. Or they may just want you to do the read cold, or wild. It all depends on what the director wants. If you feel it's easier to read to picture — and they have a scratch track set up — tell them. They may be happy to oblige. Otherwise, they may show you the spot so that you can get a feel for what they want from you. (If this is the case, you will watch the scratch track but then record your read separately.)

If you are doing a campaign (more than one spot), they may have only one scratch track to show you. (They may not have shot the other spots yet.) You'll watch the one spot they have shot just to get a feel for the campaign as a whole. You may be asked to come back again and again, as they shoot the new spots; if this happens, you will have to remember how you did the first spot so that you can recapture that same vocal quality. Sometimes they will play back the takes they liked from the original session, so that you can get a better sense of what you did before. (Refer to Appendix A for some examples of TV spots.)

RECORDING TAGS

If you are called in for the tag, you will be reading just a portion of the copy — usually the very last line. When you are booked for a commercial, you may not know that you are just doing the tag. There may be a narrator, who introduces the story; voice actors, who do the body of the spot (that is, the meat of the copy); and then you, who will do the tag — the spot's last line or catchphrase. Sometimes you'll be asked to read a tag three times, one right after the other. This is called "three in a row," or "three wild, in a row," or sometimes, "three in a row, A, B, C." You will record these lines or phrases without reading from the full copy, and, because you're reading wild, each segment of the numbered take will be slated alphabetically. For example, the sound engineer might say, "This is take fourteen A, B, and C." You will pause for a slight beat between each take. It's easier for the sound engineer to record these brief takes in groups of three rather than one at a time, and the grouping gives the client a chance to hear several reads in a row. The sound engineer may give you the timings between each read to help you get the read in the proper time. (If you run long on a read, you will know to speed up the next one, or vice versa.) You will receive direction, even for tags. Not only might the director ask you to do it again slower, faster, or with a different pacing, but he or she might also ask you to change the tone or mood.

RECORDING PROMOS

If you are called in for a promo, you'll be reading for some type of promotional ad or campaign, most likely for a television or radio station. The promo voiceover reminds viewers when a show is coming on: "Tonight on *Action 4 News*," "Later on *Grey's Anatomy*," "Next on *Dateline NBC*." Promos are different from tags because they're geared toward a very specific time frame and because the promo announcer may read several lines of copy, whereas the tag person will just state a product name or a line or phrase aimed at making the listener remember a product. As a promo actor, you may be hired to do the promos for just one television show or for a network's entire lineup of shows.

RECORDING ANNOUNCER VOICEOVERS

In a commercial, the announcer is the main narrator selling the product. When you record an announcer voiceover, the other talent whose voices appear in the spot may be there at the same session or may be booked separately. If the voice actors playing the characters in the spot (say, "Tom" and "Nancy") have already recorded their copy (say, talking about Taco Bell while playing tennis), their voiceover will be played for you, and you will work from it. You will record your part separately, and it will be edited in. The director may tell you that you have twenty-four seconds to do the announcer's part within the sixty-second spot. (The other time is used up by Tom and Nancy speaking, some music, and the sound of a tennis ball being hit back and forth.) This means that you must get your read in twenty-four seconds — although sometimes, if they can't get the read in the allotted time, they may have to cut copy. If they like the read and they don't want to cut, however, they may shorten the music track at the top or skip one tennis-ball sound effect — or even shorten Nancy and Tom's read.

RECORDING NARRATION

Narration can have several different meanings. Sometimes, it's used as a synonym for the announcer's voiceover. But the term is more commonly used for the voiceover that narrates the story in an industrial video, animated program, or live-action TV show or feature film. The narrator is the person who talks to the audience and tells the story. The narrator's voice carries you through the show.

A narration recording session is much like a regular voiceover session. If you're doing the narration for a TV spot, you may or may not be reading to a visual. If you don't read to the visual, it may be because the ad agency hasn't yet completed the spot — or they may show you the completed spot but may still want you to read wild (without the picture). Sometimes the ad agency people will feel that they'll get a better read from you if you read wild, because you will have fewer constraints.

If you are doing narration for an industrial video or feature film, it's likely that a visual prompter (a TV monitor) will be set up, so that you can read to picture. For most narration jobs, you will have more time to read because you have more copy to read. A narration might be one paragraph long, or it might run to several pages, depending on the length of the show. You will find out the length of the job when your agent calls you. If the script has been completed, your agent will get the copy ahead of time for you to go over, if he or she can. Otherwise, you will get the copy when you go to the session.

RECORDING ANIMATION VOICEOVERS

Unless you have only a couple of lines, you will be sent the script for an animation session ahead of time. At the session, you will probably be giving the same read that you gave at the audition. The director will direct you. If the session is a single, you will be alone in the booth. But if you and the other actors are hired for the day, you will each be given your own mike and headphones and you will all work together, recording each scene. (You may or may not record the scenes in the order in which they'll appear in the completed program or film.) Even if you are working with the other actors, you may be asked to do a wild line, or three in a row, depending on what the director needs. You may also be recording voices for more than one character. If that's the case, you will be working for a longer period of time with the director, who will instruct you on how he or she wants each read done.

SINGLES, DOUBLES, AND GROUP SESSIONS

If you are called in for a single, it means that you, and only you, are in the spot. The spot may include music or sound effects (added in before or after you record), but you will be the only one reading the copy for the body of the spot. This does not mean that there won't also be a tag person or announcer — just that you are the only other voice besides the announcer and/or tag person.

But often you will be the sole voice for the entire spot, reading the body as well as the announcer copy and tag line, if any. This is called reading from wall to wall (beginning to end). Note: If you do the announcer copy, the body, and the tag, you will not be paid three fees. You are not changing your voice in any way for the other roles; your voice is the same throughout the entire read, and you will only be paid one fee. This differs from animation, where you are paid for up to two characters per animated show and then a percentage, determined by the agent negotiating the deal, for every other character you do. Unless, of course, it's a non-union job and you are doing the negotiating, or it's a buyout, and you agree to a one-time-only fee.

Any session using more than one voice is a double or group read — the terms are interchangeable. There may also be an announcer, but basically it's you and the other person. You will each have your own mike and headphones if you are reading together. Even if a script calls for two or more actors to interact with each other, the others may still record during a separate session, depending on rewrites, the availability of the actors, and a number of other reasons. In this case, you will read your part wild.

In a group session, you will work with all the other actors in the spot. If the spot requires seven actors, then there will be seven actors at the session. In animation, actors sometimes double up, with one actor used for several different characters. This is because it is easy to disguise your voice in animation, where the voices are often exaggerated. In regular commercials, however, the use of the same voice for two different parts would usually be too easy to detect — unless your audition reads were so different from one another that the ad agency decides to use you for two completely different characters. (An ad agency might also decide to use the same actor for two different voices if those voices don't come up next to each other in the spot, but this is rare.) As a general rule, the agency will pull in as many actors as there are roles in the commercial.

The individual mikes and headphones will be set up for you before the session. You can choose to use the headphones or not, but it's better if everyone does the same thing, since it's easier to work off of one another if you are all on the same plane. You will be directed together. The engineer will slate and get a level from each of you, and then you will begin. Once the talkback mike is on, you are hot. This means that you are live and that everyone can hear everything you say. So say nice things!

CONTRACTS

Most likely, the contract will have been sent to the studio along with the copy. If there is no contract at the session, inform the producer once the session is over, and call your agency to let them know there was no contract and tell them the number of spots you did. If it is a union job, fill out the union papers, which the studio provides for you and then sends to your union. The producer might fax the contract straight to your agent, or he or she may ask you to fill it out and then fax it back to them for processing. Keep all of your scripts and a copy of your contract for yourself, and take them to your agency so that they can keep the copies for accounting purposes. The agency will need proof of all the work you've done to make sure you get paid.

Be scrupulous about this. I was once in a very long session. The company that hired me told my agent that I would be doing only ten tags. In fact, I did twenty. Because I had already signed the contract specifying ten tags, however, I never got paid for the additional work. Now I always check what I am doing and make sure that I never sign a contract unless it is correct. I lost thousands of dollars for that mistake, so if there's any discrepancy, make sure you tell the producer and immediately inform your agent of the problem.

▶ TIP: The "snowflake" is a great, inexpensive microphone you can purchase to send in auditions.

NON-UNION SESSIONS

Non-union work is perfectly legal. Smaller companies and companies that don't have the funds for union talent will use non-union talent, which is usually less expensive. Non-union talent negotiates the fee directly with the producer, writer, or director. There are no set fees, and the compensation might be as little as a copy of the CD and gas money. It all depends on the project budget and on how much or little you are willing to work for.

Generally there is no formal contract for a non-union job. If there is, it may be some sort of agreed-upon waiver or a buyout contract. But there may be no paperwork at all, in which case you are being paid under the table. The term *under the table* is widely used in the voiceover industry for any job that isn't union-affiliated. If you are in a union, you cannot work under the table except in some strictly limited circumstances. If you do — and you are caught — you may be fined, suspended, or even released from the union.

If you choose to do a public service announcement (PSA), the union may provide you with a waiver to sign. Check with the union. And there are some non-union, non-air jobs that you, as a union member, can do if you sign a special agreement. Rules vary from state to state, so you'll need to check your state's regulations before taking such jobs.

VOICE TO VOICE
AN INTERVIEW WITH LOREN LESTER

How did you begin in voiceovers?
I started working at the age of 16 and I was very lucky because my first agent had departments in every arena: film/TV, on-camera commercials, voiceovers, even print. Steve Tisherman, who didn't have his own agency yet, ran the voiceover department, and I give him the credit for launching my animation and commercial voiceover career. My first voiceover job was at the legendary Hanna-Barbera Studios, starring in an animated TV movie, *Five Weeks in a Balloon.*

I know you do television, film, and voiceovers. Did you begin with on-camera or VO work?
As I mentioned, my first agent had a department for everything, so I began my on-camera and voiceover career simultaneously. You can't find an agency like that now. Agencies are very specialized. Most actors these days have an agent specifically for voiceovers and another for commercial work and yet another for theatrical work. In my early years, I worked primarily on camera,

in films like the cult classic *Rock 'n' Roll High School* and TV shows like *The Facts of Life*, but I was doing a lot of voiceover at the same time. By the time I was in my late twenties, however, my on-camera career disappeared and I found myself doing a lot of guest, recurring and regular roles on a number of animated series. Eventually I was almost exclusively involved in animation as "Robin" and "Nightwing" on the various incarnations of the animated *Batman* series.

In the last few years my on-camera career has kicked into high gear again and I've done over 60 TV shows and films and dozens of on-camera commercials. Highlights include the Wes Craven film *Red Eye*, guest-starring roles on TV shows like *The Closer* and two HBO series, *Curb Your Enthusiasm* and *Hung* (where I have a recurring role).

Do you work mostly in the commercial world of voiceovers, animation, promo, trailer?
Commercial work has always been consistent, but the rest of it definitely goes in cycles. I've had periods when I was heavily involved in animation and other periods when I would be picking up work in practically every area, even promo. Lately it has been mostly commercials, but I still get some nice animation roles (such as a recurring role on the series *W.I.T.C.H.* and the upcoming series *The Avengers*).

Are you primarily known for a certain type of voiceover read? Do you often get called in for the same types of reads?
At my current voiceover agency, I'm thrilled to say that I'm given copy for everything. My agent hasn't decided what I can't do, and that's increased my odds in the crazy numbers game that we play every day looking for work. (Just about everyone agrees that it's a numbers game — you have to audition for a lot of spots in order to book the few that give you a chance to make a living — there's a definite lottery aspect to it.) I'm able to make copy sound conversational and I've been told that I have an everyman kind of voice, so I book a lot of announcer roles where I'm an enthusiastic but non-announcer-y spokesperson for the company.

How many agents do you have across the country?
I actually have three voiceover agents at my voice agency here in L.A.: one commercial agent and two animation agents (one for TV/interactive and one for features). My on-camera theatrical agent has a N.Y. and L.A. Office, and I have three agents in my L.A. on-camera commercial agency. I also have a manager for film and TV.

How many different types of demos do you currently have?
Animation, commercials, promo, and six different promos for audio books covering all genres.

Is there anything you do (outside of having representation) to go after work? Do you freelance?
I keep in touch with people I've worked with. I send postcards and emails when I'm appearing in a TV show, film, or play and I send holiday cards.

Do you have your own setup (home studio) and if so, how complex is it — ISDN, other capabilities?
It isn't complex at all, but the audio quality is such that the tracks of some of my auditions have been put right on the air. You don't have to spend a lot of money these days to have a professional home studio. I have an Audio-Technica microphone that plugs into a TASCAM US-122 that plugs into my computer. That's it. And my booth is actually a small alcove lined with a large book and record collection that gives me plenty of soundproofing.

Do you currently still have long running accounts? Do you feel the market has changed in the last ten years, and if so, how?
Yes, I have some nice repeat business for certain accounts and a few ad agencies that hire me consistently, sometimes without an audition — every actor loves that! The main difference in the business comes down to one word: demos. Many, many auditions today are for demos. Some days your agent might give you a handful of scripts, but many of those spots will be recorded at the demo rate (about half the rate for a real spot) and some won't even be recorded at all. It definitely wasn't like that 10 years ago. That changes the numbers game — that and the fact that there

are also vastly more actors competing for the work. Now you have to audition twice as much and work twice as much to earn enough money to make a living.

Do you find it difficult or easy to venture into new areas of the business, casting directors, ad agencies, etc.?
My current voiceover agent has arranged general interviews for me with animation casting directors that I've never worked for. This has really opened some doors, and because of the general interviews, I've been brought in to audition for a number of animated series over the last few months.

Any other comments, history, or bio that you'd like to add?
My advice to anyone getting into this business: Be patient. This business is like the stock market — over a lifetime you'll make consistent earnings, but during certain periods it appears like you'll never earn another dollar. Another good analogy is a rollercoaster where you're never allowed to get out. If you can deal with that, then you too might qualify for an acting career.

Animated Series:
The Avengers, W.I.T.C.H., Batman: The Brave and the Bold, The New Adventures of Batman, Batman: The Animated Series, New Kids on the Block, Defenders of the Earth, G.I. Joe, Men in Black, Sylvester & Tweety, Extreme Ghostbusters, Ahh! Real Monsters, Captain Planet, S.W.A.T. Cats, Prince Valiant, Jem, Jonny Quest, etc.

Animated Feature Films:
Sub-Zero, Ping, Thumbelina (directed by Don Bluth), *Five Weeks in a Balloon, Interactive* (partial listing), *Ultimate Spiderman* (voice of Dr. Parker), *Spiderman 2* (voice of Dr. Parker), *Batman: Rise of Sin Tzu* (voice of Nightwing/Dick Grayson),
Earth and Beyond (multiple voices)

VOICE TO VOICE

AN INTERVIEW WITH TORI HARTMAN

Tori Hartman is a voiceover actress and the owner of Gigs on the Go, an L.A. recording facility. (Visit the Web site at *www.gigsonthego.com*.)

What made you decide to take things into your own hands and build a studio?
I actually had a gig and I couldn't find a studio to work with me! I booked a few spots through an agent of mine in another city. They expected me to be a local hire (which means that I had to have my own studio and pay for my own ISDN [used for phone patching]. I didn't realize how hard it would be. I phoned a few studios, and they were very unsympathetic to my plight. I needed a place that would be open at 7 a.m. Pacific time — and since they were local spots, I was barely making $500! I found one guy who would open at that time, but for $300. The studio would be making more than me — crazy! Then I actually had a few studios tell me that I should get the ad agency to pay for my studio: One guy actually lectured me about this. Needless to say, I was embarrassed. Then at the last minute, I remembered a buddy who had a home studio about an hour away. He offered up his space — at 7 a.m., mind you — and I tossed him $100 for the trouble.

The studio was originally built for me. But the wheels were already in motion. From this experience, I learned there was a need for a comfortable, low-cost studio where artists could work. We're basically a content booth. People can record or broadcast from here. Their own facilities or other outside recording facilities do the mixing.

Our clients are the voiceover talent and the producers who like them, and folks who are on tight budgets. We've had some major producers come through here when they just need tracks laid down for a pitch that they're doing. When a few guys who did an independent movie didn't have budget for ADR, Dave set up a booth for them to do pickups. We like to think that we're here to help creative people express themselves and get their work done in a way that's affordable. I wanted a place where producers, too, could do their independent work at a low cost.

What is the goal for the studio?
To make it easy for folks to connect with and use talent here in L.A. Runaway production costs are at an all-time high. We do ISDN and phone-patch sessions from all over the world. If we can create an inexpensive alternative for producers, they will come to L.A. to get their talent. One of the most exciting calls I got was from a producer out of Dallas who told me that she would never consider using L.A. talent because she's a small shop and couldn't afford using a studio here. She's now booked a few sessions and is thrilled to get to use L.A. talent for her work.

CHAPTER 11

ADVERTISING AGENCIES, PRODUCTION COMPANIES, AND EVERYONE ELSE

IN THE WORLD OF COMMERCIALS, WHEN A CLIENT DECIDES TO RUN A CAMPAIGN, they hire an advertising agency, which comes up with the concept (with the client's input) and develops the idea from inception to fruition. Depending on the client's budget and target market, the campaign could be one radio spot (although a single spot hardly qualifies as a campaign), a series of regional radio and TV spots, or a full-blown national television and radio campaign.

The search for the voiceover talent begins after these decisions are made. If the commercials are for television, the ad agency may shoot the spot(s) and then cast the voiceover. If you are a well-known voice, spots will sometimes be created around the idea of using you; otherwise, you come into the picture much later on. Often, ad agencies bid against each other to win accounts. If an agency is competing for an account, it may need voiceover actors for the demo it produces. The demo will, hopefully, win the agency the account.

Once it has an account, the ad agency is responsible for finding the voiceover talent for the spots it produces. According to voiceover actor Michael Donovan, "Ad agencies are always looking for fresh talent. Never listen to negative input." I agree. One day when I was in San Francisco for a job, I decided to do some cold-calling. I must have hit twenty-five ad agencies. Not one person saw me. But I made connections. I asked who the creative directors and copywriters were, and I left behind copies of my CD. Who knows? Sooner or later, my effort may lead to a job.

WHAT AD AGENCIES DO

Once an ad agency has been hired, the real work begins. Agency personnel work with the client to create a spot or a whole campaign. The client may or may not have an idea for the campaign. If not, it is up to the agency to come up with the concept and the campaign itself. A number of factors come into play: budget, markets, media selection, talent (scale or celebrity, union or nonunion), and deadlines.

Advertising is a lot like other industries. Size and clout matter. The more money, staff, contacts, and talent an agency has, the bigger its accounts are likely to be. But the world of advertising also has room for upstarts. A small company with a very smart, creative ad team may compete for and win a large account simply because it has the best idea. Producers and writers often work freelance, moving from agency to agency — and bringing clients with them. If a client is happy with a writer/creative or creative director, it will often remain with them for many projects.

The ad team at the chosen agency starts creating ideas based on information the client gives them. The client will tell the ad agency what the market for a given product is — including, for example, the age range and gender of the core audience they are trying to reach. In fact, many clients will pick their ad agency based on what the ad agency has done in the past — which may give the client a good idea of whether the agency can effectively market its product to the target market. The creative team (the idea side of the agency) will come up with a slogan or campaign idea and work from there. Depending on whether the spots are for television or radio, they'll write and edit copy, develop storyboards, audition voice talent, and create a demo of the spot to show the client. The creative team will constantly work with the client to make sure that the client is happy.

Once the client approves the copy for a spot or campaign, the agency has to find the right voice talent. The agency will either call agents and casting directors in town to set up auditions or hire directly from its own stable of voice actors it has worked with successfully in the past.

THE PEOPLE INVOLVED

Quite a few people are involved in the making of a radio or TV spot. Here are some of the major participants:

THE WRITER

Once the creative team comes up with an idea, it is up to the writer to put the actual words on paper. The writer also often directs the voiceover session, making sure the talent reads the words the way he or she imagined them.

THE DIRECTOR AND THE CLIENT

Sometimes, you'll be directed by the creative director. (The whole team will have been working together closely on the campaign, and all the team members will have a feel for what the client wants.) No matter who plays this role, the director will be at the session, overseeing it to make sure the agency gets what the client wants. Although the creative team may try to convince the client to go in a certain direction (which is, after all, why they've been hired), the client has the final say on what goes to air.

THE PRODUCER

The producer is the person in charge of overseeing the entire project, from working with the client, to supervising the ad agency's work, to choosing the talent, to seeing the project through to completion. A producer can wear more than one hat in the ad world. In fact, the producer might also be the creative director or might also write and/or direct the spot — or even do the voiceover! (But that's quite uncommon.) In most cases, the producer is the liaison between the client and the talent and manages the project from inception to final product.

THE ACCOUNT SUPERVISOR

The account supervisor may work for the ad agency or the client. He or she makes sure that the project stays on budget and that the work gets done efficiently. The supervisor may come to the recording session to make sure it runs smoothly.

THE TALENT

You're the talent, and being the talent carries certain risks. For instance, you might be hired for a job that gets canceled. This might have to do with anything from a decision to change the marketing strategy, to the budget being cut, to the client having creative differences with the agency. And even if you do the session, there is no guarantee that the spot will actually run. That's just the nature of the business. You'll still get paid for the session, but you won't get residuals unless the spot actually airs.

And your job is hardly guaranteed for life even if you do a lot of commercials for a particular product. A client will stay with an agency only so long; eventually, they'll probably want a fresh approach. Of course, the agency will try to keep the client by presenting them with new and different ideas, but the client may move on anyway. When a client switches agencies, it usually means that they'll want new voiceover talent as well. When the new auditions come around, you still may be brought in to read, but you may not book the job.

FREELANCERS

Some writers and producers work freelance. They go from ad agency to ad agency, working on specific accounts. Freelance creative people may bid for jobs directly with clients, or they may be hired by an agency after the agency has won an account. Sometimes, creative people decide to become freelancers after having spent some time working for an agency. And, of course, people in advertising — just like people in every other profession — sometimes change jobs, going from one agency to another. This is why it's so important to keep track of your contacts. Knowing where the people you've worked with in the past are working now, and letting them know that you're still out there, may help you land jobs.

To keep abreast of what's going on in the advertising world, read the ad-industry trade magazines *AdWeek* and *Advertising Age*. These are informative sources that will keep you posted on who has just landed what job and what is hot in advertising right now. They also profile creative executives and let you know which accounts they are working on. Write down their names, find out their agencies' addresses, and send them a CD. Some casting directors prefer that you do not contact the ad agency on an account for which you have recently auditioned, so always ask before you submit your demo CD or send a note to the creative. Usually you can find out the names of the agency and creative director, as well as the agency's address, from the script.

By the way, not all commercials are produced by advertising agencies. Smaller businesses in smaller markets just may not have the money to hire a full-fledged ad agency to produce their spots. If Sam's Key Shop wants to do a radio spot, the "agency" might be some local guy in jeans who writes the copy and produces the spot. The voiceover work for such spots is generally non-union — and doing such jobs isn't a bad idea if you're just beginning your voiceover career.

VOICE TO VOICE

AN INTERVIEW WITH JEFF NICOSIA

Jeff Nicosia is a freelance copywriter who used to work for Chiat/Day. Chiat/Day has since merged with TBWA (famous for its Absolut Vodka ads) to become TBWA/Chiat/Day.

What is the most important aspect of the copywriter's job?
The most important thing to remember is that a copywriter's job is to write the spot. When I'm writing, I think of a voice. Then I sit down and listen to CDs (usually the house CDs of voiceover agencies) and pick voices. A common session may be selecting five or six voices. At that point I call the agencies, fax the copy, and either specifically request that client, or suggest a certain category and let the agents put their clients on CD and pick the talent from there.

What do you want from the talent you hire?
By the time a script makes it to the air, here are the things that the writer wants from the talent: Be easy to work with. Be on time. Don't get an attitude. Don't direct the writer (director), and do not rewrite the script! By the time that script has gotten into the hands of the talent, we have done our work. We want the voiceover talent to be easy, fast, and good. I love finding new talent, but there are so many voiceover people that you'd better be easy to work with.

I had to cast a spot a couple of weeks ago at the last minute and the guy wasn't available and we found another guy with a similar voice quality. It led to thirty spots! It was just as easy to keep using the same guy because he was a pleasure to work with and easy to find.

What annoys you most about talent?
Being late! The writer, producer, ad people, and sound engineer have all put in their time and money and are now waiting for you. Be on time!

How do you feel about voice actors who keep in touch by sending little notes, gifts, their new demo CDs, flyers listing their most recent jobs, things like that?
It's nice to get reminders, but don't do overkill.

Is there anything that you have a hard time finding?
"Real people" reads from actors. Most jump into their "announcer" read. Often, I get the actor into the studio and then just have to ask simple questions such as, "Where did you drive in from today?" When they start to answer in their real voice, I stop them and say, "That's the read I'm looking for." It's conversational. It's real. And, it's hard for actors to do.

Do you use beginners?
I prefer working with professionals. Beginners also announce when reading. Often, I've cast a spot from a demo and have not really known what that person is capable of. Sometimes it's hit or miss. Stage actors are not always the best voiceover actors. Finding someone with microphone experience is usually the best bet.

Do you work with celebrities?
I recently hired Mary Gross, formerly of *Saturday Night Live,* for a very sweet, ditzy-woman read. I loved working with her because she was very easy to work with and fit the spot perfectly. I would definitely hire her again.

Would you ever hire her for another type of read?
It would be interesting to have her read against type, but usually I write the spot with a particular person or type of person — a specific type of voice — in mind. I can be persuaded to go a different way if I hear something interesting.

How do you feel about hearing a woman's voice on a casting CD when you specifically asked for men?
It's interesting, and I'm not opposed to hearing them. I will admit that the first voice I tend to go for is a man's. Many of the clients are the same way. They are traditionalists and they stick to what sells. Most clients will pick a man's voice first.

What do you look for in the talent besides their voice quality?
I like a person to be flexible, show me a range of voices within their quality.

Do you do a lot of on-site casting at your ad agency? Or do you use a local voice casting agency to find talent?
In smaller markets we cast on site. We even cast non-union talent. But with the bigger markets, we work more with the CDs, Voicebank and directly with voiceover agencies.

How do you categorize women in voiceovers? How do you think that the client categorizes women in general when casting?
It used to be that the voiceover market categorized women in one of three ways. Either they are sweet announcers, little girls, or sexy. I really think that you opened up a whole new world for women. All of the sudden, women could be more accessible, likable, and still have character.

Your voice quality definitely brought quirkiness to female voiceovers that had not been around before. You changed the way that I thought of women being cast. I think you did that for a lot of advertising agencies and clients.

Well, thank you.

When you are good at what you do, copywriters tend to rehire the same people. It's easier to work with the same person. Most of the time, the client doesn't know Sally Smith from Joe Jones, so they really don't care who we pick as long as the voice fits the spot we are doing.

Any final thoughts?

Don't be late!

CHAPTER 12

THE SOUND ENGINEER AND THE SOUND BOOTH

THE SOUND ENGINEER IS THERE TO MAKE SURE YOU SOUND GREAT. This means that he or she will get a "level" by having you read the copy until the sound check is completed. You are to keep reading until the sound engineer gets exactly what he or she is looking for. The engineer is making the adjustments for the client/ad agency. He or she will have the script and will want to make sure everything is set-up before the session begins. The sound engineer runs everything technical that goes on in the voiceover session and may be used for postproduction for that same spot, as well. If so, you are brought in to read your script(s) and then the ad agency will work with the sound engineer to add appropriate SFX (sound effects), a music bed, and anything else that completes the voiceover session before it goes to air.

I once did a session with a very cranky sound engineer. The session was long, and he was not a happy camper. Well, there were a few of us in the booth, and a couple of people said some not-so-nice things, which the sound engineer heard. The lesson? The mikes pick up everything. So think before you say things about people — especially the sound engineer.

THE ROLE OF THE SOUND ENGINEER

A good working relationship between you and the sound engineer is a high priority. The sound engineer is the person working with you most closely during the session, whether the client is there in the room or not.

The sound engineer works for the recording studio. When you show up to record the job you've booked, a sound engineer will have been assigned to you and your session. A given studio may employ several engineers, but if you often do sessions at the same studio, you may work with the same sound engineer over and over again throughout the years. There are a few sound engineers whom I've known for the entire length of my career. Seeing one of them is like seeing an old friend.

The sound engineer's studio is like his or her office. When you enter, you are entering the sound engineer's world. The levels and the keyboard are set up exactly as the engineer wants them. And the engineer knows the entire process, from the phone patch to editing. The soundboard and computer allow the engineer to control all the technical aspects of the session, from making sure that your headphones work correctly, to setting up all the equipment, to keeping track of all the reads. Sometimes the engineer will even play director and help with certain reads.

The engineer plays a very valuable and important part in the whole process. He or she is responsible for adding in the music and sound effects as well as for timings and the looping and editing of a spot. The ad agency may have brought in the music track that they want to use, or the sound engineer may take a track from his or her massive collection. The engineer may also be doing the sound effects for the spot. The sound engineer is also in charge of hooking up the phone patch (if one is being used) and for getting you and the client/ad agency comfortable while making sure that you sound good and the session goes smoothly.

It's hard to overstate the engineer's importance, so you should treat him or her with respect. You want the experience with the sound engineer to run as smoothly as possible. Not only is the engineer there to make you sound good, but engineers often hear about it when clients are looking for voiceover talent, and they can tip you off to potential jobs. You never know where your next job is coming from, and the sound engineer just may send some work your way.

THE SOUND BOOTH

The sound booth is the room in which you do your voiceover work. Your copy will usually be waiting for you when you arrive. If you're working via phone patch, the copy will be faxed or emailed, and you may have to wait a few minutes to receive it. There may be several edits and copy changes during the voiceover session.

Here's what you will find in the booth:

Microphone. This will be a standing mike, whose height and angle the sound engineer will adjust until you're comfortable. Don't touch the mike: It's against policy. If you are working with a group, there will be a number of individual mikes set up, each with its own stand. Once the mikes are set, the engineer will go into the other room and get a level on your voice.

Headphones. These will be supplied for you, along with a level adjuster, which enables you to control the level of sound coming through the headphones. (Alternatively, this may be controlled by the sound engineer, and you will ask him or her to adjust the level.)

Filters. Attached to the microphone itself, the filters can be either be cone- or screen-shaped, square or round. When in use, they are placed between you and the microphone. Depending on the type of read, these may be added to help clarity or lessen the popping of Ps.

Time clock. The room may or may not contain a time clock. If it does, the clock will be set in the window between you and the sound engineer so that you can see the timing of the read as you go along. Otherwise, the engineer will tell you the time after each take.

Stand. The stand that holds the copy is like a music stand: the height and tilt are adjustable. You can adjust the stand however you want, and the sound engineer will then place the mike accordingly.

VOICE TO VOICE

AN INTERVIEW WITH LARRY WINER

Larry Winer is a mixer at The LA Studios, Inc. Prior to 1992, he worked in broadcast production at the Los Angeles office of the J.Walter Thompson ad agency. He started his career as a mixer at Margarita Mix (LA Studio's sister facility) in 1992, working on TV and radio commercials. In 1998, he moved to LA Studios to work on animation, TV and radio commercials, promos, and DVD commentary.

Can you tell us a bit about your job as sound engineer in regards to the voiceover field?

My job entails many aspects of manipulating audio — recording, editing, and mixing audio. A good voiceover record makes the process of editing and mixing go more smoothly. The voiceover record is often done at the start of a session and sets the mood for what happens the rest of the day. It's important for voiceover talent to be receptive to direction and able to adapt to different types of producers and directors. Some producers/directors will have tons of experience and some will seem to have no experience. The key for the voiceover talent is to remain calm at all times. Try to assess the mood in the control room and refrain from unnecessary chatting in the voiceover booth with other talent, which might interrupt the flow of the session.

Mainly I help the clients (producers and directors) and voiceover talent in smoothly navigating a voiceover session, while controlling the recording levels. I provide timings of lines, quickly edit between takes, and offer direction when needed. I like the talent to constantly assess the situation and offer direction only when needed.

How much input do you have with talent and direction? Is your advice influential with regards to running a voice session?

My advice is very influential in regards to running a voice session, but just like the talent I must continually assess the mood in the studio and chime in, or not, accordingly. For voiceover talent this is only learned though on-the-job experience. Thus, when studying the art of voiceover it's important to have a teacher like Terri Apple, who has years of experience in all aspects of voiceover, to prepare you for what might happen on the job.

Tell us the differences between phone patch, ISDN, MP3, and having a producer there at the session.
Often clients are not located in the same city as the voiceover talent. When this occurs, the client has several options. The first is to book a recording studio in both cities and patch via ISDN (basically a sophisticated way to conference with broadcast-quality audio between two or more places at the same time). In this instance, the client gets your audio on the spot and can start editing and mixing right away.

The second is a phone patch. The client directs you over the phone. After the session, the audio is sent to the clients. Sending options include posting files on the Internet for download, emailing files, and good old-fashioned shipping. Sometimes auditions are sent as MP3 files via email. Generally clients prefer WAV, AIFF, or SD2 files for better-quality audio.

The sessions without a producer tend to be a little more relaxed, as the talent and the engineer are the only ones in the studio.

Have you seen a decline in producers, writers, and directors being at the actual session? How great a percentage of sessions would you say are done over the phone?
In the mid-1990s there was a huge decline in producers, writers, and directors being at the actual session due to the use of ISDN technology. This allowed clients to edit and mix their radio and TV commercials at home in cities throughout the world. At that point there was perhaps a 40 to 60 percent decline in clients attending sessions. Fortunately, The LA Studios is well diversified and had plenty of work in animation and other long-form projects. Currently we do about 30 percent of our work via ISDN or over the phone. Voiceover talent needs to be taught to listen and interpret direction given remotely.

Are you involved in the final say with regards to takes?
Mostly the client has the final say in regards to voiceover takes, but I try to voice my opinion when appropriate, and when I hear something that could be a problem, such as lip-smack, timings, or the talent's earrings jingling in the background. Remember to always wear comfortable, soft clothing to the studio. A few of the old-timers put too much starch in their shirts, and it causes noise that could interfere with the voice record. Also avoid jewelry that could jingle while standing in front of the mike.

What do you think voice actors should bring to a job?
It's important for voice actors to bring a happy and positive attitude to the session. Read the room. If you like to talk a lot, be aware that the client is paying lots of money for the recording studio, so try to focus on the job and reserve small talk for before or after the session, depending on the client.

Do you see the same voice actors getting cast again and again?
In TV animation the same voice actors are getting cast again and again. Once a producer/director is accustomed to working with someone, it's tough to break the cycle. Also, stars and live action kid actors are getting cast a lot.

Radio and TV commercials also cast the same people over and over, but they tend to cast new people, too, because of conflicts and overuse.

Can you tell us about particularly bad voice sessions, due to talent, creatives, or technical people?
Some bad voice sessions are due to bad casting. Clients often hire someone that is talented but not the right voice for the job. It's not the talent's fault. The client tries to get the talent to do something they can't do naturally. Casting, casting, casting — I always say it's in the casting. That's why clients tend to stick with the same actors/actresses: they know what to expect.

You may sound great in an audition, but can you take direction? Are you good with timings? Can you improvise? Do you know how to work the mike? The bad sessions can be due to a lack of knowledge in any of these areas. If you think you can sneak by ... well, you can't. They will not cast you again if you don't have knowledge and confidence.

Lots of on-camera actors, some very famous, come in and have no idea that they have to stay still and project into the mike. They are used to a boom operator pointing the mike at their mouth.

Some sessions are just painful because of constant script changes. This is no fault of the talent, and even more reason to be patient and pleasant during the session.

Often voiceover talent is in a rush to get to their next session across town. Try not to project your rush to the client. They are the ones paying you and have nothing to do with your next session across town.

What is your idea of a good voiceover session?
The client comes in with a script that needs no changes. The voiceover talent is well cast and has experience.

The LA Studios has been doing a lot of animation. [Universal is across the street.] Do you guys hold castings, as well?
We generally do not cast at The LA Studios, Inc. Once in a while, a big studio will cast at our facility, but they are making the decisions. We do recommend people once in a while. The relationship between the studio and the talent is mutually beneficial. A lot of our business comes from voiceover talent, and a lot of the voiceover talent's business comes from our recommendations.

What advice would you give to up-and-coming talent — and even working talent — in regards to dropping off demos to recording studios?
Do not drop off demos at recording studios. We do not cast. Simple as that. Our clients — ad agencies, video editorial houses, animation companies — do all the casting. Although our suggestions to clients could get you over the hump.

As an engineer, I can manipulate a voice and make a great-sounding demo, but then the talent has to be able to do it in a real session. Make sure you have the talent to back up a well-prepared demo. And have a good agent.

What do you feel is the biggest change in the business with regards to all the home studios that have popped up over the past ten years?

Home studios have made it easier for talent to get auditions to clients. Many voiceover actors record from home. But be sure to consult with a recording professional before setting up at home, though. Overall, the booths and recording techniques don't sound as good as if you were working at a professional studio. Some of the busiest voiceover talent have home studios, and some of their setups sound far from acceptable. We often end up fixing bad sound created in a home studio. My job at The LA Studios, Inc., is to deliver the best audio product possible, so if your voice sounds technically bad it takes more time to edit and mix, costing the clients more money.

I would always recommend using a professional studio such as The LA Studios, Inc., so you get a great technical staff and support staff. Then the only thing you have to worry about is your voice. Also, the quality of the recording is not your responsibility. Oh, and don't forget the great espressos and cappuccinos.

Keep in mind that working at a recording studio also has great networking advantages. You'll meet many of your fellow voiceover actors in the lobby, and lots of clients. If you're cooped up at home, that kind of networking is not possible.

CHAPTER 13

THE UNIONS

UNIONS ARE THERE TO PROTECT YOU IN A NUMBER OF WAYS. They provide health insurance (you can qualify after making a certain amount of money). They protect your right to work and the base salary that you can make on a job. They re-negotiate contracts (per a board of union members) and create new union rules. There are two unions that represent voiceover actors: the American Federation of Television & Radio Artists (AFTRA) and the Screen Actors Guild (SAG). Both unions cover on-camera work as well as voiceovers.

Traditionally, SAG represented actors who worked in film, and AFTRA represented actors who worked in TV and radio. Since their inception, some fluidity has developed between the two, however. While AFTRA continues to cover TV actors, especially those who work on daytime TV (including soap-opera actors) and syndicated shows, some TV shows are actually covered by SAG contracts.

Each union also handles contracts for different kinds of voiceover jobs. AFTRA covers all work on radio, as well as actors who do audiobooks. Both AFTRA and SAG cover promos for TV, with AFTRA handling most of the work shot on video, and SAG handling the work shot directly on film, although, again, this division is not hard and fast. Looping, narration, and animation work for films is generally handled by SAG. Depending on the contract, work recorded directly in digital media (CDROMs, podcasts, video games) may be covered by either union. In its infancy, cable TV was a bastion of non-union work, but as it began to reach a larger and larger audience, the unions began to push cable TV stations to hire union talent. Voiceover work at cable TV stations remains largely non-union, but this situation is evolving.

The rules about how unions work and what work is handled by them can seem confusing and opaque to an outsider. Don't worry. Once you are working in the industry, the guidelines will begin to make much more sense. Your agent is there to help you navigate the various union rules and restrictions — and help you take advantage of the benefits they provide.

JOINING AFTRA AND SAG

Don't be in a hurry to join a union. Although you can join AFTRA, you probably won't want to. First of all, it's expensive (check your local pricing guide). Once you are in the union, if you don't get work, you may be put on hold or frozen for a period of time until you work (or make a base) so it may not be worth it. Just because you are in the union, does not guarantee jobs (or union auditions) will come to you. Work on putting together a great demo and getting it to casting houses to get auditions. Let the work come to you, and work your way into the union by booking jobs!

You can join AFTRA in any town at any time. You do not need to do a job to get into AFTRA — you must simply pay the initiation fee. (They will be happy to take your money.) Members join the local closest to the city or state in which they live and work. The membership fee is $1,600 although locals in some very small markets have been granted reductions in — or waivers of — this fee, so check with your local before you join. Annual dues are then calculated based on your earnings. Minimum dues are currently $63.90. For details on how to join, call your AFTRA local; AFTRA's website, *www.aftra.org*, has complete contact information.

While AFTRA only requires that you sign up and pay your dues, the eligibility requirements for SAG are more complicated. There are two ways to become a SAG member. The first is to join AFTRA, remain a paid-up AFTRA member for one year, and work at least one AFTRA-covered job during that year. (In other words, becoming eligible for SAG is one of the perks of AFTRA membership.) The other is to work on a project that's covered by SAG. According to U.S. labor law (specifically, the Taft-Hartley Act), union producers and production companies can hire non-union actors; once hired, however, the actor is given thirty days within which to join the union. If the actor is hired for two union jobs within thirty days of each other, he or she *must* join the union. For further information on SAG membership, call your SAG local; a complete list of locals can be found on SAG's website: *www.sag.org*.

There can be drawbacks to joining a union too soon. Access to union jobs means being cutting off from most non-union jobs: Once you are a member of either union, you cannot legally accept non-union work. If you do and you are caught, you can be disciplined, which can involve being fined or thrown out of the union. Union membership can also be expensive. If you join but don't make a fair amount of money from union work, you've joined just to pay dues! There is a benefit to remaining non-union as long as you can to build your resume. If the "big guys" really want you for a union job, they will hire you, and then you can join.

ONCE YOU ARE A UNION MEMBER

Once you are in the union, the only way to do non-union jobs, is to become fi-core. This means that although you will work in a non-union area and can make the money that non-union pays (per negotiation) you will not be allowed any of the union benefits. With today's economy and the opening up of non-union work, it's up to you to decide to work within a non-union market. Many actors change their name or go by a secondary name to work in the non-union world, as to not hurt their reputations or status within the union market. If you work non-union and are in the union (without going fi-core) and are found out, you can be kicked out of the union or frozen and fined for a period of time.

AFTRA and SAG protect your rights as a performer. If you eventually work in all the voiceover mediums, you will have to become a member of both unions. You don't want to do non-union work for the rest of your life. Non-union performers are usually paid lower rates than union performers; plus, the employer doesn't have to worry about benefits or residuals. This is why companies hire non-union performers: They know that they need the work, the experience, and the CD — and that they will work for comparatively little money. If they had the budget to hire a union person, they probably would.

The bottom line is that the unions are there to help you. They have health insurance plans, credit card plans, and retirement funds (if you earn enough each year). And the unions are also there to answer your questions any time you are confused or have an issue regarding a job or pay scales.

UNIONS AND EXPLOITATION

If you feel you have been exploited at a job, call your union. They will file a grievance against the person you had a problem with. Ad agencies, producers, directors, and casting directors must work within the ethical codes set forth by the unions, as well as federal and state work laws. For example, you must be paid extra if you are kept at an audition and/or session beyond a certain amount of time. If you are asked to do more work than you were originally hired to do, you must be paid more for it.

I've only encountered a problem once, when I was called in to do a demo for a commercial. When I got to the session, the writer was still playing with several different options. He had me read about fifteen different lines. Then he asked me to come up with some alternate lines on my own. Now, it's true that, once in a while, you will ad-lib or help the writer come up with a better word if nothing seems to be working. The writer doesn't generally mind your saying a word that works better than the one he or she wrote. But this was different, because the writer was asking me to come up with the entire line. He wanted my help in matching the copy to the picture. That was supposed to be *his* job. So I called my agent, who was furious that I was being asked to do double duty. As soon as I hung up with my agent, he called the writer, who promptly had me read only the lines that he had written. Nevertheless, I had already done the extra work. And even after his conversation with my agent, the writer still tried to get me to sign a standard union contract that was for less than the amount we had agreed to. With the help of the union, my agent was able to get me paid properly. The story even has a happy ending: The commercial ran and made me lots of money. It's up to you to make a judgment call if the session does not seem to be going the way it should; if not, your union is there to help.

UNIONS AND PAPERWORK

Once you are a member of the union, you need to fill out the proper form after each job that you do. For AFTRA jobs, you must send a copy of the form to your local AFTRA office within forty-eight hours of doing the job. (SAG doesn't require a copy of the form, although you should always keep a copy of the paperwork for your own records and as a backup for your agency's accounting department.) Filling out the form protects you from not getting paid and keeps the union informed about what you are doing so they can make sure that the job conformed to union rules, pay scale, and time limits — and that you are paid in a timely manner. You should be paid within two months after doing the job. If you aren't, tell your agent or call the union.

These forms are not the same as your contract, which will be faxed to the studio by the ad agency. After you fill out the AFTRA forms, fill out your contract and sign it. If the ad agency has neglected to provide a contract, inform your agent right away, and send a copy of the AFTRA forms to the agency. Even without a contract, the agency must still pay you within four to six weeks, or it will be penalized for late payment.

UNION PAY SCALES

There is a base pay scale, per union rules, for a variety of voice-over genres that you will work in throughout the years. Fee scales change through the years and there is a complete guide on either union website (or call to get a copy for any particular area of work). If you are working non-union and aren't sure what to charge for your fee, check the pay scale for that job per union rules and charge accordingly. I recommend having a knowledgeable third party negotiate for you, however. A slightly smaller fee (plus a buyout) is usually fair. A company may say that they are on a small budget, but you have to make yourself worth the rate. If they respect voice actors, they know they aren't going to get you on the cheap ($50 or $100 dollars for a spot — even if it runs three times). It isn't fair to you — or your ego — and it certainly won't lead to a future in voiceovers. Sure, it may line your pocket with a little cash, but make sure that you are getting "close to scale" on every job you take.

Both AFTRA and SAG negotiate industry-wide contracts with production companies. The contracts — which remain in effect for a period of years, after which they expire and must be renegotiated — specify pay scales, or rates, for various kinds of on camera and off-camera work. The rate schedules are available as downloadable PDF documents on the unions' websites. These schedules are extremely complicated, covering all the possibilities regarding the specific kind of work you do and where and how your work is used. Will a TV commercial for which you've done the voiceover be broadcast nationally? Regionally? Locally? How long is it? (15 seconds? 30 seconds?) Will it be on network TV? Cable? How long will it run for? How frequently? You'll be paid at different rates — and the total amount of money you earn will vary — depending on the answers to these kinds of questions.

In the best possible case, you'll be the principal (or *a* principal) off-camera voice on a spot that airs nationally on network TV. The rates schedules call this the "Program Class A" category. First off, you'll get a session fee for the recording itself. As of this writing, the session fee for off-camera principals on commercials covered by the SAG contract stands at $402.25. (The rates specified by the SAG contract differ slightly from those negotiated by AFTRA.) The schedules stipulate *minimum* rates; fees can go higher than this, but not lower. If you're a hot commodity in the voiceover field, you may be able to earn more; that's up to your agent to negotiate with the commercial's producer. By the way, SAG's minimum rates include the 10% commission that goes to your agent; AFTRA's do not, although your agent may be able to negotiate the extra 10% in advance.

Beyond the session fee, you'll be paid an additional fee each time your commercial airs. These additional payments are what are called *residuals* — and it's the residuals that can make commercial voiceover work so lucrative. For example, if you record a Program Class A commercial under the SAG contract and that ad is broadcast once, you'll receive a first-use broadcast fee of $402.25. If it airs twice, you'll receive the first-use fee *plus* a second-use fee of $96.00. If it airs three times, you'll get the firsthand second-use fees *plus* a third-use fee of $76.35. And so on. As you can probably tell by now, a nationally broadcast spot that airs frequently over a long period of time can eventually produce thousands of dollars of income for the voiceover artist.

Commercials produced under union contracts run on a thirteen-week "per spot/per cycle" basis. After thirteen weeks, the contract "begins at the top" again. If your Program Class A commercial airs for more than thirteen weeks, you will receive another session fee (for the same work, that is), and the schedule of fees for first, second, and subsequent uses again kick in. Not only that, but the total "lifespan" of a commercial contract is twenty-one months. This means your commercial can run in thirteen-week segments during the twenty-one-month period. After that, the contract expires, and the ad agency can no longer run the commercial without renegotiating with you or your agent.

Of course, other kinds of union voiceover work aren't quite as well-paying as Program Class A television commercials. Residual rates for cable-TV commercials are lower than — and are calculated differently from — those for network-TV commercials. For radio commercials, the thirteen-week cycle applies, but the per-use schedule does not — meaning that a radio commercial for which you've done the voiceover could conceivably air hundreds of times during a thirteen-week period but you will receive only one preset fee for those thirteen weeks. By the way, the unions maintain broadcast divisions that keep track of how often each commercial runs and that make sure that you get your residuals.

To get some idea of the complexity of the union contracts — which also cover things such as per-diem payments for out-of-town travel — check out the rate schedules posted on the unions' websites. Once you have an agent and are a union member, you'll find out much more about the pay scales and about how the rate schedules apply to the specific kinds of voiceover work that you do.

CONFLICTS

Union rules prohibit members from doing TV commercials for two or more different products or services that are in competition with one another if those commercials will run in the same market at the same time. For instance, you cannot do voiceovers for nationally broadcast TV commercials for two different cereal companies — if you're doing Quaker Oats, you can't do Kellogg's. Or two different sneaker manufacturers — if you book a job for Nike, you can't also book one for Reebok. You *can* do a car commercial, a cereal commercial, a feminine-hygiene product commercial, a beer commercial, and a soda commercial. Those products aren't in competition. But a Ford commercial and a Toyota commercial? Not at the same time, for the same TV market.

Radio is different. You can have radio commercials for BMW, Cadillac, and Mazda all running in the same place at the same time. The problem, of course, is that clients probably won't want you to do the voiceovers for their products' commercials if you're also working for their competitors. But it isn't against the rules. There's also no conflict between radio and TV. If you have a radio spot for Reebok and you get a national TV spot for Nike, that's okay.

Of course, it's not your fault if, say, two different shoe companies want to hire you for their TV spots. It's just against union rules. If you already have a shoe commercial running and you get called in to audition for another (for a different company), your agent probably won't send you to read for it, knowing you would have a conflict if you were to book the job. Remember, though, that commercial contracts expire after twenty-one months. If your contract has expired, you are free to audition for that other commercial, which would otherwise have been in conflict.

There's another kind of situation in which a conflict may arise. Let's say you've recorded a TV commercial for a car rental company but the ad agency, for whatever reason, has decided to put that commercial on hold. Maybe it will be broadcast at a later date, maybe not. In such a case, the agency must, under union rules, pay you a *holding fee* to prevent you from doing a commercial for another car rental company. (Like the rate schedules for commercials, holding fees apply for thirteen weeks at a time, after which the hold must be renewed.) If your commercial is on hold and you're being paid a holding fee, you can't book a job for a competitive product or service.

These rules may seem unfair to struggling voiceover actors who are in the union but don't work a lot. They may think, "It's so hard just to get one job, but then I have a chance for another and I can't even do it." As an actor, I, too, would love to do as many jobs as I possibly can, but the union has its rules, and we've got to follow them. If you are caught doing two television spots in the same market at the same time, you may be fined and thrown out of the union. Now, if the television spots aren't national — if, for example, you have a Toyota spot running locally in San Francisco and another agency wants you for a Jeep Cherokee spot that will run on the East Coast — that's fine.

UNION SCALE FOR NON-UNION WORK

As I've said elsewhere in this book — and as the unions themselves recommend — you should take all the non-union work you can get until such time as it's beneficial for you to join a union. There is a lot of non-union work out there for beginners, and by doing this work you'll build up your experience and compile material for your demo CD.

When you do a job for a company that isn't a signatory on one of the union contracts, it's up to you to negotiate your fee. So why not find out what the union scale for that kind of work is, name it as your fee, and see if they go for it? They may not, of course, but it's not a bad idea to think of the union pay scales as the industry standards — as statements of what a particular kind of voiceover work is worth, at a minimum, at this point in time. Remember, the reason they are hiring non-union talent is most likely budgetary. This can be beneficial when you are breaking into the business.

As I mentioned earlier in this chapter, the only way for union actors to work non-union jobs legally is to declare fi-core, or "financial core" status, a somewhat controversial standing within the unions that was established as the result of a lawsuit brought against AFTRA in the 1970s. Fi-core status must be declared in writing. Members with financial core status are union members and pay union dues, but they can accept non-union jobs. Although they are allowed to retain their medical, dental, and retirement benefits, they can't run for office, vote, attend union meetings, or receive union publications — ever.

While some actors see fi-core status as having the best of both worlds, allowing them to work both union and non-union jobs, others are angered by it, because it gives some union members an advantage over others in the workplace, and they therefore see it as an erosion of the very meaning of a union.

CHAPTER 14

STEREOTYPING AND TRENDS

S TEREOTYPING MEANS GETTING BOOKED FOR THE SAME "TYPE" OF READ (AND SAME VOICE) ON EVERY JOB. You do a character in a read or certain style, like Phil Buckman for Carl's Jr., and you start to suddenly get booked for that same type of read, over and over again. You cannot be asked not to do "that voice" unless you sign a contract with the company that hires you that states to not do that voice. Anything negotiated within your agency and client is okay as long as they pay you for it and it's agreed upon by all parties. I know of an actress (a very famous one) who was known for a voice in an animated series and used that voice on an answering machine for a controversial company. She got in trouble. They didn't authorize her to use that voice, even if it was just for fun. She was playing that role to sell something other than what she was being paid to sell it for. Companies can ask you to do a "version" of the style of read, for another product, but it's up to the company whether you can completely copy the exact same voice. Once you are stereotyped, it can be difficult to book work outside of that character. This is where your good acting skills come in, so that you are auditioning for things "outside of the box," or just outside of the box that was created by the read that got you stereotyped in the first place.

I get asked all the time how I came up with the voice I used for the Home Base campaign. It's a very deadpan, flat read. When I went to the audition, the description was "flat, throwaway, irony." I got the job because of my interpretation of that description. I created a character and tried to give the advertising agency what they wanted while maintaining my own personality. I didn't overanalyze or over-read it. I just came up with something that felt comfortable and different. I didn't try to be anyone else. I just did *me* and it worked.

Although I created an entire genre for women who had previously not been heard in the marketing world, that particular voice led to me being stereotyped. Suddenly, I *was* that voice. Clients would ask for a "Terri Apple voice," or the direction in the copy would say, "A Terri Apple read." Sixteen years later, it's still that way. And I, Terri Apple, still find myself saying, "Which Terri Apple do they want?"

WHAT IS STEREOTYPING?

Agents, casting directors, companies like to categorize talent by putting them into certain boxes. It makes it easier to bring them in to read. For example: "Oh, he does the flat read really great." Or, "She does quirky zany." Or, "Oh, Diane is a great young mom." Times that by hundreds because there are many voices that can fit into certain stereotypes for every job out there.

Every agent likes to categorize the talent he or she represents so that they are easier to push. For example, an agent might be representing five high-pitched women in their forties; six raspy-sounding women in their twenties; four men with a deep, "announcer" sound; and two hyper, raspy-sounding boys in their late teens. But although your agent and the casting directors you work with will fit you into a category, that's not really stereotyping. Stereotyping is something that happens in the ad world, not your agency.

You can become stereotyped if you become known for only one of the voices you do. When that voice gets a lot of air time, people may begin to associate you solely with that character.

Being stereotyped means always being asked to read in a specific way — and often being hired to do only one type of voice.

Trends develop when casting directors, writers, creatives, and clients want the same kinds of reads — a particular voice or style of voice — for many different campaigns. When a voice becomes popular, advertisers keep asking for that voice (or ones that are very similar). They may say, "Get me a Tom Bodett." (Tom is the voice for Motel 6 — flat and low-key.) Or they'll say, "Get me a Jim Cummings." Although Jim does several different characters and kinds of reads, he is best known for his strong, deep voice.

When a trend hits the airwaves and your voice matches that trend — or actually created it — stereotyping results. If you're stereotyped, you'll become known as a certain sound or sell. You may even begin to be equated with the product you're selling. I got stereotyped after doing the Home Base campaign. Before that job, I did a lot of high-energy, businesslike reads. After I'd booked Home Base, everybody wanted me to do that quirky, raspy, dry, throwaway read. I didn't realize I had created a new character for myself, nor did I know it was going to be so popular.

STEREOTYPING: THE GOOD AND THE BAD

Becoming stereotyped is a double-edged sword. It can be beneficial when you're hot: advertisers will want you for everything. And who doesn't want to be well-known in the business and to make lots of money?

But do you want to do the same character over and over? Stereotyping may even keep you from working a lot in the future. When you become overexposed, advertisers may want a voice similar to yours in tone and character, just not *your* voice. They may like the general character that you started; they just want someone to do it with less rasp or a higher pitch. Maybe they like the tone of your reads but want a new person, a new sound. They want someone *like* you; they just don't want *you*.

Or dropping product sales may indicate that your style has lost its edge. Or the client may simply want a new sound. (This may happen if your commercials get too much airplay and the ad agencies get tired of hearing you.) Whatever the reason, when a client decides it's time to change the ad campaign, *everything* usually changes, including the voiceover actor. Once the trend is over, it can be difficult to get hired at all. If you become stuck in a stereotype, you're going to have to take a little break and stop doing the type of voiceover work that you've been doing. This may mean less income for a while, but you want advertisers to stop seeing you as only that one voice. Let your agent know that you want to prove that you can do something other than what you are known for.

Continue to create new reads, and have your agent submit you for other types of auditions. This is very important. Even if the spots for which you are stereotyped are still on the air, as long as another commercial in which your voice is different is also running, you'll demonstrate your range — and show that you can do something other than what you are known for. As long as you stay individual and don't copy anyone, you will always work. Other people may steal your sound, but they cannot steal your voice. Someone may be able to ride the wave of your success for a while, but when your style of read is no longer "in," the person copying you is in trouble. What are they going to do now? Copy someone else? The point is to try to do what makes you unique.

VOICES THAT BOOK

Voices that book, are determined by a large factor on what is popular in the marketplace at that time. It can be determined by the media, or simply by a popular actor at the time. The market changes based on the kinds of sells that work — or the way in which an ad agency will set up a sell — to sell their product. The hard sell may be in, or it may be the casual sell. We just went through a big period of the "non sell" which is basically a manipulative way to saying, " I dare you to buy this product. I don't care if you do." It is actually a smart selling tool. Different products are used in the marketplace differently. Talent is hired based on how each company wants to get through to the public, how they want to be thought of, and the type of market they wish to be in.

Ad agencies are always looking for unique and fresh voices. Sometimes, they look for a distinct sound — something different from the norm. But it's not just the weird or distinctive voices that book jobs. Any interesting quality that your voice has will help. From time to time, you may be called in for a "regular Joe" style of read. If your voice has a smooth quality but not necessarily a distinct sound, you might book the job. All types of voices are needed in the voiceover business. Many different voices equals many different sells.

The fact that so many different types of voices book jobs is what makes the voiceover business so exciting. Sure, there are certain kinds of voices that stand out: Women with deep, throaty voices tend to work a lot. So do women with quirky, higher-pitched voices. Booming, deep-voiced men dominate the narration and promo markets. But these are generalizations. Every one of these "ideals" can be broken.

DOING THE RIGHT KIND OF READ

For every job you read for, it is your responsibility to understand that there is a right way and a wrong way to read. Regardless of what you are read, you have to nail the audition (or get pretty close) to book the job. The right read means delivering the copy in the right mood (per the specs) so that the right vocal quality will come out of your voice. You also must hit the beats and transitions. This is the natural set up that the copywriter wrote into the script. The wrong way is, of course, the wrong mood or wrong vocal quality, and disregarding the beats and transitions. "Throwing the read away" in the wrong way is always a wrong choice in reading. You can sound overly polished and not book the job, or you can sound overly raw and not book the job. You can be raw and green and have an understanding for how the script should be read and book the job, or you can be polished and right on the money. There's no rhyme or reason, but you must understand the steps in working on every script to have a full shot at getting the job. A casting director knows when an actor doesn't know what they are doing. With a little coaching and understanding of scripts, you can nail your reads every time — even if you've never booked a job — and increase your chances of getting through those doors!

Casting directors are looking for the right voice *and* the right delivery. Having both gets you in the game. But even then, you are one of twenty — or a hundred — other actors who also have the right vocal quality and mood.

Nailing the read to the specs when auditioning is so important. There isn't a "right" or "wrong" for reading in general, but there *is* a right read for a particular spot. There is a vocal quality that will work for that read — and you may or may not have it. Every person who auditions for a particular spot is given the same direction. Everybody who is auditioning may have a similar vocal quality. Every person auditioning for a spot may be a woman in her mid-thirties whose voice has a raspy, quirky quality. Or every person may be a man in his fifties with a deep, smoky voice. In other words, everybody "fits" the specs. The only difference will be how they read the copy. Learning to follow the specs will get you that much closer to booking the job.

APPEALING TO AD AGENCIES

You can't spend your life trying to be what everyone wants. What you can do is try be the best at what *you* do. Often, ad agencies do not know what they are looking for until they hear it. When you see a mixed group of people all auditioning for the same spot, it's obvious that the agency doesn't know exactly what it wants. You may audition for a spot whose specs ask for "male or female; twenties to fifties; warm, playful, real, and conversational." This description is very broad, and it's a good indication that the agency wants to hear a range of voices or has several different ideas in mind for the spot or campaign.

Trends have a shelf life. Whenever a trend is hot, many ad agencies will be looking for that type of read. But you can only follow your own style and personality. If you happen to fit into a trend, wonderful, but that doesn't mean you shouldn't think outside the box so that you can create a career that lasts many, many years. When the part requires authority and energy, know how to give that read. When it requires wryness and playfulness, know how to get that read, too.

BEING MORE COMPETITIVE

Be professional. Make every audition the best that it can be by being ready. Take the audition process seriously. The audition is the only time that the ad agency and client will see you in person and hear your voice *for that particular spot.* A demo CD can only tell them so much about you. They want to hear how you approach each particular job. Make sure that you treat the audition as if it's the real thing. Put the same energy into your audition as you would the job itself.

Take classes. Take every class that focuses on the areas you are interested in. Don't let your inexperience with microphones and reading copy keep you from booking jobs. Practice! Take classes! Work with other professionals! Make sure that all your demo CDs, for whichever areas you are pursuing, are up-to-date. Don't send out CDs that are five years old and loaded with old copy.

Be available! Don't get an attitude with your agent like you have better things to do than run all over town auditioning. Make sure that your agent knows that you put voiceovers first. Your career has to be your priority, even if money is tight. Take a night job if you have to, so that you will have your days free for auditions. And don't miss an audition. Missing auditions gives your agent the impression that you are not taking your job seriously, and he or she will give the next audition call to someone who is willing to compete.

Stay focused. Don't think you're going to take over the entire voiceover business. It's not going to happen. Sure, there are fortunes to be made, but you're better off being a specialist. You're not going to be the top commercial voiceover artist, the top promo person, *and* the top animation voice. There's too much work, not enough time, and — until they clone you — not enough voice. Sticking to one general area will keep you focused and competitive in that area. "Competitive" doesn't have to have a negative connotation. Being competitive means that you are in the game!

- ***A FUN EXERCISE:** Where do I fit in?*

Ask yourself the following question: Where do I fit in (right now) in the voiceover market? Am I fun and flirty? No nonsense, real? Smart, educated, and informative? Guy next door, casual?

Now, grab a piece of paper, script, magazine or write your own line of copy. Find your range and stereotype. Work without a recorder and then use a recorder for playbacks.

Start to understand where you naturally fit in now, and then begin to create other areas that you fit in. Understand this: All moods that you have in life are the same qualities you can create to sell products. You in a flirty, fun mood will have it's own vocal quality. You in a business-minded, casual mood; you in an assertive, guy-on-the-go mood, these have their own vocal qualities too. Put yourself into situations and allow the vocal quality and the rhythm of words and phrases to come out. This is how to create range and break yourself out of stereotyping.

CHAPTER 15

GENDER, ETHNICITY, AND ACCENTS

BOTH MEN AND WOMEN WORK IN ALL AREAS OF THE VOICEOVER INDUSTRY — and often compete against each other for the same jobs. But voiceover jobs for products advertised during daytime television, especially during soap operas, have traditionally gone to women. And men still tend to dominate the network promos — and much else besides.

I like knowing that I am fighting the men in what people consider to be a man's world. I have booked a lot of voiceover jobs that were originally intended for men (or for celebrities). I don't like to feel that I can't book the same amount of work as a man, so I created a market where I (and other women, too) could be up for the same kinds of jobs as men.

There's a lot of opportunity for both sexes. Certainly, Procter & Gamble's commercials lend themselves more to female voiceovers because that market is geared toward women — just as beer commercials, which are more geared toward men, generally use male voices. But there's plenty of work for everybody — including non-celebrities. (Sure, there are many celebrities who book voiceovers. In fact, many voiceover agencies have celebrity divisions strictly for celebrity voiceover talent. But if a client doesn't find the voice they are looking for within the celebrity talent pool, they will audition non-celebrities.)

THE GENDER DEBATE

The man-versus-woman debate goes on in every part of our economy. The voiceover world is no different. On any given day that I audition, there are also men auditioning — sometimes for different copy, sometimes for the same copy. I've often seen scripts for which the gender of the actor is still in play; the specs simply state, "man or woman" along with some details about mood. Sometimes an ad agency will want to hear lots of different voices of both genders before deciding which one to go with. If you're a woman and have an enlightened agent (one without a gender bias), he or she will let you read outside the "normal" reads, giving you "male copy" as well as "female copy." If your agent is creative, he or she will understand that as long as you are reading and interpreting copy the way the ad agency wants, you have a real shot for the job. It never hurts to try.

Still, there seems to be a prevailing belief that men should do most of the voiceover work. I don't believe it, and I consider it my job to expose some common myths and fallacies about men versus women in voiceovers.

NARRATORS

Typically, a narrator's voice is a voice of authority, of trust. A voice that sounds commanding. An informed, informative voice — a voice that says, "I know what I'm talking about, so listen to me." And a narrator's voice is generally low in pitch. For many people, this means a *man's* voice — but that's just not the case. A woman's voice can also have all these qualities. Whether a woman gets hired depends on the preferences — and preconceptions — of the producer, writer, and company.

Sure, some higher-pitched women complain that they don't get called for narrator/ announcer spots. But these women might be booking lots of funny or quirky spots, as well as a ton of animation work. They might also be right for Procter & Gamble–type spots, which usually run as Program Class A network spots and make lots of money in residuals. This isn't a gender issue; it's an issue of what kinds of voices sell what kinds of products.

TRAILERS

"In a land of evil...Before man walked the Earth...Before time... May 15th, in theatres everywhere."

Men also dominate the movie trailers. But that's because the action-packed films that make the big bucks are generally male-oriented. When you hear a woman on a trailer's voiceover, it's usually for a "chick flick" or a date movie (a romance, a comedy) — and these films generally don't do as well at the box office (unless they're starring Jennifer Aniston or Julia Roberts).

ANIMATION

Tiny The Tiger

Small, ferocious, not easily intimidated — except by Lola, the squirrel, whom he has a crush on.

Seeing Lola: "Will you look at those gams? She's the best looking squirrel in the place. Look how she holds those branches." (Amazed, pre-occupied, and sighing with amazement)

Seeing Dirk the Bunny: "If he talks to her, he ain't gonna have any carrots left, if you know what I mean." (Intimidating, strong yet quiet)

Women whose voices have a raspy quality sometimes provide the voices of boys in animated films and TV shows. (Bart Simpson on *The Simpsons* is famously voiced by actress Nancy Cartwright.) Men's voices are just too deep, and once a male's voice changes, it becomes too obvious if he tries to change his voice to make it sound young. More and more often, though, producers are going with real kids for child characters. Even so, animation and video games are still a wide-open market for both men and women. (Infomercials are, too.)

GENDER AND MONEY

Men dominate nighttime network promos. Women dominate daytime TV (Proctor and Gamble spots) and daytime promos. On the whole, women push more feminine products and men work the male dominated items. There certainly can be crossover where men will voice women and visa versa. Sometimes ad agencies do this to shake up the marketplace and it usually works. When you hear a voice you didn't expect, it can really add to the marketing campaign and boost sales. Men can make more money in voiceovers in certain areas, but that's true in many professions.

Still, there are successful voiceover actresses who make over half a million dollars annually, although they generally do so by putting together several animated cartoon series, some animated films, and plenty of commercials, campaigns, and promos. By contrast, men can make a lot of money by working in just one area. For instance, a man can make a million a year from one network promo contract alone. Men tend to book those promos. Networks like to use men for promos for nighttime shows because they think that men's voices bring in the mass audiences. And although both men and women do a lot of voices for animation, there are still more animated shows featuring men's voices.

ETHNICITY

Where you fit ethnically can also determine the types of voiceover jobs you will have access to — as well as what you are given to read on. This is because ad agencies and marketing companies have a specific idea of what they are looking for. Even if they don't know exactly, however, they "hear" the spot in their head and they "picture" a certain type of voiceover. When the specs call for a Caucasian male, mid-thirties, there isn't much you can do as a voice talent to book that job if you fit into another category. All together, it doesn't have to even be an ethnic issue; it can simply be age or type of voice they are looking for. Some agents and casting directors are open to bringing in a broader range of talent to read on all jobs. It isn't fair, but when a read says urban African American male, it certainly feels like it's being a bit racist. I've seen the opposite in copy as well — "an educated African American." It's very insulting, even to a Caucasian, to be labeled in a category.

Hopefully, we will be judged by vocal style alone. Understand that the way in which you read copy, say words, and where you are from in the world, hinders you only within that style of read they are asking for. You cannot be the right voice for every job, but you can create a nice niche for yourself wherever you fit in. Work with a coach to broaden your reads and work on speech patterns and accents, so that you will open yourself up to more styles of reads.

CREATING A MARKET FOR YOURSELF

No matter what your gender, work with your natural range and tone. This doesn't mean that you shouldn't be creative and have fun with mood and different vocal qualities. Just don't forget what you do best. That very trait that sounds odd or interesting may just get you the job and create a market for you. Go after the promo/narration world with the same zest that you bring to the commercial world. Study the marketplace by watching TV and listening to the radio. Notice which gender is dominating which market (and on which stations). This will give you an indication of whom to submit to and which areas to market yourself in.

You should only be competing against yourself. There is nothing you can do about everyone else at an audition, so don't worry about "beating" them, doing "better," or "winning." And you should never feel threatened by the gender issue. The voiceover work is out there, regardless of your gender. Don't worry about not booking this big promo campaign or that trailer. Put your energy where your mouth is and go get the work that you can get! Make the money that *is* there for you to make and you'll notice that you won't even be thinking about what everyone else is making or doing. Within your own gender, there are many different qualities an ad agency might be looking for. Concentrate on the here and now, the voice and talent you possess, and the voiceover career you *can* attain!

- **EXERCISE: Your Adjectives**

1. What are three adjectives that best describe you? Write them on a sheet of paper. This is where you naturally fit into the voiceover world. This doesn't mean that you cannot do other voiceover styles out there. As long as you apply your personality (mood, adjectives), you can create many voice qualities.

2. Mix and match adjectives now. Apply them as you say "That's a great shirt." Put them into different orders to see how applying and layering in order, creates a different vocal quality to your voice.

3. Remember, your vocal quality is the natural technical quality in your voice. Your vocal quality and you in a certain mood (from everyday life) will create different vocal qualities — the sell.

CHAPTER 16

BECOME A MARKETING GURU

THERE'S ONLY SO MUCH CONTROL YOU'VE GOT OVER whether you book the job or not. What you want is to work within the voiceover business and hopefully turn it into a career that will last! You are in control of making sure that you do everything you can to showcase yourself in the best light. The only "tool" you have (beside your voice) is your demo. It's your calling card, so make sure it's a good one. You also have the ability to start from scratch to build a voiceover career, as well as learn some great marketing and business tools along the way!

You may or may not make a living doing voiceovers, but if your goal is a voiceover career, you should treat it as a priority and constantly try to find work. As you book jobs, it may turn into a lucrative career.

To get work, you're going to have to market yourself, and effective marketing requires some thought. In which area of the voiceover field do you think you'd work the most? Which area of the voiceover field most excites you? If you had your dream, would you be on an animated series, have a regular promo gig for a television network, be a part of a loop group, be a DJ for a radio station, or do commercials?

I always tell my students to go after the area they are most passionate about. Learn how to analyze scripts properly, master the audition, put together a demo CD that best represents your talents, and then go after the appropriate casting directors, ad agencies, and production studios.

Your agent can only do so much. As in any business, you'll have to do some of your own marketing. In the voiceover world, the demo CD is the most effective marketing tool we have. But there are other ways you can improve your chances — by sending cards and holiday gifts to contacts, for example, or by creating a fun, appealing website. And, of course, the more jobs you do, the better known you'll become — and it's important to do everything you can to maintain those key industry relationships.

The whole point is to sell yourself. I sold myself by being assertive and taking classes. I made phone calls. I got into as many auditions as I could, read as much copy as I could, copied every commercial on TV and radio and spoke them out loud. (To this day, whenever I see an advertisement in a magazine, I read the copy aloud. I love to hear how it would sound if it were copy for an audition. It also teaches me to be better at what I do, every time I do it.)

And even though I had an agent, I still hand-delivered demo CDs to every casting director in town. I resubmitted CDs regularly and learned the casting directors' names. I wanted them to put a face to the voice. Once you get the agent, you still have to do a lot of the work. Make sure that all the casting houses know who you are. Since they get so many CDs, you will need to be unique in figuring out how to get their attention. For a long time, my J-card said, "An Apple a Day," with a picture of an apple surrounding my name. (Hey, it stood out.) Knowing how to market your voice to the proper channels is as important as landing the right agent.

The Internet, although vast, is a great venue for non-union work. Upload your demo to *www.voice123.com*, a non-union database. Lots of auditions come through there. Go to Voicebank (*www.voicebank.net*) and search for non-union talent agencies and management companies to find out if you can post your demo with them. I opened a non-union voiceover management company and I get solicitations from voice actors all the time.

But no matter what marketing approach you take, here are seven crucial steps:

1. Get a demo CD (for every genre you wish to pursue work in).
2. Make J-cards and business cards.
3. Take classes, seminars, and workouts.
4. Keep up with your business relationships.
5. Keep track of new contacts, and send over a CD and note.
6. Keep accurate records of every audition, job, ad agency, and production company.
7. Be original. Be different. Be creative. Have fun with it!

Because the way you choose to market yourself is such a personal thing — because it depends on your own career goals and your own personal style — I thought we'd spend the rest of this chapter listening to two experts. The first of the interviews that follows is with Kat Cressida, a voiceover actress who's been a very proactive advocate for her own career. The second is with Matthew Walters, booth director for the William Morris Talent Agency, who has some very interesting and useful things to say about turning your voice into a "brand."

VOICE TO VOICE

AN INTERVIEW WITH KAT CRESSIDA

Kat Cressida is a voiceover talent who really knows how to market herself and keep the industry buzz about her going. Some of Kat's recent credits include commercials for McDonald's; promos and announcing for several ESPN and ESPN2 shows; the characters Dee Dee in *Dexter's Laboratory* and Jessie the Cowgirl in *Toy Story* (both for Disney); several award-winning CD-ROM games including *Avatar, Scarface, X-Men,* and *Fantastic Four*; and a number of celebrity voice-matches for various film and animation projects. (Among the stars whose voices Kat has matched are Nicole Kidman, Kate Winslet, Joan Cusack, Kim Basinger, Keira Knightly, Reese Witherspoon, Paris Hilton, Renée Russo, Helena Bonham Carter, and Holly Hunter.)

Kat, how did you get started in the voiceover business?
I started like a lot of folks. I had worked behind the scenes in the film industry, transitioned from that to an on-camera career, and after a few years doing guest-star stuff on a lot of sitcoms and one-hour dramas, decided I wanted to move into something that would still be creative, but require a little more ... well, a little more of my training (Shakespeare) and a little less concern with whether my hair looked perfect on that particular day. I liked the on-camera world, but sitting on a set for fifteen hours waiting around for my scene to be shot didn't really suit my energy and personality. I like to be active and cram a lot into a work day, and voiceover was rumored to be much closer to that kind of energy. I was lucky, and after a few workshops and classes, I auditioned for a smaller agent and worked my way up from there.

Have you always been organized and proactive with your career?
I came from a business background, and, as I said, my first job out of college was production and then agenting in the entertainment world. So I got to see both the production behind the scenes and the business side, and it taught me a lot about networking, relationships, gratitude, marketing — and how it really works, versus the myths and fantasies I think we all tend to have growing up and in school. It's very much a business, and the most successful voiceover talent I've had the pleasure of working with — yourself included — tend to treat it as such.

You are excellent with your marketing skills and keeping up with relationships. How do you go about doing that?
That's an excellent question. I'm sitting here thinking, "Gee, do I actually have a good answer for this question?" I mean, this is the kind of question I'd love to have a succinct, simple formula for, because I myself wish it had a simple, straightforward answer! I guess the truth is, it's sort of organic and probably individual for each person. When I started out in this biz eight years ago, there were some voiceover talent that were pegged as "great marketers." And while I admired their choices, I remember thinking, "Oh, that's so not me — to be sending out monthly postcards with my most recent bookings, making the rounds to the various casting

offices with small gifts and such." That felt inauthentic for me, personally.

My strengths are creativity and intimate conversations, not mass schmooze. I wanted what I did to be more personal, I guess, so I kind of used what I'd learned while working behind the scenes and made my marketing more "one on one." If a client hires me a few times, I ask to take them to lunch. If I land a gig with a casting person or agency, I send a personalized thank-you gift — often something with a small token of my "brand," but also something fun and whimsical. I always advise students in my animation workshop: gratitude! Never underestimate appreciation. Having both a great brand and a personal approach to your marketing is, I think, a strong combination.

How much has the marketing and being creative in your choices helped you in landing and keeping contacts and jobs?
Man, these are all great questions. I would say that marketing probably does more to support the follow-through once a contact is made or a gig booked. Certainly I think it helps in supporting voice talent as a brand and helping to sort of raise your profile, but I think it's most effective once a buyer or ad agency knows you and helps keep you in their mind for the future. And I think having a well-designed, fun website certainly helps if a buyer is "shopping around" and considering you. That might be that extra nudge that helps them say yes. So I'd say, definitely, taking the time to create a fresh, personal brand in artwork and website design — and promotional gifts — can be very effective.

I've been fortunate in the support I've gotten from my graphic designer and Webmaster and gift company. I can have these vibrant, sometimes wild ideas for marketing materials: "I want it like Disneyland — fun and interactive and colorful but neat and clean and yummy." I mean, these folks are geniuses at carrying out some of these wild ideas and, better yet, not throwing their Macs at me when I change the font size of the jukebox and the color of the hot fudge or menu for the gazillionth time. Seriously.

Do you travel to meet clients?
Yes, certainly. Mostly to meet them and thank them if a working relationship has been ongoing. Meeting someone in person helps you to understand them and their work and can make working together a lot more personable. It also is nice to be able to thank clients in person.

I know that you go to the E3 convention (a game convention) every year. What else do you do to promote your career?
There are so many great events and conventions out there for so many things that are a part of the voiceover world: ProMax, E3, ComiCon, animation festivals, technology conventions, toy shows, and various award ceremonies. It can be overwhelming. There's so many great ways to not only get out there and learn about the companies and products out there but also potentially to network. But again, I recommend to folks in my animation class that you pick events that personally appeal to you, seem like something you're genuinely into, or want to learn more about. Learning what you love — and also learning what you don't necessarily connect with — can be a very powerful thing.

Example: I have always loved Disneyland. As any of my past boyfriends can (perhaps painfully) attest [to]. I'm fascinated with how it works, how its elements come together to create living entertainment. So I think it's no accident that I ended up with the tremendous honor of voicing various elements for Disneyland! I connect with that place. Take the time to ask yourself, "What gets me passionate?"

By the way, here are Kat's "marketing gurus" in Los Angeles:
- For CD design and graphic art: Lumel Design (Stephen Lumel)
- For website design and web mastering: Chris Kim Design and Grant George Design
- For CD duplication: DVD Circus (Dan and Ben)
- For promotional gifts: Unique Gifts & Wrap (Lisa Drantch, owner)

A FEW TIPS:

When marketing yourself, don't present yourself as if you are a "newbie." Don't send your demo with the list of coaches you've worked with. This won't help in booking voiceover jobs. You need to "sneak" into the voiceover market with enthusiasm and confidence. You need to act as though, although you are new to "this" market, you do have experience (no matter how minimal) in other markets. You may have never booked a job in your life, but you need to know how to read scripts when you are presented the opportunity. You need to treat this as a business, just like any other. Have fun and make friends, but treat the opportunities you receive (getting in with casting directors and ad agencies) professionally. Don't mess around when it comes to looking at scripts and knowing what you are doing. Don't waste your time getting a voice over demo before you know how to read! Don't put a great website together and lure people to a site, before you have the tools to book the jobs — if the jobs do come your way. Create a business for yourself, and have the ability to back it up. You don't want to blow a chance with someone because you sounded good once, they gave you an opportunity and you blew it by showing how green you are. Don't get cocky in an audition by saying "I can do that," unless you really can!

VOICE TO VOICE

TIPS ON VOICE BRANDING FROM MATTHEW WALTERS

Matthew Walters is a former booth director with the William Morris Talent Agency and current life coach. Matthew has had a long career in the voiceover world. Formerly with the Tisherman Agency and a former casting director with Voicetrax San Francisco, The Voicecaster, and Sight 'N' Sound Casting, he is also a voice talent. Here are his tips on "branding" your voice:

> "One of the biggest traps that voice actors (and actors in general) tend to fall into is giving away the power in their artistic choices. This is usually revealed the moment they ask 'What do they want?' or 'What do you think they're looking for?' Outside of the basic information, gender, age range, and

style, what 'they' are looking for is for you to bring something to their script to bring it to life. They want you to bring your creativity and talent to the read. They've created the concept, written the script, organized the details of producing the spot, and they want the actor to do their part, which includes more than taking direction well and having talent. Whether they say it or not, what they 'want' is your creative input in interpreting the spot. This doesn't mean taking a bizarre approach to the read; it means bringing yourself to the read and bringing the script to life.

"Bringing yourself to the read implies that, as an actor, you know what that is — that you know how to express your talent and personality in the reality of a particular script. This is not as easy or simple as it sounds. In essence, to use advertising language, you need to know your *brand*.

"To discover your brand, you need to answer several questions. The more time and thought you put into this, the more effective it will be for you. So, get out a pen and paper and take some notes.

"What are your strengths? The strengths of your voice, your skills, your range, and your talent are important to identify. Is your voice deep and resonant? Smooth or raspy? Youthful or textured with experience? Can you read quick legal copy? Do you have good diction? Great character voices? Are you good at improv? Are you funny? Do you have a quirky voice? Natural character? This is a good place to start. List seven to ten strengths and make sure they are things you are good at right now, not things you want to be good at.

"What are the strengths of your personality? Are you naturally optimistic or cynical in a funny way? Do people comment on how comfortable they feel around you? Is your honesty and integrity obvious in the way you carry yourself? Are you able to see the irony in life? What are the aspects of your personality that are obvious on the surface and what do you keep hidden from the world but have access to? You need to know who you are and how you are perceived. If you complain that you don't get the opportunity to read certain scripts because no one sees you that way, then you should ask yourself if it is you or the casting people who are unclear as to who you are. Both you and the people who hire you should have a clear idea of who you are. This doesn't mean that you can't surprise people with your range, but there needs to be an agreement on your strengths.

"What are your weaknesses? The limitations of your voice, your skills, or your talent? Do you have an accent? Bad diction? A reedy or thin voice? Do you have a pretty voice but weak acting skills? Are you too 'announcery'? Unable to do announcer copy? Once again, come up with a list of seven to ten items, and put them into three categories: weaknesses that can be improved, weaknesses that can be ignored, and weaknesses that can be turned into strengths. If you have bad diction, hire a vocal coach. Learn how to read announcer copy. Take an acting class. Or you can choose to ignore that weakness. Many animation actors choose not to do commercial copy, and vice versa. There is no shame in saying, 'That's just not what I do.' In fact, most of the time it is appreciated because you don't waste anyone's time. Sometimes that weakness can be turned into a strength. Ben Stein and Gilbert Gottfried both turned their weaknesses into their strengths. Lorenzo Music (Garfield) and Eddie Deezen also come to mind. Janeane Garofalo really only plays one type of character. Bob Newhart, as well.

"Now list how your personality, talent, and weaknesses complement each other. Is the picture getting clearer? Also, notice any contradictions. These are red flags that need to be addressed. Are you a friendly, optimistic person with a flat, uninteresting voice? Are you someone with a dark, cynical edge and a light, friendly voice? Work to bring these contradictions into harmony.

"Now let's bring your brand out into the marketplace. Are there people already doing what you do? If so, then that's a good thing. You have a product that is already proven and liked. Make a list of famous actors, voice actors, characters in movies and TV shows, and voices in current commercials that you might be compared to. You should begin to notice a pattern.

"Also, make a list of your five to ten best reads, as well as five to ten reads that people wouldn't normally think you could do and five to ten reads that you wouldn't book 90 percent of the time. Be honest with yourself. Many actors want to believe that they can do anything that is asked of them. This is not the same as what you are best at. We are attempting to narrow it down to its essence, so that not only do casting people and agents know what to do with you, but you know how to bring yourself to the copy as well. We are all unique, and if you embrace who you are, then you will bring your unique read to all of your copy without having to do any wacky voices.

"It seems that voice actors come in a few, very specific types. The Man/Woman of a Thousand Voices: This person often has limited social skills but can do about ninety-five imitations and character voices. Usually an only child who had to entertain themselves most of their childhood. The Performer: This person probably does musical theater, sings cabaret, or does standup. They like to be the center of attention and like to make people laugh. The Personality, or The Voice: This person has only one read but it is usually on a campaign. They will have limited range but do one thing very well. The Everyman/Everywoman: This person embodies everything normal and average about consumer America. Suburban, middle class, mom or dad, friendly and likeable. But not unique or remarkable. The Hipster: This person has the coolest read in the room. Probably a musician and usually someone with a little edge and texture in their voice and who somehow seems to embody all that is cool. Which are you? Do you contain bits of different types? What percentages?

"Now the final and most important step. You need to come up with a single statement that defines and describes your brand. Keep it succinct. This will be the basis of your approach to voiceover. It will also be a great way to develop your marketing materials. Good marketing will tell the casting person, agent, and producer what they will hear before they even open your CD to listen to it. You can let other people — teachers, agents, casting people, or producers — tell you who you are or you can take some time to discover it for yourself. Good luck."

MAKING A CAREER OF VOICEOVERS

Over the course of my career, I've seen many voiceover actors come and go. But I've also seen many of the same faces around for years. The core group seems to remain pretty much the same because successful voiceover actors are good actors, and good actors tend to book jobs again and again.

The voiceover market is huge. There are many areas in which to make a living. I know quite a few people who do *affiliate* work — promo work for the local stations in a particular city. From their home studios, they connect a microphone to their computers, and every day they send MP3s of their sessions to each affiliate station they do business with. Although this is currently a non-union area, you can negotiate a nice buyout rate, or flat-rate fee per job that you do, and I know people who pull in $20,000 to $50,000 a year just from the affiliate work that they pursue from home. Of course, the same rules apply in this area of voiceovers as in all the others — including having a demo CD that you can use to sell yourself. (In this case, you would need a demo CD with affiliate promos.)

The most lucrative areas of voiceovers are the national TV commercial market (with all those residuals!) and animated network TV shows. But just by booking a radio campaign with a local grocery store (where you might be brought in three times a week to record spots), you'll earn a hefty paycheck. Such a job might pay $400, three times a week. Of course, rates differ from city to city, so you need to check with AFTRA or SAG to find out what radio spots pay per session and per use in a given region.

Looping is another financially viable way to make a living. Most voiceover actors who belong to a loop group make anywhere from $100 a day (non-union) to $800 or $900 a day (union). Nothing wrong with that! If you've got the time (remembering that looping can be a full-time job), you might make $100,000 annually simply by belonging to a loop group and looping several TV shows and films per year. As I've said before, looping is tough to break into, but once you're in a group and do a great job, chances are you will become part of that group and enjoy a long and secure career.

The voiceover business is based on talent, connections, and making the opportunity to get yourself into every audition you can. Full-time voiceover actors do not have other 9-to-5 jobs; voiceovers *are* our 9-to-5 jobs. We spend most of our days running to auditions and doing voiceover sessions. On days when there is no session or audition, we have a bit of "free" time. I usually spend mine MP3ing my demo teaser to some new producers, doing mass mailings, or organizing my paperwork and updating the lists of people I've worked with. Many voiceover actors use their free time to audition for on-camera roles or to work as journalists, hosts, or on-air personalities. (Or they may have other part-time jobs on the side.)

So the real question is, how do you become a full-time voiceover actor? First, remember this: Even if you never become a full-time voiceover actor, you might still earn quite a bit of money in this business; being "part-time" simply means that you're booking less work than the full-timers do. The only thing that will make you a full-time voiceover actor is booking the jobs. The more jobs you book, the busier you will be. And the busier you become, the more you'll turn a "hobby" into a full-time career.

The voiceover world can definitely take you on a roller coaster ride. An agent of mine once told me to create a five-year plan rather than thinking year to year. Your financial situation may change over the course of five years, but the market will change as well, as will trends and styles — and interest in your voice. Knowing where you fit into the market and what areas to go after — according the plan you've made — is key to maintaining your equilibrium and keeping your career active, especially during slow periods.

TAKING THE RIGHT STEPS

There are certain steps you can take to help yourself succeed: learn your craft, make a voiceover CD, get an agent, get your demo CD out there, pursue auditions and jobs; and meet the casting directors, producers, and anyone else in your city who can help you pursue your goal. Set up a website and make your demo available on it. Get yourself on Voicebank through a legitimate agency or management company that can advertise your demo so clients will know where to find you.

Along the way, you may encounter other actors in a situation similar to yours. Sometimes, voiceover actors bond and create "workout" groups. Such groups meet at a recording studio or another place where they can practice reading copy and give each other tips on how they're doing. It's a great way to check yourself and make sure you're on the right track. It also provides different perspectives on interpreting a script with regard to mood, specs, tone, rhythm, and energy — interpretations you might not have thought of.

Booking jobs may simply be a matter of timing. Your auditions may be wonderful, but your voice may be similar to another actor who is already working quite a bit. If that's the case, you face stiffer competition, because the casting houses and producers who have worked with that other talent know what he or she is like in a voiceover session and feel comfortable working with that actor again and again. This doesn't mean that at some point you won't bring something different to a read that a producer will hear and like. That might be your chance to break in, make a good impression, and become a regular client of that particular producer. Nailing your read every time you audition, even if you don't book the job, is the way to get on the casting directors' list of actors they can depend on.

The same goes for your agent. Your agent won't worry if you don't book a job in your first two or three months. If your reads are good and you show promise, the agent will continue to bring you into the rotation of actors that he or she sends out on auditions. And you want your agent to keep sending you on auditions, even if you're not booking, so you can continue to get heard by potential clients. Remember: Ad agencies always like to hear new voices. That's what makes this profession so unique and exciting.

ONCE YOU BEGIN WORKING ...

Just try to keep on working! This is the best indication that your voice is selling products. When you're doing a lot of work, it's important to keep lists of producers' names. You'll want to remember these people when you run into them again. Before you go into a voiceover session, if you know who the producer is, look him or her up in your notes. If the name is on the list, you can remind them of the last session you worked on together. It's always nice to be remembered. Also, once you've done this new job, you can give the producer a copy of your current demo CD. You might also ask the producer for a list of the other producers and writers at the ad agency he or she is working with and send demos to all of them, too. Producers change agencies over the years and may be able to provide you with new contacts. In other words, explore every angle. And it's always nice if a producer — or a writer, for that matter — remembers you when leaving one agency for a new job at another. This, too, improves your chances of booking jobs in the future.

Expanding to other areas means establishing new contacts, making new demo CDs, and getting your agent to let you read for other kinds of jobs. Once your agent hears what you can do, he or she may add you to the list of actors sent out for other kinds of auditions.

The business is all about contacts. I know one woman who had been an on-camera actress for years, but everywhere she went, she was asked about her voice. At a dinner party, she found herself sitting next to an animation director who loved her voice so much that he hired her on the spot. One thing led to another, and she is now working full-time in animation.

I also know a working voiceover actor who used to be a doctor with his own practice. He decided he wanted to do voiceovers. (He had no acting background, mind you.) He took some classes, met some people, got a demo CD, booked some non-union jobs, then got himself an agent and started booking union jobs. He is now doing voiceovers full-time and has closed his private practice. (I also know an attorney who's in the process of making the same kind of career switch.)

Voiceover work can be very diverse. You may have one year in which you book a national campaign of ten commercials, all recorded in one session. If you do, you're set. A campaign of that magnitude can easily bring you $100,000 or more. Another year, you might mostly do radio spots. In terms of your income, it may not matter. If you book several radio spots a month, as well as some tags, you may earn quite a lot. Given the way that radio pay cycles work, if you book five or six radio spots a month and they rerun all year, you might bring in $2,000 every twelve weeks. Then throw in a television spot. Then another. How about an animation job? Or an audiobook at $2,000? Then maybe you do a buyout voiceover or narration job, too. The money adds up!

Of course, like other freelance professions, voiceover work carries some risk. But if it's security you want, stick with your 9-to-5 accounting job. This is definitely not a career in which you can count on getting the same paycheck every month. Yet you have the opportunity to bring in much more than in most 9-to-5 jobs, and the financial possibilities are limitless.

If you do go through a slow period, use that time to your benefit: go after more auditions on your own and try to drum up business however you can. The slowdown may simply be due to the time of year. You never know what's around the corner. Maybe an old commercial of yours will resurface, and you'll start to see residuals again.

This has happened to me many, many times. I'll be watching TV and suddenly see an old commercial of mine airing again. This means I can expect a check in the next few weeks (and additional checks for as long as it continues to run). If this happens to you, be sure to write down the date and time the commercial aired, as well as the channel you saw it on — just in case your agent needs to go after the money for you!

We in this business rely on our voices and on our agents. This means that you need to make sure you're with the best agency — the one that gets the most copy and works hardest for you. If you've gotten to the point where you're working in voiceovers full-time, chances are you've changed agents, moving to a larger, more prestigious agency somewhere along the way. If you are making money with that agency and getting in to the auditions, there is no reason to leave. Once you find a niche and a great agency, you don't want to rock the boat. If you're making consistently good money, you want that to continue.

To judge how well you're doing, get an overview. Don't look at just one year — the voiceover world can also be erratic. Average your income over five years — and don't worry about the inevitable ups and downs of the business. Voiceover actors who have been in the business for twenty, thirty, or even forty years understand that there are good years, bad years, and in-between years. At some point, you may have to supplement your income with a part-time job so you can continue to audition for voiceovers. But if you make investments along the way, save, and understand what a roller coaster the business can be, you will maintain your equilibrium.

Of course, not everybody in the business sees its ups and downs. Some see only the ups. Many voiceover actors get regular roles on animated series. Some promo actors never have to worry about where their next check is coming from. Getting a voiceover job with a network can pay upwards of $1 million a year. My buddy Danny Mann has been the Energizer Bunny commercials' announcer for quite a few years. Phil Buckman has been the voice of Carl's Jr. for ten years. Another friend is the voice of a network and is set for years contractually. Quite a nice chunk of cash!

What sets you apart from other voiceover actors and makes you shoot to the top in your field is having a voice that *clicks.* The advertising agencies and clients are the ones who decide what kind of voice interests them. It may be a quality that you have, a texture in your voice, or simply a personality trait that stands out. You may have a "realness" that resonates with buyers and makes the agencies choose you again and again. You may work mostly in retail or mostly in food. You may possess a sexy voice that they love for perfume or lingerie commercials. Once someone hears you, there's a good chance you'll work more. For whatever reason, your voice may catch on. You'll do one spot, then another advertiser will hear you and want you for their product, too. Or you may do a campaign for one company and get very well-known because you're on the air a lot — and this will make other companies want you. This happens all the time. This is how your voiceover "hobby" turns into an active career.

As you work more and more, you may even have several commercials or campaigns running at one time. As long as there are no conflicts (you can't do commercials for different companies making the same kind of product), you can work quite a bit.

Your agent may even want you to begin *turning down* some voiceover work. The agent may not want you to become overexposed, or may fear that you'll burn out. You don't want to become so much the "flavor of the week" that everyone will tire of your sound and not hire you next year or the year after. You want to create a career in which you can continue to be the voice of many products. Being a flash in the pan may be great for exposure (momentarily) and can make you some money, but if the spots don't run long cycles nationally, your residuals will be small and won't last as long as you'd like.

VOICE TO VOICE

AN INTERVIEW WITH DAVE SEBASTIAN WILLIAMS

Dave Sebastian Williams is an actor, voice actor, director, and the publisher of the *Voice Over Resource Guide.*

Dave, what got you started in the voiceover business?
Radio became my bread and butter in the seventies, when I landed in LA and realized acting was my future. What I didn't know at the time was that it was *voice* acting that was to become my future.
Doing commercials on the air as a Top 40 radio disc jockey was one thing, but I soon realized I needed acting and voiceover coaching. I studied with some of the top Los Angeles voiceover coaches, who gave me the direction I needed and an entrée to meet my first agent, Don Pitts.

How have you seen the business progress in the last ten years?
What's amazing to me is that so much has changed in the voiceover business, yet so much has stayed the same. What I mean is, when I was going to auditions at ad agencies early in my career, I would hear the older, seasoned actors saying many of the same things as I am hearing now from my peers: "This is the first audition I've had in two weeks; is it slow for you?" "I am so exhausted, my agent is working me too much!" "After all these years, you'd think this town would know me by now. Why can't my agent just *book* me? In all my years in the business, the one item that has changed dramatically is technology, allowing for

the decentralization of voice actors. One no longer needs to be in or near a large market to work for major accounts. Recording technology and the Internet have allowed — and will allow — all of us working voice actors to be anywhere in the world and still voice a session. We see this every day at my studio, Dave & Dave Recording, and the number of long-distance sessions over the next five to ten years will only increase.

What made you decide to start the Voice Over Resource Guide? **What has the** Voice Over Resource Guide *meant for the industry and talent?*
By 1988, my voiceover career was well established. While in the waiting room of the Voicecaster [a Los Angeles–based casting house], I reached into my back pocket and took out my very old, folded-up listing of studios and casting houses to plan how I was going to get to my next voiceover job or audition. A few of the actors in the Voicecaster waiting room noticed my tattered list and asked me for a copy. It was that night, when reflecting over the day's events, that I decided to go to press with the *Voice Over Guide*. I expanded my back pocket list by adding categories. I had a few thousand *Voice Over Guide*s printed at my expense and started handing them out wherever I went. The response was always positive. I'm thankful to the many industry people who gave insight as to how they used my six-panel, two-fold handout.

As time passed, many people asked me to expand the listings and categories, which I did. By late 1993, the *VOG* expanded to an eight-panel three-fold and I was printing and distributing five to seven thousand each quarter. Over the first ten years (1988–1998), many recording studios, production companies, workshops, and duplicators called and wanted to buy ad space in my free handout. Whatever the personal cost — humanitarianism aside — it was time to expand not only the listings but the categories as well. After much research with actors and industry insiders, I decided to launch the full-color, advertiser-supported, newsstand *Voice Over Resource Guide.* That was the summer of 1998. The newsstand *VORG* now accepts display advertising, which breathes life into it and allows many thousands of people who use it daily. I sometimes feel that the ads provide as much information about our industry as the free listings do. With hundreds of changes per issue, I feel proud of all the additions we've made along the way with our newsstand *VORG*.

January 2005 marked another milestone for the *VORG* publishers, Dave & Dave, Inc. We invited many to the grand opening of our website, *www.voiceoverresourceguide.com*. As you'll see, on the Web we have taken the opportunity to offer many more benefits to our publication. With the newsstand *VORG* and the online VORG complementing one another, we believe our industry will grow to be a more recognized thread in the fabric of America.

What do you think that advertisers are looking for today?
With all the information that I've been instrumental in providing to our industry, I still feel the one thing that advertisers are looking for today is the same thing they were looking for a hundred years ago: to stand out from the crowd and strike an emotional chord with the consumer.

How important is the way the talent behaves in a voiceover session?
It's our job as voice actors to supply that emotion with honesty. I have directed and simply observed talent achieve this in sessions in many different ways. Some actors show up late for sessions, are prima donnas, and difficult to work with, but I believe that part of the job of voice acting is to arrive on time with a terrific work ethic. After all, as I've mentioned to so many of my non-industry friends and relatives, "It ain't heavy liftin'." Those of us who have chosen voice acting as a profession should count our blessings for every session or audition we book — and act accordingly.

Do you notice a lot more fresh voices out there, with the market opening up?
The technology changes and the voice actor decentralization in our industry have doubled, maybe tripled, the number of candidates for any given job and opened these jobs to even younger, less-experienced voice actors from all over the nation. Many voiceover actors can emulate a trend, a style, an interpretation

of another actor, but it's those who find their own place and their own understanding of the meaning of the words, and who deliver those words honestly, who will work more often and sustain a career.

HANDLING THE UPS AND DOWNS

In every career, you will experience ups and downs. This is a natural occurrence in any career you may choose. The trick is to save your money and make smart choices, so when your business is down, you will know to expand your voiceover experience into other fields within that market. Maybe that means taking a loop class (or sitting in on one) and getting involved with that loop group as a voice actor. Maybe it means expanding on your experience with other languages and getting involved in dubbing. Perhaps you've always been interested in doing audiobooks. There are several production companies (in many states) that are looking for voiceover actors. This is a non-union field currently, but you can make $3,000 to $5,000 per book when negotiating for the work. When times are slow, look to other avenues for bookings. Go after other agents in smaller markets, or other states. Do another mass mailing, or join an advanced workout group. You never know who knows who and what can lead to another job. Don't simply rely on your agent for everything. Before, during, and after you have an agent, you must continue to put your "feelers" out there and make sure everything is current to get the work!

CHAPTER 17

MAKING IT IN MAJOR AND MINOR MARKETS

NEW YORK CITY, LOS ANGELES, AND CHICAGO ARE THE THREE MAJOR MARKETS IN VOICEOVERS. There are several other markets that are amazing to get work in such as Austin, Dallas, Philadelphia, Boston, and Kansas City. Basically, anywhere there are advertising agencies, production companies, radio stations and recording studios, there is an opportunity for you to book work. You don't have to live in a major market to have a successful voiceover career. It used to be that you needed to make sure you got with that one agent in that major market so that you could read for all of the "good stuff." That's no longer the case. Advertising agencies are looking for the voice, and that voice can come from anywhere and everywhere. You don't have to live where you receive auditions, you just have to receive them. There are non-union auditions and union auditions, and the ability to receive them means you are in and getting a chance to book jobs. Not every agent (no matter how great) will get every audition out there. Sometimes, ad agencies will only send auditions to particular markets or states. Other times, you will be one of hundreds reading on one particular job.

When I moved to Los Angeles in 1987, I wasn't sure what the voiceover market would be like. I found out who the agents were by calling the unions. I picked up a list of agents and began mailing out my demo with a note: "New in town. Enclosed is my demo."

Through the agencies, I found out who the casting directors were and sent out demos to them, too. I called, I dropped off demos, and I waited. I went on auditions and got an agent to send me out. Los Angeles may be a big town, but the voiceover world is small. Make sure that you are ready and that you know what you're doing. There are very few casting people and fewer agents. You don't want to show them something unpolished. Be prepared and be business-minded.

GETTING AN AGENT

When approaching agents, it is best to mail a demo CD along with a letter. The letter should be brief and professional-sounding. A resume of your work can be included on an attached sheet of paper. Call the agency first to find out the name of the appropriate person. It will either be a voiceover agent or an assistant.

Call the agent or assistant after a few days to make sure they received the CD. If you are in the area, drop the CD off in person instead of mailing it. You might get a chance to say hello — which will mean the assistant or agent can put a face with the name. They might listen to the CD and get back to you. Give them a few weeks before you call to follow up again. If they haven't listened to the CD yet, find out what day of the month they regularly listen to new submissions. If they have listened to the CD but have decided to pass on you, ask for feedback about your demo and voice. They may provide you with some information that will help in future submissions.

If you call an agency and they tell you they aren't accepting any new submissions, thank them and call another agency. There is always the possibility that an agent loves your CD but already represents someone who sounds very similar to you — and therefore sees you as a conflict of interest. Don't let this get you down. A lot of agencies do represent talent who sound similar or who will go out for the same parts. Just keep plugging away.

If you begin to feel rejected, take a class, take a break, and start over. Los Angeles and New York are great training grounds.

Not only are there a lot of casting directors and classes compared to other cities, but there are also a lot of student films being made, as well as other types of voiceover work. Read the trade papers. These include all the entertainment publications and casting magazines, including *Backstage, Hollywood Reporter,* and *Variety.* Also read the local college papers and magazines. (Voiceover auditions for industrials, commercials, films, and other projects are often listed there.)

Sample Submission Letter

[Date]

Ms. Pam Smith

Voiceover Agents Unlimited

555 Wilshire Boulevard

Hollywood, CA 90000

Dear Pam,

Per my conversation with your assistant, Brad, enclosed is my commercial demo CD. I am currently seeking voiceover representation.

I recently moved from Ohio, where I did several regional and national voiceovers. [Or name a few of the voiceover spots.]

Thank you for your consideration. I look forward to speaking with you soon.

Sincerely,

Beth R. Jones

(213) 555-1212

beth@bethrjones.com

www.bethrjones.com

Enc.

▶ **TIP: This tip comes from Dan Paschen, assistant to one of the top voiceover agents in the country.**

"One of the biggest mistakes that I see people make is that they throw themselves out of the race before the gun has been shot. Agents receive dozens of submissions every week. With that much competition and without a viable referral, your tangible submission must look good. You might have the best commercial/animation/promo voice in the world, but if your demo doesn't look professional, then it won't be perceived as such. I can't count the number of times a demo has come in blank, with 'John Doe's Voice Demo' written on the front with marker, or a cover letter greeting 'To Whom It May Concern.' Even if you're sending out dozens of packages, take the time to research exactly who you are submitting to, and always have the correct spelling of his or her name. And even though I hate saying this, call the assistant and let him or her know that your demo is coming. Assistants have almost no time for calls like this, but you're also fighting your own battle, and if your name gets remembered, then you might up your chances of getting heard once your demo arrives. (Call between three and five in the afternoon.) A perfect presentation doesn't guarantee anything, but at least it puts you at the starting line and can give you peace of mind that you didn't waste the postage."

COVER ALL THE CASTING HOUSES

You don't need an agent, or manager, to send your demos out to casting houses, production companies, ad agencies and recording studios. Your name, phone number and a good demo gets you in the door. Of course, having your name with a respectable agency that has their own connections, certainly is beneficial. You don't have to wait to get in to audition and book jobs. They may even make a call for you, if they like what they hear and like how you read. What they don't like is playing phone tag, having to re-arrange schedules, and dealing with talent who are unprofessional in their manners. So, if you are called to read directly, call back immediately without the changing time or causing any problems. Be on time, and do your audition well. You don't want them not to call you in because you were difficult to deal with or late!

While you are looking for an agent (*and* once you have one), send your CD out to all the casting houses. The routine is the same: Mail your CD with a submission letter. Enclose a resume if you have one. If you have a website, make sure the cover note gives the site's address. Start relationships. Get to know people. If you've done other work that is not on the CD, let them know. If you have a spot that's currently running, tell them. You have to start somewhere. Casting directors are more apt to take a chance on a newbie and bring you in if they like your demo CD and voice.

In a market so inundated with fresh talent, how are you ever going to stand out? By doing something different. Gift baskets can be an excellent way to get your foot in the door. Spending a few bucks to impress a future agent who may potentially make you hundreds of thousands of dollars isn't a bad first impression to make. Have other original ideas? Follow through on them.

SUBMIT TO ADVERTISING AGENCIES, PRODUCTION COMPANIES, AND PROMO HOUSES

Okay. By now you're definitely getting an idea of what to do. To submit your CD to advertising agencies, production companies, and promo houses, follow the same guidelines as those listed above, with one exception: Don't make the follow-up call, especially if it's just a general submission. The person receiving your CD will listen to it, time permitting. You may or may not ever hear back. Keep a running list of people you've contacted over the years. Add this person to your list. Send everyone on the list a card at the holidays. Send a note once a year with a list of the new commercials you have running. Email them a 1-minute teaser of your demo, which is easy for them to download and easier for them to listen to than a full demo. (You can always mail them the full demo, as well.)

If someone at an ad agency specifically asks for a copy of your CD, submit it along with a note. In this case it's okay to call to make sure they got it. They may not have anything for you at the time, but you never know what they may be working on down the line. By the way, the CDs you submit will not be returned to you. That's why you have to make lots of copies. Today, you can send quite a few via MP3 as an attachment. You can market to a certain number of potentials (at a time), concentrate on that area, and send away.

VOICE TO VOICE

AN INTERVIEW WITH LINDA JACK

Linda Jack is one of the top voiceover agents in Chicago.

"I started in the business as the first children's agent in Chicago. Voiceover was my favorite part of the business — versus print and on-camera. When I switched to a different agency, I accepted the challenge of building up the voiceover department. I initially worked in on-camera as well as voiceover, but eventually voiceover took all my time and energy.

"Linda Jack Talent was started in 1992. I had been working for Emilia Lorence, Ltd., and felt it was necessary to strike out on my own. My partner in the new agency was a former ad agency writer and producer, Mike Jablonski, who happened to be my husband. Mike passed away in August 2005. I did not want to continue as Linda Jack Talent, so a new agency was formed. Mickey Grossman had been the head of the on-camera department at LJT since we opened, and he and I formed a new corporation, Grossman & Jack Talent, which opened on March 1, 2006.

"I listen for voice quality and interpretive skill in new talent, and I check my gut reaction, my hunch. I look for prospective voice talent by listening to actors when they are talking here in the office, by going to the theater, or by getting recommendations on hot new on-camera talent and testing them in the audition studio. If someone I trust and respect in the business recommends a talent, I will try to check him or her out.

"With the popularity of Internet casting, I don't know if it's as time- and cost-effective to travel to market the talent, although I'm sure if I asked the talent, they would believe that it would be worthwhile. I just don't know how much time ad agency creatives have to receive sales calls.

"We have some video game and animation auditions here in Chicago, but promos and the affiliate market are nil. My experience with affiliates was very limited, and very low paying, so that it really isn't worth our time and energy.

"I have mixed emotions about Voicebank. We're competing against the entire nation. Sometimes we hit it and get the booking, and other times it seems that we're sending auditions into the great void. But what's our choice? You have to participate in the game if you want to win. Still, I question the number of submissions that are actually listened to by the ad agency creatives.

"Unsolicited demos, generally speaking, end up in the circular file. So many come in, and we have limited time to listen to them. And we already have such a large number of actors to care for and promote that we are very limited on the number of new talent we can represent. A new talent usually has to know someone I trust in order for me to pay attention to her or him.

"Occasionally, talent will go to an ad agency for an audition, or to a casting director's office. But the majority of the auditions are recorded in the talent agency's studio.

"There are voiceover classes at Act One and Acting Studio Chicago that I recommend. You should also practice reading out loud.

"I think the market is very tight here, with the exception of bringing in new, young talent. We have such a strong theatrical community — these are wonderful actors for voiceover work. And the way the business has changed in the last several years, in Chicago it's difficult to make a living strictly through voiceover work any more.

"Whew! That pretty much does it."

▶ TIP: Knowing where to look to pursue particular jobs is key in determining your success. Don't go after major animation movies, spend the money on a great demo, and take tons of classes, if you live in a really small town and don't have access to those auditions. Pursue the potential work you can get where you live. Then, work outside of that within the surrounding states to further your options. You can definitely book a job in New York City if you live in San Diego, if you receive the audition. But if they only are holding "in house" auditions, you won't receive the audition, even if you have an agent in New York City. There is plenty of work out there, when you look and pursue it in the right venues!

CHAPTER 18

TOOLS, TIPS, AND TRICKS

EOPLE WHO ARE NEW TO THE VOICEOVER BUSINESS usually have a lot of questions — and I find that I get asked the same ones again and again. This final chapter gives my answers to some of these FAQs, as well as some specific tips on running your business as a voiceover actor.

How do I find the copy to read?
There are only a few ways to get the copy. You may see a notice for an upcoming audition online and pursue it that way. Or someone may know you and call you in. Otherwise, the copy goes from the ad agency to the casting directors and voiceover agents. For non-union jobs, you just need to pound the pavement, making contact with local production companies, radio stations, and ad agencies.

Do I tell people my union status?
Yes. Never lie. Any client can call the union to check if you are *current* — that is, a current member of the union whose dues are paid up. If you are booked for a job and aren't in the union (or are not current) you may be fined — as may the ad agency for hiring you — and you have a chance of ruining your reputation. If an agency likes you and wants to hire you for a job despite the fact that you are not a union member, they will "Taft-Hartley" you — that is, they'll take the first step in the process of your joining the union. (See Chapter 13 for more information on joining the unions.) Some casting directors have specific projects for which they are looking for non-union actors only. If they like your voice, they'll bring you in despite your non-union status.

Can I do "under the table" jobs if I'm in the union?
No. Not if you are signed by an agency. Or not legally, anyway. If you book a job under the table, it means that you are taking a job that the agency didn't get for you. If you get caught doing a non-union job, you can be dropped and/or fined by your union, and your agency may also drop you. If it's a union job, the agency will find out — and your agent will know that he or she didn't get you the job. If someone wants you for a job, always tell him or her to call your agent before hiring you. If it's not a scale job, talk to your agency. If you aren't union, they may negotiate a lower salary so you can still do the job. If you are in the union, there are certain jobs that you can do anyway, if you sign a waiver.

How do I choose the best agent for me?
Well, in some cases you may not have many agents to choose from. In many cities, the pool of agents handling voiceover talent isn't that large. In some smaller markets, there may only be one or two. In any case, you've got to talk to them to find out if they get a lot of copy and how well connected they are to the casting people and ad agencies in town. Also, ask them if they're on Voicebank, which gives them access to castings all across the United States.

Make your choice from there. You may prefer to go with a smaller, "boutique" agency that, because it handles fewer people, can give you more attention, or you may like a larger, corporate-style agency that has a little more clout and whose agents may know more people. However, it's easy for a newcomer to get lost in the shuffle at a large agency, and if you don't book right away, you may find yourself not being called in very much — or at all. When you're starting out, smaller is generally better —especially if you haven't yet booked any jobs. It's just like any other business: you have to work your way up to the big guys. There's nothing wrong with starting small — if you're booking jobs! As long as the voiceover agency has a recording booth and regularly gets copy, you have as much chance of booking a job as anyone.

How long will the contract I sign with an agency last?
You can only sign for up to one year when you first join an agency. That's the union rule. After the one-year contract's up, you have

the option of signing for anywhere from one year to three years. If you have a good relationship with your agent, the standard is three years. But if you are at all unsure, just sign for one year at a time. An agent may like you but not be sure if he or she wants to sign you right away. The agent may want to test the waters first by taking you on a trial basis. This is called "pocketing," or "hip-pocketing." If you're pocketed, you will have all of the perks of a regular client. If you begin to book jobs, the agent will most likely offer you a contract. The pocketing process differs from place to place. In California, you may only sign with one agent at a time. In New York City, you may be pocketed with several. In general, though, most agents like to know that you are working with them alone.

But can't I have different agents in different cities?
It is not unusual for voiceover talent to work in different markets, and you may have different agents representing you in those markets. In that case, the agent who sends you out on the audition would be the one to negotiate the fee and receive the commission. If you move from one city to another, you will need to find a new agent to represent you in that new location. But if you are just on vacation and happen to find out about some auditions where you're vacationing — or your agent sets up meetings for you with casting directors in that town — your agent is still your agent.

You and your agent must work all of this out ahead of time. If you do not have a signed contract with your agent (that is, if you've been pocketed) and you are going back and forth between cities, as long as your agent and you are okay with your being sent out by other people, it's fine. If there is no contract, you are not legally bound.

What is an agent's commission?
The standard union rule is 10%. Managers generally get a 15% commission. If you have both an agent and a manager, this means you'll be giving away 25% of your fees. But it also means you'll have more help and may be able to book more jobs.

What is non-air, non-broadcast work?

A non-air, non-broadcast voiceover session is for a job that the ad agency is not planning to air. Non-air, non-broadcast demos are often created by ad agencies competing for corporate accounts against other agencies. They are also used as industrials — instructional films that are shown exclusively within the company that produces them and never on a broadcast medium. Such scripts generally have the verbiage "non-air" or "non-broadcast" written on them. Such jobs are paid at a different rate than jobs for broadcast. If it's a union job, you will be paid even if the spot never airs. Your agent will negotiate the payment, using standard union rates.

Who calls whom about an audition?

Casting agents usually call talent agents the day before an audition. Your agent will then spend a great deal of time calling voice clients to give them the information. A good agent will know your schedule. My agent always pleasantly surprises me when I go into the office in the morning to read and he says, "So, you've got a twelve, a one fifteen, and a four o'clock." He knows my day to the minute. This is why it is so important to be available. If you cannot be available one hour of one given day, you *must* call your agent and let him or her know so that you can be booked out. Otherwise, they may accept an audition for you for which you can't show up. The agent ends up looking bad — and you look unprofessional.

Some days, you might not get any calls. That just means there is nothing for you to read. Or you might just go into your voice agency, read one piece of copy, and leave. This is normal. Sometimes it's just slow. Don't panic about it. Calls can come in any time of the workday. Writers spend the morning writing the promos, the afternoon getting them approved, and the evening recording them. Promos air very quickly.

What if I can't make it to an audition?

Communicate with your agency. Your agent will alert the casting house. Emergencies happen, of course, and you can't always get to an audition on time. If you're in a group read, you may be holding up several people. Voiceover actors usually have a busy day running from audition to session — that is, if they're lucky enough to be working and running around — so they are all on a tight schedule.

If you don't have an agent, call the company directly. If, for whatever reason, you can't make it, try to reschedule for later or earlier in the day. (Generally, voiceover auditions don't go on for two or three days in a row. They get the call, hold the audition, send those takes on to the client, and it's over.) Don't be a no-show. Always call. The voiceover community remains relatively small, and if you don't show, they will remember and consider you irresponsible.

When do auditions take place?
You must be available any time between 9:00 AM and 6:00 PM to audition. If you live on the West Coast and the client is on the East Coast, you may be called in even earlier. Being available whenever your agent calls you for an audition or a session can mean success in this business.

Do I always have to audition to get a job?
Sometimes (although rarely), well-known, established voiceover talent will get a booking from a referral — or an ad agency that knows your voice will just book you for a spot without auditioning you. You may also be recommended for a job. But even then, you will often have to read for the part and compete for the job against other people — even if your name is on the copy as a "special request." I can't tell you the number of times that I've been specially requested, have read for the part, have done a great read — and still didn't get the job. Somebody did *me* better than I could! Can you believe it? It happens time and time again. This business is about auditioning and reading, over and over again.

What about out-of-town jobs?
Your voiceover agent handles all the jobs you book, including the out-of-town jobs. If you book a job that requires you to travel out of town, the agent will arrange everything.

If you are out of town and book a job on your own while you are there, your agent will still be the one to negotiate the terms (and will still make his or her commission). It doesn't matter where you go. If you have an agent representing you, that person is your agent for as long as you are legally bound by the contract.

What if I do a bad job at an audition or on a job that I've booked?
We all have bad days. You can rarely go back in to re-read once you've left the voiceover session. (If you really feel like you could truly have nailed a read and you know how to fix it, walk back in and ask to try again.) If you feel that the producer or writer isn't happy with what you've done, the time to say something is during the voiceover session. You might ask, "What else can I give you? Are you happy with the reads that we did? Do you think you got what you needed?" Or ask the casting director to lay down an alternate read. But don't assume you will get to read every piece of copy twice. Having an alternate way to read a script is the actor's job — and the director may not be interested in hearing it. If he or she is, make sure the read is really different. And remember, we can sometimes be bad judges of what we think copy should sound like — or of what we sound like. Let another person be the judge. The casting director or booth director usually knows what the client is looking for and is there to help you during a read.

Can I practice reading with other people for a double or group spot?
If you're paired or grouped together by the casting director at an audition and you all want to read it together a few times before auditioning, go ahead. There may also be times when you will read the copy "wild." This means that you're asked to audition alone but to read the copy as if you were responding to another person or other people. Timing and rhythm are still important, as are the beats of the copy.

How do I make sure that I am being sent out on all auditions I might be right for?
Trust your agent to make the right decisions. If the audition is "in-house" (at your agency), then the audition process is up to

the agency, and they will bring you in for what they think you are right for. Deciding who gets called to auditions outside your agency is not necessarily in your agent's power, however. Of course, he or she recommends voiceover actors to casting directors and ad agencies, but it is up to the outside agency to decide whom to see for which audition. This is where you come in. Get to know the casting directors. Make sure they've got your demo CD. (Your agent may not want you sending them out, if the agency already does it. So ask before you do.) It's important for every casting director and ad agency to get to know your voice and to realize you are out there as a talent. This is something you can do regardless of whether you have an agent or not.

What if I'm at an audition and I see that there's another job I want to read for?
There may indeed be more than one audition going on. But the client or agency has called you in for a specific audition and for a specific reason. If you see something else that you feel you'd be right for (and the direction fits your description) ask the casting director if you can read. He or she may agree to let you read — or not.

Even though you may be vocally right for a role, a casting director can only read a certain number of actors. They have their top five choices, and the ad agency may have specified its own choices. Or maybe they had ten other voiceover actors they thought could nail the read better than you. Do not make a habit of throwing yourself in front of people, demanding to audition. You have to work your way up the chain and earn your spot in the audition world. It is a competitive market, and the casting directors will bring in people they know can book. Eventually, they always bring a few new voices into the mix because ad agencies and clients always like to hear new voices. Everyone wants to find hot new talent.

What about callbacks?
Generally, voice talent is booked after the first audition they record; callbacks are rarer in voiceovers than in on-camera work. But sometimes a client needs to hear the voice again or has

trouble deciding between a few people. Treat the callback the same as the initial audition. Ask the casting director for more specific direction. The casting director may have new information, or he or she may simply tell you, "They aren't sure what they want," "They want to hear you again," or "They want to hear a variety of reads."

When you do a callback, mood and point of view become, if anything, even more important than usual. You may come into the audition in a certain mood, but you will have to "marry up" to the read that you did before — the one that they liked so much (which is the reason you got the callback in the first place). Remembering the mood that you read with before will make it much easier for you to go into your read while keeping it fresh. Maybe you missed the rhythm or wording on something the first time around and you'll catch it this time. Maybe you'll come up with a second take that's different and refreshing!

What should I do during a session?
Your job is to give the people who hired you what they are looking for. Listening to the producer who is directing you in the session is the most important thing you can do. Don't make too many suggestions. Apply the principles of breaking down a script, following the direction, applying the mood, and doing your work. A session can get frustrating, but the problems that arise usually don't have to do with the talent. There is a lot of work going into the session.

You are only one part of a large group. There are a lot of people to please in a voiceover session. The writer is worried about the director, the director is worried about the sound engineer, the sound engineer is trying to get your levels technically right for the session, and so on. You are all aiming at the same goal: doing the best work for the product and the client. Be friendly and professional, and to do the best job you can in a timely manner. If you can make this process easier for everyone else, they will appreciate it — and it may ensure that you book many more jobs in the future. Just remember: You're lucky to be where you are. You beat out a lot of other people for this job. So just count to ten and begin again if you get frustrated. Make sure you don't leave a session on a bad note.

When do I get the dough?
Usually, about four to six weeks after the job. Your agent will take out his or her 10% before sending you the check. Non-union talent is either paid at the session or receives a check directly from the client. If you have been waiting for payment longer than six weeks, call your agency's accounting department, and it will find out what's going on. AFTRA and SAG have rules about when actors must be paid; if you are not paid in a timely fashion, the client and ad agency will be penalized, and you will receive a late fee.

How do residuals work?
Every time a commercial recorded by union talent airs, the actor(s) involved get paid. But you do not receive a separate check for each time the commercial appears. Residuals come in chunks; the intervals are based on various union rules. For example, if a commercial runs seventeen times in a week, you may get one check for all the air dates — not seventeen separate checks.

The Federal Communications Commission (FCC) tracks how many times each commercial runs. The unions also keep track of this information. And the ad agency involved is supposed to inform you each time the campaign is rerun. Most of the time, ad agencies are good about calling your agent and paying the required recycle fees. But sometimes a commercial is rerun and you aren't paid, and you have to chase down your money. If you see or hear your commercial on the air, always jot down the information. If you don't receive the proper residuals, call your agent.

Non-union work never pays residuals. All non-union work is considered a "buyout"; you agree to let that company run your spot for a certain length of time (very often in perpetuity) for a one-time "buyout" payment. If you are non-union, get the agreed-upon money as soon as you are done with the job, to avoid having to chase after that company later on.

What if the check amount isn't right — for instance, suppose they pay me for one job when I actually did three?
Call the ad agency's accounting department and tell them. They may need to see a copy of the contract that you signed at the job. If you don't sign a contract, keep all the information about the person hiring you for the job. (This is a good reason to keep your copy of the contract.) As long as you signed for three jobs, they owe you for the other two. If there is a further problem, talk to your agent. He or she will straighten everything out so that you are paid the right amount.

I once did a job for a car rental agency. It ran locally in one market, and they paid me for the initial cycle. Then I found out that it was running again. They hadn't paid me. I called my agent, who called the advertising agency, which sent me my cycle fee plus a late charge. You can't always check to make sure that people are honest, but you hope you are getting paid what you should be.

How do contracts work?
When you are at a session, you should make sure that the paperwork you sign clearly and accurately states the amount of work that you've done. Nothing is sent in advance; it is up to you to sign the appropriate paperwork that will be waiting for you after the session. One copy goes back to the agency, another copy goes to your agent, and a third is for you for your records.

Signing a contract is equivalent to agreeing to the terms and conditions it describes — including terms about payment. If there is a discrepancy between what the contract says and the work you actually performed, don't sign it until you speak to your agent. Let your agent negotiate for you and rectify the situation. If you're unsure about how many spots, tags, or changes you recorded or should be paid for, don't sign the contract. Call your agent, fax it over to your agency, and let your agent advise you on how to proceed.

Should I ever work for free?
Voiceover work for not-for-profit or charitable organizations generally takes the form of public service announcements (PSAs), and this work is usually done pro bono — that is, for free. If you

TOOLS, TIPS, AND TRICKS

are recommended for a PSA job or you read for one and get the job, you must decide whether to take it or turn it down.

When you are first starting out, you should try to go after as many of these jobs as you can. They are often for a great cause, and they can also benefit you in the long run. These are great opportunities to get your voice out there, to work with some great producers and writers, and to teach you how to work in a voiceover session. There's nothing like on-the-job training! Always request a copy of the work to include on your demo CD.

Your agent may also suggest working for free if an ad agency asks you to record a non-air, non-broadcast demo — if he or she believes the spot may eventually air and lead to big bucks later on if the ad agency wins the account. The decision is up to you, of course, but it's not a bad idea to take advantage of opportunities that can lead to big-paying jobs. Even if the project is scrapped, the session gives you exposure to the ad agency team, which, depending on where you are in your career, can be valuable in and of itself and lead to paying work in the future.

How do I follow the trend of what the current "sound" is?

There are always trends and stereotypes out there. There are seasons and years when it seems that everyone sounds the same or has the same attitude. Where do you fit in? Is your voice current with the trends and market? Well, you really can't worry if your voice is "in" or "out." Certainly, having a vocal style that is trendy helps, but you still have to go through the regular channels to break into the business. You can't simply call an agency, ask to speak to the head of the voiceover department, and say, "My voice is very 'in' right now. You need me." Remember, the business overall is about *personality.* Trends and styles come and go, and the business goes through constantly changing waves and cycles. There will be auditions in which you're asked to sound like somebody, to have a similar attitude to somebody, or to try to be close to somebody. Do *not* change your voice to impersonate that person. If they want Rosie O'Donnell, they will hire her or someone who sounds very similar in tone and attitude. But if they ask for a Rosie O'Donnell type of read, then follow that *style* of read. Learn where your *niche* lies — find where you fit as a stereotype in the voiceover world. What types of sells/reads do you see yourself doing? Who is your competition?

How do I come up with different characters?
Play with your voice. Take an animation class. Watch cartoons. Draw a character (even a stick figure), give it a name, and make up three sentences that the character might say. Come up with a voice. Try another voice. See what comes out. You've just created an animation character! This is the same exercise that many animation classes have you do. It's very helpful.

How do I send out demo CDs to people?
Send them in a CD jewel case and CD envelope or email. A custom-made jewel case to cover the CD (a J-card) is more common on the West Coast market. On the East Coast, agents, casting directors, and ad agencies expect a simple CD cover with your name and some straightforward graphics. On the West Coast, graphics tend to get a bit more dynamic and fun.

Always include a note to the person receiving the CD. You can mass-mail to ad agencies and production houses. You can hand deliver your CD with a little cookie basket. Be creative. Walking the CD in to casting directors with a little goody bag is a nice way to get seen and be heard. You can certainly try to walk your CD in to a voiceover agent's office, but most likely you won't get past the assistant. (That's okay, though. The assistant can deliver the voiceover CD to the agent.) Remember, your demo (or a shortened version) can also be sent as an MP3 file via email.

What about gifts for clients?
During the holidays, it's always a nice gesture to send a basket or other small gift. Keep up with your contacts. It's good to send cards to regular clients, but large, expensive gifts aren't necessary. A lot of people do a special holiday voiceover demo CD or a novelty gift. Try to think of something that will stand out. Anything with your name on it should always be fun and alluring. Be creative.

Do I really need more than one type of demo CD?
Commercial jobs make up at least 70% of the business. At a minimum, I recommend that you have a commercial CD that represents the different moods within your range and really shows off what you can do. If you work — or want to work — mainly in animation, make sure you have an animation CD, as well. You can still book jobs in other voiceover areas, but when you venture seriously into promo or narration, it's essential that the producers hear you do these types of reads. So it becomes important to have specific demo CDs for each type of job.

Having a different demo CD for each aspect of the business can, however, become very expensive. Alternatively, a single demo CD can have several categories of reads — just be sure to identify which track is which on the face of the CD and on the J-card, so the recipients can listen to the relevant tracks.

What if I have a commercial CD, an animation CD, and a promo CD? How do I know which to send where?
Commercial CDs go to commercial casting directors and ad agencies; animation CDs go to animation casting directors, animation production houses, and studios; and promo and narration CDs go to networks and production companies. Audiobook CDs go to audiobook publishers. Keep multiple copies. Your agent needs several of each kind to give or send out as needed, and so do you. (It's even a good idea to keep several copies in your car — or, if you live in New York and travel by bus, subway, and taxi, in your shoulder bag — so that you always have them to hand out when the opportunity arises.)

How do I open my range to read for animation, promos, audiobooks, industrials, and narration?
Talk with your agent and let him or her know you would like to read in other areas. Your agent may recommend that you take a class if he or she feels you aren't ready. The agent might also recommend a demo producer to you, so that you can add these specific areas to your CD. Some agencies have stronger voiceover departments than others. Some may even be known specifically for their animation or promo departments. As you learn more

about the business and these other areas of the voiceover trade, you'll learn which agencies are strong in which areas.

How do I book more jobs?

The Internet has provided more venues to search for jobs than when I first started in the business. Although the business is competitive, the voiceover actor has many more places to look for jobs — from colleges, to the vast number of production companies, to the video game world. This market has gotten huge over the last ten years, and producers are always looking for voices. The more your voice is out there, the more work you will book. *A* leads to *B.* It's your job to pull yourself up through the ranks. Get your demo CD out to whomever you think can potentially book you for a job. Send thank-you notes when you're starting out, especially after a booking. Being cordial goes a long way.

How much will I work? (Or, should I quit my night job?)

Once you are working, your schedule may vary from week to week. You may go to ten auditions one week and then may not get called at all for a few weeks. Your agent may not call you one week but then call you several times the next week. Sometimes there's a lot, and sometimes there's not.

Don't be picky about which auditions you go to. Let your agent do the picking — he or she is trying to build your career, just as you are. Hopefully, you and your agent talked about your game plan when you signed up with the agency. You might have said, "Send me out on everything; I don't care what I book," or "I really want to only do animation." Whatever that game plan is, your agent is now working for you, trying to get you the best jobs that are out there.

You can definitely go on other auditions, if you come across them. Your agent may not know about a certain audition that a friend tells you about. If your friend sets up the audition, let your agent know, or have your agent call to set up the audition. Your agent won't always know about everything that's out there. Keep your ears open! An audition can pass you by. There's nothing you can do about it. Work at meeting all the casting directors you can and getting on their good side, so you don't miss any opportunities.

If your agent seems only to be sending you out for radio auditions, talk with him or her. The agent may feel that you aren't ready for television copy. Radio is a little easier to break into. It's easier to book, and there's less competition. Once you're reading for television, you are going up against a lot of pros who work a lot. Radio feels a little less intimidating — more realistic for newcomers.

What about vacations?

If you're going to take a vacation, the best time to do it is during the late summer months, because this is the slowest time in the advertising world. Ad agencies tend to be busiest whenever a holiday is around the corner. Try to keep your vacations brief, unless you're traveling to a city that has a recording facility from which you can do your voiceover work. (Check this in advance.) Some voiceover agents will fax or email you the copy and allow you to MP3 the material back to the office.

You will want to be gone as few weekdays as possible, since it's during the week that all the auditions come in. Being gone on long trips keeps you out of competition. Ad agencies won't hold the auditions for you. Everyone works on a deadline, so be available and hustle!

Once I work, will I always work?

Maybe…. One can only hope. I know many people who work all the time — and have for many years. On the other hand, your voiceover work might be a hobby that never gets off the ground. To succeed, you need patience, perseverance, and talent. Once you've got those three things, you're on your way.

Once you begin to book a job here and there, you need to keep up the momentum. How do you do that? Through having a good agent, keeping up with your relationships, and constantly marketing yourself. The good news is that once you've established relationships and start booking voiceover jobs, you will be on advertisers' radar. Maybe they'll even begin to create campaigns around you. Each year, you may find more and more work, and you may even begin to branch out into other voiceover areas. The only logic to the voiceover business is that *there is no logic.* As long as you know that anything can happen at any time (just as in life), you're on your way. Take a shot. What's the worst that can happen? You go back to your 9-to-5 with a renewed vigor and confidence — and maybe some fun new voices to amuse your coworkers with.

Or you begin a successful, lucrative, amazing career in the voiceover industry that lasts a lifetime!

KEEPING TRACK

Here's a checklist of things to do to help you keep track of your business:

- Send out thank-you notes, new CDs, and cards whenever you change agents. Occasionally, you should send out "just keeping in touch" cards.
- Keep your records carefully filed in case your union, your agent, or a producer has a question. You may need to have the information handy.
- Know when you should be getting paid for each job. (Again: four to six weeks is usually about right, but some jobs can take up to eight weeks to pay. If it goes on any longer than that, check with your agent or call the ad agency). Also know *what* you should be getting paid and in what cycle the spot is running so you can keep track of your money.
- Keep a record of all the spots you have running — and know which potential jobs might create a conflict for you.
- Keep a running list so that you always have some idea of what kind of spots you are auditioning for and booking and the casting houses you are frequenting.

ABOUT DEMO CDS

And here are a few helpful pointers about your demo CDs:

- Resubmit your CD to ad agencies every two months or so — especially to the ones that have used you in the past. If

they bring you in, you do not need to keep supplying them. They already know you. Sending a flyer announcing a new job that is running is okay, as long as you don't bother casting people personally. They are busy. Although relationships are important, the one between you and your agent is the most important.
- Keep your CD current. Add new spots as you book. Take old spots off your CD that no longer apply. Keep up with trends.
- Use your signature voice (the voice that most closely resembles your personality) on the first track of CD. Show the range of your voice on your commercial demo CD.
- Send demo CDs to appropriate places.
- Take an animation class with a casting director, producer, or director to get to know them and to build up a "stable" of your own voices for use on your animation CD.
- Don't write your own copy. Make sure you are using real spots for your demo CD.
- Let someone who has knowledge of the voiceover business listen to your demo.
- Don't overpower your demo CD with music and sound effects. The point of the demo is to show your vocal range and moods.

AFTER A SESSION

After each recording session, make a copy of the contract and fax or send it to your agent for accounting. Then staple a copy of the contract to the script you've just read, noting the date and time of the job, the ad agency's name, and the writer's name. File your copy, so that you know where to find it if you need it. A friend of mine keeps track of everything on her computer. It's good to be able to look back and see what kinds of jobs you were getting at what time — and to see how the market has changed. It also doesn't hurt to have past job information so you can send current voiceover CDs to people who hired you in the past. You never know when you might get booked on another job with a company you haven't worked for in quite some time.

VOICE TO VOICES
ADVICE FROM WORKING VOICEOVER ACTORS

"I always used to carry around a list of the studios every time I got sent on an audition. I felt that somehow it made me more alert and better prepared."

— *Dave*

"I find that I like to read in the mornings, when my voice is deeper and throatier. By the afternoon, it seems to have smoothed out, and I don't feel as competitive for the same kinds of roles."

— *Beth*

"When I'm preparing for an audition, and the copy is in front of me, I read through it two times first. Then I take a highlighter and highlight all the words I think should be said brighter or stronger. I also pre-plan which way the words are going to go at the end of each sentence — up or down. This helps me feel like I know what I'm saying when I go on in there to read."

— *Debbie*

"I get nervous when I see a lot of other people auditioning. I feel as though they'll like everyone except me. When I read, I sometimes try to disguise or change my voice, hoping they'll like that better than my natural sound. My agent inevitably calls me and tells me to go back to being me."

— *Kristen*

"I know that for every job, there's at least a room full of other men who could read that copy the same or better. I read the copy once, find a character out of my 'pocket' of characters, and read the copy that way, no matter what the director asks for. At least I feel it makes me stand out and maybe I'll get the job because I was different."

— *David*

"I live in the Midwest, so I don't feel the sweat of competition so much. I'll basically be called directly to read for some part. When I do have to audition, I make sure to go over the copy several times, reading it different every time. I read the copy until I mentally tell myself that I am the only possible voice for that role, which makes me give a better reading. Thinking that another person couldn't possibly get that job helps me make strong vocal choices."

— *Barbara*

"I do a lot of promo work, but I think it's because they hear a booming voice come through. I guess they like my delivery, and I always pretty much do the same delivery. I don't put much emphasis on any words; I just read the copy with my voice. Other voiceover actors may put too much emphasis on words, make too much out of the promo, because they think that they need to sound loud or pushy. I think women are used more for intimate promos and daytime talk shows, where there is a more female audience. The networks and production companies like to use women more for day and men more for night."

— *John*

"I just go in and be myself. I try not to think of what another voiceover actor would do. The competition side of it freaks me out. If I thought about that all the time, I wouldn't be able to read the copy. A lot of these people are my friends, so, of course, I want everyone to get the job. I just try to do what I do and wing it."

— *Steve*

SKIN THE CAT
SECRET TERMS THAT ARE FREQUENTLY USED IN VOICEOVERS

Tighten it up: take less breaths, read with less pauses; same read only a bit faster, but don't sound like you're going faster.

Loosen it up: have more fun with it; come into beginnings and ends of reads a bit smoother, more simple. You're coming in too strong, you're reading too polished and formal.

Pull it back: same reading only a little bit "less." This doesn't mean to read without the smile now, or change your mood, this simply means the exact same read, only a little less.

Have more fun with it: again, too formal; a bit more playful, looser, flirty, more smile, maybe a bit brighter. This depends on where you were before the direction.

You have 5 seconds (or whatever time) to play with: This means you have more time to work within the read. This may simply be a breathing negotiation on your part, or a mood change (however small). They may ask you to read a bit slower all together, but keep the same mood.

We have to pick up 5 seconds (or whatever time): This means you are reading too long and you must go quicker. The trick here is that they may love the read and not want you to do anything, except find a way to "make it work." Your job as a voice actor is to be able to follow direction and understand how to make something work that may run long. Simply getting more comfortable with the copy (practicing) may give you the time you are looking for. Understanding that you can breeze through certain parts of the copy — and still emphasize what they want — is a trick in the voiceover business as well.

Add warmth (or any adjective): This means, from wherever you are in your read — right there — they need you (for the next read) to simply add warmth. Nothing else. Do not take anything away from how you were reading before. Do not go slower, get bigger, or change any other direction they have given you up to this point. When you are given a direction, note, or adjective, your job is to know how to add (or remove) simply that one note they are giving you without losing all the work you have done up to that point within the voice session.

You nailed it: You read the read exactly how they wanted it read.

Let's do one for safety: This means that you nailed it, but either there were problems with popping of Ps, some mouth noises, problems with the sound engineer side or technical aspect, or they simply want a second take for "insurance" in case that one isn't good for whatever reason. Sometimes, they like to do a second take just to get an "alternate," or sometimes better, version of the first time. Once you get comfortable in your reads, you will understand how to do one for safety without making it bigger or trying to outdo yourself. Just relax and stay in the same world they direct you in.

An alternate read: This is a second read (a second chance) in an audition to book the job. You should know how to show them another way of looking at the same script (that still fits the specs) but can lead to another vocal quality from you. This does not mean changing the read entirely or going outside of the box of "friendly, warm." (Or whatever they are looking for.) Understanding how to create another version of "friendly, warm" that brings out a different read and different quality of your voice is what creates an alternate choice.

Just play with it: This means that you can "play" within the read. Improvising can be okay, as long as you aren't changing entire scripts. They want to hear some different choices. They want to see how creative you are and what you can bring to the script.

Make it your own: This is another way to show them who you are. When a read "isn't your own," it sounds like you are reading from a script already written. You don't own it. The person who books the job made the script his or her own. This sounds like the voice actor is reading/talking (in that mood) directly to a person, he or she owns the copy, and it sounds like it is coming out of his or her mouth. He or she knows how to act and create the mood and moment — as if it's coming directly from him or her and not written by a writer.

Wild lining: There are several terms to wild lining.

1. When reading three in a row of any line(s), and they are labeled A, B, and C.
2. When you are reading alone (even if there are other actors in the script). This happens when you are booked separately so that the director/writer can work with you one-on-one. You may also read audition copy "wild" (alone) in the sound booth. No booth director will read the other copy.
3. You may wild line to time. (They have to get the read in a certain amount of time.)
4. You may wild line to make sure you nail the mood.
5. You may do a line reading and wild line. (The director or writer will say the line in exactly the way they want you to read it.)

Give me a level: This is for the sound engineer, and/or booth director. You will read the copy in exactly the way you plan to read it for the audition/session. They are getting levels on their side for the recording.

Slate your name: This simply means to say your name (first and last) before you begin your read. You will say your name, take a slight beat, and continue with the copy. Sometimes the booth director, or casting director will slate for you.

Slate your name and character: If asked, you will slate your name and character. "Sue Smith as announcer." "Sue Smith as Jenny." "Sue Smith as Roxanne the Squirrel."

Keep a journal of terms you don't know or learn on the job and write them down here, so that you can refer back to them.

AFTERWORD

I've had a very successful run (and hopefully still chugging) career that's spanned over 30 years since I first began. It's had it's ups and downs. There have been years when I've worked less than others. And there have been years when I've worked more. But, overall, it's been a great experience that turned into a career. I don't think I started out thinking it would one day become my career, but that's exactly what has happened. Through living in Los Angeles and New York City and working in film/TV (as an actress) and writing (books, film, and TV), I've realized that voiceover work has sustained me and allowed me the freedom to pursue these other areas. I no longer wish to be sitting on a set for 15-hour days versus sitting in a booth for an hour. I no longer wish I was running around the world signing autographs. Instead, I'm quite happy to not be recognized on my way to the gym, thanks! I appreciate where this voiceover career has taken me, the gift I've been given with my voice — thanks, Mom — and the choices I've made to make the most of my career. By pursuing other avenues within the voiceover business, I could become a working, staple voiceover talent.

I've written this book to enlighten people about the voiceover world. Hopefully, I've opened your eyes to the ins and outs of commercial voiceovers as well as some of the less well-known kinds of voiceover jobs. I hope I've answered your questions and that this book will help you create a fun and lucrative career for yourself. Although I've done voiceovers for more than twenty-five years, I only began to do voiceovers full-time when I landed a successful campaign — the Home Base campaign — at the age of twenty-five. Obviously, when I started I was in high school, then college, and then I took some part-time jobs in Los Angeles when I first moved here. I worked at a talent agency, as a waitress, for a producer — a few different jobs, but I always made sure I kept time to audition for voiceovers while pursuing acting and writing as well.

I was one of the lucky ones. But I have to tell you that I see many of the same faces around all the time — people who've been doing voiceovers for years (which means they're doing something right to book the jobs!). At the same time, I see many *new* faces, too, which means the industry is always looking for new talent to bring to the mix. This business is ever-expanding and definitely not going away! So no matter where you are in your voice journey, know this: It never ends. No matter where you live, start your voiceover journey now! Don't worry about Hollywood, New York, or Chicago right off. Focus on getting the bait first. Then worry about the big fish.

AND GOOD LUCK!

Terri

ONE FINAL THOUGHT

A CONVERSATION BETWEEN THE QUEEN OF VOICEOVERS AND THE JINGLE QUEEN

As a final thought, I had to include this brief interview I had with Linda November, the "Jingle Queen." Linda's career, which spans several decades, demonstrates that with talent, determination, and a little luck, your career can take you just about anywhere. She has over 22,000 jingles to her credit. At one time, she had over 700 jingles playing simultaneously on national TV and radio. Her most famous jingle remains "Meow, meow, meow, meow" for the Meow Mix cat food commercials.

Linda, they call you the Jingle Queen in the voiceover world! How did you get your start in the business?
I met Dick Williams, Andy's brother, and Ray Charles of Perry Como fame, and they started hiring me 'cause I sight read beautifully. So, I did a zillion record dates, TV shows, and it took me seven years to become a success. That's when I did my first jingle—the rest was history. I sang over 22,000 jingles in 32 years.

Did you have a singing background?
I was a child prodigy. I sang and played piano at the age of 4. I have perfect pitch as well.

Did you have one agent throughout your career?
Never ever had an agent—much to their chagrin, hee! Just Artists' Service that the agencies and music houses called to book me.

The market has changed quite a bit. Can you give us any insight into how you perceive the business today?
The business as we knew it—the Golden Age of Advertising—is dead and buried.

Can you give us any good "jingle" stories?
The best was when I recorded the original Meow Mix and they wouldn't show me the film until after I sang because they said I'd cry when I saw it—and they were right. It was a phenomenon.

Can you chat just a little about SAG and AFTRA?
SAG and AFTRA have wonderful benefits, and we all earned every penny we made—no matter how many millions!

What, if any, was the highlight or best time you ever had in your career?
That's really tough. From working with Sinatra, Frankie Valli, Dionne Warwick, Humperdinck, James Moody, Michel Legrand, Burt Bacharach, Steve Tyrell, Streisand and the list goes on and on and on—it was the greatest experience a little Jewish kid born in Brooklyn could have.

APPENDIX A

SAMPLE COPY

This appendix contains sample copy for a variety of voiceover jobs. As you practice with these scripts, remember to go through the following steps with each new piece of copy you encounter:

1. Read the copy to yourself all the way through.
2. Read the specs and/or any direction.
3. Apply the proper point of view and mood.
4. Start to add adjectives to get as specific as you can.
5. Choose a person to tell the story to.
6. Read the copy aloud all the way through until you're comfortable.
7. Come up with an alternate read.

Now you're ready for your audition. Do remember that — although scripts can sometimes be overwritten — the closer you are in mood, the closer you'll be in time.

NARRATION

"Bright Ideas" Story
In 1984, Sherry Winters had an idea — an idea that would change the way people walked. The idea started as a concept. The concept turned into a reality. Today, Sherry Winters is a star athlete and cross-country walker ...

AUDIOBOOKS

For sample audiobooks, pick up any book and begin reading. What is your mood? With audiobooks, depending on the topic, you will generally be authoritative and objective and will move along at an even pace. You are the narrator, and the reader will want to be able to follow the story without hearing a lot of overselling or overacting. A nice narrative voice is required. Now record your read, play it back, and listen to it. Remember that there are two versions of many audiobooks: abridged and unabridged. The unabridged version is the full text of the book, as published. The abridged version is condensed. Often, celebrities are hired to read the shorter (abridged) versions, while scale voiceover actors record the unabridged versions.

TAGLINES

Only at Alfie's. Get it right now.
Get your burger's worth.
If it doesn't get all over the place, it's not in your face.
Welcome home. To us.
It's about time.
More for your money.
More bang for your buck.

RADIO SCRIPT

60 seconds
Winer, Broad, & Reed Advertising

SPECS
Male: Friendly, casual, with a good sense of comedic timing. Not forced.
Female announcer: Sassy, friendly, and likeable.

MAN: Hi. You may have met me the other day in the grocery aisle, but you were in too big of a hurry to stop and say hello. I was there, all by my lonesome, because my buddies were all purchased and no one bothered to restock me. I know what you're thinking. So what? I can just go to another shelf, which is what you did, by the way — and purchase that other brand... . Ooh, the thought of this is giving me dizzy spells. Let me take a minute. Anyway, I'm here, begging for you to give me a try. Really. I can't stand being all alone. I look around and it just seems like everyone is having a

party — without me! Help. Can't you come back to the store and pick me up? Oh, wait, who's that? [Muffled sounds of being picked up.] Well, too late now. Gotta run. Somebody loves me ... yea, yea! [Excited but muffled as customer walks off.]
ANNOUNCER: Add Crispy Delight Croutons to your next salad, stuffing, or favorite meal, and see what happens. Crispy Delight Croutons. In your grocer's aisle. And try our new spicy Picante Croutons.

RADIO SCRIPT

60 seconds
Napa Wine Country — Napa Vineyard

SPECS
Keep it real, conversational, upbeat, and moving along.
Woman: Calm, cool, and collected.
Waiter: Professional, warm, and helpful; a bit condescending.
Announcer: Flat, cool, hip, conversational.
SFX: Restaurant noise

WOMAN [*through a car window*]: Excuse me. I'm trying to find Napa Vineyard. I'm a bit lost.
WAITER: Napa Vineyard in Napa Country?
WOMAN: Yes. Am I close?
WAITER [*Stifled laugh*]: Ma'am, you're in Kansas.
WOMAN [*shocked*]: Kansas, California?
WAITER: No, Kansas, Kansas. You know, Dorothy? Kansas?
WOMAN [*looking around*]: Oh, yeah, now I see the cornfields. Must have gotten turned around.
WAITER: What you're going to need to do is turn around and follow the smell.
WOMAN: The smell?
WAITER: Right. Fresh air. Keep following it. Then you'll start to smell grapes. Then you'll see happy people dancing. You're getting close.
WOMAN: Great. Thanks.
SFX: Starts to drive off.
WAITER [*yelling after her*]: Ma'am? Ma'am!

SFX: Car keeps driving. We hear the clank of cans as she drives off.
WAITER [*reading from a sign on the back of the car*]: "Just married?" Wonder where her husband is?
ANNOUNCER: Napa Vineyard. Follow your nose.

TV PROMO COMMERCIAL

VIDEO	AUDIO
Dog groomer grooms dog.	Today on *Grooming Fifi* ...
Fifi gets shaved.	So maybe life for Fifi is a little boring.
A TV plays.	
A servant stands by with cookies.	
Fifi gets a pedicure.	
Fifi yawns.	Sometimes a dog's life is exactly like it seems.
Groomer dries Fifi.	On an all-new *Grooming Fifi*. Today at four.

TV PROMO SCRIPTS

#1
Tonight
On *CSI*
(SOT) "Get him here, now."
On an episode you won't want to miss.
(SOT) "We've still got time."
CSI. Tonight at nine/eight central, only on [NETWORK].

#2
Tonight at nine.
News that matters
In trying times.
Channel 8.
Cincinnati's only news station to watch.

APPENDIX A

TV COMMERCIAL SCRIPT

60 seconds

SPECS

Male or female. Twenties to fifties. Conversational, in on the joke, friendly but not selly or smiley. Matter-of-fact. Some rasp or edge okay. Try two different ways. For the second, maybe warm it up a bit. Keep it real.

VIDEO	**AUDIO**
We open on a woman cleaning out her refrigerator. She is singing while sitting in a recliner	In life, there are people who like to clean ...
Cut to:	
A man sitting on a lazy recliner, snoring.	... and those who don't.
Cut to:	
The woman sitting in a recliner smiling at herself in a mirror.	Those who like to preen ...
Cut to:	
The man now lying in the lazy recliner, still snoring.	... and those who don't.
Cut to:	
Recliner. Front, back, changing positions.	The all new NELL recliner with automatic settings to fit your lifestyle.
Cut to:	
The man on his stomach, flat out, still snoring.	Or, your sleep style.
Tag: The new NELL recliner.	

ANIMATION SCRIPT

The Adventures of Robbie the Squirrel

Robbie: Precocious eight-year-old, leader of the pack. Manipulative but loving, fun, and playful.

Robbie's Mom: Patient, warm, nurturing. Protects her son at all costs. Had a difficult birth, so she's extra cautious with Robbie.

Chuck: Robbie's best friend. Lost half his tail in a lawnmower mishap. Sweet and kind of dorky. Follows his best friend, Robbie, everywhere, even to the bathroom.

Penelope: Robbie's older sister. Future ballerina. Always in a tutu. Hair always on top of her head. Doesn't speak much and when she does has a strange accent (like a Valley Girl, maybe?). A bit arrogant, but just has a lot on her plate.

Ext. Tree. Daytime.
Robbie is sitting outside the tree with his best friend, Chuck. They're very busy folding papers. Chuck has a computer in front of him.

Robbie: [*folding papers*] So, once we've created the supersonic rock ...

Penelope waltzes by. Robbie stops.

Robbie: We're having a secret meeting.

Penelope: [*still dancing*] Please ...

Chuck: Hi, Penelope.

Robbie covers his mouth. Chuck shuts up. Penelope rolls her eyes while doing ballet moves and exits frame. Robbie's Mom enters with freshly baked cookies on a tray.

Mom: Hi, sweetie. Hi, Chucky. How about some homemade cookies with fresh nuts?

The boys grab cookies and eat them quickly. Robbie covers the papers. Chuck sits on the computer.

Robbie: Thanks, Mom. We've got to get back to business.

Mom leans down, pinches Robbie's cheek, and walks out.

APPENDIX A

MY SIX-MONTH TO ONE-YEAR GOALS/PLAN

Date:

1. Where I am right now in the world of voiceovers:

2. Where I want to be in six months to a year:

3. What tools I have/need: (1 min. voiceover demo(s), classes/coaching/groups):

4. Casting directors/producers/advertising agencies/agents that I know:

5. My goal to meet new casting directors/agents/advertising agencies/production companies:

6. Mass mailing to advertising agencies/casting directors:

7. Other interests within the voiceover world and how to achieve those goals:

APPENDIX B

RESOURCES

AGENTS AND MANAGERS

LOS ANGELES AND SOUTHERN CALIFORNIA

AGENTS

Abrams Artists Agency (AAA)
9200 Sunset Boulevard, 11th Floor
Los Angeles, CA 90069
(310) 859-0625
www.abramsartists.com

Arlene Thornton & Associates
12711 Ventura Boulevard, Suite 490
Studio City, CA 91604
(818) 760-6688
www.arlenethornton.com

Artist Management Agency/San Diego
835 Fifth Avenue, Suite 411
San Diego, CA 92101
(619) 233-6655
www.artistmanagementagency.com

Artist Management Agency/Santa Ana
261 Bush Street
Santa Ana, CA 92701
(714) 972-0311
www.artistmanagementagency.com

Cassell-Levy
843 North Sycamore Avenue
Los Angeles, CA 90038
(323) 461-3971

Cunningham, Escott, Slevin and Doherty (CESD Voices)
10635 Santa Monica Boulevard, #130
Los Angeles, CA 90025
(310) 475-2111
www.cesdvoices.com

Daniel Hoff Agency
5455 Wilshire Boulevard
Los Angeles, CA 90036
(323) 932-2500
www.danielhoffagency.com

Danis, Panaro & Nist (DPN)
9201 West Olympic Boulevard
Los Angeles, CA 90212
(310) 432-7800

Don Buchwald & Associates
6500 Wilshire Boulevard, Suite 2200
Los Angeles, CA 90048
(323) 852-9555
www.buchwald.com

Hervey/Grimes Talent Agency
10561 Missouri Avenue, Suite 2
Los Angeles, CA 90025
(310) 475-2010

Imperium 7 Talent Agency (i7)
9911 West Pico Boulevard, Suite 1290
Los Angeles, CA 90035
(310) 203-9009
www.imperium-7.com

APPENDIX B

Independent Artists
9601 Wilshire Boulevard, Suite 750
Beverly Hills, CA 90210
(310) 550-5000

Innovative Artists
1505 Tenth Street
Santa Monica, CA 90401
(310) 656-5172

Kazarian/Spencer & Associates
11969 Ventura Boulevard, 3rd Floor
Studio City, CA 91604
(818) 755-7570
www.ksawest.com

Marian Berzon Talent Agency
336 East 17th Street
Costa Mesa, CA 92627
(800) 266-2778

N2N Entertainment
1230 Montana Avenue, Suite 203
Santa Monica, CA 90403
(310) 394-2900

Osbrink Agency
4343 Lankershim Boulevard, Suite 100
Universal City, CA 91602
(818) 760-2488

Paradigm Talent & Literary Agency
360 North Crescent Drive, North Building
Beverly Hills, CA 90210
(310) 288-8000

Sandie Schnarr Talent
8500 Melrose Avenue, Suite 212
West Hollywood, CA 90069
(310) 360-7680
www.sandischnarrtalent.com

Solid Talent
6608 Lexington Avenue
Hollywood, CA 90038
(323) 978-0808
www.solidtalent.com

Special Artists Agency
9465 Wilshire Boulevard, Suite 890
Beverly Hills, CA 90212
(310) 859-9688

Sutton, Barth & Vennari
145 South Fairfax Avenue
Los Angeles, CA 90036
(323) 938-6000
www.sbvtalentagency.com

TGMD Talent Agency
6767 Forest Lawn Drive, Suite 101
Los Angeles, CA 90068
(323) 850-6767
www.tishermanagency.com

United Talent Agency
9580 Wilshire Boulevard, 5th Floor
Beverly Hills, CA 90212
(310) 273-6700
www.unitedtalent.com

VOX
5670 Wilshire Boulevard, Suite 820
Los Angeles, CA 90036
(323) 655-8699
www.voxusa.net

Wallis Agency
4444 Riverside Drive, Suite 204
Burbank, CA 91505
(818) 953-4848

William Morris Endeavor Agency
One William Morris Place
Beverly Hills, CA 90212
(310) 859-4289
www.wma.com
(Also in New York, Nashville, London, Miami Beach, and Shanghai)

UNIONS

AFTRA
(American Federation of Television & Radio Artists)
National Headquarters
5757 Wilshire Boulevard, 9th Floor

Los Angeles, CA 90036
(323) 634-8100
www.aftra.com
(Locals throughout the United States)

SAG
(Screen Actors Guild)
National Headquarters
5757 Wilshire Boulevard
Los Angeles, CA 90036
(323) 954-1600
www.sag.com
(Locals throughout the United States)

CASTING SERVICES

A. C. Productions Casting
4106 West Burbank Boulevard
Burbank, CA 91505
(818) 954-9931

ArttWorx Voice Casting
4862 Excelente Drive
Woodland Hills, CA 91364
(818) 225-7864
www.arttworxvo.com

Beard Boy Productions Casting
14451 Chambers Road #250
Tustin, CA 92780
(714) 734-0372

Bert Berdis & Company
1956 North Cahuenga Boulevard
Hollywood, CA 90068
(323) 462-7261
www.bertradio.com

Blanca Valdez Casting
1001 North Poinsettia Place
West Hollywood, CA 90046
(323) 876-5700
www.blancavaldez.com

Blupka Productions Casting
13223 Ventura Boulevard #G
Studio City, CA 91604
(818) 763-8500
www.blupka.com

Carroll Voiceover Casting
6767 Forest Lawn Drive, Suite 203
Los Angeles, CA 90068
(323) 851-9966

Cashman Commercials Casting
4310 West Victory Boulevard
Burbank, CA 91506
(661) 222-9300

Chris Borders TikiMan Casting
30062 Happy Sparrow Lane
Laguna Niguel, CA 92677
(949) 363-9548

Danny Goldman & Associates Casting
1006 North Cole Avenue
Hollywood, CA 90038
(323) 463-1600
www.dannygoldman.com

Davis Glick Entertainment (DGE)
3280 Cahuenga Boulevard West, 2nd Floor
Los Angeles, CA 90068
(323) 851-2233
www.davisglick.com

Dawn Hershey, CSA/Blindlight Casting
8335 Sunset Boulevard Suite #307
West Hollywood, CA 90069
(323) 337-9090

Elaine Craig Voice Casting
6464 Sunset Boulevard, 11th Floor
Los Angeles, CA 90028
(323) 469-8773
www.elainecraig.com

Famous Radio Ranch Casting
13440 Ventura Boulevard
Sherman Oaks, CA 91423
(818) 465-0150
www.radio-ranch.com

Funny Farm & Sons Casting
4470 Sunset Boulevard, Suite 200
Los Angeles, CA 90027
(323) 667-2054

APPENDIX B

Ginny McSwain Voiceover Casting
(818) 548-7174

Kalmenson & Kalmenson Voice Casting
5730 Wish Avenue
Encino, CA 91316
(818) 342-6499
www.kalmenson.com

Loop Troop/ADR Voice Casting
859 Hollywood Way, Suite 411
Burbank, CA 91505
(818) 239-1616
www.looptroop.net

Mambo Casting
489 South Robertson Boulevard
#101
Los Angeles, CA 91505
(323) 655-7200

Marc Graue Voice Over Casting
3421 West Burbank Boulevard
Burbank, CA 91505
(818) 953-8991
www.marcgraue.com

Radioville Casting/Julie Roux & Company
(323) 962-1882
www.julieroux.com

Sandy Holt Voice Casting
Los Angeles, CA
(310) 271-8217

Sheila Manning Casting
332 South Beverly Drive
Beverly Hills, CA 90212
(323) 852-1046

Sight 'N' Sound Casting
10707 Magnolia Boulevard
North Hollywood, CA 91606
(818) 845-9551

Terry Berland Casting
2329 Purdue Avenue
Los Angeles, CA 90064
(310) 775-6608
www.terryberlandcasting.com

The Voicecaster
1832 West Burbank Boulevard
Burbank, CA 91506
(818) 841-5300
www.voicecaster.com

Voices Voicecasting
11340 Moorpark Street
Studio City, CA 91602
(818) 716-8865
www.voicesvoicecasting.com

Wally Burr's No-BS Voice Casting
(818) 763-2618

RECORDING STUDIOS

Visit **www.voiceoverresourceguide.com** *for a complete list of studios in the LA area.*

A Z Los Angeles
1657 Twelfth Street
Santa Monica, CA 90404
(310) 581-8081
www.azlosangeles.com

Absolute Post
2633 North San Fernando Boulevard
Burbank, CA 91504
(818) 842-7966
www.absolutepost.tv

AudioBanks
1660 Ninth Street
Santa Monica, CA 90404
(310) 581-1660
www.audiobanks.com

Bell Sound
916 North Citrus Avenue
Los Angeles, CA 90038
(323) 461-3036
www.bellsound.com

Bennett Group
2017 South Westgate Avenue
West Los Angeles, CA 90025
(310) 979-0191

VOICEOVERS ◎ APPLE

Big Joe Sound
1410 Second Street, Suite 300
Santa Monica, CA 90401
(310) 394-3100
www.bigjoesound.com

Blupka Productions
13223 Ventura Boulevard, 2nd Floor
Studio City, CA 91604
(818) 763-8500
www.blupka.com

Buzzy's Recording
6900 Melrose Avenue
Los Angeles, CA 90038
(323) 931-1867
www.buzzysrecording.com

The Complex Studios
3234 Purdue Avenue
West Los Angeles, CA 90064
(310) 477-1938
www.thecomplexstudios.com

Dave & Dave Recording Studios
4352 Lankershim Boulevard
Toluca Lake, CA 91602
(818) 508-7578
www.everythingvo.com

Davis Glick Entertainment (DGE)
3280 Cahuenga Boulevard West,
2nd Floor
Los Angeles, CA 90068
(323) 851-2233
www.davisglick.com

Eleven
1231 Lincoln Boulevard
Santa Monica, CA 90401
(310) 562-2911

The Famous Radio Ranch
1140 North La Brea Avenue
Los Angeles, CA 90038
(323) 462-4966
www.radio-ranch.com

Five Guys Named Moe
11027 Weddington Street
North Hollywood, CA 91601
(818) 753-7500
www.5moes.com

Garden Of Sound
(323) 230-8249
www.gardenofsound.com

Juice
1648 Tenth Street
Santa Monica, CA 90404
(310) 460-7830
www.juicewest.com

Juniper Post
801 South Main Street
Burbank, CA 91506
(818) 841-1244
www.juniperpost.com

LA Studios
3453 Cahuenga Boulevard West
Hollywood, CA 9068
(323) 851-6351
www.lastudios.com

Larson Studios
6520 Sunset Boulevard
Hollywood, CA 90028
(888) 598-4863
www.larson.com

Latté Mix Studios
1548 Ninth Street
Santa Monica, CA 90401
(310) 260-9838

Levels Audio Post
1026 North Highland Avenue
Hollywood, CA 90038
(323) 461-3333
www.levelsaudio.com

Lime Studios
1528 Twentieth Street
Santa Monica, CA 90404
(310) 829-5463
www.limestudios.tv

APPENDIX B

Marc Graue Voiceover Recording Studios
3421 West Burbank Boulevard
Burbank, CA 91505
(818) 953-8991
www.marcgraue.com

Margarita Mix Hollywood
6838 Romaine Street
Los Angeles, CA 90038
(323) 962-6565

Margarita Mix Santa Monica
1661 Lincoln Boulevard, Suite 101
Santa Monica, CA 90404
(310) 396-3333

Matchframe Video
610 North Hollywood Way
Burbank, CA 91505
(818) 840-6800
www.matchframe.com
(Also in San Antonio and Austin)

McCoy Productions
10707 Magnolia Boulevard
North Hollywood, CA 91601
(818) 985-2303
www.mccoysound.com

Mix Magic Post Sound
839 North Highland Avenue
Hollywood, CA 90028
(323) 466-2442
www.mixmagic.com

N.O.V.A. Productions
3575 Cahuenga Boulevard West, Suite 630
Los Angeles, CA 90068
(323) 969-0949

Novastar Digital Sound Services
6430 Sunset Boulevard, Suite 103
Los Angeles, CA 90028
(323) 467-5020
www.novastarpost.com

Oracle Post Burbank
4720 West Magnolia Boulevard
Burbank, CA 91505
(818) 752-2800
www.oraclepost.com

Oracle Post Santa Monica
3232 Nebraska Avenue
Santa Monica, CA 90404
(310) 449-5550
www.oraclepost.com

Outlaw Sound
1608 North Argyle Avenue, 1st Floor
Hollywood, CA 90028
(323) 462-1873
www.outlawsound.com

Patches Sound
1627 North Gower Street, #2
Los Angeles, CA 90028
(888) 833-8191
www.digitalpatches.com

Point 360 Burbank
1133 North Hollywood Way
Burbank, CA 91505
(866) 968-4336
(818) 556-6700
www.point360.com
(Also in Hollywood, Los Angeles, San Francisco, Dallas, Chicago, and New York)

POP Sound
625 Arizona Avenue
Santa Monica, CA 90401
(310) 458-9192
www.popsound.com

Post Logic Studios LA
1800 North Vine Street
Hollywood, CA 90028
(323) 461-7887
www.postlogic.com

Private Island Trax
6671 Sunset Boulevard, Suite 1550
Hollywood, CA 90028
(323) 856-8729

VOICEOVERS ◉ APPLE

Ravenswork
1611 Electric Avenue
Venice, CA 90291
(310) 392-2542
www.ravenswork.com

Riverton Productions
5319 Craner Avenue
North Hollywood, CA 91601
(818) 505-0181

Rocket Surgery
220 Main Street, Suite D
Venice, CA 90291
(310) 450-4600
www.rocketsurgery.com

Salami Studios
10733 West Magnolia Boulevard
North Hollywood, CA 91601
(818) 754-6611
www.salamistudios.com

Shoreline Studios
100 Wilshire Boulevard, Suite 150
Santa Monica, CA 90401
(310) 394-4932

Skylark Sound Studios
1100 North Hollywood Way, Suite E
Burbank, CA 91505
(818) 562-1550
www.skylarksound.com

Sound Advice
1023 North Cole Avenue
Hollywood, CA 90038
(323) 462-7505
www.sound-advice.com

Stewart Sound
204 North Broadway Avenue, Suite N
Santa Ana, CA 92703
(714) 973-3030
www.stewartsound.com

Todd-AO Burbank
900 North Seward Street
Los Angeles, CA 90028
(818) 840-7116
www.toddao.com

Todd-AO Hollywood
900 Seward Street
Hollywood, CA 90028
(323) 962-4000
www.toddao.com

Todd-AO Radford
4024 Radford Avenue
Studio City, CA 91604
(818) 487-6000
www.toddao.com

Todd-AO West
3000 Olympic Boulevard
Santa Monica, CA 90404
(310) 315-5000
www.toddao.com

VoiceTrax West
12215 Ventura Boulevard, #205
Studio City, CA 91604
(818) 487-9001
www.voicetraxwest.com

Waves Sound Recorders
1956 North Cahuenga Boulevard
Hollywood, CA 90068
(323) 466-6141
www.wavessoundrecorders.com

Westlake Audio
7265 Santa Monica Boulevard
Los Angeles, CA 90046
(323) 851-9800
www.westlakeaudio.com

World Digital Studios
13848 Ventura Boulevard, Suite 4-D
Sherman Oaks, CA 91423
(818) 385-1000

World Wide Wadio
6464 Sunset Boulevard, Suite 1180
Los Angeles, CA 90028
(323) 957-3399
www.wadio.com

TRAINING

Visit **www.voiceoverresourceguide.com** *for a complete list of voiceover classes in the LA area.*

ACE YOUR AUDITIONS
Terri Apple
Terapp3@aol.com
www.TerriApple.com
NYC, LOS ANGELES (Phone, private, in person)
(310) 251-0038

Act With Your Voice
Sale Butler Studios
Studio City, CA
(818) 766-3318

Lauren Adams
Voice Box Studios
West Hollywood, CA
(323) 953-3617

Adler-Zimmerman Animation Workshop
Burbank, CA
(818) 759-1515

Aliso Creek Voiceover Workshop
4106 West Burbank Boulevard
Burbank, CA
(818) 954-9931
www.alisocreek.net

Arttworxs Coaching by Phone
(818) 225-7864
www.arttworxvo.com

Dan Balestrero
13700 Marina Pointe Drive, Suite 623
Marina del Rey, CA 90292
(310) 575-4321
www.masteringvoiceover.com

Michael Bell's Voice Animation Workshop
Hollywood, CA
(818) 784-5107
Michael Bell is a well-known and well-respected voiceover actor who has done TV series, specials, CD-ROMs, and animated feature films. His work includes roles in Homeward Bound 2, *the GI Joe series and movie,* Scooby Doo, Jonny Quest, Voltron: Defender of the Universe.

Bob Bergen's Animation Voiceover Workshop
VoiceTrax West
12215 Ventura Boulevard, Suite 205
Studio City, CA
(818) 999-3081
www.bobbergen.com

Bla Bla Bla Voiceover
Latté Mix Studios
1548 Ninth Street
Santa Monica, CA 90401
(310) 338-9476
www.bla-bla-bla.info
(Spanish only)

Susan Blu's Voiceover Workshops
Blupka Productions
(818) 509-1483
www.blupka.com/news.htm
Sue is a wonderful producer, casting director, and teacher. Her highly regarded classes emphasize animation. Her strong suit is helping students develop characters that will lead to future work. Sue has produced and directed many prime-time animated shows. A prominent casting director in Los Angeles, she is very open to new talent. She is also the coauthor of Word of Mouth, *another excellent book on voiceovers.*

Jocelyn Blue's Sound-Like-A-Pro Voiceover Workshop
Glendale, CA
(818) 242-7881
Jocelyn is a well-known, successful voiceover actress in both commercials and animation.

Beverly Bremers' Voicercise
Orange County/San Diego, CA
(949) 874-0616
www.beverlybremers.com
www.voicercise.net

Wally Burr's No-BS VO Counseling & Coaching
Burbank, CA
(818) 763-2618

Carroll Voice Casting
6767 Forest Lawn Drive, Suite 203
Los Angeles, CA 90068
(213) 851-9966
Owner Carroll Day Kimble — casting director, producer, teacher, and private coach — gets some wonderful copy and is very loyal to the people she loves. She is a patient coach and casting director and is a great person from whom to learn how to interpret copy. She will teach you the ins and outs of the business and what "they" are looking for — which can lead to booking the job.

The Cashman Cache of Voice Acting Techniques
26136 North Twain Place
Stevenson Ranch, CA 91381
(661) 222-9300
www.cashmancommercials.com

Louise Chamis Voiceover Workshops
Studio City, CA
(818) 985-0130

Elaine Craig Voice Casting
6464 Sunset Boulevard, 11th Floor
Los Angeles, CA 90028
(323) 469-8773
www.elainecraig.com
Owner Elaine Craig — casting director, producer, and director — has been in business for years, and her classes are some of the best regarded in Los Angeles.

Brian Cummings's Class Act Workshop
Snazmodyne Studios
Santa Clarita, CA
(323) 497-8900

Delores Diehl's Voiceover Connection
691 South Irolo Street, Suite 212
Los Angeles, CA 90005
(213) 384-9251
www.voconnection.com

Ear Prompter Training
San Fernando Valley, CA
(818) 802-0497

Robert Easton Master Class
Toluca Lake, CA
(323) 828-9285

Famous Radio Ranch Casting
13440 Ventura Boulevard
Sherman Oaks, CA 91423
(818) 465-0150
www.radio-ranch.com
At the ranch, students learn to interpret copy, as well as the ins and outs of radio dialogue.

Pat Fraley Teaches
Los Angeles, CA
(818) 400-3733
www.patfraley.com
(Also offered in New York and San Francisco)

Joanie Gerber
Studio City, CA
(323) 654-1159

Leigh Gilbert, Voiceover Coach
West Hollywood, CA
(323) 692-5704

Ed Greenberg's ImproWorks Workshop
West Los Angeles, CA
(310) 399-3654
www.improworks.com

Linda Hess Looping Coach
Hollywood, CA
(661) 222-7255

APPENDIX B

Robb Holt's Voiceover Workshop
Bell Sound Studios
916 North Citrus Avenue
Hollywood, CA 90038
(818) 762-4045

Sandy Holt's Commercial/ Animation VO Classes
Los Angeles, CA
(310) 271-8217

Jeff Howell's Private Training
Hollywood, CA
(323) 252-6690

Kalmenson & Kalmenson Voiceover Workshops
105 South Sparks Street
Burbank, CA 91506
(818) 342-6499
www.kalmenson.com
Cathy and Harvey Kalmenson maintain a full roster of teachers who provide classes in animation and commercial voiceovers at all levels. Their studio teaches the fundamentals, then brings students in to read when they think they are right for a job. Harvey and Cathy, hardworking and talented professionals, get wonderful copy and always treat talent with the utmost respect. Working in such an environment enhances students' reads — and opens many doors.

LA KidsAct with Trisha Simmons
Sherman Oaks, CA
(818) 771-7879
www.lakidsact.com

Larry Moss's Dialect Gym and Voiceover Workout
West Los Angeles/Santa Monica, CA
(310) 395-4284

Learning Annex
11850 Wilshire Boulevard, Suite 100
Los Angeles, CA 90025
(323) 478-6677
www.learningannex.com

Loop Troop
859 Hollywood Way, Suite 411
Burbank, CA 91505
(818) 239-1616
www.looptroop.com

Ginny McSwain Animation Voiceover Classes
VoiceTrax West
12215 Ventura Boulevard, Suite 205
Studio City, CA 91604
(818) 548-7174

Avery Schreiber Improvisational Workout
Actors Creative Workshop
10523 Burbank Boulevard, Suite 206
North Hollywood, CA 91601
(818) 767-5625
www.acwclasses.com
Since the death of Avery Schreiber in 2002, Karly Rothenberg, his student and apprentice, has carried on his legacy, utilizing his methodologies and revolutionary approach to improvisation in this course. Karly, a coach and actress in her own right, has appeared on cable and network TV and in films.

Susan Silo Voiceover Workshops
(818) 725-3820
www.susansilo.com
Susan is a very talented actress, doing both voiceover and on-camera work. Her animation work includes roles in The Smurfs, Captain Planet, and Felix the Cat. Her coaching focuses on voice manipulation and learning new voices.

Cynthia Songé's Voiceover Workshops
Studio City/Los Angeles, CA
(818) 509-1483
www.blupka.com

Karen Strassman
Accent Reduction and Dialect Coach
(323) 253-4214

Tobias Entertainment Group
(800) 995-2096
www.tobiasent.com

Lori Tritel's The Voice Actor's Perspective
(310) 951-3664
www.loritritel.com

The Voicecaster Casting and Workshops
1832 West Burbank Boulevard
Burbank, CA 91506
(818) 218-2342
www.voicecaster.com

Voices
4051 Radford Avenue, Suite A
Studio City, CA 91604
(818) 980-5659
Mary Lynn Wissner, a well-respected casting director and producer, as well the facility's owner, teaches ongoing classes. She gets a lot of great copy and is willing to see new people and help mold careers.

Nancy Wolfson's Braintrax Audio
Brentwood, CA
(310) 472-4480
www.braintraxaudio.com
(Also in New York, Las Vegas, and Nashville)

Rick Zieff's Unbelievably Fun Voiceover Classes
Hollywood, CA
(323) 651-1666

DEMO PRODUCERS

Visit www.voiceoverresourceguide.com *for a complete list of demo producers in the LA area.*

Terri Apple
(310) 251-003
www.terriapple.com
LA, NYC (Can produce from anywhere to anywhere)

Lauren Adams
Voice Box Studios
West Hollywood, CA
(323) 953-3617

Chuck Duran
World Digital Studios
13848 Ventura Boulevard, Suite 4D
Sherman Oaks, CA 91423
(818) 358-1000
www.voiceover-demos.com

Susan Blu
(818) 509-1483
www.blupka.com

Jocelyn Blue Demo Production
(818) 242-7881

Louise Chamis
(818) 985-0130

Dave & Dave
4352 Lankershim Boulevard
Toluca Lake, CA 91602
(818) 508-7578
www.everythingvo.com

Eliza Doolittle Demos
(323) 828-9285

Jodi Gottlieb
(818) 783-9605

Marc Graue
3421 West Burbank Boulevard
Burbank, CA 91505
(818) 953-8991
www.marcgraue.com

Sandy Holt CD Production
Los Angeles, CA
(310) 271-8217

Jeff Howell
The Atlantis Group
429 Santa Monica Boulevard, Suite 250
Santa Monica, CA 90401
(310) 458-9098
www.atlantisgrouprecording.com

CD DUPLICATION

Armadillo Digital Audio
6855 Vineland Avenue
North Hollywood, CA 91605
(818) 980-6895
(818) 980-6700

AT&T Duplicating
5301 Rosewood Avenue
Los Angeles, CA 90004
(323) 466-9000

Audio CD & Cassette
12426 1/2 Ventura Boulevard
Studio City, CA 91604
(818) 762-2232
www.acdc-cdr.com

CDS Compact Disc Service
634 West Broadway
Glendale, CA 91204
(800) 599-9534
www.cdsg.com

Clonetown
3131 Cahuenga Boulevard West
Los Angeles, CA 90068
(323) 850-6608
www.clone-town.com

Dave & Dave Duplication
4352 Lankershim Boulevard
Toluca Lake, CA 91602
(818) 508-7578
www.everythingvo.com

Disc Makers
3445 Cahuenga Boulevard West
Los Angeles, CA 90068
(866) 707-0012
www.discmakers.com
(Also in New York, Seattle, Chicago, San Francisco, Atlanta, and Puerto Rico)

Dynamite Dubs
12215 Ventura Boulevard, Suite 205
Studio City, CA 91604
(818) 769-8800

N.S.I. Sound and Video
105 South Sparks Street
Burbank, CA 91506
(818) 848-1004

Post Digital Services
3575 Cahuenga Boulevard West, Suite 521
Universal City, CA 90068
(323) 845-0812

LOOP GROUP

Loop Ease
Sandy Holt
(310) 271-8217

NEW YORK (AND OTHER EAST COAST)

AGENTS

Abrams Artists Agency (AAA)
275 Seventh Avenue, 26th Floor
New York, NY 10001
(646) 486-4600
www.abramsartists.com
Contact: J. J. Adler

Access Talent
171 Madison Avenue, Suite 900
New York, NY 10016
(212) 331-9600
(212) 684-7795
www.accesstalent.com
Contact: Linda Weaver

Ann Wright Representatives
165 West 46th Street, Suite 1105
New York, NY 10036
212-764-6770
Contact: Ann Wright

Arcieri & Associates, Inc.
305 Madison Avenue, Suite 2315
New York, NY 10165
(212) 286-1700
Contact: Steven Arcieri

Atlas Talent
36 West 44th Street, Suite 1000
New York, NY 10036
(212) 730-4500
Promos: Jonn Wasser
Commercial: David Coakley

The Carson-Kolker Organization
419 Park Avenue South, Suite 607
New York, NY 10016
(212) 221-1517
Contact: Jenevieve Brewer

**Cunningham, Escott, Slevin and Doherty
(CESD Voices)**
257 Park Avenue South, Suite 900
New York, NY 10010
(212) 477-1666
www.cedvoices.com
Contacts: Billy Collura, Sharon Bierut
Promos: Donna Mancino, Nate Zeitz

Don Buchwald & Associates (DBA)
10 East 44th Street
New York, NY 10017
(212) 867-1200
www.buchwald.com
Head of department: Robyn Stecher
Agent contacts: Katherine Ryan, Robyn Starr
Promos: Robin Steinfeld

Frontier Booking International
1560 Broadway, Suite 1110
New York, NY 10036
(212) 221-0220
www.frontierbooking.com
Contact: Heather Finn

Generation TV
20 West 20th Street, Suite 1008
New York, NY 10011
(646) 230-9491
Contact: Dina Torre
(Teens and early twenties only)

Ingber & Associates
274 Madison Avenue, Suite 1104
New York, NY 10016
(212) 889-9450
Contacts: Carole R. Ingber, Amy E. Davidson

Innovative Artists
235 Park South, 7th Floor
New York, NY 10003
(212) 253-6900
Contacts: Allen G. Duncan, Luanne Regis

Jordan, Gill & Dornbaum, Inc.
1133 Broadway, Suite 623
New York, NY 10010
(212) 463-8455
Contact: David McDermott

Paradigm Talent & Literary Agency
500 Fifth Avenue, 37th Floor
New York, NY 10010
(212) 703-7540

Videoactive Productions
1780 Broadway, Studio 804
New York, NY 10019
(212) 541-6592
www.videoactiveprod.com
Contacts: Steve Garrin, Ted Sluberski

William Morris Endeavor Agency
1325 Avenue of the Americas
New York, NY 10019
(212) 586-5100
www.wma.com
Contact: Marc Guss

UNIONS

AFTRA
(American Federation of Television & Radio Artists)
260 Madison Avenue, 7th Floor
New York, NY 10016
(212) 532-0800
www.aftra.com

SAG
(Screen Actors Guild)
360 Madison Avenue, 12th Floor
New York, NY 10017
(212) 944-1030
www.sag.com

CASTING SERVICES

Beth Melsky Casting
928 Broadway, Suite 300
New York, NY 10010
(212) 505-5000
www.bethmelsky.com
Contact: Beth Melsky

Chantiles Vigneault Casting Inc.
39 West 19th Street, 12th Floor
New York, NY 10011
(212) 924-2278
(866) 924-2278
www.cvcasting.com
Contacts: Sharon Chantiles, Jeffrey Vigneault

Charles Rosen Casting
247 West 38th Street, 7th Floor
New York, NY 10018
(212) 929-2339
www.crcasting.com
Contact: Charles Rosen, Scott Wojcik

Donald Case Casting, Inc.
386 Park Avenue South, Suite 809
New York, NY 10016
(212) 889-6555
www.donaldcasecasting.com
Contact: Donald Case

Donna DeSeta Casting
525 Broadway, 3rd Floor
New York, NY 10012
(212) 274-9696
www.donnadesetacasting.com
Contact: David Cady

Eileen Haves Talent
16 East 85th Street, Suite 4E
New York, NY 10028
(212) 249-0033
Contact: Eileen Haves

Godlove & Company Casting
151 West 25th Street, 11th Floor
New York, NY 10011
(212) 627-7300
www.godlovecasting.com
Contact: Jennifer Sukup

Impossible Casting
122 West 26th Street, Suite 600
New York, NY 10001
(212) 255-3029
www.impossiblecasting.com
Contact: Danny Farag

Jodi Collins Casting
9 Desbrosses Street, Suite 520
New York, NY 10013
(212) 625-0115
Contact: Jodi Collins

Judy Keller Casting
247 West 38th Street, 7th Floor
New York, NY 10018
(212) 463-7676
www.judykellercasting.com
Contact: Judy Keller

Kipperman Casting
12 West 37th Street, 3rd Floor
New York, NY 10018
(212) 736-3663
www.kipperman.com
Contacts: Anthony Pichette, Greg Levins

Liz Lewis Casting Partners
129a West 20th Street, Ground Floor
New York, NY 10011
(212) 645-1500
www.lizlewiscastingpartners.com

Mike Lemon Casting, C.S.A.
413 North Seventh Street, Suite 602
Philadelphia, PA 19123
(215) 627-8927
www.mikelemoncasting.com

Pomann Sound
2 West 46th Street, PH
New York, NY 10036
(212) 869-4161
(877) 4PO-MANN
www.pomannsound.com

Stark Naked Productions, Inc./ Elsie Stark Casting
39 West 19th Street, 12th Floor
New York, NY 10011
(212) 366-1903
Contacts: Elsie Stark, Elizabeth Gans, Rawleigh Moreland

ONLINE CASTING/AUDITIONS

Craig's List
www.craigslist.org
Choose New York and then TV/Film/Video/Radio

Donna Summer/Voicecasting
www.voicecasting.com

Voiceover Miami
3899 Sheridan Street, #514
Hollywood, FL 33021
(800) 473-1454
www.voiceover-usa.com
Contact: Gary Travers

RECORDING STUDIOS

Audio Department
119 West 57th Street, Suite 400
New York, NY 10019
(212) 586-3503

Buttons Sound
2 West 45th Street, Suite 603
New York, NY 10036
(212) 764-8650
www.buttonssound.com

Broadway Sound
1619 Broadway, 4th Floor
New York, NY 10019
(212) 333-0700
www.broadwayvideo.com

HSR|NY (Howard Schwartz Recording)
420 Lexington Avenue, Suite 1934
New York, NY 10170
(212) 687-4180

Nutmeg Audio Post
45 West 45th Street, 6th Floor
New York, NY 10036
(212) 921-8005
www.nutmegaudiopost.com

Point 360 New York
114 West 26th Street
New York, NY 10001
(800) 211-8994
(212) 627 2216
www.point360.com

Post Logic Studios NY
435 Hudson Street, 7th Floor
New York, NY 10014
(212) 520-3150
www.postlogic.com

Sound Hound
45 West 45th Street, 4th Floor
New York, NY 10036
(212) 575-8664
www.soundhound.com

Sound Lounge
149 Fifth Avenue
New York, NY 10010
(212) 388-1212
www.soundlounge.com

Soundtrack New York
936 Broadway
New York, NY 10010
(212) 420-6010
www.soundtrackgroup.com
(Also in Boston)

TRAINING

Wendy Dillon
(212) 246-9611

Don Morrow Voiceover Training
Danbury, CT
(203) 748-0378
www.donmorrowvoiceovers.com

Edge Studios Voice Design Group
307 Seventh Avenue, Suite 1007
New York, NY 10001
(212) 868-EDGE
www.edgestudio.com
(Also in Washington, DC, and Connecticut. Also offers remote/tele-training)

The Great Voice Company
110 Charlotte Place
Englewood Cliffs, NJ 07632
(800) 333-8108
www.greatvoice.com/voiceoverworkshop.html

Marla Kirban Voiceover
630 Ninth Avenue, Suite 1104
New York, NY 10036
(212) 397-7969
www.marlakirbanvoiceover.com

Mike Lemon Casting
413 North Seventh Street, Suite 602
Philadelphia, PA 19123
(215) 627-8927
www.mikelemoncasting.com

New York Voiceover Academy
2224 Hewlett Avenue
Merrick, NY 11566
(516) 783-7499
www.newyorkvoiceoveracademy.com

Pat Fraley Teaches
(818) 400-3733
www.patfraley.com
(Classes in New York as well as in L.A.)

Scott Shurian Voiceover Workshops
(800) 496-1776
www.voscott.com
(Also Los Angeles and Salt Lake City)

Stoller System Dialect Coaching & Design
(917) 319-7448

The Ted Bardy Studio
153 West 27th Street, Suite 301
New York, NY 10001
(212) 769-7666
www.tedbardy.com

Weist-Barron
35 West 45th Street, 6th Floor
New York, NY 10036
(212) 840-7025
www.weistbarron.com

Nancy Wolfson's Braintrax Audio
Brentwood, CA
(310) 472-4480
www.braintraxaudio.com
(Offered in Los Angeles, Las Vegas and Nashville, too)

MANAGEMENT

ASE Talent Management
New York City/Los Angeles
(310) 251-0038

Michael Katz Talent Management
Personal Manager
P.O. Box 1925
Cathedral Station
New York, NY 10025
(212) 316-2492

MJC Entertainment
443 Greenwich Street, 5th Floor
New York, NY 10013
(212) 965-8432
Contact: Tara Boragine

Take One
P.O. Box 2128
Greenport, NY 11944
(866) 580-2228
Contact: Beth Allen

CD DUPLICATION

Disc Makers
16 West 18th Street
New York, NY 10011
(212) 645-0312
(800) 466-3470
www.discmakers.com
(Also in Los Angeles, Washington, Chicago, San Francisco, Atlanta, and Puerto Rico)

CHICAGO

AGENTS

Grossman & Jack Talent
230 East Ohio Street, Suite 200
Chicago, IL 60611
(312) 587-1155

Naked Voices
865 North Sangamon, Suite 415
Chicago, IL 60622
(312) 563-0136
www.nakedvoices.com

Voices Unlimited
541 North Fairbanks Court, #2735
Chicago, IL 60611
(312) 832-1113
www.voicesunlimited.com

UNIONS

AFTRA Chicago
One East Erie, Suite 650
Chicago, IL 60611
312-573-8081
www.aftra.com

SAG Chicago
One East Erie, Suite 650
Chicago, IL 60611
312-573-8081
www.sag.com

CASTING

O'Connor Casting Company
1017 West Washington, Suite 2A
Chicago, IL 60607
(312) 226-9112
www.oconnorcasting.com

VOX: Chicago
Recording facility/casting
400 South Green Street, Suite 318
Chicago, IL 60601
(312) 666-7911
Contact: David Lewis

RECORDING STUDIOS

Audio Producers Group
35 West Wacker Drive, 2nd Floor
Chicago, IL 60601
(312) 220-5400
www.audioproducersgroup.com

Audio Recording Unlimited
400 North Michigan Avenue, Suite 1900
Chicago, IL 60611
(312) 527-7000
www.aruchicago.com

Point 360 Chicago
430 Erie Street
Chicago, IL 60610
(800) 211-8993
(312) 280-8949
www.point360.com

TRAINING

The Chicago Actors Studio
20 West Hubbard Street, Suite 2E
Chicago, IL 60610
(773) 645-0222
www.actors-studio.net

Harlan Hogan
(312) 427-5264
www.harlanhogan.com
Harlan's website includes a very useful listing of voice coaches in all regions of the United States, as well as in Canada.

CD DUPLICATION

Disc Makers
562 West Washington Boulevard
Chicago, IL 60661
(800) 468-9353
(312) 441-9622
www.discmakers.com

PUBLICATIONS

Numbers listed are for subscriptions.

The Voiceover Resource Guide
Dave Sebastian Williams
Dave & Dave
4352 Lankershim Boulevard
Toluca Lake, CA 91602
vorg@everythingvo.com
The Resource Guide is an extensive directory to every casting director, agent, production house (for promos, animations, trailers, and commercials), J-card service, CD production and dubbing facility, and demo director.

Acting Magazine
Box 468054
Atlanta, GA 31146
www.actingmagazine.com

Advertising Age
711 Third Avenue
New York, NY 10017
(888) 288-5900
www.adage.com

Animation Magazine
30941 West Agoura Road, Suite 102
Westlake Hills, CA 91361
(818) 991-2884
www.animationmagazine.net

BackStage
770 Broadway, 4th Floor
New York, NY 10003
(646) 654-5700
www.backstage.com

BackStage West
5055 Wilshire Boulevard
Los Angeles, CA 90036
(323) 525 2356
www.backstage.com

Broadcasting and Cable
www.broadcastingcable.com

Fade In
289 S. Robertson Boulevard, Suite 465
Beverly Hills, CA 90211

VOICEOVERS ◉ APPLE

(310) 275-0287
(800) 646-3896
www.fadein.com

Hollywood Reporter
5055 Wilshire Boulevard, 6th Floor
Los Angeles, CA 90036
(323) 525-2150
(866) 525-2150
www.hollywoodreporter.com

Ross Reports
8721 Santa Monica Boulevard, Suite 700
Los Angeles, CA 90069
(877) 570 9662
www.therossreports.com

Screen **magazine**
676 North LaSalle Street, Suite 300
Chicago, IL 60610
(312) 640-0800
www.screenmag.tv
This magazine, which covers Chicago, the Midwest, and Texas, also publishes The Screen Magazine Production Bible, a guide to production services containing more than 2,300 listings in 134 production categories and available both in print and online.

Variety
5700 Wilshire Boulevard
Los Angeles, CA 90036
and
360 Park Avenue South
New York, NY 10010
(866) 698-2743
www.variety.com

ONLINE VOICEOVER RESOURCES, BLOGS, WEBSITES

www.actorsaccess.com

www.actorspace.com

www.brainboxtalent.com

www.castingaudition.com

www.everythingvo.com

www.studiocenter.com

www.TerriApple.com (Sign up for monthly newsletter, online workouts and more)

www.voice123.com

www.voicebank.net

www.voicehunter.com

www.voiceover.com (Magazine and Podcast)

www.voiceover-casting.com

The Voiceover Boblog
www.bobsouer.com/blog

Vox Daily Blog
www.blogs.voices.com/voxdaily/

EVENTS

Promax, Comi-con, E3, Backstage Yearly event (New York/LA)

GLOSSARY

ADR: Audio dialogue replacement. Another term for **looping** or **walla**.

AFTRA: American Federation of Radio & Television Artists. One of the **unions** to which voiceover actors belong.

Alternate read: A more personalized interpretation of audition copy sometimes provided by a voiceover actor after auditioning strictly within the given **specs**.

Animatic: The **rough cut** of a commercial, an animatic is unfinished — without either color or music.

Announcer: A voiceover actor is a **spot**'s announcer, although other actors may read other parts of the copy.

Authoritative: Script direction asking voiceover actors to sound knowledgeable about the subject matter — to make the **read** informative.

Billboard: To overly enunciate the name of a product during a **read**.

Bleed-through: Noises from headphones that get picked up because of the placement of the microphone. Causes of bleed-through include standing in the wrong place or placing the headphones too high above the mike.

Book out: To tell your agency you are not available for auditions or sessions at a certain time or on a certain day.

Burn: To transfer digital information to a CD or DVD.

Button: A word or short phrase — usually humorous — improvised by a voiceover actor at the end of a radio spot.

Buyout: An agreement to do the voiceover for a commercial or program for one lump sum — that is, without **residuals**.

Cable: A **spot** that runs on cable stations only.

Cans: Headphones.

Caress: Script direction asking voiceover actors to play with certain words — to emphasize, elongate, and warm them up.

Cheesy: Script direction asking voiceover actors to push the characterization and really go out on a limb.

Class-A Program: Commercials broadcast on national networks that pay top **union scale**.

Cold read: To audition without having previously seen the script.

Cone: A cone-shaped Styrofoam filter that fits over a microphone to ensure the actor's voice is recorded clearly.

Conversational: Script direction asking voiceover actors to keep phrasing honest and informal.

Cut: To stop a **take**. Used mostly in **looping**, or **ADR**, work.

Cue up: To align the timing and speed of sound and visuals. The **sound engineer** cues up the voice **track** to the visuals and timings of the **spot** according to the specifications of the ad agency and client. The engineer may also cue up music.

Double: A **spot** for two or more actors.

Double scale: Getting paid twice the scale amount set by the **union**.

Doughnut: An insert during a voiceover, often in the form of dialogue between the opening announcer and **tagline**. Voiceover actors are sometimes hired just for the doughnut.

Dubbing: Matching a translation of dialogue spoken by movie or TV actors to the mouth movements and emotional expressions of those actors speaking that dialogue in the original language of that film or program.

Ext.: Exterior.

Feedback: An unpleasant whining or whistling sound made by a microphone, resulting from amplified output returning through the microphone as input.

Filter: One of various devices used on microphones to clarify sound recording.

Financial core (fi-core): A status selected by some **union** members that enables them to work **non-union** jobs but strips them of many union benefits.

Flat: Script direction asking voiceover actors to read without emphasis.

Full voice: Script direction asking voiceover actors to read loudly, using their whole voice.

GFX: Graphics.

Graphic lower third: The bottom third of the TV screen image, reserved for the station ID and the show's tune-in time.

Graphic upper third: The top third of the TV screen image, reserved for the name of the show.

Have fun with it: Script direction asking voiceover actors to relax; directors often use it if they feel actors are stiff and need to loosen up.

High energy: Script direction asking voiceover actors to add liveliness and keep the script moving or flowing.

Hip pocket client: An actor who has been taken on by an agent on a trial basis, without a contract; also called a "pocket client."

Holding fee: Actors receive a holding fee if a commercial is not aired immediately but is instead held for a later air date.

Hot: When a microphone is on, it is hot. Also, when a mike is feeding back, it is sometimes called "hot."

Industrial: A **non-air**, **non-broadcast** film or video usually made for instructional or training purposes for a specific corporation.

Intimate: Script direction asking voiceover actors to read more softly, closer to the microphone.

J-card: The paper cover inside a CD case — or jewel box (hence the J) — that contains information about the artist and tracks on the CD itself.

Land patch: See **phone patch**.

Level: A sample of how the **read** will actually sound, a level is provided by the actor for the **sound engineer** so any technical issues can be worked out prior to the actual recording.

Local: The **union** chapter in a particular state or locality.

Looping: Background sound effects and noises for TV and film.

Master: The original copy of a **spot**. Copies are **burned** off of the main copy in **post-production**.

Mix: To mix a **spot**, an engineer will combine the music with the dialogue and, for film or television, edit the entire piece together with the picture.

MP3: MPEG audio layer 3. Because this computer file format compresses digital audio data so efficiently, large audio files — like

GLOSSARY

demo CDs — can be sent via email.

Music bed: The music that will be laid behind the voiceover.

National: A commercial that runs in every state.

National network: A commercial that runs in every state on a network station.

Network: A commercial that runs on a network affiliate station.

Non-air, non-broadcast: A **spot** or program not intended to run on any broadcast medium, including **industrials** and advertising agency demos.

Non-union: A voiceover job with a company that has not signed an agreement with **SAG** or **AFTRA**.

Off-the-cuff: Script direction asking voiceover actors not to emphasize the words but rather to read conversationally, or in a throwaway manner.

On air: Hot and on with the client for a **phone patch**.

Open it up: Script direction asking voiceover actors to take more time for the **read** or stretch it out.

Over scale: Anything you are paid over the **scale** established by the **union**.

Per spot per cycle: To ensure actors are paid for each **spot** they record for every **thirteen-week cycle** it runs, contracts include the phrase "per spot per cycle."

Phone patch: The digital patching system for a type of **read** that is done completely via telephone.

Phones: Headphones.

Pick it up: Script direction asking voiceover actors to hurry the pace or move things along; directors will ask actors to pick it up if they are reading too slowly.

Pitch: Refers to where on a musical scale someone's voice falls — the actual number of cycles per second at which it vibrates.

Play with: Script direction asking voiceover actors for a less straightforward **read** — to have more fun with the script.

Playback: To listen to what has just been recorded.

Pocket client: See **Hip pocket client**.

Pop filter: A specific type of microphone filter designed to soften the popping sound of Ps.

Post-production: A catchall term for all the production work (for example, editing) that is performed on a **spot**, program, or film after the images have been shot and the voiceovers recorded.

Promo: The on-air advertising for a TV show, radio program, or film.

Pull back: Script direction asking voiceover actors to keep it simple. Directors will ask actors to pull back if they are overacting.

Read: A voiceover **spot**. Also, the way an actor performs a voiceover spot.

Real: Script direction asking voiceover actors to keep it conversational and sounding like real people.

Regional: A **spot** that runs in more than one city, but not nationally.

Re-record: When a voiceover actor is paid another **session fee** and asked to record additional **takes** of a commercial.

Residuals: The money paid to **union** voiceover actors each time their work airs on TV or radio.

Reuse: What voiceover actors are paid when a **spot** is rerun.

Rhythm: The pace at which an actor speaks.

Romance it: Script direction asking voiceover actors to lovingly emphasize a certain word or phrase.

Rough cut: The initial, interim edit of a **spot**. See also **animatic**.

SAG: Screen Actors Guild. One of the **unions** for voiceover actors.

Safety: After directors get the **read** they want, they often record a safety — another, similar read to have as a backup, in case something is technically wrong with the one they prefer. Safeties should follow the same intonation and mood of the preferred read.

Scale: The lowest base **union** fee for a job.

Scale plus ten: The lowest base **union** fee plus the 10 percent commission paid to the agent. The extra 10 percent is paid by the employer; it does not come out of the actor's base pay.

Scratch track: An unfinished or **animatic** version of a commercial for the **spot** being read. Scratch tracks are assembled by the ad agency.

Session fee: The payment for the first commercial recording during a session. If two **spots** are recorded, the actor receives one session fee and payment for the other spot; if one spot and two **tags** are recorded, the actor is paid one session fee and two tag fees, and so on. The actor is always paid one — and only one — session fee per session.

SFX: Sound effects.

Shelved: When a voiceover actor is purposely not sent out on auditions by his or her agency.

Sides: Audition copy for animation, narration, or TV.

Single: A **spot** read by one actor from start to finish.

Slate: Information about what is about to occur. At the beginning of an audition, actors slate their name and agent. In a session, the number of the **spot** is slated before each take.

Slot mix: Music that has been premixed by the **sound engineer**.

SOT: Formerly an acronym for "sound on tape," the term now refers to sound on CD — that is, the sound already from a TV program being promoted that is included in the promo itself.

Sound booth, sound studio: The recording facility in which the actor records the voiceover.

Sound engineer: The person who works with the actor in the session, handling technical and editing issues. The liaison between talent and client.

Specs: Instructions for how to interpret and perform copy at an audition or session.

Speeding: Rolling; getting ready to record.

Split the difference: Script direction asking voiceover actors for a performance somewhere in the middle of two previous **reads**.

Spot: A commercial.

Stand: The table used to hold copy below the microphone stand.

Stereotyped: When an actor is typecast, or only picked to play a certain type of character or do a certain style of **read**.

Straight read: Script direction asking voiceover actors for a businesslike, knowledgeable, matter-of-fact **read**, providing just the facts. A straight read is different from an **authoritative** read.

Stretch: Script direction asking voiceover actors to lengthen the duration of, or elongate, a word.

Synching: Matching your dialogue with another voice or your own voice from an earlier **take**.

Taft-Hartley Act: A federal law that protects you from being forced to join a **union** until you are hired for two union jobs within a thirty-day period.

Tag, tagline: The selling point or highlight phrase at the end of a **spot**.

GLOSSARY

Tag out: A promo's standard wrap-up line. For example, "Judge Judy. She's ready to rule."

Take: Each attempt at recording a **read** during a session. The **sound engineer** calls out, "Take One," or "Take Two," and so on, in sequence, before the voiceover actor begins to read the **spot**.

Talk-back mike: A sound studio microphone used by **sound engineers** who are outside the recording booth to communicate with actors while they are recording.

Thirteen-week cycle: The maximum time during which a client can run a **spot**, after which, according to **union** rules, either the commercial must be pulled or the actor's payment cycle must begin anew.

Three in a row: If a voiceover actor is asked to redo a word or a phrase during a session or audition, it will usually be recorded three times in succession: A, B, and C.

Tighten it up: Script direction asking voiceover actors to read more quickly.

Time code: A digital readout on the **sound engineer**'s board that helps actors with timings while reading dialogue.

Time compression: Digitally trimming a **spot** by taking out air — or small silences — between words.

Timing: The duration of a **spot**. A 37-second spot must be read in 37 seconds — no more, no less.

To picture: Reading the voiceover copy while watching the visual for that **spot** on a monitor or TV.

Tracks: Any type of music, background noise, or laugh track that a **sound engineer** uses with **spots**.

Trailer: A short promotional piece for a movie, a trailer almost always uses a voiceover to tie scenes from the film together.

Tune-in time: The time when the program being promoted will air.

Under the table: Working without the knowledge of your agent.

Union: An organization for actors that protects their rights in the workplace, guarantees them certain wages, prevents non-union members from working at union facilities, and offers a range of benefits, including health care.

Upgrade: The fee paid to a voiceover actor if a client decides to air a **spot** originally recorded as **non-air, non-broadcast**.

Voice bank: An online service used by casting directors, voice agents, and creative directors looking to hire voiceover actors, a voice bank is a collection of samples of voiceover actors' work. Agents also use them to showcase their voiceover talent, and ad agencies download samples from them for their clients to listen to.

Voice matching: See **dubbing** and **looping**.

Wall-to-wall: When a single actor reads an entire **spot** — the **announcer** copy, the body, and the **tag**.

Walla: Another term for **looping**.

Wild: To record lines for a **double** or group **spot** without the other actors present.

Wild lines: Specific lines isolated from the rest of the script for recording. Usually done **three in a row**: A, B, and C.

Wild spot: A **spot** that runs an unspecified number of times during a **thirteen-week cycle**. Actors are usually paid a flat fee for such a spot, which can be local or regional.

INDEX OF TERMS

accents, 40, 41, 54, 107, 298
acting, 32, 37, 40, 72, 115, 24, 210, 243
ADR (audio dialogue replacement), 122, 124, 126. *See* looping
ad agencies, 13, 22, 23, 27, 41, 54, 63, 65, 73, 170, 186, 234
auditions, 21, 23, 25, 30, 37, 40, 53, 60, 178, 204, 211, 216
charging for CDs, 47, 49, 120, 189, 190, 194, 195
contracts, 57, 202, 257, 280, 286, 340
copy, 19, 24, 28, 33, 34, 69, 79, 104, 166
demo CDs and demos, 12, 49; and stereotyping, 19, 158, 290, 291, 297
African Americans and voiceover business, 186, 187, 301
AFTRA, 15, 21, 58, 162, 207, 280, 281, 284; and dues, 281; and financial core (FICORE), 289; and scale, 21, 57, 216; and Taft Hartley, 331; and union vs. non-union, 15, 21, 60, 64, 74, 258
agency demos, contracts, 257; and copy, 104, 109, 157; demo CD for, 12, 23, 139, 189; and demos, 12, 23, 184; and recording sessions, 245, 246, 250, 252; and stereotyping, 158, 290; and talent agents, 200
advertising industry, 57, 264
affiliate TV scripts, 358; and promos for, 139, 181
animation, 86, 121, 131, 178, 184; and agents, 200; auditions for, 228; characters for, 22, 98; classes for, 208; copy for auditions, 104; demo CD for, 189; demos for, fees for, 12, 23, 193; house minute for, 189; scripts for, 189; callbacks, 172; submitting demo CD to, 189, 191; and talent agencies, 197; casting houses, 327, audiobooks, 141

INDEX

booth, recording booth, 165, 245; and recording studio, 247; and booth director, 37, 165
branding, 158, 310
breathing, 105
buyouts, 59, 257
callbacks, 172
class A commercials, 280; cycles of (*see* unions) 280; residuals (*see* unions) 280; cold reading, 157
classes, 23, 206
doubles, 255
dubbing, 131, 180
foreign language, 96
group reads, 255. *See* doubles
health insurance, 281
phone patch, 248

POV (point of view), 100
radio copy, 34, 104
representation, 200, 326, 362
re-records, 247
scripts (*see* copy); breaking down, analyzing, genres, stereotyping, all aspects of, 51, 104, 109, 86; trailer copy, 140; rhythm of/beats of 34, 51; submitting to ad agencies, 317; submitting to casting houses, 317; submitting to agents, 58, 200; submitting to production companies, 264, 328
sessions (voiceover) 255, 257
TV copy, 37, 51, 109
voiceover classes, 23, 206, 207, 208

ABOUT THE AUTHOR

Terri Apple "the queen of voiceovers," writer, and actress is one of the top voiceover actresses in the country. With a voiceover career spanning 30 years, she is the author of the number one book in its field, *Making Money In Voiceovers* and the updated *Voiceovers: Everything You Need to Know About How to Make Money with Your Voice*.

Terri is also an actress as well as an accomplished writer with TV and feature film acting credits that include the winner of the Sundance Film Festival for short film in 2005. She wrote, has the rights to, and will be producing *Undefeated: The Rocky Marciano Story*, currently in development. A TV pilot, *Bomb Squad*, has been optioned and is soon to be in development as well.

Terri also owns ASE Talent Management, a boutique management company that represents voiceover artists.

To contact Terri, click on www.terriapple.com

{ THE MYTH OF MWP }

In a dark time, a light bringer came along, leading the curious and the frustrated to clarity and empowerment. It took the well-guarded secrets out of the hands of the few and made them available to all. It spread a spirit of openness and creative freedom, and built a storehouse of knowledge dedicated to the betterment of the arts.

The essence of the Michael Wiese Productions (MWP) is empowering people who have the burning desire to express themselves creatively. We help them realize their dreams by putting the tools in their hands. We demystify the sometimes secretive worlds of screenwriting, directing, acting, producing, film financing, and other media crafts.

By doing so, we hope to bring forth a realization of 'conscious media' which we define as being positively charged, emphasizing hope and affirming positive values like trust, cooperation, self-empowerment, freedom, and love. Grounded in the deep roots of myth, it aims to be healing both for those who make the art and those who encounter it. It hopes to be transformative for people, opening doors to new possibilities and pulling back veils to reveal hidden worlds.

MWP has built a storehouse of knowledge unequaled in the world, for no other publisher has so many titles on the media arts. Please visit www.mwp.com where you will find many free resources and a 25% discount on our books. Sign up and become part of the wider creative community!

Onward and upward,

Michael Wiese
Publisher/Filmmaker

FILM & VIDEO BOOKS
TO RECEIVE A FREE MWP NEWSLETTER, CLICK ON WWW.MWP.COM TO REGISTER

SCREENWRITING | WRITING

And the Best Screenplay Goes to... | Dr. Linda Seger | $26.95
Archetypes for Writers | Jennifer Van Bergen | $22.95
Bali Brothers | Lacy Waltzman, Matthew Bishop, Michael Wiese | $12.95
Cinematic Storytelling | Jennifer Van Sijll | $24.95
Could It Be a Movie? | Christina Hamlett | $26.95
Creating Characters | Marisa D'Vari | $26.95
Crime Writer's Reference Guide, The | Martin Roth | $20.95
Deep Cinema | Mary Trainor-Brigham | $19.95
Elephant Bucks | Sheldon Bull | $24.95
Fast, Cheap & Written That Way | John Gaspard | $26.95
Hollywood Standard – 2nd Edition, The | Christopher Riley | $18.95
Horror Screenwriting | Devin Watson | $24.95
I Could've Written a Better Movie than That! | Derek Rydall | $26.95
Inner Drives | Pamela Jaye Smith | $26.95
Moral Premise, The | Stanley D. Williams, Ph.D. | $24.95
Myth and the Movies | Stuart Voytilla | $26.95
Power of the Dark Side, The | Pamela Jaye Smith | $22.95
Psychology for Screenwriters | William Indick, Ph.D. | $26.95
Reflections of the Shadow | Jeffrey Hirschberg | $26.95
Rewrite | Paul Chitlik | $16.95
Romancing the A-List | Christopher Keane | $18.95
Save the Cat! | Blake Snyder | $19.95
Save the Cat! Goes to the Movies | Blake Snyder | $24.95
Screenwriting 101 | Neill D. Hicks | $16.95
Screenwriting for Teens | Christina Hamlett | $18.95
Script-Selling Game, The | Kathie Fong Yoneda | $16.95
Stealing Fire From the Gods, 2nd Edition | James Bonnet | $26.95
Talk the Talk | Penny Penniston | $24.95
Way of Story, The | Catherine Ann Jones | $22.95
What Are You Laughing At? | Brad Schreiber | $19.95
Writer's Journey – 3rd Edition, The | Christopher Vogler | $26.95
Writer's Partner, The | Martin Roth | $24.95
Writing the Action Adventure Film | Neill D. Hicks | $14.95
Writing the Comedy Film | Stuart Voytilla & Scott Petri | $14.95
Writing the Killer Treatment | Michael Halperin | $14.95
Writing the Second Act | Michael Halperin | $19.95
Writing the Thriller Film | Neill D. Hicks | $14.95
Writing the TV Drama Series, 2nd Edition | Pamela Douglas | $26.95
Your Screenplay Sucks! | William M. Akers | $19.95

FILMMAKING

Film School | Richard D. Pepperman | $24.95
Power of Film, The | Howard Suber | $27.95

PITCHING

Perfect Pitch – 2nd Edition, The | Ken Rotcop | $19.95
Selling Your Story in 60 Seconds | Michael Hauge | $12.95

SHORTS

Filmmaking for Teens, 2nd Edition | Troy Lanier & Clay Nichols | $24.95
Making It Big in Shorts | Kim Adelman | $22.95

BUDGET | PRODUCTION MANAGEMENT

Film & Video Budgets, 5th Updated Edition | Deke Simon | $26.95
Film Production Management 101 | Deborah S. Patz | $39.95

DIRECTING | VISUALIZATION

Animation Unleashed | Ellen Besen | $26.95
Cinematography for Directors | Jacqueline Frost | $29.95
Citizen Kane Crash Course in Cinematography | David Worth | $19.95
Directing Actors | Judith Weston | $26.95
Directing Feature Films | Mark Travis | $26.95
Fast, Cheap & Under Control | John Gaspard | $26.95
Film Directing: Cinematic Motion, 2nd Edition | Steven D. Katz | $27.95
Film Directing: Shot by Shot | Steven D. Katz | $27.95
Film Director's Intuition, The | Judith Weston | $26.95
First Time Director | Gil Bettman | $27.95
From Word to Image, 2nd Edition | Marcie Begleiter | $26.95
I'll Be in My Trailer! | John Badham & Craig Modderno | $26.95
Master Shots | Christopher Kenworthy | $24.95
Setting Up Your Scenes | Richard D. Pepperman | $24.95
Setting Up Your Shots, 2nd Edition | Jeremy Vineyard | $22.95
Working Director, The | Charles Wilkinson | $22.95

DIGITAL | DOCUMENTARY | SPECIAL

Digital Filmmaking 101, 2nd Edition | Dale Newton & John Gaspard | $26.95
Digital Moviemaking 3.0 | Scott Billups | $24.95
Digital Video Secrets | Tony Levelle | $26.95
Greenscreen Made Easy | Jeremy Hanke & Michele Yamazaki | $19.95
Producing with Passion | Dorothy Fadiman & Tony Levelle | $22.95
Special Effects | Michael Slone | $31.95

EDITING

Cut by Cut | Gael Chandler | $35.95
Cut to the Chase | Bobbie O'Steen | $24.95
Eye is Quicker, The | Richard D. Pepperman | $27.95
Film Editing | Gael Chandler | $34.95
Invisible Cut, The | Bobbie O'Steen | $28.95

SOUND | DVD | CAREER

Complete DVD Book, The | Chris Gore & Paul J. Salamoff | $26.95
Costume Design 101, 2nd Edition | Richard La Motte | $24.95
Hitting Your Mark, 2nd Edition | Steve Carlson | $22.95
Sound Design | David Sonnenschein | $19.95
Sound Effects Bible, The | Ric Viers | $26.95
Storyboarding 101 | James Fraioli | $19.95
There's No Business Like Soul Business | Derek Rydall | $22.95
You Can Act! | D.W. Brown | $24.95

FINANCE | MARKETING | FUNDING

Art of Film Funding, The | Carole Lee Dean | $26.95
Bankroll | Tom Malloy | $26.95
Complete Independent Movie Marketing Handbook, The | Mark Steven Bosko | $39.95
Getting the Money | Jeremy Jusso | $26.95
Independent Film and Videomakers Guide – 2nd Edition, The | Michael Wiese | $29.95
Independent Film Distribution | Phil Hall | $26.95
Shaking the Money Tree, 3rd Edition | Morrie Warshawski | $26.95

MEDITATION | ART

Mandalas of Bali | Dewa Nyoman Batuan | $39.95

OUR FILMS

Dolphin Adventures: DVD | Michael Wiese and Hardy Jones | $24.95
Hardware Wars: DVD | Written and Directed by Ernie Fosselius | $14.95
On the Edge of a Dream | Michael Wiese | $16.95
Sacred Sites of the Dalai Lamas– DVD, The | Documentary by Michael Wiese | $24.95

To Order go to *www.mwp.com* or Call 1-800-833-5738